ARCTIC OCEAN
50-51

Greenland
50-51

Alaska &Western Canada
22-23

CONTINENTAL MAP:
NORTH AMERICA
20-21

Eastern Canada
24-25

CANADA

Pacific
States
36-37

Central &
Mountain States
32-33

Great Lakes
30-31

Northeastern
States
26-27

UNITED STATES
OF AMERICA

Southwestern
States
34-35

Southern States
28-29

PACIFIC OCEAN
128-129

ATLANTIC
OCEAN
52- 53

Mexico
38-39

Central America &
the Caribbean
42-43

Northern
South America
44-45

CONTINENTAL MAP:
CENTRAL & SOUTH AMERICA
40-41

Brazil
46-47

CONTINENTAL MAP:
OCEANIA
130-131

New Zealand
134

Southern
South America
48-49

ANTARCTICA
50-51

THE EYEWITNESS

ATLAS

OF THE

WORLD

BURROW.

THE ◉ EYEWITNESS

ATLAS
OF THE
WORLD

DORLING KINDERSLEY
LONDON • NEW YORK • MOSCOW • SYDNEY

CONSULTANTS

Consultant editor
Dr. David R. Green, Department of Geography, King's College

Digital mapping consultant
Professor Jan-Peter A. L. Muller, Professor of Image Understanding and Remote Sensing,
Department of Photogrammetry and Surveying, University College London

Digital base map production
Department of Photogrammetry and Surveying, University College London:
Philip Eales (Producer) • Kevin Tildsley • David Rees •
James Pearson • Peter Booth • Tim Day • Planetary Visions Ltd

Contributors
Peter Clark, Former Keeper, Royal Geographical Society, London •
Martin McCauley, Senior Lecturer in Politics,
School of Slavonic and East European Studies, University of London

Dorling Kindersley would also like to thank
Dr. Andrew Tatham, Keeper, and the Staff of the Royal Geographical Society, London,
for their help and advice in preparing this Atlas

Project art editor: Nicola Liddiard
Project editors: Elizabeth Wyse and Caroline Lucas
Project cartographer: Julia Lunn

Editorial: Jayne Parsons • Phillip Boys • Chris Whitwell • Donna Rispoli •
Margaret Hynes • Ailsa Heritage • Sue Peach • Laura Porter

Design: Lesley Betts • Rhonda Fisher • Paul Blackburn • Jay Young

Cartography: Roger Bullen • Michael Martin • James Mills-Hicks • James Anderson •
Yahya El-Droubie • Tony Chambers • Simon Lewis • Caroline Simpson

Illustrations: John Woodcock • Kathleen McDougall • Mick Gillah • David Wright

Photography: Andy Crawford • Tim Ridley • Steve Gorton

Picture research: Clive Webster • Charlotte Bush •
Sharon Southren • Frances Vargo • Caroline Brook

Editorial director: Andrew Heritage
Art director: Chez Picthall
Production: Susannah Straughan

A DORLING KINDERSLEY BOOK

First published in Great Britain in 1994
by Dorling Kindersley Limited,
9 Henrietta Street, London WC2E 8PS
Visit us on the World Wide Web at http://www.dk.com

Copyright © 1994 Dorling Kindersley Limited, London
Reprinted in 1994
Second Edition 1995
Adapted for this edition 1997

Reproduced by Colourscan, Singapore

CONTENTS

NORTH AMERICA • 20-21

CENTRAL AND SOUTH AMERICA • 40-41

EUROPE • 54-55

AFRICA • 86-87

NORTH AND WEST ASIA • 102-103

SOUTH AND EAST ASIA • 114-115

OCEANIA • 130-131

THE EARTH IN SPACE

THE EARTH IS ONE OF NINE PLANETS that orbit a large star – the Sun. Together they form the solar system. All life on Earth – plant, animal and human – depends on the Sun. Its energy warms our planet's surface, powers the wind and waves, drives the ocean currents and weather systems, and recycles water. Sunlight also gives plants the power to photo-synthesize – to make the foods and oxygen on which organisms rely.
The fact that the Earth is habitable at all is due to its precise position in the solar system, its daily spin, and an annual journey round the Sun at a constant tilt. Without these, and the breathable atmosphere that cloaks and protects the Earth, it would be as barren as our near-neighbours Venus and Mars.

Asteroid belt

Mars 687 days *Jupiter 12 years*

Uranus 84 years *Mercury 88 days* *Earth 365 days (1 year)*

Venus 225 days

Neptune 165 years *Saturn 29 years*

Pluto 248 years

THE SOLAR SYSTEM
Although the planets move at great speeds, they do not fly off in all directions into space because the Sun's gravity holds them in place. This keeps the planets circling the Sun. A planet's "year" is the time it takes to make one complete trip round the Sun. The diagram shows the length of the planet's year in Earth-days or Earth-years.

THE SUN
The Sun is 1,392,000 km (865,000 miles) across. It has a core temperature of 14 million°C and a surface temperature of 5,500°C.

Jupiter -150°C

Saturn -180°C

Venus 465°C *Mars -23°C*

YOU CAN USE THIS SENTENCE TO REMEMBER THE SEQUENCE OF PLANETS: MANY VERY EAGER MOUNTAINEERS JOG SWIFTLY UP NEW PEAKS.

Mercury Day: 430°C Night: -180°C
Earth 15°C

Pluto -230°C

Venus 108,200,000 km (67,200,000 miles)
Jupiter 778,330,000 km (483,000,000 miles)

Uranus -210°C
Neptune -220°C

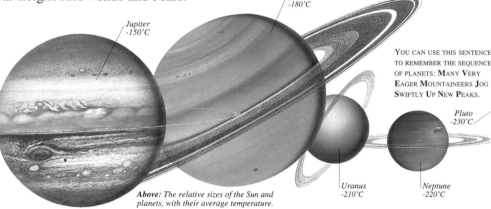
Above: The relative sizes of the Sun and planets, with their average temperature.

| *Mercury 57,910,000 km (36,000,000 miles)* | *Earth 149,500,000 km (92,900,000 miles)* | *Mars 227,940,000 km (141,600,000 miles)* | *Saturn 1,426,980,000 km (886,700,000 miles)* | *Uranus 2,870,990,000 km (1,783,000,000 miles)* | *Neptune 4,497,070,000 km (2,800,000,000 miles)* | *Pluto 5,913,520,000 km (3,670,000,000 miles)* |

Above: The planets and their distances from the Sun.

THE LIFE ZONE: THE EARTH SEEMS TO BE THE ONLY HABITABLE PLANET IN OUR SOLAR SYSTEM. MERCURY AND VENUS, WHICH ARE CLOSER TO THE SUN, ARE HOTTER THAN AN OVEN. MARS, AND PLANETS STILL FARTHER OUT, ARE COLDER THAN A DEEP FREEZE.

Huge solar flares, up to 200,000 km (125,000 miles) long, lick out into space

THE FOUR SEASONS
The Earth always tilts in the same direction on its 950 million-km (590 million-mile) journey around the Sun. This means that each hemisphere in turn leans towards the Sun, then leans away from it. This is what causes summer and winter.

DECEMBER 21ST (SOLSTICE)
Summer in the Southern hemisphere; winter in the Northern hemisphere. At noon, the Sun is overhead at the Tropic of Capricorn. The South Pole is in sunlight for 24 hours, and the North Pole is in darkness for 24 hours.

MARCH 21ST (EQUINOX)
Spring in the Northern hemisphere; autumn in the Southern hemisphere. At noon, the Sun is overhead at the Equator. Everywhere on Earth has 12 hours of daylight, 12 hours of darkness.

It takes 365 days 6 hours 9 minutes 9 seconds for the Earth to make one revolution around the Sun. This is the true length of an Earth "year"

To North Star

The Earth travels around the Sun at 107,244 km per hour (66,600 miles per hour)

The Earth takes 23 hours 56 minutes 4 seconds to rotate once. This is the true length of an Earth "day"

Sun

JUNE 21ST (SOLSTICE)
Summer in the Northern hemisphere; winter in the Southern hemisphere. At noon, the Sun is overhead at the Tropic of Cancer. The North Pole is in sunlight for 24 hours, and the South Pole is in darkness for 24 hours.

SEPTEMBER 21ST (EQUINOX)
Autumn in the Northern hemisphere; spring in the Southern hemisphere. At noon, the Sun is overhead at the Equator. Everywhere on Earth has 12 hours of daylight, 12 hours of darkness.

South Pole

24 HOURS IN THE LIFE OF PLANET EARTH
The Earth turns a complete circle (360°) in 24 hours, or 15° in one hour. Countries on a similar line of longitude (or "meridian") usually share the same time. They set their clocks in relation to "Greenwich Mean Time" (GMT). This is the time at Greenwich (London, England), on longitude 0°. Countries east of Greenwich are ahead of GMT. Countries to the west are behind GMT.

Noon everywhere on this meridian

	0°	15°W	30°W	45°W	60°W	75°W	90°W	105°W	120°W	135°W	150°W	165°W
Noon at:	Greenwich	Dakar	E. Greenland	Rio de Janeiro	Caracas	New York	Mexico City	Calgary	Los Angeles	E. Alaska	Honolulu	(Pacific Ocean)
Greenwich time:	1200 hrs	1100 hrs	1000 hrs	0900 hrs	0800 hrs	0700 hrs	0600 hrs	0500 hrs	0400 hrs	0300 hrs	0200 hrs	0100 hrs

MOON AND EARTH

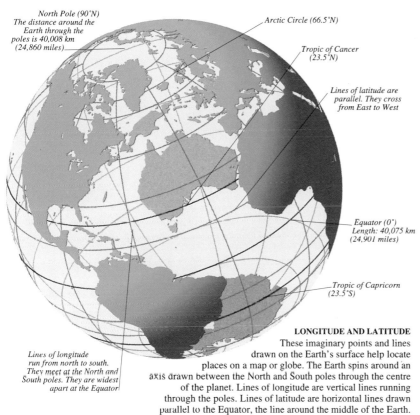

Craters made by collision with meteors

The Moon is a ball of barren rock 3,476 km (2,156 miles) across. It orbits the Earth every 27.3 days at an average distance of 384,400 km (238,700 miles). The Moon's gravity is only one-sixth that of Earth – too small to keep an atmosphere around itself, but strong enough to exert a powerful pull on the Earth. The Moon and Sun together create tides in the Earth's oceans. The period between successive high tides is 12 hours 25 minutes. The highest (or "spring") tides occur twice a month, when the Moon, Sun and Earth are in line.

The Moon's surface temperature falls from 105°C in sunlight to -155°C when it turns away from the Sun

MAGNET EARTH

The Earth acts like a gigantic bar magnet. As the Earth spins in space, swirling currents are set up within its molten core. These movements generate a powerful magnetic field.

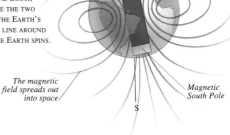

Magnetic North Pole, close to the true North Pole

THE GEOGRAPHICAL NORTH AND SOUTH POLES ARE THE TWO ENDS OF THE EARTH'S AXIS, THE LINE AROUND WHICH THE EARTH SPINS.

The magnetic field spreads out into space

Magnetic South Pole

North Pole (90°N) The distance around the Earth through the poles is 40,008 km (24,860 miles)

Arctic Circle (66.5°N)

Tropic of Cancer (23.5°N)

Lines of latitude are parallel. They cross from East to West

Equator (0°) Length: 40,075 km (24,901 miles)

Tropic of Capricorn (23.5°S)

Lines of longitude run from north to south. They meet at the North and South poles. They are widest apart at the Equator

LONGITUDE AND LATITUDE

These imaginary points and lines drawn on the Earth's surface help locate places on a map or globe. The Earth spins around an axis drawn between the North and South poles through the centre of the planet. Lines of longitude are vertical lines running through the poles. Lines of latitude are horizontal lines drawn parallel to the Equator, the line around the middle of the Earth.

DIAMETER OF EARTH AT EQUATOR: 12,756 KM (7,927 MILES). DIAMETER FROM POLE TO POLE: 12,714 KM (7,900 MILES). MASS: 5,988 MILLION, MILLION MILLION TONNES (TONS).

THE ATMOSPHERE

An envelope of gases such as nitrogen and oxygen surrounds our planet. It provides us with breathable air, filters the Sun's rays and retains heat at night.

Height in km (miles)

INTERPLANETARY SPACE

COMMUNICATIONS AND SOME ASTRONOMICAL SATELLITES 35,880 km (22,295 miles)

EXOSPHERE 500–2,000 km (300–1,240 miles) Outer limit of atmosphere

40,000 (25,000)

SPACE STATION 300 km (186 miles)

THERMOSPHERE 80–500 km (50–300 miles)

SPACE SHUTTLE 300–600 km (186–372 miles)

500 (300)

MESOSPHERE 50–80 km (31–50 miles)

WEATHER BALLOON up to 50 km (31 miles)

80 (50)

STRATOSPHERE 15–50 km (9–31 miles)

OZONE LAYER 15–30 km (9–18 miles)

PASSENGER AIRCRAFT 8–16 km (5–10 miles)

CLOUDS Usually below 10 km (6 miles)

SKYDIVING Typical leap: 4 km (2.5 miles)

HELICOPTER Usually below 2.5 km (1.5 miles)

KITE Usually below 0.1 km, (0.06 miles)

TROPOSPHERE 0–15 km (0-9 miles)

50 (31)

Sea level

WINDS AND CURRENTS

Cold air descends from the poles towards the Equator

Warm air and water travel to the poles from the Equator

Air circulates between the poles and the Equator in stages called "cells"

Winds and currents do not move in straight lines because the Earth spins

The world's winds and ocean currents are caused by the way the Sun heats the Earth's surface. More heat energy arrives at the Equator than at the poles because the Earth is curved and tilted. Warm air and warm water carry much of this energy towards the poles, heating up the higher latitudes. Meanwhile cool air and water moves back towards the Equator, lowering its temperature.

180°	165°E	150°E	135°E	120°E	105°E	90°E	75°E	60°E	45°E	30°E	15°E	0°
Wellington 2400 hrs	(Pacific Ocean) 2300 hrs	Sydney 2200 hrs	Tokyo 2100 hrs	Manila 2000 hrs	Jakarta 1900 hrs	Dacca 1800 hrs	Karachi 1700 hrs	Muscat 1600 hrs	Baghdad 1500 hrs	Cairo 1400 hrs	Berlin 1300 hrs	Greenwich 1200 hrs

THE EARTH'S STRUCTURE

THE EARTH IS IN SOME WAYS like an egg, with a thin shell around a soft interior. Its hard, rocky outer layer – the crust – is up to 70 km (45 miles) thick under the continents, but less than 8 km (5 miles) thick under the oceans. This crust is broken into gigantic slabs, called "plates", in which the continents are embedded. Below the hard crust is the mantle, a layer of rocks so hot that some melt and flow in huge swirling currents. The Earth's plates do not stay in the same place. Instead, they move, carried along like rafts on the currents in the mantle. This motion is very slow – usually less than 5 cm (2 in) a year – but enormously powerful. Plate movement makes the Earth quake and volcanoes erupt, causes immense mountain ranges such as the Himalayas to grow where plates collide, and explains how over millions of years whole continents have drifted across the face of the planet.

DRIFTING CONTINENTS
Currents of molten rock deep within the mantle slowly move the continents. Over time, they appear to "drift" across the Earth's surface.

Pangaea

200 MILLION YEARS AGO
All of today's continents were joined in one supercontinent, called Pangaea. It began to break up about 180 million years ago.

"Africa"
"India"
"Atlantic Ocean" opening up

120 MILLION YEARS AGO
The Atlantic Ocean splits Pangaea into two. India has broken away from Africa.

"North America"
"Asia"
"India"
"Australia"
North America
Europe
Asia
India
"Antarctica"
South America
Australia
Africa
Antarctica

40 MILLION YEARS AGO
India is moving closer to Asia. Australia and Antarctica have separated.

TODAY
India has collided with Asia, pushing up the Himalaya Mountains.

50 MILLION YEARS IN THE FUTURE?
If today's plate movements continue, the Atlantic Ocean will be 1,250 km (775 miles) wider. Africa and Europe will fuse, the Americas will separate again, and Africa east of the Great Rift Valley will be an island.

Great Rift Valley, now sea

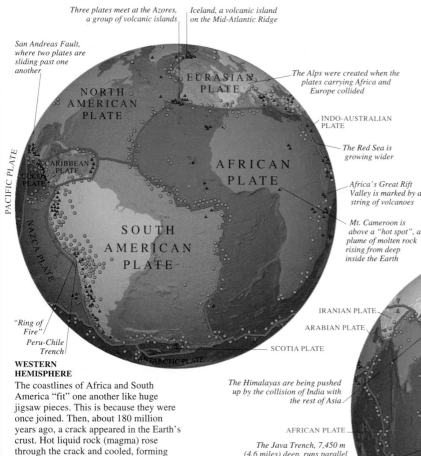

Three plates meet at the Azores, a group of volcanic islands

Iceland, a volcanic island on the Mid-Atlantic Ridge

San Andreas Fault, where two plates are sliding past one another

The Alps were created when the plates carrying Africa and Europe collided

EURASIAN PLATE

NORTH AMERICAN PLATE

INDO-AUSTRALIAN PLATE

The Red Sea is growing wider

CARIBBEAN PLATE

COCOS PLATE

AFRICAN PLATE

Africa's Great Rift Valley is marked by a string of volcanoes

PACIFIC PLATE

Mt. Cameroon is above a "hot spot", a plume of molten rock rising from deep inside the Earth

NAZCA PLATE

SOUTH AMERICAN PLATE

"Ring of Fire"
Peru-Chile Trench

ANTARCTIC PLATE

WESTERN HEMISPHERE
The coastlines of Africa and South America "fit" one another like huge jigsaw pieces. This is because they were once joined. Then, about 180 million years ago, a crack appeared in the Earth's crust. Hot liquid rock (magma) rose through the crack and cooled, forming new oceanic crust on either side. As the ocean grew wider, the continents moved apart. The process continues today.

The "Ring of Fire" passes through Japan.

Mariana Trench, 11,033 m (6.8 miles) deep, where an ocean plate dives into the mantle

EURASIAN PLATE

IRANIAN PLATE

ARABIAN PLATE

PHILIPPINE PLATE

PACIFIC PLATE

SCOTIA PLATE

The Himalayas are being pushed up by the collision of India with the rest of Asia

AFRICAN PLATE

The Java Trench, 7,450 m (4.6 miles) deep, runs parallel to a long chain of active volcanoes in Southeast Asia

INDO-AUSTRALIAN PLATE

ANTARCTIC PLATE

The Hawaiian islands lie over a "hot spot"

Highly volcanic New Zealand lies on the "Ring of Fire"

KEYBOX

▲	*Major active volcano*
●	*Major earthquake*
►◄	*Colliding plates*
▲▼	*Sliding plates*
◄►	*Spreading plates*

THE ATLANTIC OCEAN IS GROWING WIDER BY 2.5 CM (1 IN) A YEAR – ABOUT THE SAME SPEED THAT FINGERNAILS GROW. THE NAZCA PLATE IS SLIDING THREE TIMES FASTER UNDER SOUTH AMERICA, PUSHING UP THE ANDES.

EASTERN HEMISPHERE
Most earthquakes and volcanoes occur around the edges of crustal plates (or plate margins). Australia, in the middle of the Indo-Australian plate, has no active volcanoes and is rarely troubled by earthquakes. Things are very different in neighbouring New Zealand and New Guinea, which lie on the notorious Pacific "Ring of Fire". The Ring is an area of intense volcanic activity which forms a line all the way round the Pacific rim, through the Philippines, Japan and North America, and down the coast of South America to New Zealand.

THE LAYERED EARTH

The Earth has layers, like an egg. The core is made of metals such as iron and nickel. This is surrounded by a rocky mantle and a thin crust.

Crust (solid)

Mantle (solid rock and liquid magma)

Inner core (solid)

Outer core (liquid)

Ocean

Oceanic crust, 5-8 km (3-5 miles) thick

Solid mantle, up to 50 km (30 miles) thick

Liquid mantle

Continental crust, up to 70 km (45 miles) thick

Lithosphere (all crust plus solid layer of mantle). Up to 120 km (75 miles) thick

CRUST

Crust is of two kinds: continental and oceanic. Continental crust is older, thicker and less dense. Beneath the crust is a solid layer of mantle. Together, these form the lithosphere, which is broken into several plates. These float on the liquid mantle layer.

| CRUST | MANTLE | OUTER CORE | INNER CORE |

15°C (59°F) 3,000°C (5,400°F) 4,000°C (7,200°F) 4,500°C (8,100°F)

6,370 km (3,955 miles)
5,000 km (3,100 miles)
3,000 km (1,850 miles)
Sea level

TEMPERATURE AND DEPTH

Our planet is a nuclear-powered furnace, heated from within by the breakdown of radioactive minerals such as uranium. Temperature increases with depth: 100 km (60 miles) down it is 1,350°C (2,460°F), hot enough for rocks to melt.

Magma rising along centre of ridge

Ocean

Magma from molten mantle

Solid mantle

SPREADING PLATES

When two plates move apart, molten rock (magma) rises from the mantle and cools, forming new crust. This is called a constructive margin. Most are found in oceans.

Deep ocean trench opens where plate dives

Mountain

Volcano

Oceanic plate dives into mantle

COLLIDING PLATES THAT DIVE

When two ocean plates or an ocean plate and a continent plate collide, the denser plate is forced under the other, diving down into the mantle. These are destructive margins.

Valley Mountain

Continent A

Continent B

Line of collision

Continental crust crumples

COLLIDING PLATES THAT BUCKLE

When two continents collide, their plates fuse, crumple and push upwards. Mountain ranges such as the Himalayas and the Urals have been formed in this way

Fault

Plate

Plate

SLIDING PLATES

When two plates slide past one another, intense friction is created along the "fault line" between them, causing earthquakes. These are called conservative margins.

ICELAND, MID-ATLANTIC RIDGE

Most constructive margins are found beneath oceans, but here in volcanic Iceland one comes to the surface.

VOLCANO, JAVA

Diving plates often build volcanic islands and mountain chains. Deep ocean trenches form offshore.

FOLDING STRATA, ENGLAND

The clash of continental plates may cause the Earth to buckle and twist far from the collision zone.

SAN ANDREAS FAULT

A huge earthquake is expected soon somewhere along California's San Andreas Fault, seen here.

EXPLOSIVE VOLCANO

About 50 of the world's 600 or so active volcanoes erupt each year. Explosive pressure is created by the build-up of magma, gases, or super-heated steam.

Crater

Cloud of ash, gases and steam

Lava flows

Main vent (opening)

Cone of ash and lava from old eruptions

SOME MAJOR QUAKES AND ERUPTIONS

This map shows some of the worst natural disasters in recorded history. Over one million earthquakes and about 50 volcanic eruptions are detected every year. Most are minor or occur where there are few people, so there is no loss of human life or great damage to property. But crowded cities and poorly-constructed buildings are putting ever-greater numbers at risk.

Direction of ocean plate movement

HOT SPOT, HAWAII

Hawaii is on a "hot spot" in the Earth's crust. This is a plume of hot magma that rises from the mantle and breaks through the thin ocean crust to feed a volcano. As the crust moves, the volcano is carried away, but the hot spot stays, forming a new volcano.

Maui

Chain of older islands, now eroded to below sea level

Oahu: no longer sits over the hot spot. No volcanic eruptions for over 2 million years

Hawaii rises more than 10,000 m (33,000 ft) from the ocean floor

Hot spot

Peru (Quake 1970) 67,000 killed

India (Quake 1993) 30,000 killed

Japan (Quake 1923) 143,000 killed

San Francisco, USA (Quake 1906) 700 killed

Italy (Quake 1908) 75,000 killed

China (Quake 1976) 242,000 killed

Ruiz (Volcano 1985) 22,000 killed

Mt. Pelée (Volcano 1902) 30,000 killed

Vesuvius (Volcano AD 79) 20,000 killed

Krakatau (Volcano 1883) 36,000 killed

Tambora (Volcano 1815) 92,000 killed

SHAPING THE LANDSCAPE

LANDSCAPES ARE CREATED AND CHANGED – even destroyed – in a continuous cycle. Over millions of years, constant movements of the Earth's plates have built its continents, islands and mountains. But as soon as new land is formed, it is shaped (or "eroded") by the forces of wind, water, ice and heat. Sometimes change is quick, as when a river floods and cuts a new channel, or a landslide cascades down a mountain slope. But usually change is so slow that it is invisible to the human eye. Extremes of heat and cold crack open rocks and expose them to attack by wind and water. Rivers and glaciers scour out valleys, the wind piles up sand dunes, and the sea attacks shorelines and cliffs. Eroded materials are blown away or carried along by rivers, piling up as sediments on valley floors or the sea bed. Over millions of years these may be compressed into rock and pushed up to form new land. As soon as the land is exposed to the elements, the cycle of erosion begins again.

ICE ACTION, ALASKA
Areas close to the North Pole are permanently covered in snow and ice. Glaciers are rivers of ice that flow towards the sea. Some glaciers are more than 60 km (40 miles) long.

KEYBOX

Area covered in ice today	Area drained by major river
Ice and snow 18,000 years ago	Protected coastline
Desert	Coast affected by tidal swell
Wind direction (simplified)	Coast affected by storm waves

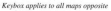

Keybox applies to all maps opposite

THE "ROOF OF NORTH AMERICA"
Steeply-sloping Denali (also called Mt. McKinley), Alaska, is North America's highest mountain at 6,194 m (20,320 ft). It is a fairly "young" mountain, less than 70 million years old. The gently sloping Appalachians in the east of the continent are very much older. Once, they were probably higher than Denali is today. But more than 300 million years of ice, rain and wind have ground them down.

SEA ACTION, CAPE COD
Cape Cod, a sandy peninsula 105 km (65 miles) long, juts out like a beckoning finger into the Atlantic Ocean. Its strangely-curved coastline has been shaped by wave action.

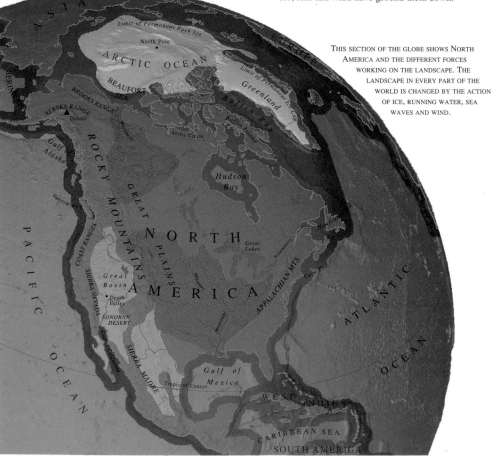

THIS SECTION OF THE GLOBE SHOWS NORTH AMERICA AND THE DIFFERENT FORCES WORKING ON THE LANDSCAPE. THE LANDSCAPE IN EVERY PART OF THE WORLD IS CHANGED BY THE ACTION OF ICE, RUNNING WATER, SEA WAVES AND WIND.

WIND ACTION, DEATH VALLEY
Death Valley is the hottest, driest place in North America. Its floor is covered in sand and salt. Winds sweeping across the valley endlessly reshape the loose surface.

WATER ACTION, MISSISSIPPI
The Mississippi River and its many tributaries frequently change course. Where two loops are close together, the river may cut a new path between them, leaving an "ox-bow lake".

Ice floats because it is less dense than sea water

Only one-ninth of an iceberg shows above sea level

A GLACIER REACHES THE SEA
When a glacier enters the sea, its front edge or "snout" breaks up and forms icebergs – a process called calving. These "ice mountains" are then carried away by ocean currents.

ICE COVER   *See keybox opposite*

Greenland's icecap
Area covered by ice today
ARCTIC
Alps
Himalayas
Area covered by ice 18,000 years ago
NORTH AMERICA
EUROPE
ASIA
SOUTH AMERICA
AFRICA
AUSTRALIA
ANTARCTICA
ANTARCTICA
Key on p.10
Ice once covered much more land than today
Andes   Drakensberg
Australian Alps
Southern Alps

NORDFJORD, NORWAY
One sign of glacial action on the landscape is the fjord. These long, narrow, steep-sided inlets are found along the coasts of Norway, Alaska, Chile and New Zealand. They mark the points where glaciers once entered the sea.

Rock eroded here
Rock fragments and sand deposited here
Hard rock headland broken into small sections
Advancing sea waves
Bay
Headland

COASTAL ATTACK
The ceaseless push and pull of waves on a shore can destroy even the hardest rocks. The softest rocks are eroded first, leaving headlands of hard rock that survive a little longer.

COASTAL EROSION   *See keybox opposite*

Northwest Europe's shorelines are heavily eroded by Atlantic storms
Permanent ice protects Antarctica's shores
Key on p.10
The southern tip of South America is notorious for its devastating storms
The Mediterranean Sea is enclosed by land, so there is little coastal erosion
Islands help protect Asia's mainland from advancing waves

WAVE POWER
The powerful action of waves on an exposed coast can erode a coastline by several metres (feet) a year.

The sheltered slope is steeper than the slope facing the wind
Dunes advance when sand particles are blown over the top of the dune
Wind direction

DESERT DUNE
Dunes are slow-moving mounds or ridges of sand found in deserts and along some coastlines. They only form when the wind's direction and speed is fairly constant.

THE GREAT DESERTS   *See keybox opposite*

Great Basin   Sahara   Arabian
Kara Kum
Takla Makan
Key on p.10
Atacama
Namib
Kalahari   Thar   Gobi
Great Victoria

NAMIB DESERT, SOUTHERN AFRICA
The sand dunes seen in the centre of the picture are about 50 m (160 feet) high. Winds are driving them slowly but relentlessly towards the right. Not all deserts are sandy. Wind may blow away all the loose sand and gravel, leaving bare rock.

This crescent-shaped "ox-bow" lake was once a meander
Old river channel, now filled with sand and gravel
New river channel
Sand and gravel deposited here so bank grows
Direction of flow
Swift currents on outer bends cut steep banks

MEANDERS
River banks are worn away most on the outside of bends, where water flows fastest. Eroded sand and gravel are built up into banks on the inside of bends, in slower-moving water.

THE LARGEST RIVER BASINS   *See keybox opposite*

Mackenzie   Mississippi
Ob'   Yenisey
Lena   Amur
Key on p.10
Amazon
Paraná   Niger
Congo
Nile   Ganges
Yangtse

WINDING RIVER, ALASKA
The more a river meanders across a plain, the longer it becomes and the more slowly it flows.

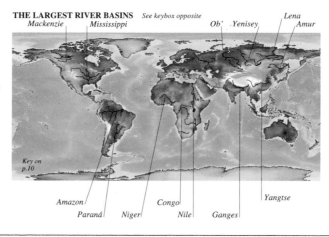

CLIMATE AND VEGETATION

THE EARTH IS the only planet in our solar system which supports life. Most of our planet has a breathable atmosphere, and sufficient light, heat and water to support a wide range of plants and animals. The main influences on an area's climate are the amount of sunshine it receives (which varies with latitude and season), how close it is to the influence of ocean currents, and its height above sea level. Since there is more sunlight at the Equator than elsewhere, and rainfall is highest here too, this is where we find the habitats which have more species of plants and animals than anywhere else: rainforests, coral reefs and mangrove swamps. Where rainfall is very low, and where it is either too hot, such as in deserts, or too cold, few plants and animals can survive. Only the icy North and South Poles, and the frozen tops of high mountains, are practically without life of any sort.

WEATHER EXTREMES
Weather is a powerful influence on how we feel, the clothes we wear, the buildings we live in, the colour of our skin, the plants that grow around us, and what we eat and drink. Extreme weather events such as heatwaves, hurricanes, blizzards, tornadoes, sandstorms, droughts and floods, can be terrifyingly destructive.

TORNADO
Tornadoes are whirlwinds of cold air that develop when thunderclouds cross warm land. They are extremely violent and unpredictable. Windspeeds often exceed 300 km (180 miles) per hour.

TROPICAL STORMS
These devastating winds develop when air spirals upwards above warm seas. More air is sucked in and the storm begins to move. They bring torrential rain, thunder and lightning and destruction.

DROUGHT
Long periods without water kill plants. Stripped of its protective covering of vegetation, the soil is easily blown away.

OCEAN CURRENTS
Currents are a powerful influence on climates. They are like great rivers in the ocean that carry warm water (orange) away from the Equator and cold water (blue) towards the Equator.

Labrador current, *Equatorial currents*, *Gulf Stream*, *Benguela current*, *Oya Shio current*, *North Pacific current*, *California current*, *E. Greenland current*, *Canaries current*, *Monsoon Drift*, *Brazil current*, *Peru current*, *Antarctic circumpolar current*, *Agulhas current*, *W. Australia current*

NORTH AMERICA, EUROPE, ASIA, AFRICA, SOUTH AMERICA, AUSTRALIA, ANTARCTICA

MAIN STORM ZONES
Storms combine very high winds with heavy rainfall (tropical storms) or driving snow (blizzards). Typhoons, cyclones, hurricanes and willy-willies are regional names for tropical storms.

Tropical storms, *Hurricanes, August to October*, *Blizzards*, *Blizzards, November to March*, *Typhoons, April to December*, *Areas prone to flooding*, *Willy-willies, December to April*, *Cyclones, May to December*

TEMPERATURE
Average temperatures are very different around the world. Areas close to the Equator are usually hot (orange on the map); those close to the Poles usually cold (deep blue). The hottest areas move during the year from the Southern to the Northern hemispheres.

Average January temperature

Arctic Circle, Tropic of Cancer, Equator, Tropic of Capricorn, Antarctic Circle

Average July temperature

Highest: 58°C (136°F), Saharan Libya

Lowest: -89°C (-129°F), Antarctica

RAINFALL
The wettest areas (grey) lie near the Equator. The driest are found close to the tropics, in the centre of continents, or at the poles. Elsewhere, rainfall varies with the season, but it is usually highest in summer. Asia's wet season is known as the monsoon.

Average January rainfall

Average July rainfall

Arctic Circle, Tropic of Cancer, Equator, Tropic of Capricorn, Antarctic Circle

Highest in 1 year: 11.68 m (460 in), Hawaii

Lowest: No rain in more than 14 years, Atacama

BROADLEAF FOREST
Temperate climates have no great extremes of temperature, and drought is unusual. Forests usually contain broad-leaved trees, such as beech or oak, that shed their leaves in autumn.

TUNDRA
As long as frozen soil melts for at least two months of the year, some mosses, lichens and ground-hugging shrubs can survive. They are found around the Arctic Circle and on mountains.

NEEDLELEAF FOREST
Forests of cone-bearing, needleleaf trees such as pine and fir cover much of northern North America, Europe and Asia. They are evergreen and can survive long frozen winters. Most have tall, straight trunks and down-pointing branches. This reduces the amount of snow that can settle on them. The forest floor is dark because leaves absorb most of the incoming sunlight.

TRAVELLING SOUTHWARD FROM THE NORTH POLE, A NUMBER OF DISTINCT LIFE ZONES OR "BIOMES" CAN BE SEEN. PLANT AND ANIMAL LIFE IS CLOSELY ADAPTED TO LOCAL CLIMATE.

North Pole

Arctic Circle

Tundra

NORTH AMERICA

Needleleaf Forest

Broadleaf Forest

EUROPE

Mediterranean

MEDITERRANEAN SEA

Tropic of Cancer

CARIBBEAN SEA

ATLANTIC

AFRICA

Hot Desert

Dry Woodland

Tropical Grassland

Equator

Tropical Rainforest

PACIFIC OCEAN

SOUTH AMERICA

Tropical Rainforest

Dry Woodland

OCEAN

Dry

Tropical Grassland

Tropic of Capricorn

Andes

B

For more detailed mapping of vegetation zones, see the individual maps that introduce each continent.

ANTARCTICA

South Pole

MEDITERRANEAN
The hot dry summers and warm wet winters typical of the Mediterranean region are also found in small areas of Southern Africa, the Americas and Australia. Mediterranean-type vegetation can vary from dense forest to thinly spread evergreen shrubs, like these.

MOUNTAIN
Vegetation changes with height because the temperature drops and wind increases. Even on the Equator, mountain peaks can be covered in snow. Although trees may cloak the lower slopes, at higher altitudes they give way to sparser vegetation. Near the top, only tundra-type plants can survive.

TROPICAL RAINFOREST
The lush forests found near the Equator depend on year-round high temperatures and heavy rainfall. Worldwide, they may contain 50,000 different kinds of trees and support several million other plant and animal species. Trees are often festooned with climbing plants, or covered with ferns and orchids that have rooted in pockets of water and soil on trunks and branches.

DRY WOODLAND
Plants in many parts of the tropics have to cope with high temperatures and long periods without rain. Some store water in enlarged stems or trunks, or limit water losses by having small, spiny leaves. In dry (but not desert) conditions, trees are widely spaced, with expanses of grassland between, called savannah.

HOT DESERT
Very few plants and animals can survive in hot deserts. Rainfall is low – under 10 cm (4 in) a year. Temperatures often rise above 40°C (104 °F) during the day, but drop to freezing point at night. High winds and shifting sands can be a further hazard to life. Only specially adapted plants, such as cacti, can survive.

NORTH-SOUTH CROSS-SECTION THROUGH EUROPE AND AFRICA

5,000 (16,404)

Mediterranean-type vegetation

Tundra-type vegetation
Mountain

Tropical rainforest

Temperate rainforest

Dry woodland

Dry woodland

Tundra-type vegetation

Temperate grassland

Tundra-type vegetation

Tropical grassland

Tropical grassland

Mediterranean

Tundra

Needleleaf forest

Needleleaf forest

Broadleaf forest

Hot desert

Mediterranean-type vegetation

Sea level 0

-4,000 (-13,123)

Metres (feet)

A
Arctic Ocean

Lapland

Black Sea

Turkey

Mediterranean Sea

Tropic of Cancer

Ruwenzori Range

Tropic of Capricorn

Drakensberg

Indian Ocean

B

The line running between points 'A' and 'B' on the map is the line of the cross-section

PEOPLE AND PLANET

SOON, THERE WILL BE 6,000 million people on Earth, and numbers are rising at the rate of about one million every week. People are not distributed evenly. Some areas, such as parts of Europe, India and China, are very densely populated. Other areas – particularly deserts, polar regions and mountains – can support very few people. Almost half of the world's population now lives in towns or cities. This is quite a recent development. Until 1800, most people lived in small villages in the countryside, and worked on the land. But since then more and more people have lived and worked in much larger settlements. A century ago, most of the world's largest cities were in Europe and North America, where new industries and businesses were flourishing. Today, the most rapidly-growing cities are in Asia, South America and Africa. People who move to these cities are usually young adults, so the birth rate amongst these new populations is very high.

A CROWDED PLANET?
If the 5.5 billion people alive today stood close together, they could all fit into an area no larger than the small Caribbean island of Jamaica. Of course, so many people could not live in such a small place. Areas with few people are usually very cold, such as land near the poles and in mountains, or very dry, such as deserts. Areas with large populations often have fertile land and a good climate for crops. Cities support huge populations because they are wealthy enough to buy in everything they need.

KEYBOX

Orange represents towns and cities

• City with more than 1 million people.

● City with more than 10 million people

THERE ARE JUST OVER 400 MILLION PEOPLE IN NORTH AMERICA. NEARLY 7 IN 10 LIVE IN A CITY.

NORTH AMERICA

New York
14.6 million

Los Angeles
10.1 million

Mexico City
20.9 million

JAMAICA

Rio de Janeiro
11.7 million

SOUTH AMERICA

São Paulo
18.7 million

Buenos Aires
11.7 million

THERE ARE ABOUT 300 MILLION PEOPLE IN SOUTH AMERICA. MORE THAN 7 IN 10 LIVE IN A CITY.

MILLIONAIRE CITIES 1900
Less than a century ago there were only 13 cities with more than one million people living in them. All the cities were in the northern hemisphere. The largest was London, with seven million people.

MILLIONAIRE CITIES 1950
By 1950, there were nearly 70 cities with more than one million inhabitants. The largest was New York.

SAHARA, AFRICA
The Sahara, like all deserts, is thinly populated. The Tuareg of the northern Sahara are nomads. They travel in small groups because food sources are scarce. Their homes have to be portable.

MONGOLIA, ASIA
Traditionally, Mongolia's nomadic people lived by herding their animals across the steppe. Today, their felt tents, or *gers*, are often set up next to more permanent houses.

AMAZONIA, SOUTH AMERICA
The Yanomami people gather plants in the rainforest and hunt game, but they also grow crops in small forest gardens. Several families live together in a "village" under one huge roof.

MALI, AFRICA
The Dogon people of Mali use mud to construct their elaborate villages. Every family has its own huts and walled areas in which their animals are penned for the night.

WORLD POPULATION GROWTH 1500–2020
Each figure on the graph represents 500 million people.
Note: One billion is 1,000 million.

The world's population in 1500 was about 425 million

The world's population in 1600 was about 545 million

The world's population in 1700 was about 610 million.

1500

1600

1700

POOR SUBURB
Densely-populated "shanty towns" have grown on the fringes of many cities in the developing world. Houses are usually built from discarded materials.

RICH SUBURB
Cities are often surrounded by areas where the richest people live. Population densities are low, and the houses may be luxurious, with large gardens or swimming pools. People in these suburbs rely on their cars for transport. This allows them to live a great distance from places of work and leisure in the city centre.

Land covers less than a third of the Earth's surface.

OCEAN 71%
LAND 29%

Only one-tenth of the total land area can grow crops.

TOO COLD 17%
TOO DRY 24%
POOR SOILS 49%
SUITABLE FOR CROPS 10%

CULTIVATION
Only a small proportion of the Earth's surface can grow crops. It may be possible to bring more land – such as deserts – into production, but yields may be low and costly.

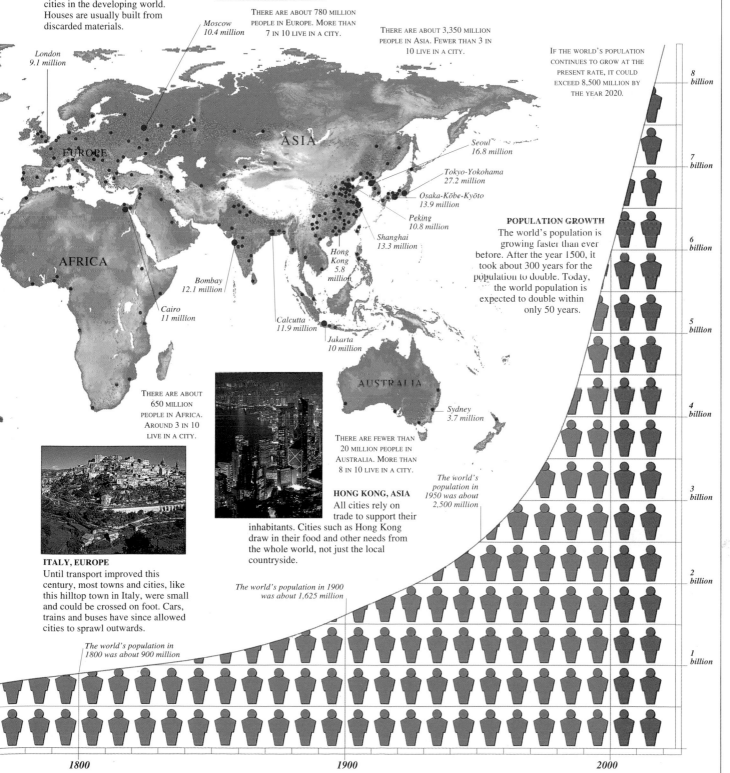

THERE ARE ABOUT 780 MILLION PEOPLE IN EUROPE. MORE THAN 7 IN 10 LIVE IN A CITY.

THERE ARE ABOUT 3,350 MILLION PEOPLE IN ASIA. FEWER THAN 3 IN 10 LIVE IN A CITY.

IF THE WORLD'S POPULATION CONTINUES TO GROW AT THE PRESENT RATE, IT COULD EXCEED 8,500 MILLION BY THE YEAR 2020.

Moscow
10.4 million

London
9.1 million

EUROPE

ASIA

Seoul
16.8 million

Tokyo-Yokohama
27.2 million

Osaka-Kōbe-Kyōto
13.9 million

Peking
10.8 million

Shanghai
13.3 million

AFRICA

Hong Kong
5.8 million

Bombay
12.1 million

Cairo
11 million

Calcutta
11.9 million

Jakarta
10 million

AUSTRALIA

POPULATION GROWTH
The world's population is growing faster than ever before. After the year 1500, it took about 300 years for the population to double. Today, the world population is expected to double within only 50 years.

THERE ARE ABOUT 650 MILLION PEOPLE IN AFRICA. AROUND 3 IN 10 LIVE IN A CITY.

Sydney
3.7 million

THERE ARE FEWER THAN 20 MILLION PEOPLE IN AUSTRALIA. MORE THAN 8 IN 10 LIVE IN A CITY.

The world's population in 1950 was about 2,500 million

HONG KONG, ASIA
All cities rely on trade to support their inhabitants. Cities such as Hong Kong draw in their food and other needs from the whole world, not just the local countryside.

8 *billion*
7 *billion*
6 *billion*
5 *billion*
4 *billion*
3 *billion*
2 *billion*
1 *billion*

ITALY, EUROPE
Until transport improved this century, most towns and cities, like this hilltop town in Italy, were small and could be crossed on foot. Cars, trains and buses have since allowed cities to sprawl outwards.

The world's population in 1900 was about 1,625 million

The world's population in 1800 was about 900 million

1800

1900

2000

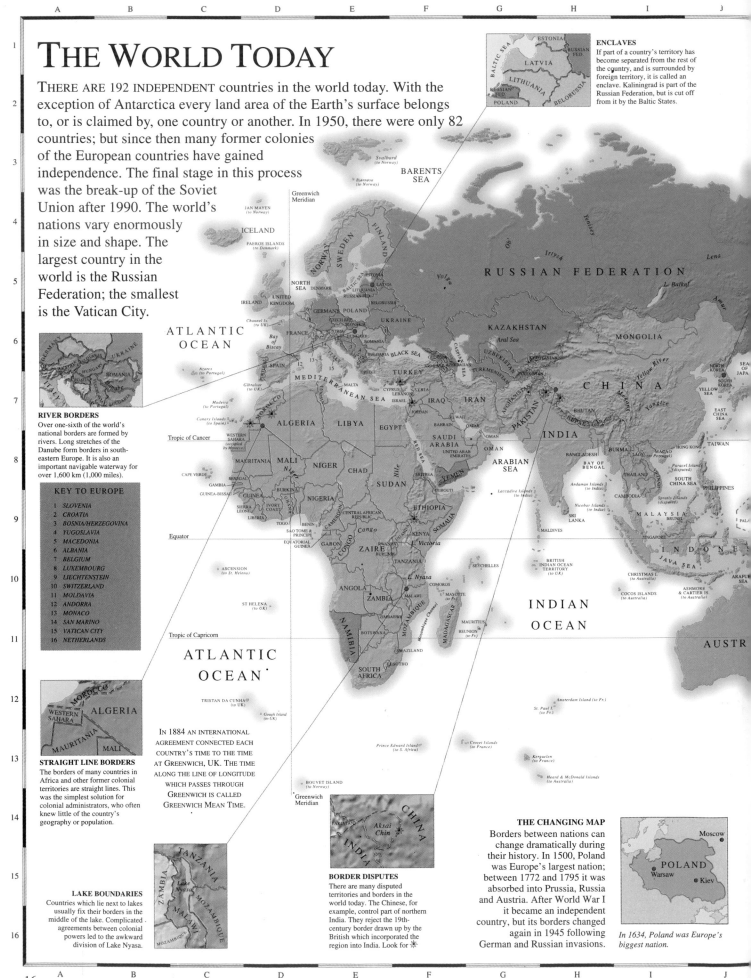

THE WORLD TODAY

THERE ARE 192 INDEPENDENT countries in the world today. With the exception of Antarctica every land area of the Earth's surface belongs to, or is claimed by, one country or another. In 1950, there were only 82 countries; but since then many former colonies of the European countries have gained independence. The final stage in this process was the break-up of the Soviet Union after 1990. The world's nations vary enormously in size and shape. The largest country in the world is the Russian Federation; the smallest is the Vatican City.

ENCLAVES
If part of a country's territory has become separated from the rest of the country, and is surrounded by foreign territory, it is called an enclave. Kaliningrad is part of the Russian Federation, but is cut off from it by the Baltic States.

RIVER BORDERS
Over one-sixth of the world's national borders are formed by rivers. Long stretches of the Danube form borders in south-eastern Europe. It is also an important navigable waterway for over 1,600 km (1,000 miles).

KEY TO EUROPE
1. SLOVENIA
2. CROATIA
3. BOSNIA/HERZEGOVINA
4. YUGOSLAVIA
5. MACEDONIA
6. ALBANIA
7. BELGIUM
8. LUXEMBOURG
9. LIECHTENSTEIN
10. SWITZERLAND
11. MOLDAVIA
12. ANDORRA
13. MONACO
14. SAN MARINO
15. VATICAN CITY
16. NETHERLANDS

STRAIGHT LINE BORDERS
The borders of many countries in Africa and other former colonial territories are straight lines. This was the simplest solution for colonial administrators, who often knew little of the country's geography or population.

IN 1884 AN INTERNATIONAL AGREEMENT CONNECTED EACH COUNTRY'S TIME TO THE TIME AT GREENWICH, UK. THE TIME ALONG THE LINE OF LONGITUDE WHICH PASSES THROUGH GREENWICH IS CALLED GREENWICH MEAN TIME.

LAKE BOUNDARIES
Countries which lie next to lakes usually fix their borders in the middle of the lake. Complicated agreements between colonial powers led to the awkward division of Lake Nyasa.

BORDER DISPUTES
There are many disputed territories and borders in the world today. The Chinese, for example, control part of northern India. They reject the 19th-century border drawn up by the British which incorporated the region into India. Look for ✻

THE CHANGING MAP
Borders between nations can change dramatically during their history. In 1500, Poland was Europe's largest nation; between 1772 and 1795 it was absorbed into Prussia, Russia and Austria. After World War I it became an independent country, but its borders changed again in 1945 following German and Russian invasions.

In 1634, Poland was Europe's biggest nation.

K L M N O P Q R S T

MILITARY BORDERS
At the end of World War II, Korea was occupied by Soviet and American troops. In 1950, after the troops were withdrawn, the communist north attempted to invade the south. In 1953, North and South Korea were divided along the 38° line of latitude. This border has remained heavily fortified.

THE LONGEST BORDER
The border between the USA and Canada is the longest in the world. It cuts through the centre of the Great Lakes. To the west of Michigan, the border runs along the 49° line of latitude. The border slices through the American territory of Point Robert, separating it from the rest of the USA.

ARCTIC OCEAN

International Date Line

BEAUFORT SEA

Greenland (to Denmark)

Baffin Bay

Alaska (to USA)
Yukon
Mackenzie

BERING SEA

Great Slave L.

Hudson Bay

Gulf of Alaska

CANADA

ATLANTIC OCEAN

JAPAN

PACIFIC OCEAN

Missouri

UNITED STATES OF AMERICA

St Pierre and Miquelon (to France)

KEY TO CARIBBEAN
17 CAYMAN IS. (to UK)
18 NAVASSA (to USA)
19 ARUBA (to Neth.)
20 NETHERLANDS ANTILLES (to Neth.)
21 ST. VINCENT AND GRENADINES
22 MARTINIQUE (to Fr.)
23 TURKS AND CAICOS IS. (to UK)
24 ST. CHRISTOPHER AND NEVIS
25 MONTSERRAT (to UK)
26 BRITISH VIRGIN IS. (to UK)
27 VIRGIN IS. (to USA)
28 ANTIGUA AND BARBUDA
29 ANGUILLA (to UK)
30 GUADELOUPE (to Fr.)

Bermuda (to UK)

Mississippi

Gulf of Mexico

BAHAMAS

MIDWAY IS. (to USA)

Hawaii (to USA)

Revillagigedo Islands (to Mexico)

MEXICO

CUBA

23 DOMINICAN REPUBLIC
17 18 HAITI
JAMAICA
PUERTO RICO
BELIZE
GUATEMALA
HONDURAS
EL SALVADOR
NICARAGUA
CARIBBEAN SEA
COSTA RICA
PANAMA

26 29
28
27 30
24 25 DOMINICA
SAINT LUCIA
21 BARBADOS
22 GRENADA
19 20 TRINIDAD & TOBAGO

NORTHERN MARIANAS IS. (to USA)

WAKE I. (to USA)

MARSHALL ISLANDS

JOHNSTON ATOLL (to USA)

MICRONESIA

KINGMAN REEF (to USA)
PALMYRA ATOLL (to USA)

Clipperton Island (to France)

HOWLAND I. (to USA)
BAKER I. (to USA)

Jarvis Island (to USA)

Galápagos Is. (to Ecuador)

VENEZUELA
COLOMBIA
ECUADOR
PERU
SURINAM
FRENCH GUYANA (to Fr.)
GUYANA

NAURU

PAPUA NEW GUINEA

SOLOMON ISLANDS

TUVALU

TOKELAU (to NZ)

KIRIBATI

WESTERN SAMOA
WALLIS & FUTUNA (to Fr.)
AMERICAN SAMOA (to USA)

Amazon
Peru
BRAZIL

Claimed by Argentina
CHILE ARGENTINA

CORAL SEA

CORAL SEA IS. (to Australia)

VANUATU

NEW CALEDONIA (to France)

FIJI

TONGA

NIUE (to NZ)

COOK ISLANDS (to NZ)

FRENCH POLYNESIA (to Fr.)

BOLIVIA

PARAGUAY

Claimed by Chile

PITCAIRN IS. (to UK)

Easter Island (to Chile)

San Ambrosio Island (to Chile)
San Félix I. (to Chile)

Juan Fernández Islands (to Chile)

ARGENTINA
CHILE
Paraná
Uruguay

MOUNTAIN BORDERS
Mountain ranges such as the Pyrenees, Alps and Himalayas form natural borders between many countries. In the Andes, border disputes between Chile and Argentina centred on finding the highest point in the mountain range which divided them.

INDONESIA

Darling
Murray

NORFOLK I. (to Australia)

Lord Howe Island (to Australia)

NEW ZEALAND

TASMAN SEA

Chatham Island (to NZ)

Bounty Island (to NZ)

Antipodes Islands (to NZ)

Auckland Islands (to NZ)

Campbell Island (to NZ)

MacQuarie Island (to Australia)

PACIFIC OCEAN

THE WORLD IS DIVIDED INTO 24 TIME ZONES. THE 180° LINE OF LONGITUDE IS CALLED THE INTERNATIONAL DATE LINE. PLACES JUST WEST OF THIS LINE ARE 24 HOURS AHEAD OF PLACES TO THE EAST. SO, BY TRAVELLING EAST ACROSS THE DATE LINE YOU CAN GO BACK A WHOLE DAY.

FALKLAND IS. (to UK)

SOUTH GEORGIA (to UK)

SOUTH SANDWICH IS. (to UK)

Peter the First Island (to Norway)

International Date Line

PRUSSIA
Warsaw
RUSSIA
Moscow
Kiev
AUSTRIA

From 1772, Poland was part of Austria, Russia and Prussia.

POLAND
Warsaw
Moscow
Kiev

After World War I, Poland became a nation again.

POLAND
Warsaw
Moscow
Kiev

After World War II, the Polish borders were again redrawn.

KEYBOX

Present-day countries established before 1990.

New countries created since 1990.

International borders

Disputed borders

CANADA
Strait of Georgia
Point Robert
USA

Key to maps: Certain symbols will appear on every spread, and are listed below. These symbols represent physical features, or the country's infrastructure: borders, transport, settlement.

International border: Border between countries which is mutually recognized.

De facto border: Border used in practice, but not mutually agreed between two countries.

Claimed border: Border which is not mutually recognized – where territory belonging to one country is claimed by another.

Map area division: This line indicates that a country is treated on two different spreads in the Atlas. It is not an international border.

River border: International borders of any of the first three categories which run along rivers or lakes.

Wadi border: International borders of any of the first three categories which run along wadis (seasonal watercourses).

State border: Border used in some large countries to show their internal divisions.

Main road

Main railway

Main canal

Main oceanic shipping route

PARIS   Capital city

ALBANY   State or administrative capital

Lyons   Major town

Tampico   Other important town

⊕   Major international airport

⊕   Major port

River

Waterfall

Wadi (seasonal watercourse)

Lake

Seasonal lake

▲ 3,000 m   Spot height of mountains

▼ -3,000 m   Spot depth of oceans

Abbreviations: The following abbreviations are used on maps:

Arch. = Archipelago	Pen. = Peninsula
C. = Cape	R. = River
Fr. = France	Res. = Reservoir
L. = Lake	Fed. = Federation
I. = Island	W. = Wadi
Is. = Islands	UK = United Kingdom
Mts. = Mountains	USA = United States
Neth. = Netherlands	of America
NZ = New Zealand	

HOW TO USE THIS ATLAS

THE MAPS IN THIS ATLAS are organized by continent: North America; Central and South America; Europe; Africa; North and West Asia; South and East Asia; Oceania. Each section of the book opens with a large double page spread introducing you to the physical geography – landscapes, climate, animals and vegetation – of the continent. On the following pages, the continent is divided by country, or group of countries. These pages deal with the human geography; each detailed map is supplemented by photographs, illustrations and landscape models. Finally, a glossary defines difficult terms used in the text, and the index provides a list of all place names in the Atlas and facts about each country.

CONTINENT SPREAD

Key to symbols: This keybox lists major physical features which appear on the continental maps

Key to natural vegetation: The world is broken up into areas which are defined by the plants and animals which live there

Locator map: This world map shows where the continent is located

Image key: This natural vegetation colour and symbol box locates the type of landscape on the map to which the photograph refers

⚠ Threatened species: This symbol indicates that the future of certain plants and animals is uncertain

Cross-section: Find 'A' and 'B' on the map, and draw an imaginary line between them. The cross-section is a slice through the Earth along this line

Lines of longitude and latitude: A grid of imaginary lines around the globe used to locate places

COUNTRY SPREAD

Flags: The flag of each nation is positioned next to the country. Population figures are also given

Scale bar: This shows you how distance on the map relates to kilometres and miles

Compass point: This will show you the direction of North

Locator map: This small map shows you the location of each country in relation to the continent to which it belongs

Reference grid: The letters and numbers around this grid help you to locate places listed in the index. For an explanation on how to use the grid, see Index, page 137

Keybox: A keybox on each spread lists the symbols which appear on the map. These symbols have been chosen to illustrate particularly important or interesting aspects of the country

HOW THIS ATLAS WAS MADE

MAKING UP-TO-DATE and accurate maps of the world is a complicated process which draws upon the skills of geographers, researchers, cartographers (or map-makers) and designers. The maps in the *Eyewitness Atlas of the World* are completely new. They have been created using the latest computerized techniques. At the heart of this process was the development of a computerized model of the Earth. Computers store vast amounts of information. Cartographers used this technology to create precise maps, which may be regarded as the most accurate representation of the Earth's surface achieved in atlas form.

MAPS AND PROJECTIONS

Map-makers have a problem: the Earth is round, but a map is flat. In order to represent a curved surface on a flat page, the image of the Earth's surface needs to be stretched and distorted. The mathematical way of achieving this is by using a projection. There are three main types of projection used in this atlas.

CYLINDRICAL PROJECTION
This is most commonly used to make maps of the whole world. The image is rolled out to form a rectangular shape. The image becomes distorted as it moves away from the Equator towards the poles.

CONIC PROJECTION
This is useful for making regional maps and is most often used in this atlas. Distortion occurs as lines converge as they move away from the centre of the map.

ORTHOGRAPHIC PROJECTION
This kind of projection is useful for mapping polar regions. The image appears as though you were looking at the Earth from Space. Distortion increases as you move away from the centre of the map.

THE EARTH MODEL

To create a faithful representation of the Earth's relief – the shape of coastlines, mountains, valleys and plains – an enormous model of the Earth (called a "terrain model") was constructed using a computer. This was achieved by combining and processing various sets of data. Then other features, such as roads, railways, place names and coloured vegetation areas, were added to complete each map.

Points on the grid represent height values

HEIGHT DATA
A grid was created which covers the whole of the Earth's surface. Each point on the grid has an accurate height value. The grid was fed into the computer, and formed the basic framework for the terrain model.

Data records the height of individual hills and mountains

LARGE SCALE MAPS
For large-scale maps, this basic framework was combined with a data set of land heights, which record the height of the summit of every hill and mountain. This produced a much more detailed framework for the terrain model.

Lines join the height points to create a model

PRODUCING THE TERRAIN MODEL
The computer then transformed these elevation points into a basic terrain model known as a wire-frame model. The computer does this by joining the individual height points with lines, creating a realistic image of the Earth's surface.

Colour is added to the wire-frame model

THEMATIC MODELS
Models such as these appear on various pages throughout the Atlas. By adding various layers of extra information and annotations, they are a useful diagrammatic way of showing how the landscape of a particular region works.

Artificial light source, imitating the action of the Sun

A SMOOTH SURFACE
To create the main maps, the computer processed these models even further. Firstly, a smooth surface to the model was created (a process known as interpolation). An artificial light source within the computer was then used to create the effect of hill-shading. This light source imitates the action of the Sun, casting highlights and shadows across the landscape. The coastline was then added to the map.

The terrain model after interpolation

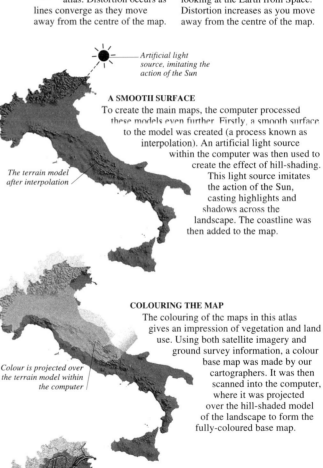

COLOURING THE MAP
The colouring of the maps in this atlas gives an impression of vegetation and land use. Using both satellite imagery and ground survey information, a colour base map was made by our cartographers. It was then scanned into the computer, where it was projected over the hill-shaded model of the landscape to form the fully-coloured base map.

Colour is projected over the terrain model within the computer

THE COMPLETE MAP
Lastly, the remaining map information – rivers, roads, railways, borders, place names and other symbols – were carefully compiled from the most up-to-date sources. These were traced into the computer and combined with the coloured landscape image to create the finished map.

Roads and railways are added to the coloured terrain model

Raccoon
Procyon lotor
Length: 66 cm (26 in)

Desert swallowtail
Papilio coloro
Wingspan: 7 cm (3 in)

Collared lizard
Crotaphytus collaris
Length: 35 cm (14 in)

NORTH AMERICA

NORTH AMERICA FORMS a gigantic downward-pointing triangle, out of which two great bites have been taken – Hudson Bay and the Gulf of Mexico. Huge parallel mountain chains run down the eastern and western sides. The oldest are the Appalachians to the east, which have been worn away by wind and rain for so long that they are now considerably lower than the younger Rockies to the west. The vast landscape between the mountain chains is very flat. There are large forests in the north, while the central Great Plains are covered by grasslands on which huge herds of bison once roamed. North America is a continent of climatic extremes. In the farthest north, temperatures drop to a freezing -66°C (-87°F), and a dome of ice up to 3 km (2 miles) thick covers Greenland. In the hot deserts of the south-west, temperatures can soar to 57°C (134°F).

Triceratops, a vegetarian dinosaur that lived in western North America 70 million years ago.

Douglas fir cone
Pseudotsuga menziesii
Length: 8 cm (3 in)

Road runner
Geococcyx californianus
Length: 60 cm (2 ft)

Loggerhead turtle
Caretta caretta
Length: 1.2 m (4 ft)

AUTUMN IN ALASKA
Only tundra – short grasses, low shrubs and small trees – can survive the northern climate. In the brief Alaskan summer plants burst into bloom, changing colour in the autumn.

THE ROOF OF AMERICA
When water-laden ocean air rises over the Alaska Range, moisture freezes and falls as snow. It is so cold that mountain slopes as low as 900 m (3,000 ft) are always snow-covered.

Eutrephoceras, which lived in North America 100 million years ago. It swam by squirting water out of its body cavity.

VOLCANIC ACTIVITY
The volcanic island of Iceland is part of the Mid-Atlantic Ridge. Intense heat generated deep underground creates bubbling hot mud pools and hot springs.

Coast redwood
Sequoia sempervirens
Height: 100 m (330 ft)

Priscacara, a perch that swam in North America's lakes and rivers 50 million years ago.

RIVERS, TREES AND GRASSLAND
For millions of years rivers flowing east from the Rockies have deposited silt on the Great Plains. This has helped to create a deep and very fertile soil which supports huge areas of grassland.

NORTHERN FORESTS
Forests grow across most of the northern region and on cold mountain slopes. These contain mostly needleleaf trees which are well suited to growing in cold conditions.

RAINFORESTS
Temperate rainforests thrive between the Pacific and the Coast Ranges. Their lush growth is made possible by heavy rainfall carried inland by moist ocean winds.

Bald eagle
Haliaeetus leucocephalus
Wingspan: 2.2 m (7 ft)

DRY WINDS AND SAND DUNES
Dry winds blowing from the centre of the continent, combined with the lack of rain, are responsible for the extensive deserts in the south-west. Because the climate is so dry, vegetation is sparse.

OKEFENOKEE SWAMP
Okefenokee Swamp is part of the complex river system of the south-east. This large wetland area has a warm climate, providing a haven for reptiles such as alligators and snakes. It is also an important resting place for many migratory birds.

American beaver
Castor canadensis
Length: 1.6 m (5 ft)

DESERT RIVER
The brown silt-laden waters of the Colorado River have cut a spectacular gorge through solid rock – the Grand Canyon. It is nearly 2,000 m (6,135 ft) deep.

KEY TO SYMBOLS

▲	*Mountain*
△	*Volcano*
	Mangroves
	Wetlands
	Coral reef
	Plate margins showing direction of movement

DESERT TREES
With searing temperatures and low rainfall, deserts are home to plants which are adapted to conserve water, like cacti and the Joshua Trees shown here.

CROSS-SECTION THROUGH NORTH AMERICA

Coast Ranges
Pacific Ocean
Rocky Mts.
Great Basin
Great Plains
Mississippi
Lake Michigan
Lake Erie
Appalachians Mts.
Cape Cod
Atlantic Ocean

3,000 (9,843)
Sea level 0
-4,500 (-14,764)
Metres (feet)

A
Length: 5,800 km (3,600 miles)
B

KEY TO NATURAL VEGETATION

Mountain	Tundra
Temperate rainforest	Needleleaf forest
Cold desert	Temperate grassland
Mediterranean-type	Broadleaf forest
Hot desert	Tropical rainforest
Dry woodland	

Hooded seal
Cystophora cristata
Length: 3 m (10 ft)

Moose
Alces alces
Shoulder height: 2 m (7 ft)

21

WESTERN CANADA AND ALASKA

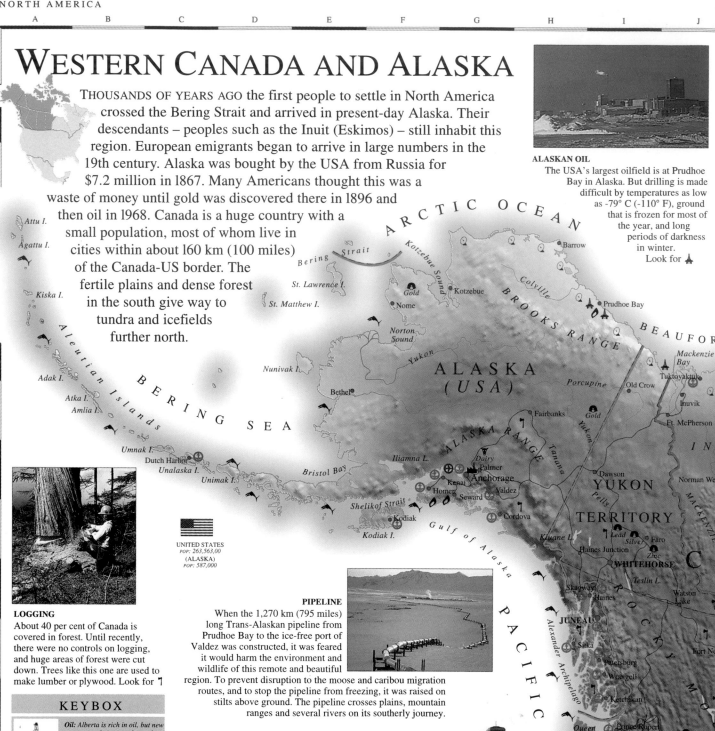

THOUSANDS OF YEARS AGO the first people to settle in North America crossed the Bering Strait and arrived in present-day Alaska. Their descendants – peoples such as the Inuit (Eskimos) – still inhabit this region. European emigrants began to arrive in large numbers in the 19th century. Alaska was bought by the USA from Russia for $7.2 million in 1867. Many Americans thought this was a waste of money until gold was discovered there in 1896 and then oil in 1968. Canada is a huge country with a small population, most of whom live in cities within about 160 km (100 miles) of the Canada-US border. The fertile plains and dense forest in the south give way to tundra and icefields further north.

ALASKAN OIL
The USA's largest oilfield is at Prudhoe Bay in Alaska. But drilling is made difficult by temperatures as low as -79° C (-110° F), ground that is frozen for most of the year, and long periods of darkness in winter.
Look for ⚓

UNITED STATES
POP: 263,563,00
(ALASKA)
POP: 587,000

LOGGING
About 40 per cent of Canada is covered in forest. Until recently, there were no controls on logging, and huge areas of forest were cut down. Trees like this one are used to make lumber or plywood. Look for ⌐

PIPELINE

When the 1,270 km (795 miles) long Trans-Alaskan pipeline from Prudhoe Bay to the ice-free port of Valdez was constructed, it was feared it would harm the environment and wildlife of this remote and beautiful region. To prevent disruption to the moose and caribou migration routes, and to stop the pipeline from freezing, it was raised on stilts above ground. The pipeline crosses plains, mountain ranges and several rivers on its southerly journey.

KEYBOX

Oil: *Alberta is rich in oil, but new sources are being sought, such as the tar sands near Athabasca where the oil has to be separated from the sand. Look for* ⚓

Border: *The world's longest undefended border runs between Canada and the USA. People and goods can cross it with few restrictions. Look for* ⇅

Radar: *The joint Canada-US Distant Early Warning system has been a key component in the defence of the North American continent since 1957. Look for* ⛆

🐂	Cattle	⛑	Mining
🌾	Cereals	🎖	Coal
🔨	Timber	⬦	Gas
🐟	Fishing	⚙	Industrial centre

CALGARY STAMPEDE

The city of Calgary in Alberta started life as a centre of the cattle trade. Although today it is an oil centre, its cowboy traditions are continued in the Stampede, a huge rodeo held every July. For ten days spectators watch displays that include bronco-busting, bull-riding and chuck-wagon racing.

VANCOUVER

This city began as a small settlement for loggers and is now a major port. Grain from Canada's prairies and timber from its forests are shipped from Vancouver's ice-free harbour to countries across the Pacific. The city has attracted many immigrants; at first from Europe, then Asia and, most recently, from Hong Kong.

Brilliant autumn colours in British Columbia.

Mountains are mirrored in Lake Louise, Alberta.

Caribou roam the northern parts of Canada and Alaska.

TRANSPORT

In a country as vast as Canada, transport is vital. When the Canadian Pacific Railway was completed in 1885, the country's east and west coasts were linked for the first time. Roads like the Trans-Canada Highway also helped to open up the country, especially the wilderness areas. Here, a highway crosses a spectacular part of Alberta.

SALMON FISHING

The main fish caught on Canada's west coast is the Pacific salmon. The bulk of the catch is canned. The cans are made at aluminium smelting plants like the one at Kitimat, where the plant is powered by hydro-electricity produced by the damming and reversing of the Nechako River. Look for

Pacific salmon

Edmontonia, a dinosaur once found in Alberta.

KWAKIUTL

The Kwakiutl, among the first peoples to settle along Canada's west coast, were skilled artisans. Families displayed their wealth and prestige in posts carved with animal and human figures. Other carved pieces were created for the *potlach*, a celebration of gift giving. When this was banned in 1884, many artifacts were destroyed. Since the 1950s, native artists have revived the traditional techniques.

SNOWSHOES

Snowshoes, made from wooden frames strung with animal gut or leather strips, were once essential for winter travel. They are still used in areas where vehicles, such as snowmobiles, cannot manoeuvre.

THE PRAIRIES

Grain production on the vast prairies of western Canada is highly mechanized; one farmer can harvest several hundred hectares (acres) single-handed. After the grain is cut, it is stored in huge grain elevators like these before being sent by rail to cities or ports. Railways were the key to the development of farming on the prairies. Look for

Harvesting grain on the fertile prairies of Saskatchewan.

CANADA
POP: 29,248,000
(WESTERN CANADA)
POP: 8,062,000

0   100   200   300   400   500   600   700 KM
0 50 100 150 200 250 300 350 400 MILES

### Map labels

Nares Strait, Ellesmere I., Axel Heiberg I., Queen Elizabeth Islands, Baffin Bay, Mackenzie King I., Bathurst I., Lead, Devon I., Melville I., Cornwallis I., Zinc, Resolute, Lancaster Sound, Parry Is., McClure Strait, Viscount Melville Sound, Banks I., Prince of Wales I., Gulf of Boothia, Somerset I., Baffin I., BAFFIN, Davis Strait, Prince Charles I., Cumberland Sound, Pangnirtung, Amundsen Gulf, Victoria I., McClintock Channel, King William I., Foxe Basin, Iqaluit, Frobisher Bay, Hudson Strait, KITIKMEOT, Coppermine, NORTHWEST TERRITORIES, Great Bear L., Southampton I., Contwoyto L., Gold, Garry L., Coats I., KEEWATIN, FORT SMITH, Lac la Martre, Dubawnt L., Chesterfield Inlet, CANADA, Rankin Inlet, YELLOWKNIFE, Fort Simpson, Great Slave L., Nonacho L., Eskimo Pt, Hudson Bay, Hay River, Fort Revolution, Fort Smith, Uranium City, Seal, Churchill, L. Athabasca, Uranium, Wollaston L., Silver, Copper, Fort Vermilion, Cree L., Uranium, Reindeer L., Zinc, Gold, MANITOBA, Nelson, Fort St John, Lesser Slave L., Frobisher L., Lynn Lake, Nickel, Hayes, Dawson Creek, Beef, Potassium, Thompson, Grande Prairie, Athabasca, SASKATCHEWAN, Flin Flon, Copper, ALBERTA, Jasper, Leduc, EDMONTON, Lloydminster, North Battleford, Prince Albert, The Pas, L. Winnipeg, ONTARIO, Wetaskiwin, Saskatchewan, Wheat, Red Deer, Dairy, Wheat, Saskatoon, Yorkton, L. Winnipegosis, Drumheller, Potash, Melville, Trans-Canada Highway, Selkirk, Calgary, Swift Current, Wheat, Moose Jaw, REGINA, Brandon, WINNIPEG, Medicine Hat, Lethbridge, Wheat, Weyburn, Dairy, Cranbrook, Beef, Estevan, UNITED STATES OF AMERICA

EASTERN CANADA

THE VIKINGS WERE THE FIRST Europeans to visit eastern Canada in about AD 986. Then, in the 15th and 16th centuries two expeditions, one from England and one from France, reached Canada and each claimed it. Traders and fur trappers from the two countries followed, setting up rival trading posts and settlements. The struggle for territory led to war between Britain and France. The French were forced to give up their Canadian territories to Britain in 1763, but the French language is still spoken in the province of Quebec today. Canada eventually achieved effective independence from Britain in 1867. Today, southern Quebec and Ontario form eastern Canada's main industrial region, containing most of its population and two of its largest cities – Montreal and Toronto. The Hudson Bay area, while rich in minerals, is a wilderness of forests, rivers and lakes. Snowbound for much of the year, it is sparsely inhabited except by Inuit in the far north.

The Toronto Sky Dome, a huge stadium which seats 50,000.

FRENCH / ENGLISH
Most Canadians speak English, but the country is officially bilingual – as can be seen from the use of both French and English on this stamp which commemorates the province of New Brunswick.

The sap of the sugar maple tree is made into syrup and sugar. The maple leaf is Canada's national symbol.

CANADA
POP: 29,248,000
(EASTERN CANADA)
POP: 19,738,000

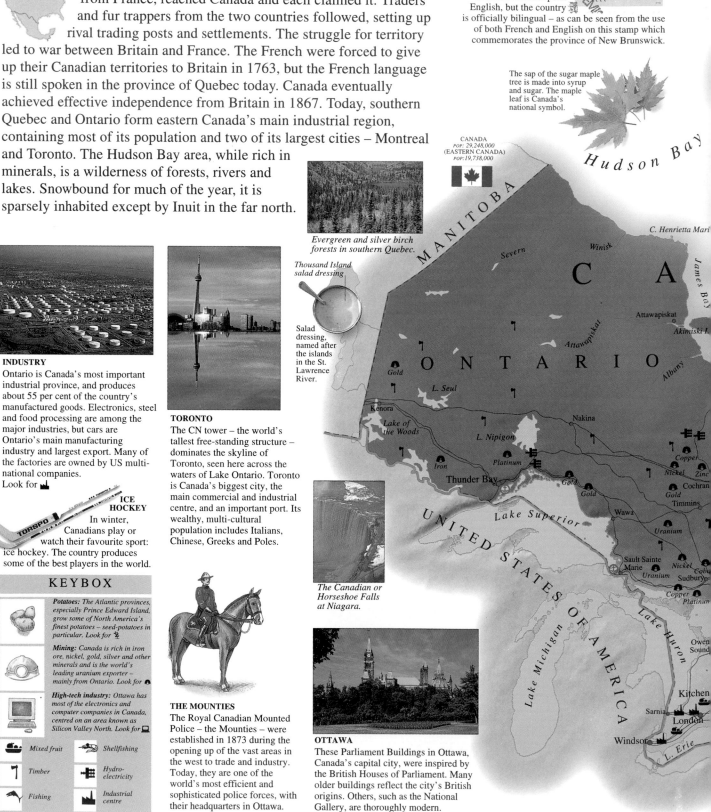

Evergreen and silver birch forests in southern Quebec.

Thousand Island salad dressing

Salad dressing, named after the islands in the St. Lawrence River.

INDUSTRY
Ontario is Canada's most important industrial province, and produces about 55 per cent of the country's manufactured goods. Electronics, steel and food processing are among the major industries, but cars are Ontario's main manufacturing industry and largest export. Many of the factories are owned by US multi-national companies. Look for 🏭

ICE HOCKEY
In winter, Canadians play or watch their favourite sport: ice hockey. The country produces some of the best players in the world.

TORONTO
The CN tower – the world's tallest free-standing structure – dominates the skyline of Toronto, seen here across the waters of Lake Ontario. Toronto is Canada's biggest city, the main commercial and industrial centre, and an important port. Its wealthy, multi-cultural population includes Italians, Chinese, Greeks and Poles.

KEYBOX

Potatoes: The Atlantic provinces, especially Prince Edward Island, grow some of North America's finest potatoes – seed-potatoes in particular. Look for 🌱

Mining: Canada is rich in iron ore, nickel, gold, silver and other minerals and is the world's leading uranium exporter – mainly from Ontario. Look for ⛑

High-tech industry: Ottawa has most of the electronics and computer companies in Canada, centred on an area known as Silicon Valley North. Look for 💻

🐟	Mixed fruit	🦐	Shellfishing
🌲	Timber	⚡	Hydro-electricity
🎣	Fishing	🏭	Industrial centre

THE MOUNTIES
The Royal Canadian Mounted Police – the Mounties – were established in 1873 during the opening up of the vast areas in the west to trade and industry. Today, they are one of the world's most efficient and sophisticated police forces, with their headquarters in Ottawa.

The Canadian or Horseshoe Falls at Niagara.

OTTAWA
These Parliament Buildings in Ottawa, Canada's capital city, were inspired by the British Houses of Parliament. Many older buildings reflect the city's British origins. Others, such as the National Gallery, are thoroughly modern.

MANITOBA

Hudson Bay

C. Henrietta Mari

Severn
Winisk

CANADA

James Bay

Attawapiskat
Akimiski I.

ONTARIO

Gold
L. Seul
Albany

Kenora
Lake of the Woods
Nakina

L. Nipigon
Iron
Platinum
Thunder Bay
Gold
Gold

Copper
Nickel Zinc
Cochran
Gold
Timmins

Uranium
Wawa

UNITED STATES
Lake Superior

Sault Sainte Marie
Uranium
Nickel Cob
Sudbury
Copper
Platinum

OF AMERICA

Lake Michigan

Lake Huron

Owen Sound

Kitchen
Sarnia
London
Windsor
L. Erie

K L M N O P Q R S T

A polar bear mother and cubs
on the ice in Hudson Bay.

JAMES BAY
Canada uses its rivers to produce more
hydro-electric power than any other
nation. In the remote James Bay region
of Quebec, five hydro-electric power
complexes are planned to utilize
the area's powerful rivers. So
far, only the Grande
Rivière complex has been
completed. Look for

NEWFOUNDLAND
Until recently, Newfoundland's
economy was largely dependent on
fishing. Now, however, the mining and
timber industries are being developed
and the island boasts two of Canada's
largest paper mills. Oil is also a major
industry.

Sawn log

FOREST PRODUCTS
Wood and other products from
its forests earn Canada twice
as much as agriculture
does. Newsprint is a
major export in Ontario,
Quebec and the
Atlantic provinces. It
is made from wood
pulp. Look for

C. Chidley
Akpatok I.
Ungava Bay

LABRADOR SEA

Inukjuak
Kuujjuaq
Rivière aux Feuilles

Belcher Is.
(NW Territories)

Kuujjuarapik

Grande Rivière
de la Baleine

Caniapiscau

Schefferville

Nain
Hopedale
Makkovik
Cartwright

Caniapiscau Res

N A D A

NEWFOUNDLAND

Smallwood
Reservoir
Goose Bay
Port Hope
Simpson

La Grande
Rivière

La Grande Rivière
H.E.P. Project

Churchill
Falls

Belle I.

Eastmain

Ross Bay
Junction

Iron
Labrador City
Iron

Newfoundland
Corner Brook
Grand Falls
Clarenville
ST. JOHN'S

Rivière de Rupert

Manicouagan Res

Havre-Saint-Pierre

Strait of Belle Isle

Moosonee

Q U E B E C

L. Mistassini

Sept-Îles

Île d'Anticosti

Gulf of St. Lawrence

Channel-Port-
aux-Basques
Cabot Strait

Placentia
Bay
C. Race

Copper
Zinc
Silver
Gold

Silver
Copper
Chibougamau

Gold

St. Lawrence

Gaspé

Îles de la
Madeleine

Grand
Banks

ST PIERRE
ST PIERRE & MIQUELON
(to France)

Gold
L. Saint-Jean
Jonquière
Chicoutimi

Copper
Bathurst

PRINCE
EDWARD
ISLAND

Sydney

L. Abitibi
Silver Gold
Val-d'Or

Gouin Res

Silver
Zinc Lead
NEW
BRUNSWICK

CHARLOTTE-
TOWN

A T L A N T I C   O C E A N

La Tuque

QUEBEC

Grand
Falls

Moncton

Ottawa
Silver
North
Bay

Trois-Rivières

Trans-Canada
Highway
Drummondville

Laval

Sherbrooke

FREDERICTON

NOVA
SCOTIA
Truro

Saint John

HALIFAX

OTTAWA

Gatineau
Montreal

St. Lawrence
Seaway (Canal)

Bay of Fundy

Liverpool
Yarmouth

Barrie
Peterborough
Kingston

C. Sable

ST. LAWRENCE SEAWAY
This 3,500 km (2,200 mile) long
waterway follows the St.
• Lawrence River and the Great
Lakes to the heart of Canada's
industrial region. Ocean-going
ships of many nations pass
through the 16 locks which climb
183 m (600 ft) from sea level to
the level of Lake Ontario.

TORONTO
Hamilton
Niagara
Falls

Lake Ontario

Niagara
Peninsula

Atlantic cod

U N I T E D   S T A T E S   O F   A M E R I C A

FISHING
Off Canada's eastern coast is a
shallow continental shelf called the
Grand Banks, which is one of the world's
richest fishing areas. Many types of fish are caught
there, the most valuable being cod. However, the area
has been overfished and stocks of fish must now be
carefully conserved. Canada has taken control of
all fishing within 320 km (200 miles)
of its coastline and hardly any
commercial cod fishing is
allowed. Look for

FRUIT GROWING
The Niagara Peninsula
is the strip of land
between Lake Erie and
Lake Ontario. These huge lakes affect
the climate in this area, making it milder. The
peninsula has rich soils, so a wide range of
fruit can be grown, including peaches,
cherries, apples and grapes. Look for

Apple
Cherry
Peach

N

0 50 100 150 200 250 300 350 400 KM
0   50   100   150   200   MILES

NORTHEASTERN UNITED STATES

THE FIRST INHABITANTS of Northeast America were the Native peoples, who made their living for thousands of years from fishing and farming. These peoples were among the first to encounter settlers from Europe in the 16th century, and their numbers were drastically reduced by warfare and contact with European diseases. Many of the first settlers, such as the Puritan pilgrims who sailed to Cape Cod on board the *Mayflower*, were victims of religious persecution, determined to found a brave new world in America. Most settlers were English, and they called the newly-discovered territory New England. They cleared land for farming, founded universities, built churches and established cities. Thanksgiving, celebrated throughout America, commemorates the end of the *Mayflower* pilgrims' first year and their successful harvest. Northeast America, with its rich mineral resources, good harbours and fast-flowing rivers, was the first area on the continent to become industrialized and urbanized. By the mid-19th century, immigrants from Europe were flocking to the USA, many of them settling in New York, or in other East Coast cities. Today, this region is the most densely populated and heavily industrialized area of the United States.

THE HUDSON-MOHAWK GAP
New York became the East Coast's leading port thanks to its fine harbour and its location at the mouth of the Hudson River. The Hudson connects with the Mohawk River, giving the city access to the continent's interior; mineral resources and industrial produce were transported along this route.

The spectacular Niagara Falls near Buffalo, New York State.

THE AMISH
This isolated Amish farmstead near Lancaster, Pennsylvania, is run without any modern technology. The Amish are a Protestant sect who came to America from Switzerland in the 18th century. They live by farming, weave all their own clothes and use horses for transport.

PUMPKINS
Pumpkins are grown all over New England, and pumpkin pie is a favourite American dish. Pumpkins are also hollowed out to make Jack O'Lanterns for the Hallowe'en festival.

TOMATO SOUP
Many of the fruit and vegetables for the region's big cities, especially New York, are grown in the fruit and vegetable farms, called market gardens, of New Jersey (known as "the Garden State"). Tomatoes are grown in huge quantities, and made locally into tinned tomato soup. Look for 🛒

Severe winter weather is common in New England.

NEW ENGLAND BERRIES
Cranberries and blueberries both come from New England and large quantities are grown there. Cranberries are used in sauces, especially to go with roast turkey at Thanksgiving. Blueberries are sweeter, and are often used in pies.

Blueberries
Cranberries

KEYBOX

Sailing: *Yachting is a popular pastime on New England's Atlantic coast. The Bermuda Race starts from Rhode Island. Look for* ⛵

Universities: *There are more centres of further education and research and development in New England than in any other part of the USA. Look for* 🖥

Maple syrup: *Both sugar and syrup are obtained from the sap of maple trees. Vermont is the USA's main producer. Look for* ⚓

🐂	Cattle	🚢	Fishing port
🐔	Poultry	⛏	Coal
🛒	Market gardening	🏭	Industrial centre
🐟	Fishing	💻	High-tech industry

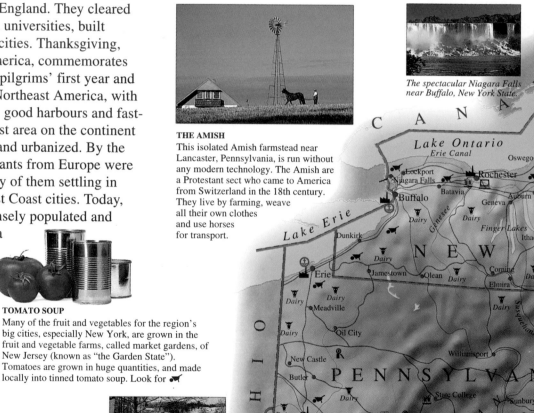

CANADA

Lake Ontario
Erie Canal
Oswego
Lockport
Niagara Falls
Buffalo
Batavia
Rochester
Geneva
Auburn
Genesee
Finger Lakes
Ithaca
Dairy
Dairy
Corning
Dunkirk
Dairy
NEW
Erie
Jamestown
Olean
Dairy
Elmira
Dairy
Lake Erie
Dairy
Dairy
Meadville
Dairy
Dairy
Oil City
Susquehanna
Williamsport
New Castle
State College
Sunbury
Butler
PENNSYLVAN
Dairy
Pittsburgh
Indiana
Altoona
Lewistown
Johnstown
Washington
Monessen
HARRISBURG
Dairy
Uniontown
Carlisle
Gettysburg
Lancaster
York
WEST VIRGINIA
APPALACHIAN
MARYLAND
OHIO

UNITED STATES
POP: 263,563,000
(NORTHEASTERN STATES)
POP: 51,806,000

Elevation map labels: Adirondack Mts. · Albany · Hudson Valley · Utica · Hudson R. · Mohawk R. · Syracuse · Rochester · Long Island · L. Ontario · New York City · Appalachian Mountains

0	25	50	75	100	125	150	175 KM
0	25		50		75		100 MILES

MARITIME NEW ENGLAND
The Atlantic Ocean off New England teems with fish, and many people in this region make their living from fishing. Many towns grew wealthy as fishing and whaling ports: today, clams, mussels, lobsters, oysters and scallops are caught in large quantities. Maine lobster and clam chowder (a thick soup) are New England delicacies. Look for ➤

VERMONT IN AUTUMN
The state of Vermont has a very small population, and much of its income comes from tourism. Visitors come to Vermont for fishing, hiking, skiing and, above all, its breathtaking mountain scenery. It is at its best in autumn, when the leaves change colour. The red leaves of the maple trees are especially striking.

Minke whales are found off the coast of Cape Cod in the summer.

Portable telephone set

HIGH-TECH
High-technology industries, such as electronics and computers, are concentrated in the Boston region and in eastern New Jersey. Universities provide expertise in research and development. There are more engineers and scientists in New Jersey than in any other state. Look for 🖥

Bright yellow taxis are used in New York City.

The rugged Maine coast is popular with summer visitors.

WOODEN ARCHITECTURE
The clapboard buildings of New England copy stone and brick architecture in wood. The town of Portsmouth, New Hampshire, has outstanding examples of 18th-century wooden houses; many were built for merchants and sea captains.

RHODE ISLAND RED
Rhode Island is the smallest state in the USA. It has, however, given its name to a chicken, the Rhode Island Red, bred in the state in 1857. Used for both meat and eggs, Rhode Island Reds are now reared in Europe as well as America. Although Rhode Island is mainly industrial, poultry and dairy farming are still important. Look for 🐓

Rhode Island Red cockerel

THE BIG APPLE
New York City is home to many book publishers, television networks and major newspapers, dominating the national media. The stock exchange on Wall Street is the largest in the world, handling over 100 million shares a day. Nearly 100 of the largest companies in the USA are based here, and many banks have headquarters in the city.

INDUSTRIAL BLIGHT
By 1900, Pennsylvania was heavily industrialized, with vast coal mines, steel mills and a heavy engineering industry. In recent years oil has replaced coal, manufacturing has declined and steel mills have closed. Today, much of Pennsylvania's industrial landscape is a desolate wasteland.

The Statue of Liberty stands at the entrance to New York harbour.

NEW YORK CITY
New York, with a population of over 7 million, is the USA's largest city. Always a major port of entry for immigrants, New York is a mix of different peoples. Manhattan is the commercial and cultural centre of the city. The Manhattan skyline and Statue of Liberty are world-famous.

A B C D E F G H I J

THE SOUTHERN STATES

THIS PART OF THE USA can be divided into three broad regions. To the north, the ridges and valleys of the Appalachian Mountains form a hilly landscape, rich in coal deposits. Immediately to the south and west, the cotton-belt states, with fertile land and a warm, moist climate, are ideal for agriculture. The tropical, humid Gulf region has rich fishing resources; large cargo ports and oil terminals also line the coast. By the 19th century the South had developed an agricultural economy, based on tobacco, rice, indigo and especially cotton, cultivated by African slaves. The northern states believed that slavery in the southern states was wrong, and should be abolished. The South's defeat in the Civil War that followed devastated the region. Today, the South's economy is more varied, thanks to the discovery of oil reserves in the Gulf region and the development of industry. Florida, has experienced great population growth in recent years, becoming the fourth-largest state in the 1980s. Its population includes retired people from other states and refugees from Cuba, the Caribbean and Latin America.

Horses graze on a Kentucky farm, in the Bluegrass country.

ATLANTA
The commercial centre of the region is Atlanta, which is the hub of the South's transport network, and has one of the world's busiest airports. Raw materials flood into Atlanta and manufactured goods pour out: clothes, books, iron and steel products and Coca Cola are all made here.

DERBY DAY
Kentucky is called the "Bluegrass State" after the grasslands around the city of Lexington, which provide superb grazing for livestock. This area has the world's greatest concentration of stud farms for breeding thoroughbred horses. The Kentucky Derby, held at Louisville, is one of the world's most famous horse races.

Orange
Lemon
Florida produces three-quarters of the USA's oranges and grapefruits.
Grapefruit
Lime

KEYBOX

Soya beans: The main crop in the South is the soya bean. Used for oil, margarine and livestock feed, it has found both domestic and export markets. Look for ✿

Coal: Coal, mined from the rich reserves of the Appalachian Mountains, is being overtaken by oil and gas. Look for ⚒

High-tech industry: The South, with its skilled labour force and good communications, is attracting many high-tech industries. Look for ▭

Space centre: The Space Shuttle is launched from the Kennedy Space Center, the launch site of the US Space programme. Look for ▲

🌾 Cereals	🐟 Fishing	
🍃 Citrus fruit	⚓ Oil	
🥜 Peanuts	⛏ Mining	
⚓ Cotton	🏭 Industrial centre	
🚬 Tobacco	🎣 Tourism	

JAZZ
Jazz saxophone
Jazz developed in New Orleans in the early 1900s. Originally it was the music of the bands who marched through the streets, playing at funerals and weddings. Jazz combined many influences – "blues" and spirituals (sung by slaves) and popular songs. Wind instruments are accompanied by drums, piano and double bass.

MISSISSIPPI
Steamboats carry tourists on scenic trips along the Mississippi, one of the world's busiest waterways. Barges transport heavy cargoes from the industrial and agricultural regions near the Great Lakes to the Gulf Coast.

KING COTTON
Cotton, grown on large plantations using slave labour, was once the basis of the Southern economy. Today, it is still grown on farms in some parts of the South. Look for ⚓

Okra
Prawn
Gumbo is a spicy seafood and vegetable stew from Louisiana.

BOURBON
Maize is one of Kentucky's major crops. It is used for making Bourbon whisky, which is a worldwide export.

RETIREMENT STATE
Nearly 30 per cent of Florida's inhabitants are over 55 years old. Large numbers of people retire to Florida, lured by its climate and sports facilities. Many settle in retirement developments or in the coastal cities.

### Map labels
MISSOURI
OKLAHOMA
Fayetteville
BOSTON MTS.
White R.
Black R.
Fort Smith
ARKANSAS
L. Ouachita
North Little Rock
Memphis
Hot Springs
LITTLE ROCK
Aluminium
Pine Bluff
Ouachita
Arkansas
Mississippi
TEXAS
Shreveport
Greenville
Maize
Monroe
Yazoo
Maize
Red R.
LOUISIANA
JACKSON
Alexandria
Meri
MISSISSIPP
Maize
Pearl
Lake Charles
Lafayette
Hattiesbur
BATON ROUGE
L. Pontchartrain
Gulfport
Marsh I.
New Orleans
Biloxi
Sulphur
Sulphur
Breton Sound
Mississippi Delta

A B C D E F G H I J

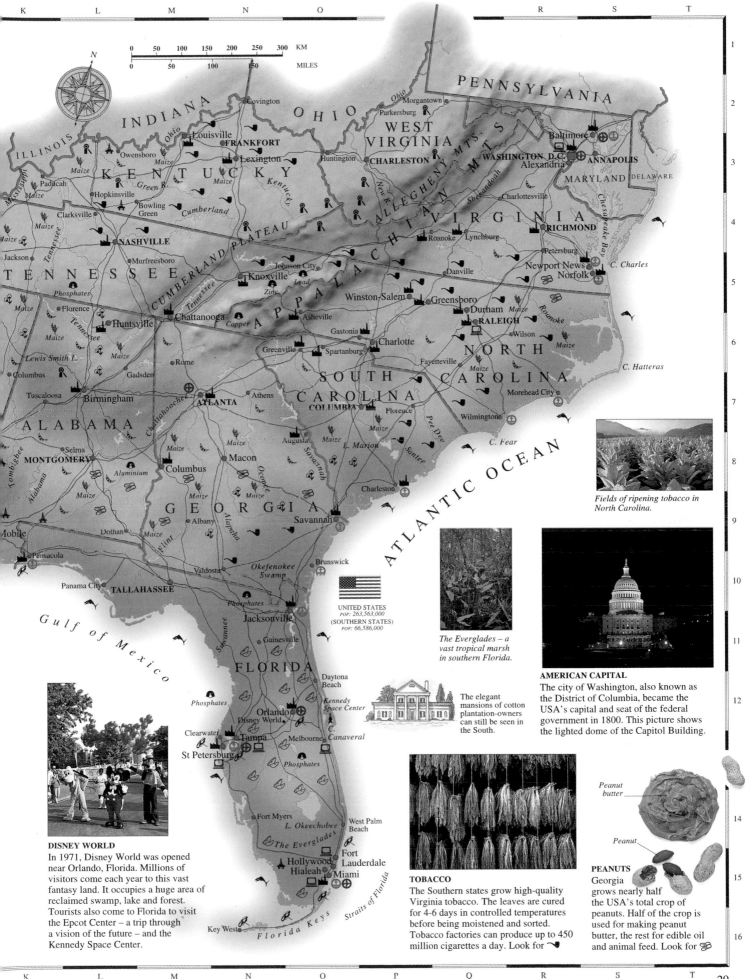

KM
0 50 100 150 200 250 300
0 50 100 150
MILES

ILLINOIS
INDIANA
OHIO
PENNSYLVANIA
Covington
Morgantown
Parkersburg
WEST VIRGINIA
Louisville
FRANKFORT
Owensboro
Lexington
Huntington
CHARLESTON
WASHINGTON D.C.
Baltimore
Alexandria
ANNAPOLIS
MARYLAND
DELAWARE
Paducah
KENTUCKY
Maize
Maize
Hopkinsville
Charlottesville
Clarksville
Bowling Green
Cumberland
VIRGINIA
RICHMOND
Roanoke
Lynchburg
Petersburg
Newport News
C. Charles
NASHVILLE
Murfreesboro
Johnson City
Danville
Norfolk
Jackson
Knoxville
Lead
Winston-Salem
Greensboro
TENNESSEE
Phosphates
Zinc
Asheville
Durham
Maize
Florence
Copper
Gastonia
RALEIGH
Wilson
Huntsville
Chattanooga
Charlotte
NORTH
Roanoke
Lewis Smith L.
Greenville
Spartanburg
CAROLINA
Maize
Columbus
Rome
Fayetteville
C. Hatteras
Tuscaloosa
Gadsden
SOUTH
Maize
Morehead City
Birmingham
ATLANTA
Athens
CAROLINA
ALABAMA
Chattahoochee
COLUMBIA
Florence
Wilmington
MONTGOMERY
Selma
Maize
Maize
Augusta
Maize
L. Marion
Santee
C. Fear
Aluminium
Columbus
Macon
Savannah
Charleston
Mobile
Albany
GEORGIA
Maize
Oconee
ATLANTIC OCEAN
Dothan
Alapaha
Flint
Pensacola
Okefenokee Swamp
Brunswick
Panama City
TALLAHASSEE
Valdosta
UNITED STATES
POP: 263,563,000
(SOUTHERN STATES)
POP: 66,586,000
Gulf of Mexico
Phosphates
Jacksonville
Suwannee
Gainesville
FLORIDA
Daytona Beach
Kennedy Space Center
Orlando
Disney World
C. Canaveral
Clearwater
Tampa
Melbourne
St Petersburg
Phosphates
Fort Myers
L. Okeechobee
West Palm Beach
The Everglades
Fort Lauderdale
Hollywood
Hialeah
Miami
Key West
Florida Keys
Straits of Florida

Fields of ripening tobacco in North Carolina.

The Everglades – a vast tropical marsh in southern Florida.

AMERICAN CAPITAL
The city of Washington, also known as the District of Columbia, became the USA's capital and seat of the federal government in 1800. This picture shows the lighted dome of the Capitol Building.

DISNEY WORLD
In 1971, Disney World was opened near Orlando, Florida. Millions of visitors come each year to this vast fantasy land. It occupies a huge area of reclaimed swamp, lake and forest. Tourists also come to Florida to visit the Epcot Center – a trip through a vision of the future – and the Kennedy Space Center.

The elegant mansions of cotton plantation-owners can still be seen in the South.

TOBACCO
The Southern states grow high-quality Virginia tobacco. The leaves are cured for 4-6 days in controlled temperatures before being moistened and sorted. Tobacco factories can produce up to 450 million cigarettes a day. Look for 🖝

Peanut butter

Peanut

PEANUTS
Georgia grows nearly half the USA's total crop of peanuts. Half of the crop is used for making peanut butter, the rest for edible oil and animal feed. Look for

THE GREAT LAKES

THE FIVE GREAT LAKES of North America – Erie, Ontario, Huron, Michigan and Superior – together form the largest area of fresh water in the world. The states of Indiana, Illinois, Michigan, Ohio, Wisconsin and Minnesota, all of which border on one or more of the lakes, are often called the industrial and agricultural heartland of the United States. This region is rich in natural resources, including coal, iron, copper and timber, and there are large areas of fertile farmland on the flat plains of the prairies. First explored by French traders, fur trappers and missionaries in the 17th century, the region began to attract large numbers of settlers in the early 1800s. Trading links were improved by the opening of the Erie Canal in 1825, which connected the region to the Atlantic Coast, while the Mississippi and other rivers gave access to the Gulf of Mexico and the rest of the continent. When railways reached the region in the 1840s, cities such as Chicago grew and prospered as freight-handling centres. Steel production and the car industry later became the main industries in the region. In recent years, a decline in these traditional industries has led to high unemployment in some areas.

Wall-eyes live in the Great Lakes, but their numbers are falling due to pollution.

HOGS
In the 19th century, huge numbers of animals from all over this region were sent to the stock-yards in Chicago for slaughter and processing. Rearing livestock is still important in Illinois. Maize and soya beans, both grown locally, are used as animal feed. Look for

HAMBURGERS
Hamburgers are America's own fast food, first produced on a massive scale in Illinois in the 1950s. It has been calculated that in every second of the day, 200 Americans are eating a hamburger. American-style hamburger take-aways can now be found all over the world.

THE WINDY CITY
Chicago is situated at the southern tip of Lake Michigan. It gets its nickname – the Windy City – from the weather conditions in this area. Chicago was ideally positioned for trading with the Midwest region, and quickly became a wealthy modern city. By 1900 it had vast complexes of lumber mills, meat processing factories, railway yards and steel mills.

COLD WINTERS
The Great Lakes region has severe winters, and Minnesota, in particular, suffers from heavy snow-storms. Parts of the Great Lakes themselves can freeze over in winter, and lakeside harbours can be frozen from December to early April.

Cherries: One-third of the world cherry crop is grown along the shores of Lake Michigan. Look for

Iron ore: Iron ore deposits are found around the shores of Lake Superior. It is mined, processed, then shipped to industrial centres in pellet form. Look for

	Cattle		Soya beans
	Hogs		Coal
	Cereals		Oil
	Sugar beet		Industrial centre
	Market gardening		Vehicle manufacture

Baseball and fielder's glove. Baseball is the USA's national game.

MILWAUKEE BEER
The Great Lakes region has attracted many immigrants, especially from Germany, the Netherlands and the Scandinavian countries. Milwaukee, where many Germans settled, is home to several of the USA's largest breweries.

PRAIRIE LANDS
The fertile soil and hot, humid summers make the flat expanses of the Midwestern prairies ideal for farming. Nearly half of the world's maize crop is grown on the huge farms in this region.

An isolated farm on the open prairies of Illinois.

CORNFLAKES
Food processing is a major industry throughout this agricultural region. Wisconsin, for example, is the major producer of canned peas and sweet corn in the USA. Corn and wheat-based breakfast cereals are exported all over the world from Battle Creek, Michigan. Look for

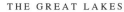

LAKESIDE HOLIDAYS
The lakes attract millions of visitors a year. Summer holiday homes line accessible parts of the shores, and huge marinas have been built for the pleasure-craft that sail on the lakes.

Over 10,000 loons, the state bird of Minnesota, spend the summer on its lakes.

A wooded island in Minnesota.

UNITED STATES
POP: 263,563,000
(GREAT LAKES STATES)
POP: 47,233,000

Parts of the shores have been eroded by water, endangering buildings

LAKES UNDER THREAT
Heavy industry around the shores of the Great Lakes has caused disastrous water pollution. In some regions, fish are now unsafe to eat and swimming is dangerous. In addition, changes to the weather, such as heavy rainfall and cooler temperatures, have led to much higher water levels. Lakeside holiday towns are often flooded, threatening tourism. Many houses, perched precariously on the lakes' crumbling shores, are under threat.

Model of a 1956 Ford Fairlane

THE MOTOR CITY
In the early 20th century Detroit became the centre of a revolution in transport when two engineers, Henry Ford and Ransom Olds, began mass-producing cars there. Today, Detroit is still the centre of the American car industry, with several of the USA's biggest car manufacturers based in the city. Look for

TAMLA MOTOWN
In 1961 Berry Gordy, a worker from the Ford factory in Detroit, launched the Tamla Motown record label to promote local black talent. Motown artists, such as Smokey Robinson, the Supremes and Stevie Wonder, perfected the unique style of "soul" music.

OPEN HIGHWAYS
The Great Lakes states have benefited from their central location and well-developed rail and water transport systems. The region is also well served by roads – Indianapolis has more major highways than any other American city.

A farmhouse and barn in the rich farm country of Indiana.

Robie House, Chicago, (built 1910) was designed by the world-famous US architect, Frank Lloyd Wright.

KM
0   50   100   150   200   250
MILES
0   25   50   75   100   125   150

N

A B C D E F G H I J

CENTRAL AND MOUNTAIN STATES

The foothills of the snow-covered Rockies in Montana.

THIS REGION INCLUDES the lowlands on the west bank of the Mississippi River, the vast expanses of the Great Plains, and the majestic Rocky Mountains. In climate, it is a region of extremes: hot summers alternate with cold winters, and hailstorms, blizzards and tornadoes are frequent events. Once home to large numbers of Native Americans and great herds of buffalo, the plains were settled in the 19th century; the Native Americans were pushed on to reservations and the buffalo slaughtered. Originally dismissed as a desert because of low rainfall and lack of trees, the Great Plains proved to be one of the world's great agricultural regions; today, vast amounts of cereals are grown on mechanized farms, and cattle are grazed on huge ranches. The Rockies are rich in minerals, and reserves of coal, oil and natural gas are being exploited.

Shredded wheat

AGRICULTURAL INDUSTRIES

A great range of cereals are grown in the Midwest and transported to local cities for processing. Iowa has the largest cereal processing factory in the world, and it is in the cities of this region that many cereals are prepared for the world's breakfast tables. Cities also provide storage facilities for grain and cereals, as well as markets for grain, livestock and farm machinery.

Corn flakes *Oats* *Toasted rice*

COWBOYS

Cattle are raised on the Great Plains and foothills of the Rocky Mountains. Ranches often have thousands of cattle. In summer, mounted cowboys herd cattle to upland pastures and drive them back to the ranch for the winter. Cattle are then taken to markets in nearby towns for cattle auctions. Look for 🐂

WYOMING COAL

Wyoming now leads the USA in coal production. Coal from the West is in demand because it has a lower sulphur content than coal mined in the East, and causes less pollution when burnt. Shallow coal reserves are extracted from open-cast mines, like this one, which spoil the landscape. Look for ⛏

Fossils of dinosaurs, such as *Tyrannosaurus*, have been found in the foothills of the Rockies.

KEYBOX

Aerospace industry: Both Wichita and St. Louis are centres of aircraft production. They have recently been hit by a slowdown in the US economy. Look for ✈

Irrigated agriculture: The Ogallala Aquifer is a vast underground reserve of water, which is tapped to water crops in this dry region. Look for 🌱

🐂	Cattle	⛏	Coal
🌾	Cereals	🛢	Oil
🌿	Potatoes	⬭	Gas
⛏	Mining	🏭	Industrial centre

Railway towns are now surrounded by agricultural land

A central route over the Rockies links mining towns

Main east-west railway route

To Minnesota and Chicago

Snake River valley: potato farming on fertile flood-plain

MODEL OF ROCKY MOUNTAINS

The Rocky Mountains divide the North American continent in two; rivers to the west of the range flow towards the Pacific, while those to the east drain into the Arctic and Atlantic oceans and the Gulf of Mexico. First explored by fur trappers and traders in the 19th century, the mountain passes were used by settlers on their way west. Miners followed the settlers, and the mining towns of Montana were established. By 1869, the Transcontinental railroad had crossed the Rockies, linking the Pacific Coast with the rest of the country.

FARMING

Maize is the main crop in Iowa, while wheat is more important in the centre of this region. Nearer the Rockies, the rainfall decreases and wheat farming gives way to cattle ranching. Farming in the Midwest is large-scale and mechanized. These vast wheatfields in Nebraska stretch to the far horizon. Farmers often produce more than they can sell. Look for 🌾

A B C D E F G H I J

TOURISM

Huge carvings of the heads of four great American presidents – Washington, Lincoln, Jefferson and Theodore Roosevelt – can be seen at Mount Rushmore in South Dakota. Millions of people have visited the monument since its completion in 1927. The mountainous scenery and wildlife of this region attract tourists from all over the world.

Only 800 grizzly bears are left in the USA; many live in the mountains of Wyoming and Idaho.

BISON

Millions of bison (American buffalo) used to roam the Great Plains. Native Americans hunted them for food and used their hides to make clothing and shelters. Settlers and railway workers virtually wiped out the bison herds in the late 19th century, killing them for food and profit. Today, the bison population is protected and there are now about 50,000 bison living on reserves.

UNITED STATES
POP: 263,563,000
(CENTRAL & MOUNTAIN STATES)
POP: 19,050,000

The Badlands of North and South Dakota have been eroded into hills and gullies.

ON THE ROAD

An extensive road network holds this vast, sparsely-inhabited region together. Highways often run through long stretches of nearly empty land, fringed by gas stations, motels and roadside restaurants. Cars are a necessity in much of the West; in Wyoming, children of 14 can drive to school.

Popcorn, roasted and puffed-up maize, is a Midwestern export.

The Grand Teton Mountains, northern Wyoming.

GOLD RUSH

In 1874, gold was found in the Black Hills of South Dakota, a region sacred to the Sioux people. The discovery sparked a major gold rush; towns sprang up overnight, fortunes were won and lost, gambling and crime flourished. The area is still rich in minerals – South Dakota's Homestake gold mine is the biggest in the country. Look for ⚒

Broad-brimmed hats are still an essential part of the cowboy's wardrobe.

0 50 100 150 200 250 300 350 KM
0   50   100   150   200 MILES

THE SOUTHWESTERN STATES

THE SOUTHWESTERN USA is a region of deserts and high plateaux, broken by the ridges of the southern Rocky Mountains. Many different Native American peoples lived in the Southwest. The region still has the country's largest concentration of Native Americans. The first Europeans to settle in this region were Spaniards who came north from Mexico. This mixed Spanish and Native American heritage is reflected in the region's folk art, architecture and foods. American settlers in Texas rebelled against Mexican rule in 1836, and Texas was annexed to the USA a decade later. The rest of the region became part of the USA after the Mexican War of 1846-48. Gold and silver mining and cattle-ranching attracted settlers to the region in the late 19th century, and oil became a major part of Texas's economy in the 20th century. The region's natural beauty draws tourists from all over the world.

Jordan Mormon Temple, Utah

MORMON CITY
Salt Lake City in Utah is the headquarters of the Latter-day Saints, or Mormons. They settled in Utah in the 1840s, after fleeing from the eastern states, where they had been persecuted for their beliefs. There are now more than six million Mormons worldwide.

NAVAJO RUGS
Many Navajo people live on a vast reservation in Arizona and New Mexico. They still practise weaving, pottery, silver-working and other traditional crafts. Navajo rugs are woven into geometric patterns, and coloured with natural dyes, such as juniper and blackberry.

The Saguaro cactus thrives in the deserts of Arizona.

An 11th-century pottery bowl, made by the Mogollon people.

KEYBOX

High-tech industry: *The space programme has attracted high technology industries to the area. Look for* 💻

Irrigated agriculture: *Sprinklers fixed on central pivots create circular oases of green fields in the arid landscape. Look for* 🌿

Dams: *Acute water shortages are being remedied by the construction of dams on the region's rivers. Look for* ▦

Military bases: *The first nuclear bombs were tested in New Mexico and Nevada. Military installations are common in the region. Look for* III

🐂	Cattle	🛢	Oil
🌾	Cereals	◉	Gas
⚓	Cotton	🏭	Industrial centre
⛑	Mining	⛷	Skiing

THE GREAT OUTDOORS
Riding, trekking, canoeing, skiing and fishing are just some of the outdoor activities which draw tourists to the Southwest. But the region's main attraction is the Grand Canyon. About 10,000 visitors each year navigate the Canyon's dangerous waters on rubber rafts, and many others explore it on foot or by donkey.

TAOS
The *pueblo*, or village, of Taos in New Mexico is built of unbaked clay brick, called *adobe*. This style of building dates back to the Pueblo people, who lived in the region a thousand years ago, farming maize, cotton, beans and squash.

These strangely shaped rocks in Monument Valley, Arizona, have been carved by the wind.

THE GRAND CANYON
Over the last million years, the Colorado River has cut its way through the rocky plateaux of northern Arizona. At the same time, the plateaux have risen. This combined action has formed the largest land gorge in the world – the Grand Canyon. It is more than 1.6 km (1 mile) deep, and 350 km (220 miles) long. Some of the oldest rocks in North America have been found at the base of the canyon.

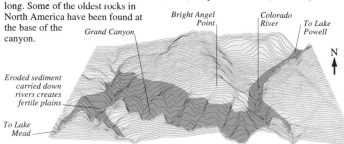

Eroded sediment carried down rivers creates fertile plains

To Lake Mead

Grand Canyon

Bright Angel Point

Colorado River

To Lake Powell

N

### Map labels
OREGON, IDAHO, BLACK ROCK DESERT, Mercury, Beef, Bear L., Winnemucca, GREAT BASIN, Beef, Great Salt L., Brigham City, Logan, Rye Patch Res., Humboldt, Gold, Elko, Ogden, Pyramid L., Bountiful, SALT LAKE CITY, Reno, Sparks, Tooele, Zinc, Orem, CARSON CITY, NEVADA, Copper, L. Utah, Provo, L. Tahoe, Walker L., Ely, Beef, Silver, UTAH, Sevier L., Salina, Nellis Air Force Range, Beef, Bryce Canyon, Uranium, Iron, L. Powell, Nevada Test Site, Glen Canyon Dam, Uranium, North Las Vegas, L. Mead, Bright Angel Point, Monument Valley, Las Vegas, Grand Canyon, PAINTED DESERT, Henderson, Hoover Dam, COLORADO PLATEAU, Davis Dam, Flagstaff, Beef, ARIZONA, Parker Dam, Prescott, Colorado, Theodore Roosevelt L., Salt, SONORAN, Glendale, Scottsdale, Copper, PHOENIX, Mesa, Copper, Yuma, Central Arizona Project, Imperial Dam, Colorado Project, Luke Air Force Range, Casa Grande, Copper, Copper, Silver, DESERT, Copper, Tucson, Beef, Copper, Douglas, CALIFORNIA

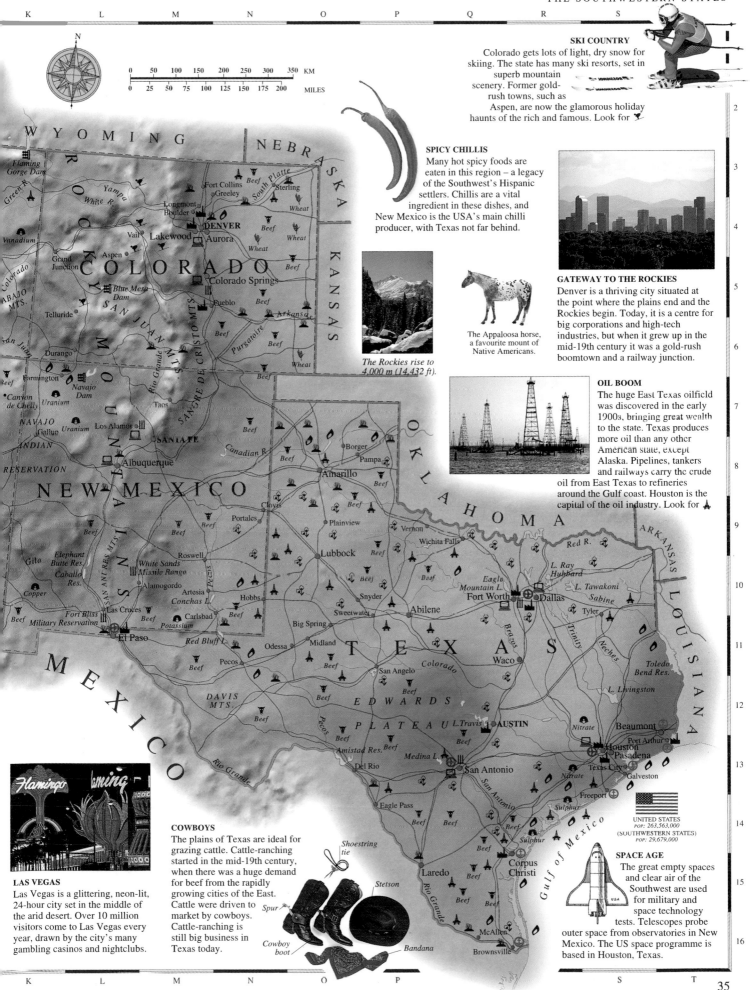

SKI COUNTRY
Colorado gets lots of light, dry snow for skiing. The state has many ski resorts, set in superb mountain scenery. Former gold-rush towns, such as Aspen, are now the glamorous holiday haunts of the rich and famous. Look for 🎿

SPICY CHILLIS
Many hot spicy foods are eaten in this region – a legacy of the Southwest's Hispanic settlers. Chillis are a vital ingredient in these dishes, and New Mexico is the USA's main chilli producer, with Texas not far behind.

The Rockies rise to 4,000 m (14,432 ft).

The Appaloosa horse, a favourite mount of Native Americans.

GATEWAY TO THE ROCKIES
Denver is a thriving city situated at the point where the plains end and the Rockies begin. Today, it is a centre for big corporations and high-tech industries, but when it grew up in the mid-19th century it was a gold-rush boomtown and a railway junction.

OIL BOOM
The huge East Texas oilfield was discovered in the early 1900s, bringing great wealth to the state. Texas produces more oil than any other American state, except Alaska. Pipelines, tankers and railways carry the crude oil from East Texas to refineries around the Gulf coast. Houston is the capital of the oil industry. Look for ⚒

LAS VEGAS
Las Vegas is a glittering, neon-lit, 24-hour city set in the middle of the arid desert. Over 10 million visitors come to Las Vegas every year, drawn by the city's many gambling casinos and nightclubs.

COWBOYS
The plains of Texas are ideal for grazing cattle. Cattle-ranching started in the mid-19th century, when there was a huge demand for beef from the rapidly growing cities of the East. Cattle were driven to market by cowboys. Cattle-ranching is still big business in Texas today.

Shoestring tie

Stetson

Spur

Cowboy boot

Bandana

UNITED STATES
POP: 263,563,000
(SOUTHWESTERN STATES)
POP: 29,679,000

SPACE AGE
The great empty spaces and clear air of the Southwest are used for military and space technology tests. Telescopes probe outer space from observatories in New Mexico. The US space programme is based in Houston, Texas.

THE PACIFIC STATES

THE PACIFIC COAST STATES boast some of the most varied scenery in the USA. California, for example, contains the snow-capped peaks of the Sierra Nevada Mountains and the lowest point in North America – Death Valley. Much of California is arid, with farming dependent on irrigation, while vast forests and well-watered fertile valleys are characteristic of Washington and Oregon. American settlers began to cross the Rockies to the Pacific coast in the 1840s. California became part of the USA as a result of the Mexican-American War (1846–48), and the discovery of gold in 1848 led to its rapid settlement. All three states are now major agricultural producers and centres of high-technology industry. In the early 1960s, California became the USA's most highly-populated state. Despite recent problems, the state's economy rivals those of many wealthy nations.

AGRICULTURE
California alone produces half of the USA's fruit and vegetables. Fertile soils and a warm climate have contributed to the state's success, but dry conditions mean that much of the state's farmland has to be irrigated. California's main crops are cotton and grapes. Look for 🍇

Almond

Avocado pear

Peach

Plum

TIMBER
Oregon and Washington are the USA's major timber producers. The region's cedar and fir forests supply one-third of the country's softwood timber. The trees are cut into logs at one of the thousands of sawmills in the forests and then floated down rivers on rafts to the large coastal cities. Some of the wood is made into paper at pulp-mills like the one pictured here. Much of the region's timber is exported to Japan. Tree-felling has reduced the region's stocks of mature trees; efforts are now being made to plant more trees. Look for 🌲

AEROSPACE
The Boeing Corporation, the world's largest aircraft manufacturer, is based in Seattle.
Boeing is the city's main employer, and any decline in orders can result in unemployment. California is a major producer of military aeroplanes; cuts in US defence spending have badly affected this region. Look for ✈

Boeing 767 aircraft

California redwoods are evergreen trees, which can reach 100 m (330 ft).

Washington's Mount Rainier is permanently snow-covered.

Fortune-cookie, served in San Francisco's Chinese restaurants

IMMIGRATION
California attracts many immigrants from Asia and South America. Many Chinese immigrants have settled in San Francisco's Chinatown. This area of the city is a magnet for the Chinese community, and is famous for its exotic shops and restaurants. Immigrants from Latin America, especially Mexico, make up a growing part of the state's population.

SILICON VALLEY
Santa Clara Valley, south of San Francisco, has one of the largest concentrations of high-technology industry in the world. Over 3,000 firms there specialize in micro-electronics and computer hardware and software. US manufacturers face increasing competition from the Far East. Look for 💻

Computer discs capable of storing vast amounts of information

SAN FRANCISCO
San Francisco is located on one of the world's finest natural harbours, and is the West Coast's trade and shipping centre. San Francisco is built on a hilly peninsula, with some of the steepest streets in the world. San Francisco suffers from frequent earthquakes as it is situated right on the San Andreas Fault. The city's large skyscrapers are specially designed to withstand earthquakes.

Waves batter the rugged Pacific coast of Oregon.

DESERT ENERGY

The resources of the Californian landscape – wind and sun – are being tapped to provide new sources of energy. This has become necessary as strict laws now forbid the building of power plants near Los Angeles. Wind farms have been built in the San Gorgonio Pass area. Solar energy is harnessed by complexes of mirrors. This force reflected light onto a central boiler, converting water to steam which is used to generate electricity.

The sand dunes of Death Valley in eastern California.

UNITED STATES
Pop: 260,563,000
(PACIFIC STATES)
Pop: 38,981,000

Green abalone shells found off the Californian coasts are used to make jewellery.

LOS ANGELES

Los Angeles is a vast, sprawling city, stretching for 100 km (60 miles) along the Pacific coast. The city has grown rapidly over the last 100 years, and is a focus for migrants from the rest of the USA. Today, it consists of many separate residential centres, which are linked by an extensive road system, but it in the 1930s. Most residents are dependent on cars for transport. The city suffers from pollution because it is surrounded by mountains which stop car fumes escaping.

DREAM CITY

Hollywood in Los Angeles is the capital of the world's film and television industry. Although many major studios are no longer based here, the glamour of Hollywood's heyday – from 1915-1950 – lingers on. Many film stars still live here.

Denim jeans were first made in the 1850s for miners during the California gold-rush.

TOURISM

Over 100 million visitors a year come to California. The state offers a wide range of activities: spectacular national parks; attractions such as Disneyland and Hollywood; and the superb Pacific coastline. Venice Beach in Los Angeles is a magnet for visitors. Jugglers, mime artists, folk-singers and body builders throng the sea-front. Fads such as roller-skating and skate-boarding have spread from Venice Beach across the country. Look for 📷

WINE

Raisins, which were discovered when grapes withered on the vine, and grapes are major crops in California. The wide range of wines made here reflects the varied climates in the state. Look for 🍇

White grapes

Raisins

KEYBOX

Mixed fruit: Washington produces one-third of the USA's apple crop, grown in irrigated valleys east of the Cascade Range. Look for 🍎

Irrigated agriculture: Fertile but dry land in central California is irrigated, via canals and dams, by water from the mountains to the west. Look for 🌾

Borders: Millions of Mexicans cross the border into California, many illegally. The border is patrolled by mounted guards and helicopters. Look for ✕

Military bases: San Diego has the largest concentration of naval bases in the USA. Deserts in California are also used for weapons testing. Look for ✈

🍇 Wine	🛢 Oil
🌿 Cotton	🏭 Industrial centre
🪵 Timber	✈ Aerospace industry
🎣 Fishing	💻 High-tech industry
⛏ Mining	📷 Tourism

HOLLYWOOD

PACIFIC OCEAN

Potassium

Death Valley

A R I Z O N A

N E V A D A

C A L I F O R N I A

S I E R R A   N E V A D A

C O A S T   R A N G E S

S O N O R A N   D E S E R T

M O J A V E   D E S E R T

Colorado

M E X I C O

Crescent City
Eureka
Medford
Grants Pass
Ashland
Weed
Alturas
Klamath Falls
Upper Klamath L.
Goose L.
Clear L.
Eagle L.
Redding
Shasta L.
Chico
Napa Valley
Santa Rosa
Petaluma
Novato
San Francisco
Oakland
Concord
San Jose
Santa Clara Valley
Santa Cruz
Monterey
Salinas
Sacramento
Stockton
Vacaville
McClellan Air Base
Gold
Sta. Tahoe
Mono L.
Yosemite National Park
Modesto
Merced
San Joaquin
Fresno
Tungsten
Bishop
Death Valley
Potassium
China Lake Naval Weapons Center
San Luis Obispo
Santa Maria
Vandenburg Air Force Base
Santa Barbara
Ventura
Oxnard
Bakersfield
Mojave
Edwards Air Base
Barstow
Hollywood
Los Angeles
Glendale
Pasadena
Long Beach
Huntington Beach
Santa Ana
Riverside
San Bernardino
San Gorgonio Pass
Palm Springs
Salton Sea
Oceanside
San Clemente
Miramar Naval Air Station
San Diego
Brawley

KM
MILES
250
200
150
100
50
0
150
100
50
0

N

MEXICO

THE LAND OF MEXICO consists of a dry plateau crossed by broad valleys and enclosed to the west and east by mountains, some of which are volcanic. Baja California, the Yucatan Peninsula and along the country's coasts are the main low-lying areas. Mexico was first occupied by civilizations such as the Maya and Aztec, who built magnificent cities containing plazas, palaces and pyramids. Lured by legends of fabulous hoards of gold and silver, Spanish conquistadores invaded Mexico in 1519 and destroyed the existing civilizations. For 300 years the Spanish ruled the country, unifying it with their language and the Roman Catholic religion. Mexico succeeded in winning its independence from Spain by 1821. Today, most Mexicans are mestizo – which means they are descendants of the native peoples and the Spanish settlers. Although half the population lives in towns, many people still inhabit areas only accessible on horseback, but rail and air transport are improving. So much of the country is mountainous or dry that only 12 per cent of the land can be used for farming. Mexico has vast oil reserves and mineral riches, but suffers from over-population and huge foreign debts. Closer links with the USA promise to strengthen Mexico's economy in the future.

MEXICO
POP: 95,365,000

Cedros Island, off the north-west coast of Mexico.

Skeleton made of papier mâché

THE DAY OF THE DEAD
Mexicans believe that life is like a flower; it slowly opens and then closes again. During the annual festival of the Day of the Dead, the streets are decorated with flowers, and ghoulish skeletons are everywhere.

TEXTILES
Although today many fabrics are machine-made, some Mexicans still practise their traditional art of hand-weaving colourful textiles. This *sarape*, part of the traditional Mexican dress for men, is worn over the shoulder.

Teeth made of shell

Aztec mask, inlaid with turquoise, depicting a god.

AGRICULTURE
Although Mexico is rapidly industrializing, over half the working population still makes its living from farming. They grow crops like maize, beans and vegetables, and raise cattle, sheep, pigs and chickens.

Cacti growing on Mexico's dry central plateau.

SPIKED DRINKS
The desert and dry regions of Mexico are home to many varieties of the spiny-leaved *agave* plant. Juice from two varieties is used to make the alcoholic drinks, *tequila* and *mezcal*. The *agave* plant is grown on plantations, then cooked, crushed and fermented. The drink is exported worldwide.

KEYBOX

Tourism: Resorts like Acapulco attract thousands of visitors to Mexico each year. Tourism is now a vital source of foreign currency. Look for 🏖

Maquiladora: American raw materials are brought across the border to supply factories, or maquiladora, where labour costs are lower. Look for ⚒

🌾	Cereals	🐟	Fishing
⚜	Sugar cane	⛏	Mining
☕	Coffee	⛽	Oil
🌿	Cotton	🏭	Industrial centre
🌲	Forest products	▲	Archaeological site

Popocatépetl 5,452 m (17,900 ft)

Iztaccíhuatl 5,286 m (17,350 ft)

Ribbon development along railway routes

Mountains prevent pollution escaping

Lake Texcoco

Uncontrolled expansion of suburbs

Limit of urban area

Centre of Mexico City

N

MEXICO CITY
The Aztec capital, Tenochtitlán, was built on islands in Lake Texcoco. The city was destroyed by the Spanish, but modern-day Mexico City is built on the ruins. By AD 2000 it is expected to be the world's largest city, containing over 20 million people. Mexico City is very polluted because it is surrounded by a ring of mountains which stop polluted air from cars and factories escaping.

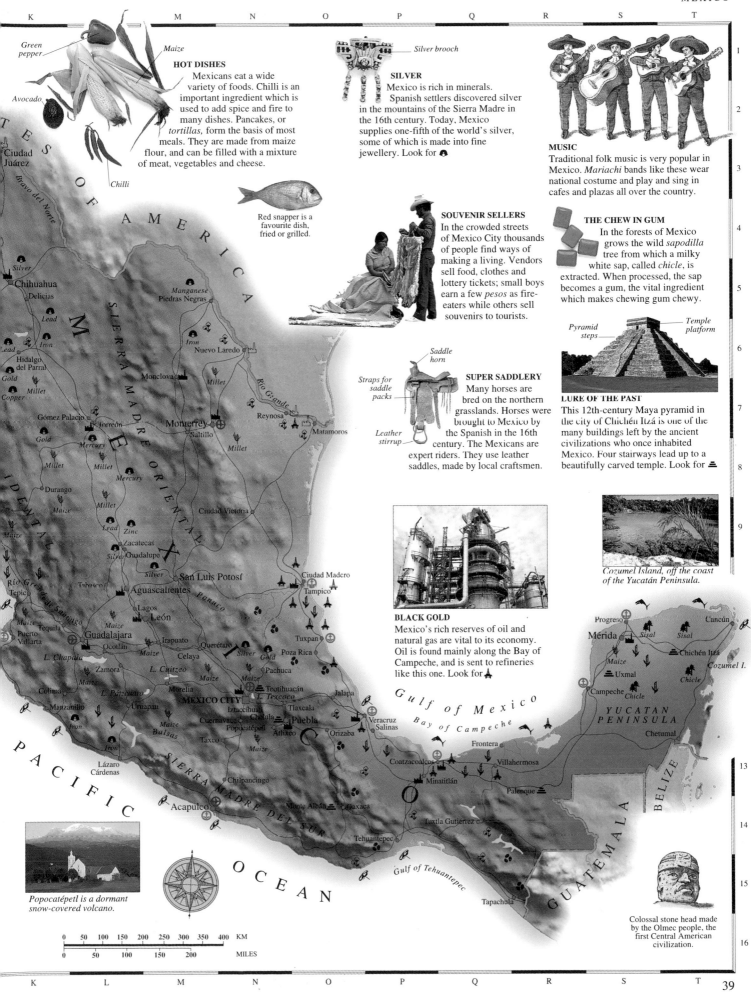

K L M N O P Q R S T

HOT DISHES

Mexicans eat a wide variety of foods. Chilli is an important ingredient which is used to add spice and fire to many dishes. Pancakes, or *tortillas,* form the basis of most meals. They are made from maize flour, and can be filled with a mixture of meat, vegetables and cheese.

Green pepper

Maize

Avocado

Chilli

Red snapper is a favourite dish, fried or grilled.

SILVER

Silver brooch

Mexico is rich in minerals. Spanish settlers discovered silver in the mountains of the Sierra Madre in the 16th century. Today, Mexico supplies one-fifth of the world's silver, some of which is made into fine jewellery. Look for 💍

MUSIC

Traditional folk music is very popular in Mexico. *Mariachi* bands like these wear national costume and play and sing in cafes and plazas all over the country.

SOUVENIR SELLERS

In the crowded streets of Mexico City thousands of people find ways of making a living. Vendors sell food, clothes and lottery tickets; small boys earn a few *pesos* as fire-eaters while others sell souvenirs to tourists.

THE CHEW IN GUM

In the forests of Mexico grows the wild *sapodilla* tree from which a milky white sap, called *chicle,* is extracted. When processed, the sap becomes a gum, the vital ingredient which makes chewing gum chewy.

Pyramid steps

Temple platform

SUPER SADDLERY

Saddle horn

Straps for saddle packs

Leather stirrup

Many horses are bred on the northern grasslands. Horses were brought to Mexico by the Spanish in the 16th century. The Mexicans are expert riders. They use leather saddles, made by local craftsmen.

LURE OF THE PAST

This 12th-century Maya pyramid in the city of Chichén Itzá is one of the many buildings left by the ancient civilizations who once inhabited Mexico. Four stairways lead up to a beautifully carved temple. Look for ⛪

Cozumel Island, off the coast of the Yucatán Peninsula.

BLACK GOLD

Mexico's rich reserves of oil and natural gas are vital to its economy. Oil is found mainly along the Bay of Campeche, and is sent to refineries like this one. Look for 🛢

Popocatépetl is a dormant snow-covered volcano.

Colossal stone head made by the Olmec people, the first Central American civilization.

STATES OF AMERICA

Ciudad Juárez
Bravo del Norte
Silver
Chihuahua
Delicias
Lead
Lead
Iron
Hidalgo del Parral
Gold
Copper
Millet
Gómez Palacio
Gold
Torreón
Mercury
Millet
Millet
Durango
Mercury
Maize
Lead
Zinc
Zacatecas
Silver Guadalupe
Silver
San Luis Potosí
Tabasco
Aguascalientes
Lagos
León
Maize
Tepic
Río Grande de Santiago
Maize
Puerto Vallarta
Tequila
Guadalajara
Ocotlán
Maize
L. Chapala
Zamora
L. Cuitzeo
Colima
Maize
L. Pátzcuaro
Manzanillo
Uruapan
Maize
Iron
Lázaro Cárdenas
Acapulco

Piedras Negras
Manganese
Iron
Nuevo Laredo
Monclova
Millet
Río Grande
Reynosa
Monterrey
Matamoros
Saltillo
Millet
Ciudad Victoria
Celaya
Irapuato
Querétaro
Silver Gold
Pachuca
Morelia
Teotihuacán
MEXICO CITY
L. Texcoco
Iztaccíhuatl
Tlaxcala
Cuernavaca
Cholula
Popocatépetl
Puebla
Taxco
Atlixco
Orizaba
Maize
Maize Balsas
Chilpancingo

Ciudad Madero
Tampico
Panuco
Tuxpan
Poza Rica
Jalapa
Veracruz Salinas
Orizaba
Coatzacoalcos
Minatitlán

SIERRA MADRE ORIENTAL

SIERRA MADRE DEL SUR

Monte Albán
Oaxaca
Tehuantepec
Tuxtla Gutiérrez
Tapachula
Gulf of Tehuantepec

PACIFIC OCEAN

Gulf of Mexico
Bay of Campeche
Frontera
Villahermosa
Palenque
Chetumal

YUCATAN PENINSULA
Progreso
Cancún
Mérida
Sisal
Sisal
Chichén Itzá
Maize
Cozumel I.
Uxmal
Chicle
Campeche
Chicle

GUATEMALA
BELIZE

0 50 100 150 200 250 300 350 400 KM
0 50 100 150 200 MILES

Toco toucan
Ramphastos toco
Length: 60 cm (24 in)

Emerald tree boa
Corallus caninus
Length: 1.8 m (6 ft)

Geoffroy's spider monkey
Ateles geoffroyi
Length: 1.5 m (5 ft)

CENTRAL AND SOUTH AMERICA

SOUTH AMERICA is shaped like a giant triangle that tapers southward from the Equator to Cape Horn. A huge wall of mountains, the Andes, stretches for 7,250 km (4,500 miles) along the entire Pacific coast. Until three million years ago South America was not connected to North America, so life there evolved in isolation. Several extraordinary animal groups developed, including sloths and anteaters. Many unique plant species originated here too, such as the potato and tomato. South America has the world's largest area of tropical rainforest, through which the River Amazon and its many tributaries run. Central America is mountainous and forested.

□ TROPICAL TOBAGO
Coconut palms grow along the shores of many Caribbean islands. Palms have flexible trunks that enable them to withstand tropical storms.

Mahogany
Swietenia macrophylla
Height: 25 m (82 ft)

△ VOLCANIC ISLANDS
One of the extinct volcanic craters of the Galápagos Island group breaks the surface of the Pacific Ocean. Like other isolated regions of the world, many unique species have evolved here, such as the giant tortoise 1.2 m (4 ft) long.

✦ SEA-DWELLING TREES
Mangroves grow along tropical coastlines. The tangled roots of Pinuelo mangroves create ideal homes for tiny aquatic species.

□ PAMPAS
Giant grasses up to 3 m (10 ft) high grow on Argentina's dry southern Pampas. Here, further north, more plentiful rainfall supports a few scattered trees.

Alpaca
Lama pacos
Height: 1.5 m (5 ft)

Archaeogeryon, a crab that lived in this region 20 million years ago.

□ THE FOREST FLOOR
Tropical rainforest trees form such a dense canopy that little sunlight or rain can reach the ground 70 m (200 ft) below. Rainforest soils are easily washed away when the trees and plants are removed.

□ THE BLEAK SOUTH
Patagonia's cold desert environment contrasts starkly with the lush hot forests of Amazonia. Plants take root in the cracks of bare rock, and grow close to the ground to survive icy winds.

△ VOLCANIC ANDES
Steam and smoke rises from Villarrica, an active volcano. Many peaks in the Andes are active or former volcanoes. Despite the intense heat within these lava-filled mountains, the highest are permanently covered in snow – even those on the Equator.

Passion flower
Passiflora caerulea
Across flower: 15 cm (6 in)

BIRTH OF A RIVER
The snow-capped peaks of the Andes are the source of the Amazon, the world's second longest river. It is 6,570 km, (4,080 miles) long.

□ ▲ DRY ATACAMA DESERT
The Atacama Desert is the world's driest place outside Antarctica. Rain has not fallen in some areas for hundreds of years. Winds that pass over cold coastline currents absorb no moisture.

CROSS SECTION THROUGH SOUTH AMERICA

Peru-Chile Trench | Andes | Selvas | Guiana Highlands | Barbados
Pacific Ocean | Amazon Basin | Amazon | Atlantic Ocean

4,500 (14,764)
0 Sea level
-6,000 (-19,686)
Metres (feet)

A   Length: 4,400 km (2,700 miles)   B

Giant anteater
Myrmecophaga tridactyla
Length: 2 m (7 ft)

Galápagos fur seal
Arctocephalus galapagoensis
Length: 1.8 m (6 ft)

Ocelot
Felis pardalis
Length: 1.7 m (6 ft)

NORTH AMERICA

100° 80° 60° Tropic of Cancer 40° 20°

Gulf of Mexico
Bahamas
Nares Plain
ATLANTIC

Caicos Is.
Turks Is.
Puerto Rico Trench
Hispaniola ▼8605m
Leeward Is.
NORTH AMERICAN PLATE
SOUTH AMERICAN PLATE
Mt. Pelée 1397m ■ B

Mexico Basin
Yucatán Basin
Cuba
Jamaica
Greater Antilles
Lesser Antilles
Venezuelan Basin
Windward Is.
Barbados
Mid-Atlantic Ridge
AFRICAN PLATE
SOUTH AMERICAN PLATE

SIERRA MADRE
4210m ▲ ▲ Santa Maria 3768m
CARIBBEAN SEA
Colombian Basin
Trinidad
Tobago
Demerara Plain
Equator

Middle America Trench
NORTH AMERICAN / CARIBBEAN PLATE
L. Nicaragua
Gulf of Darien
Magdalena
CARIBBEAN PLATE
SOUTH AMERICAN PLATE
Orinoco Delta
Ceará Plain

CENTRAL AMERICA
Isthmus of Panama
Gulf of Panama
LLANOS
Orinoco
Angel Falls 980m ▲2810m
C. de São Roque

Guatemala Basin
Cocos Ridge
Probable plate margin
△Ruiz 5400m
GUIANA HIGHLANDS
Negro
Branco
Amazon
Marajó I.

East Pacific Rise
COCOS PLATE
NAZCA PLATE
Amazon Basin
SOUTH AMERICA

PACIFIC
Galápagos Is.
△Cotopaxi 5896m
Chimborazo 6267m
Putumayo
Marañón
Juruá
Purus
Madeira
Tapajós
Xingu
Tocantins
Araguaia
SELVAS
Brazil Basin

Galapagos Rise
Peru-Chile Trench
ANDES
▲Huascaran 6768m
Ucayali
São Francisco
Sobradinho Res.

Peru Basin
SOUTH AMERICAN PLATE
NAZCA PLATE
L. Titicaca
PLATEAU OF MATO GROSSO
BRAZILIAN ▲2890m HIGHLANDS

Sala y Gómez Ridge
Nazca Ridge
Sajama 6520m △ L. Poopó
Guallatiri 6060m △
ATACAMA DESERT
Paraguay
Itaipú Res.
Tropic of Capricorn
Santos Plateau
OCEAN

▲ A
-8064m
Ojos del Salado 6880m
Cerro Bonete 6872m
Iguaçu Falls 64m
Paraná
Uruguay
Rio Grande Rise

Chile Basin
Peru-Chile Trench
GRAN CHACO
Plate
Mirim Lagoon

Roggeveen Basin
Mercedario 6770m
Aconcagua 6960m
△Tupungatito 5640m
Salado
PAMPAS
Argentine Basin

East Pacific Ridge
NAZCA PLATE
ANTARCTIC PLATE
△Villarrica 2840m
Colorado
Negro
Salinas Grandes Salt Marsh -46m

NAZCA PLATE
Chile Rise
Chiloé I.
Falkland Escarpment
South Georgia Basin

Mornington Plain
PATAGONIA
Falkland Is.
South Georgia
-8325m
South Sandwich Trench

PACIFIC PLATE
Strait of Magellan
TIERRA DEL FUEGO
Cape Horn
SOUTH AMERICAN PLATE
SCOTIA PLATE
SCOTIA PLATE
ANTARCTIC PLATE

Probable plate margin
Drake Passage
Antarctic Circle

Bellingshausen Plain
ANTARCTICA
80°

The Triton shell can be found from Central America to Brazil.

■ GREAT WATERS
The Iguaçu Falls in Brazil are spectacular. Water thunders over the rim from November to March, but at other times slows to almost a trickle.

Common Chilean tarantula
Grammostola spatulatus
Length: 10 cm (4 in)

KEY TO SYMBOLS
▲ Mountain
△ Volcano
Mangroves
Wetlands
Coral reef
Plate margins and direction of movement

KEY TO NATURAL VEGETATION
Tropical grassland
Mountain
Mediterranean-type
Broadleaf forest
Cold desert
Tropical rainforest
Dry woodland
Temperate rainforest
Temperate grassland
Hot desert

CENTRAL AMERICA AND THE CARIBBEAN

THE TROPICAL REGION of Central America and the Caribbean was settled by hunters and farmers many thousands of years ago. By 300 BC the Maya had established a sophisticated civilization on the mainland – ruins of their pyramids and temples can still be seen deep in the forests of Guatemala. The Maya, as well as the native peoples who lived on the Caribbean islands, were almost wiped out by European explorers who arrived in the 15th century. From this time, European nations, in particular the British, French, Spanish and Dutch, competed for control of the region and some countries did not gain independence until recently. Europeans brought slaves from Africa to work on vast sugar plantations. In the last few decades, tourism has enriched the Caribbean, but in Central America, poverty and civil wars are still major problems.

A Jamaican beach, devastated by a hurricane.

Great Bahama Bank

CUBA
POP: 11,172,000

HAVANA (LA HABANA)
Matanzas
Copper Pinar del Río
I. de la Juventud (I. of Pines)
Cienfuegos
Santa Clara
Camagüey
Jardines de la Reina
Gulf of Guacanayabo

GUATEMALA
POP: 10,000,000

M E X I C O

Altun Ha
Tikal
Belize City
Flores
Belize
BELMOPAN
San Ignacio

BELIZE
POP: 200,000

G U A T E M A L A
Cobán
Huehuetenango
Quezaltenango
Sololá
Mazatenango
Nickel
L. Izabal
Gulf of Honduras
Puerto Barrios
Zacapa
Puerto Cortés
Copán
San Pedro Sula
La Ceiba
Trujillo
GUATEMALA CITY
Santa Rosa
Escuintla

B E L I Z E

G R E A T E R

Little Cayman
GEORGETOWN *Grand Cayman*
Cayman Brac
CAYMAN ISLANDS *(to UK)*

JAMAICA
POP: 2,572,000

Savanna-la-Mar
Montego Bay
Aluminium
Spanish Town

JAMAICA

C A R I B B E A N

Conches from the shallow waters of the Caribbean are edible.

HONDURAS
POP: 5,600,000

H O N D U R A S
Comayagua
La Esperanza
Juticalpa
TEGUCIGALPA
Patuca
Caratasca Lagoon
Coco

EL SALVADOR
POP: 5,400,000

Santa Ana
La Libertad
SAN SALVADOR
San Miguel
EL SALVADOR
San Lorenzo
Choluteca
Somoto
Estelí
Jinotega
Matagalpa
Gold
Copper
Puerto Cabezas

NICARAGUA
POP: 4,100,000

The ancient Maya temple of Altun Ha is hidden deep in the rainforest of Belize.

NICARAGUA
Since Nicaragua became independent in 1838 it has been devastated by civil war and foreign interference. During the 1980s, a desperate conflict took place between the socialist government and the right-wing Contras, supported by the USA. Although democracy has now been restored, little progress has been made in fighting the huge problems of poverty, ill-health and homelessness.

KEYBOX

Archaeological sites: Great civilizations, such as the Maya, flourished in Central America from 300 bc. They built temples, palaces and cities. Look for ⛩

Shellfishing: Shrimps and lobsters thrive in the mangrove swamps on the coasts of Central America, which provide rich feeding grounds. Look for 🦐

Shipping registry: Ships from all over the world fly Panama's flag. They register there because of low fees and limited controls on the labour force. Look for 🚩

↓	Sugar cane	🌿	Tobacco
	Bananas	🌲	Timber
	Coffee	⛏	Mining
	Cocoa	🏭	Industrial centre
	Cotton		Tourism

Chinandega
Corinto
León
L. Managua
Boaco
MANAGUA
Juigalpa
Granada
Rivas
L. Nicaragua
Bluefields
San Carlos
Liberia
Río Grande
San Juan

N I C A R A G U A

P A C I F I C   O C E A N

C O S T A
Puntarenas
Alajuela
SAN JOSE
Cartago
Gulf of Nicoya
R I C A

COSTA RICA
POP: 3,300,000

Puerto Limón

Swamps near the Honduran coast.

Bocas del Toro

RURAL MARKETS
Many Guatemalans live in small villages, growing maize and beans and making brightly-coloured cloth, baskets, pottery and wood carvings. These goods, as well as fruit and tobacco, are sold at local markets.

Mosquito Gulf
David
Panama Canal
Colón
Copper
Penonomé
PANAMA CITY
Santiago
Gulf of Chiriquí
Gulf of Panama
San José I.
Isla del Rey
Chitré
Coiba I.
Las Tablas
La Palma
Gulf of Darien

P A N A M A

C O L O M B I A

Hot pepper sauce, made with spicy chillis, is used all over the region.

N

| 0 | 50 | 100 | 150 | 200 | 250 | 300 | 350 | 400 | KM |

| 0 | 50 | 100 | 150 | 200 | MILES |

PANAMA
POP: 2,600,000

L M N O P Q R S T

BANANAS
Bananas are a major export for many Central American countries, especially Honduras. Refrigerated cargo ships enable green bananas to be exported as far afield as Europe. Locally, bananas have many uses: they are eaten raw, cooked or dried and used to make beer. Look for 🍌

Molasses

Rum, made from cane juice

Sugar cane

SUGAR
Sugar cane thrives in the tropical climate of the Caribbean. The cane stalks are shredded and crushed, producing raw cane juice, which can be used to make molasses, or refined to make crystallized sugar. Look for ⬇

Grenada supplies a quarter of the world's nutmeg.

A TOURIST PARADISE
The beautiful islands of the Caribbean offer tourists sun, coral reefs, sailing, swimming and diving. Tourism has brought wealth to the region. The Bahamas, for example, attract two million visitors a year.

Seeds and oil from annatto trees are used in local cooking.

Cloves — *Mace*

Cinnamon stick — *Bay leaf*

VOODOO
Voodoo religion was brought to Haiti by African slaves. Voodoo rites try to make contact with the dead, and involve animal sacrifices, dancing, drumming and chanting.

Jamaican Blue Mountain coffee is prized by experts.

Saffron

Ground cinnamon

ISLE OF SPICES
Grenada is the only island in the western world where spices grow abundantly. Nutmeg, mace, cinnamon, cloves, bay leaves and saffron are cultivated. The island's main exports are cocoa and nutmeg.

St. Eustatius, a volcanic island in the Caribbean.

BAHAMAS POP: 281,000

Little Abaco
reeport
Grand Bahama
Great Abaco
Berry Is.
NASSAU
New Providence
Eleuthera
Andros I.
Cat I.
San Salvador
Great Exuma
Rum Cay
Long I.
Crooked I.
Acklins I.
Mayaguana

ATLANTIC OCEAN

BAHAMAS

Victoria de las Tunas
Holguín
Bayamo
Nickel
Colbalt
Santiago de Cuba
Guantánamo
Guantánamo Bay (to USA)
Windward Passage

Great Inagua
Caicos Is.
GRAND TURK
Turks Is.

TURKS & CAICOS ISLANDS (to UK)

DOMINICAN REPUBLIC POP: 8,050,000

Port Antonio
KINGSTON

SEA

Port de Paix
Cap-Haïtien
Montecristi
Gonaïves
Puerto Plata
Santiago
Île de la Gonâve
San Francisco de Macorís
HAITI
Jérémie
Les Cayes
Gold
PORT-AU-PRINCE
Nickel
Samaná
Aluminium
Ibeme?
L. Enriquillo
DOMINICAN REPUBLIC
Aluminium
SANTO DOMINGO
La Romana

HAITI POP: 7,328,000

ANTILLES

Mona Passage
Mayagüez
SAN JUAN
Ponce
PUERTO RICO (to USA)
St Croix
Christianstad

VIRGIN ISLANDS (to USA)
CHARLOTTE AMALIE
BRITISH VIRGIN ISLANDS (to UK)
ROAD TOWN

ANGUILLA (to UK)
THE VALLEY
St Martin (to France & Neth.)
St Eustatius (to Neth.)

LEEWARD ISLANDS

CUBAN CIGARS
Tobacco was grown in western Cuba long before the arrival of Europeans, who were amazed at the sight of native Americans smoking rolled-up leaves. World-famous cigars earn Cuba foreign currency – badly needed by the only communist state left in the western hemisphere. Look for 🚬

CARIBBEAN CRICKET
Cricket is a reminder of the West Indies' colonial past. It is played today in many of the former British colonies and passionately followed, especially in Barbados.

CARIBS
A native American people, the Caribs inhabited many of the islands of the Caribbean and part of the mainland. The warlike Caribs were almost wiped out by the Europeans, although a few hundred survive today on Dominica.

Carib Indian necklace

An idyllic palm-fringed beach in Martinique.

LESSER ANTILLES

WINDWARD ISLANDS

ANTIGUA & BARBUDA
BASSETERRE
ST KITTS & NEVIS POP: 44,000
ST JOHNS
MONTSERRAT (to UK)
PLYMOUTH
Antigua
Barbuda
ANTIGUA & BARBUDA POP: 69,000

GUADELOUPE (to France)
BASSE-TERRE
Basse Terre
Grande Terre
Pointe-à-Pitre
Marie Galante

DOMINICA
ROSEAU
DOMINICA POP: 71,000

MARTINIQUE (to France)
FORT-DE-FRANCE

ST LUCIA
CASTRIES
ST. LUCIA POP: 144,000

PANAMA CANAL
One of the world's busiest waterways, the Panama Canal links the Atlantic and Pacific Oceans. It was completed in 1914 and is 80 km (50 miles) long. About 12,000 ships a year use the canal; half the cargo is carried to or from America.

LESSER ANTILLES
ORANJESTAD
ARUBA (to Neth.)
WILLEMSTAD
Curaçao
Bonaire
Kralendijk
NETHERLANDS ANTILLES

Percussion instrument, or Guiro

Wooden maraca

CARIBBEAN MUSIC
The music of the Caribbean, such as Calypso and reggae, shows a strong African influence. Songs often provide witty commentaries on events and personalities. Like Calypso, steel bands originated in Trinidad.

Steel drum, made from an oil drum

ST VINCENT & THE GRENADINES
KINGSTOWN
St Vincent
The Grenadines
ST. VINCENT & THE GRENADINES POP: 113,000

BARBADOS
BRIDGETOWN
BARBADOS POP: 262,000

GRENADA
ST GEORGE'S
GRENADA POP: 92,000

TRINIDAD & TOBAGO
Tobago
Scarborough
PORT OF SPAIN
Trinidad
San Fernando
TRINIDAD & TOBAGO POP: 1,317,000

VENEZUELA

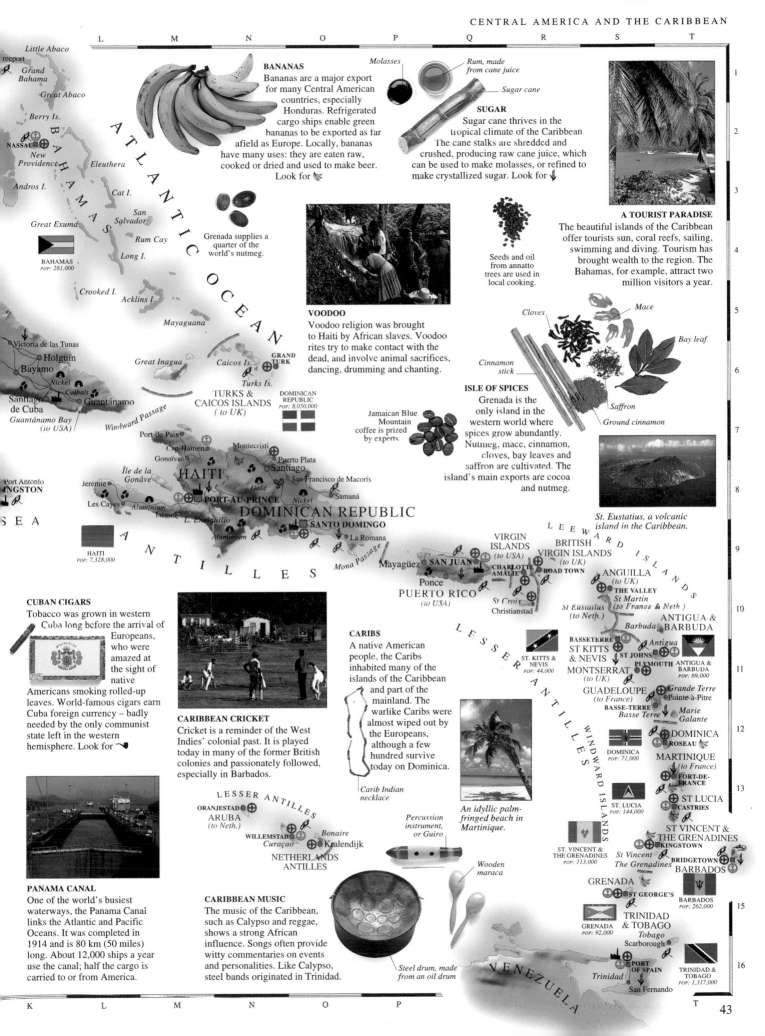

NORTHERN SOUTH AMERICA

THIS REGION IS DOMINATED by the volcanic peaks and mountain ranges of the Andes. The powerful Incas ruled much of this area in the 15th century, and large numbers of their descendants still live in Peru, Bolivia and Ecuador today. In the 16th century, Spanish conquistadores reached South America, swept the Incas and other native peoples aside, and colonized the region from Venezuela to Bolivia. Although all the countries except French Guiana are now independent republics, independence has brought many problems, such as military dictatorships, high inflation, organized crime, the illegal drug trade and huge foreign debts. Many of the cities are overcrowded, but large numbers of people still flock there from the countryside, looking for jobs.

SHRIMPS

Shrimps living in the muddy waters of Ecuador's mangrove swamps have become the country's second most important source of foreign currency, after oil. But, as the industry expands, it is destroying the mangroves – the shrimps' natural habitat. Look for

CARACAS

The discovery of oil in 1917 made Venezuela the richest country in the region. Its capital, Caracas, was built with oil money. Modern motorways and skyscrapers dominate the city, but many people live in shanty towns on the surrounding hillsides.

MARKET DAY

Brightly dressed in their traditional Andean clothes and hats, local people display their wares in the market of the Peruvian town of Pisác. They sell fruit and vegetables, together with pottery and clothes produced for the tourist trade.

The lush Caribbean coastline of northern Venezuela.

Hammered gold
A figure made by ancient Colombian craftsmen.

EMERALDS

Some of the world's finest emeralds are mined near Bogotá, the capital of Colombia. Long before the Spanish invaded the country in search of gold, native peoples mined the emeralds for their gold jewellery and ceremonial objects. Look for

Emerald

Cinchona leaves
Quinine from the bark of the Peruvian cinchona tree is used to treat malaria.

The ancient Inca city of Machu Picchu in the Peruvian Andes.

Flags / Populations

SURINAM POP: 470,000

VENEZUELA POP: 20,490,000

GUYANA POP: 843,000

COLOMBIA POP: 35,624,000

ECUADOR POP: 12,063,000

### Map labels

FRENCH GUIANA (to France)
SURINAM
GUYANA
VENEZUELA
COLOMBIA
ECUADOR
BRAZIL
PANAMA

CARIBBEAN SEA
Gulf of Venezuela
Gulf of Darien
Gulf of Guayaquil
PACIFIC OCEAN

CAYENNE
Kourou
Macouria
St Laurent-du-Maroni
Albina
Marowijne
PARAMARIBO
Brokopondo
Kabalebo Res.
New Amsterdam
Fort Wellington
Brownsweg
Berbice
Courantyne
Essequibo
GEORGETOWN
Bartica
Mazaruni
Suddie
Maharuma
Lethem
Santa Elena
Ciudad Guayana
Ciudad Bolívar
Guri Res.
Tucupita
Maturín
Cumaná
Barcelona
La Asunción
Margarita I.
Puerto Ayacucho
San Fernando de Apure
San Juan de los Morros
Maracay
CARACAS
La Guaira
Valencia
Puerto Cabello
San Carlos
Guanare
Barinas
San Felipe
Coro
Barquisimeto
Maracaibo
L. Maracaibo
Cabimas
Mérida
San Cristóbal
Puerto Carreño
Puerto Inírida
Mitú
Arauca
Yopal
Tunja
BOGOTÁ
Cúcuta
Bucaramanga
Santa Marta
Riohacha
Valledupar
Barranquilla
Cartagena
Sincelejo
Montería
San Andrés
Providence Islands
Villavicencio
San José del Guaviare
Florencia
Mocoa
Neiva
Ibagué
Manizales
Pereira
Armenia
Palmira
Cali
Buenaventura
Popayán
Pasto
Quibdó
Bello
Medellín
Leticia
Iquitos
QUITO
Ibarra
Santo Domingo de los Colorados
Esmeraldas
Manta
Portoviejo
Montecristi
Babahoyo
Latacunga
Ambato
Riobamba
Milagro
Cuenca
Guayaquil
Machala
Loja
Piura
Sullana

Rivers
Orinoco
Apure
Meta
Guaviare
Magdalena
Cauca
Caquetá
Putumayo
Napo
Amazon
Marañón
Negro

Resources labels
Gold, Aluminium, Diamonds, Iron, Beef, Bauxite

Scale
600 KM
MILES 350 300 250 200 150 100 50
0 100 200 300 400 500

N

PANAMA HATS
Panama hats are made of fibre from a palm tree that grows in the coastal forests of Ecuador. One hat can take up to three months to make.

COCAINE
The steep slopes of the Andes are ideally suited to growing the coca bush. The native peoples have always chewed coca leaves to protect themselves against cold and altitude sickness. But the drug cocaine, made from the leaves, is now a major world problem. Today, Colombia's economy is virtually dependent on the illegal export of cocaine.

Coca leaves

HIGHEST RAILWAY
Peru's railways are the highest in the world. The single-track railway from Lima to Huancayo in the Andes zigzags through tunnels and over wooden bridges, reaching an altitude of 4,843 m (15,885 ft) where it crosses through one of the passes.

OTAVALO PEOPLE
Woollen rugs woven by the Otavalo people from Ecuador are sold all over the Americas and Europe. The Otavalo have developed new techniques, such as replacing traditional natural dyes with synthetic ones.

Rug decorated with llamas, the traditional Andean pack animals

Strap handle

Clay body

Water jar, found at the ancient Inca city of Cusco in Peru.

Llamas grazing on the high plains of the Andes in Bolivia.

BRAZIL

BOLIVIA
POP. 8,256,000

PERU
POP. 24,314,000

PARAGUAY

ARGENTINA

CHILE

The Andes are the world's longest chain of mountains.

The native peoples of the Andes were the first to grow potatoes.

LIMA
Pizarro, a leader of the Spanish *conquistadores*, founded Peru's capital city in the 16th century, and his bones are buried in the cathedral on the Plaza de Armas, the main square in the city's centre.

Lima Cathedral

PACIFIC OCEAN

CORPUS CHRISTI
Every town commemorates its patron saint with a festival. Events, such as this colourful procession on Corpus Christi Day in Cusco, Peru, combine the religious beliefs of the native peoples with Christian ceremonies.

LAKE TITICACA
Stretching across the border between Bolivia and Peru is the world's highest lake, Lake Titicaca, 4,000 m (13,000 ft) above sea level. The Uru people sail on the lake in boats of woven reeds.

ANDEAN CULTIVATION
On the steep hillsides of the Andes, every scrap of soil must be made to work efficiently. Like their Inca ancestors, Andean farmers suit the crop to the temperature, which gets lower higher up the mountains. This region is the original home of the potato, which can be grown successfully at high altitudes.

Permanent snow and ice

Inland river valleys: sugar, coffee

3,000 m (9,850 ft)

2,000 m (6,550 ft)

1,000 m (3,280 ft)

Altiplano: high plateaux between mountains used for grazing animals

Highland areas: barley, potatoes, wheat

Temperate zone: coffee, tobacco, corn

Coastal lowland: sugar, cacao, bananas, rice

Sea level

N

Pacific Ocean floor

Peru-Chile Trench: c.6,000 m (19,686 ft) below sea level

KEYBOX

Bananas: Bananas are grown as a cash crop in Ecuador's tropical lowlands. Ecuador is now the world's main exporter. Look for 🍌

Oil: Oil is vital to Venezuela's economy; today the country's oil revenues account for 80 per cent of its export earnings. Look for 🗼

Archaeological sites: The remains of many magnificent ancient cities and temples can still be seen in the Andes. Look for 🏛

Space centre: The European Space Agency launches its rocket, Ariane, from its rocket base at Kourou, French Guiana. Look for 🚀

🐂	Cattle	🪵	Timber
〰	Rice	🐚	Shellfishing
➤	Sugar cane	⚫	Mining
☕	Coffee	🏭	Industrial centre

45

BRAZIL

OCCUPYING NEARLY HALF of South America, Brazil possesses the greatest river basin in the world. The Amazonian rainforest, which covers some two-thirds of the country, is a vast storehouse of natural riches, still largely untapped. But land is needed for agriculture, ranching and new roads, and each year vast tracts of forest are cleared. The Portuguese colonized the country in the 16th century, intermarrying with the local population. They planted sugar in the northeast, working the plantations with slaves brought from Africa. With a further influx of Europeans, Brazil is now one of the world's most populous and ethnically diverse democracies. A land of opportunity for some – like those in the industrial region round São Paulo – it is one of poverty and deprivation for many, especially in the northeast. In spite of improved industrial output, Brazil still has high unemployment and huge foreign debts.

BRAZIL NUTS

Sometimes known as the *inferno verde*, or green hell, Brazil's vast rainforest is home to an astonishing variety of animals and plants from which products – such as chemicals, drugs and rubber – can be made. Scattered through the forest are Brazil nut trees. Their nuts can be eaten, or crushed to make an oil used in cosmetics. Look for 🌰

Nuts fit into shell, like segments of an orange

Shelled nut

NATIVE PEOPLES

There were once some two million native people in Amazonia. Today only about 240,000 survive. This Xingu girl is fortunate: she was born into a tribe which lives in a protected area of the Amazon rainforest. The well-being of many peoples is threatened by disease, the ever-shrinking rainforest and by logging, farming and gold prospecting.

FOOTBALL

Football is an all-consuming passion for millions of Brazilians. It is played in every back street and on every open space, even on the beach at Rio. Sometimes the ball is only a coconut. During the World Cup, Brazil comes to a standstill.

Conga drum

DANCE MUSIC

Transported to the north-eastern region of Brazil to work on the sugar plantations, African slaves brought with them the musical rhythms of their homelands. Their music has blended with other musical influences to produce the music for dances, such as the *samba* and the *lambada*. The instruments include this drum, called a *conga*.

Grandillas, one of the many exotic fruits found in Brazil.

A huge treetrunk in the depths of the Brazilian rainforest.

A stretch of coast near Salvador in the northeast.

BRAZIL
POP: 163,577,000

ATLANTIC OCEAN

COLONIAL LEGACY

When the Portuguese arrived in Brazil in the 16th century, they brought their distinctive style of architecture. At the heart of many towns and cities in modern Brazil lie cobbled streets, squares and churches. The historic town of Ouro Prêto – centre of the 18th-century gold rush – remains today as a perfect example of a 16th century town.

CARNIVAL

Every year, just before Lent, Rio de Janeiro erupts into carnival. Often called "The Biggest Party on Earth", carnival involves five days of music and dance. The main event is the competition to find the most outrageous costumes and best decorated floats as they parade through the city to the sound of *samba* music.

The huge statue of Christ the Redeemer which towers over Rio de Janeiro.

Guanabara Bay provides access to the sea

Rio-Niterói Bridge

Suburbs have grown rapidly

Rio de Janeiro

From Rio, good road and rail routes lead inland

Favelas lacking sanitation and other amenities

Favelas on steep slopes vulnerable to heavy rain

N

RIO DE JANEIRO

Once the capital of Brazil, the beautiful city of Rio de Janeiro sprawls among the bays, islands and hills around Guanabara Bay. The city acts like a magnet, drawing people from poor rural areas who come in search of work. A bad lack of housing has given birth to endless shanty towns, called *favelas*, which creep up the hillsides and crowd every piece of land unfit for other development.

STEEL

Attracted by Brazil's steel industry, cheap labour and plentiful electricity, several multinational companies have invested money in the country. US and European car manufacturers have established successful factories around São Paulo. Look for 🚗

Brazilian-made Fiat saloon

ORANGE JUICE

Oranges are grown in the region around São Paulo, where the climate is frost-free. Over a million tonnes are picked each year. Most of it is processed into orange juice concentrates. Brazil now supplies 85 per cent of the world's orange juice, exporting it mainly to the USA and Europe. Look for 🍊

BRASILIA

In the mid-1950s the government of Brazil decided to build a new capital city in the sparsely inhabited central plateau region. Built in the shape of an aeroplane, the futuristic city of Brasília became the country's official capital in 1960. The wide boulevards and open spaces contain spectacular buildings, such as this cathedral.

GOLD MINING

Brazil has vast mineral reserves. This huge human anthill is the result of a gold rush which began in the 1980s near the Serra Pelada. Thousands of prospectors – called *garimpeiros* – burrow into the hillsides hoping to find gold. Look for ⚒

COFFEE

Coffee originated in Africa, but Brazil is now the world's largest producer. When the trees have shed their white blossoms, the green berries ripen into red "cherries". Each cherry contains two seeds, or coffee beans, which are washed, dried and roasted. Look for ●●

The wings of the *Morpho* butterfly are often used to decorate jewellery.

The Iguaçu River as it drops over the Iguaçu Falls.

KEYBOX

Cattle: Vast areas of Brazilian rainforest have been destroyed to clear the land for cattle-ranching. Look for ▼

Sugar cane: In the 1970s Brazil began to make an alternative to petrol out of sugar cane, but now falling oil prices have made this uneconomic. Look for

Aerospace industry: In recent years Brazil has been successful in developing an aerospace industry, designing planes that are sold worldwide. Look for ✈

Bananas	Tobacco
Citrus fruit	Timber
Coffee	Forest products
Cocoa	Mining
Soya beans	Industrial centre
Cotton	Vehicle manufacture

ATLANTIC OCEAN

BRAZILIAN HIGHLANDS

SERRA DOS PARECIS

BOLIVIA

PARAGUAY

ARGENTINA

URUGUAY

Salvador
Feira de Santana
Ibotirama
Barreiras
Gold
Nickel
Beef
São Francisco
BRASÍLIA
Goiânia
Gold
Uberlândia
Ribeirão Prêto
Campinas
São Paulo
Santos
São José dos Campos
Juiz de Fora
Ouro Prêto
Belo Horizonte
Vitória
Rio de Janeiro
C. de São Tomé
Manganese
Gold
Diamonds
Zinc
Lead
Iron
Diamonds
Iron
Uranium
Furnas Res.
Ilha Solteira Res.
Curitiba
Joinville
Florianópolis
Lead
Zinc
Iron
Londrina
Campo Grande
Cuiabá
Gold
Corumbá
Iron
Manganese
Paraguay
Paraná
Uruguay
Iguaçu
Iguaçu Falls
Itaipu Res.
Passo Fundo
Santa Maria
Pôrto Alegre
Rio Grande
Pelotas
Copper
Patos Lagoon
Mirim Lagoon

600
500
400
300
200
100
0

SOUTHERN SOUTH AMERICA

ALL FOUR COUNTRIES in this region were colonized in the 16th century by Spain. With the exception of Argentina, their populations are almost entirely mestizo – people of mixed Spanish and native descent. In Argentina, 98 per cent of the population is descended from European settlers, as the native peoples were killed or driven out by the immigrants. Argentina falls into three regions: the hot, damp lands of the Gran Chaco in the north, the grasslands of the Pampas in the centre and the barren plateau of Patagonia in the south. Argentina gets its wealth from the rich soil of the Pampas, where cereals are grown and vast herds of sheep and cattle graze. The Pampas spills into neighbouring Uruguay, where sheep provide the country with its main export: wool. Paraguay's economy is mainly dependent on agriculture. Chile lies coiled like a snake along the western side of the Andes, its head in the mineral-rich Atacama Desert and its tail in the icy wastes of the south. These countries all suffer from high inflation, unstable governments and poverty.

THE PEOPLES OF THE CHACO

Only five per cent of Paraguay's population live in the grasslands and swamps of the Gran Chaco. The main people still living there are the Guaranís, the first inhabitants of Paraguay. A smaller group, the Macá, make money by selling colourful hand-woven cloth and goods, like this bag, to tourists.

PARAGUAY
POP: 4,576,000

ASUNCION

Plaza Constitución is just one of many squares whose beautiful Spanish buildings still stand in Asunción, Paraguay's capital and only large city.

ITAIPU DAM

On the mighty Paraná River is one of the world's largest hydro-electric projects, the Itaipú Dam. This joint venture between Brazil and Paraguay boosted Paraguay's economy, creating jobs for thousands of people.
Look for

MAINLY MEAT

In the late 19th century, processing and packing meat became an important industry in Uruguay. Today, tinned meats, such as corned beef, are still a major export.
Look for

Tomatoes were first grown in South America.

URUGUAY
POP: 3,240,000

COPPER

Near Calama, Chile, shining metal is extracted from the largest open-cast copper mine in the world. Giant trucks remove thousands of tonnes (tons) of ore a day. However, the world price of copper is now falling, causing severe economic problems in Chile. Look for

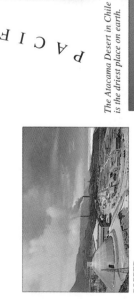

The Atacama Desert in Chile is the driest place on earth.

48

TEXTILES

Uruguay is covered by flat plains which provide grazing land for vast flocks of sheep. The country is a major world exporter of wool. Some articles, like this scarf, are still hand-made. Look for ❤.

Hand-made woollen scarf

ARGENTINA
POP: 35,298,000

The rolling plains and grass-lands of Uruguay.

BUENOS AIRES

Argentina's capital, Buenos Aires, is one of the largest cities in South America and one of the world's great ports. Situated on the River Plate estuary, the city has a large population, including many Italians. The broad, tree-lined avenues, theatres and cafés reflect the city's European heritage.

The leaves of the ilex tree are used to make a refreshing hot drink, called *maté*.

One of the windswept islands of Tierra del Fuego.

THE END OF THE WORLD

Ushuaia in Argentina is one of the world's most southerly towns. It is situated on the chain of islands at the tip of South America called Tierra del Fuego. The name means "land of fire" in Spanish. Ushuaia was once a port for whaling ships. It is now a modern town and busy centre for tourists.

ATLANTIC OCEAN

Dolores
Maize
Maize
Necochea
Mar del Plata
Olavarría
Azul
Wheat
Tres Arroyos
Beef
Bahía Blanca
Wheat
Beef
Wheat
Colorado
Viedma
Beef
Negro
Gulf of San Matías
Valdés Peninsula
Rawson
Santa Rosa
Beef
San Antonio Oeste
Puerto Madryn
Trelew
Chubut
Neuquén
Gulf of San Jorge
Comodoro Rivadavia
Caleta Olivia
Puerto Deseado
Deseado
Zapala
L. Nahuel Huapi
L. Calhué Huapí
Puerto Moreno
San Carlos de Bariloche
L. Buenos Aires
Esquel
Coihaique
ChileChico
Cochrane
Viedma
Puerto Santa Cruz
Calafate
Río Gallegos
Bahía Grande
Río Grande
TORRES DEL PAINE
Puerto Natales
Punta Arenas
Porvenir
Strait of Magellan
Puerto Williams
Ushuaia
TIERRA DEL FUEGO
Beagle Channel
Cape Horn

PATAGONIA
ANDES
CHILE
ARGENTINA
PAMPAS

Uranium
Wheat
Beef

Concepción
Chillán
Los Angeles
Angol
Temuco
Valdivia
Osorno
Puerto Montt
Chaitén
Chiloé I.
Castro

San Fernando
Curicó
Talca
Linares
Bío-Bío
Lebu
Coronel
Caquenes
Teno

LAPIS LAZULI

Lapis lazuli, a deep blue-coloured semi-precious stone has been used in jewellery for thousands of years. The world's most important sources of this stone are many miles apart – near Ovalle in Chile and in Afghanistan. Look for ◆.

Silver and lapis lazuli ring

Silver and lapis lazuli necklace

Rock containing calcite, pyrite and blue lazurite

CHILEAN WINE

The Spanish first brought wine to Chile. Their vines thrived in the Mediterranean climate of the valleys near Santiago. Later, French, then German settlers imported vines. Look for ❧.

THE PAMPAS

In the heart of Argentina lie vast areas of grassland, called the Pampas, where great herds of sheep and cattle roam. Their hides, meat and wool are all exported. But *gauchos*, the Argentinian equivalent of the US cowboy, are fast disappearing. Look for ❧

RAINFALL IN THE SOUTH

The contrasting climates of this region are caused by the Andes. Damp winds from the Pacific Ocean are forced up over the mountains. The air cools as it rises, and rain falls. As it descends on the eastern side of the mountains, the air is dry and warms up. So the west is wet, the east is dry.

Over 2,000 mm (over 80 inches)
1,500–2,000 mm (60–80 inches)
500–1,500 mm (20–60 inches)
250–500 mm (10–20 inches)
Under 250 mm (10 inches)

Andes
Prevailing winds
ATLANTIC OCEAN
PACIFIC OCEAN
Continental shelf
c.2,000 m (6,560 ft) below sea level
Valdés Peninsula
Tierra del Fuego

CHILE
POP: 14,435,000

Spectacular peaks of the Torres del Paine in Chile.

KM / MILES
500 / 300
400 / 250
300 / 200 / 150
100 / 50
0

N

KEYBOX

🌾 Cereals: These are grown in the rich soils and ideal climate of the Pampas. Argentina is one of the world's great cereal exporters. Look for 🌾	Cotton
	Tobacco
📖 Mennonites: Large areas of the Chaco in Paraguay are farmed by communities of these Christians who came originally from Germany. Look for 📖	Fishing
	Mining
	Oil
Cattle	Industrial centre
Sheep	Sugar cane
	Wine

49

A B C D E F G H J

THE ANTARCTIC

THE CONTINENT OF ANTARCTICA has such a cold, harsh climate that no people live there permanently. The land is covered by a huge sheet of ice up to 2 km (1.2 miles) thick, and seas around Antarctica are frozen over. Even during the short summers, the temperature barely climbs above freezing, and the sea-ice only partly melts; in winter, temperatures can plummet to -80° C (-112° F). Few animals and plants can survive on land, but the seas around Antarctica teem with fish and mammals. The only people on the continent are scientists working in the Antarctic research stations and tourists, who come to see the dramatic landscape and the unique creatures that live here. But even these few people have brought waste and pollution to the region.

Icebergs are huge blocks of ice which float in the sea.

KRILL
Krill are the main food of the baleen whale. Japanese and Russian ships catch about 400,000 tonnes (tons) of krill each year, threatening the whales' food supply. Mainly used for animal feed, krill are also considered a delicacy in Japan. Krill gather in such huge numbers that they are visible from aeroplanes or even satellites.

Adélie penguins live in huge colonies on rocks or Antarctic pack ice.

VARIOUS NATIONS CLAIMED TERRITORY IN ANTARCTICA WHEN IT WAS FIRST DISCOVERED IN THE 19TH CENTURY. THESE CLAIMS HAVE BEEN SUSPENDED UNDER THE 1959 ANTARCTIC TREATY (SIGNED BY 39 NATIONS). STATIONS CAN BE SET UP FOR SCIENTIFIC RESEARCH, BUT MILITARY BASES ARE FORBIDDEN.

ATLANTIC OCEAN

SCOTIA SEA

South Orkney Is. (to UK)
Elephant I. (to UK)
South Shetland Is. (to UK)
Larsen Ice Shelf
Anvers I. (to USA)

Drake Passage

Fimbul Ice Shelf
Georg van Neumayer (to Germany)
Novalazarevskaya (to Russian Fed.)
Syowa (to Japan)
Lutzow-Holm Bay

QUEEN MAUD LAND

Riiser-Larsen Ice Shelf

Halley (to UK)
Belgrano II (to Argentina)
Filchner Ice Shelf
Ronne Ice Shelf

WEDDELL SEA
PALMER LAND

INDIAN OCEAN
ENDERBY LAND

Crozet Is. (to France)
Kerguelen I. (to France)
Heard I. (to Australia)

Mawson (to Australia)
C. Darnley
Amery Ice Shelf
Mackenzie Bay
Prydz Bay
Lambert Glacier
West Ice Shelf

SOUTH POLAR PLATEAU

Antarctic fishing fleets are reducing stocks of the cod icefish.

Siple (to USA)
Peter the First I. (to Norway)

BELLINGSHAUSEN SEA
ELLSWORTH MTS.
TRANSANTARCTIC MTS.

• South Pole
Amundsen-Scott (to USA)

Vostok (to Russian Fed.)
Mirnyy (to Russian Fed.)

DAVIS SEA
Shackleton Ice Shelf

These mountains are on Anvers Island, which lies off the Antarctic peninsula.

MARIE BYRD LAND
AMUNDSEN SEA

Getz Ice Shelf
C. Colbeck

Ross Ice Shelf
Scott Base (to New Zealand)
McMurdo Sound

ROSS SEA
VICTORIA LAND
WILKES LAND

Vincennes Bay
Cape Poinsett
Porpoise Bay

PACIFIC OCEAN

C. Adare
Balleny Is.
Dumont d'Urville (to France)

ANTARCTIC TOURISM
Cruise liners have been bringing tourists to the Antarctic region since the 1950s. About 2-3,000 visitors a year observe the harsh beauty of the landscape and its extraordinary wildlife from the comfort of cruise ships.
Look for 📷

| 0 | 250 | 500 | 750 | 1000 | 1250 | 1500 | KM |
| 0 | 250 | 500 | 750 | 1000 | | | MILES |

WHALES
Whales thrive in the seas around the Antarctic, which are rich in plankton and krill, their main food sources. Large-scale whale-hunting started in the 20th century, and the numbers of whales soon fell. In 1948 the International Whaling Commission was set up to regulate the numbers and species of whales killed, and to create protected areas. Look for ✲

Blue whale

RESEARCH
The scientific base in this picture is the US Amundsen-Scott station, which is built underground at the South Pole. Scientists at the Antarctic research stations are monitoring changes to the weather and environment. Look for ◠

POLLUTION
The Antarctic research stations have yet to find effective ways of disposing of their waste. Although some of it is burnt, tins, bottles, machine parts and chemicals are often simply dumped near the bases, spoiling the area's natural beauty. The only solution to the problem is to take the rubbish out of Antarctica. Look for ☠

KEYBOX

Oil: Much of the polar region is rich in oil, but the difficulty of drilling and moving oil, as well as environmental concerns, have slowed exploitation. Look for ⚒

Penguin grounds: Penguin breeding grounds are found near Antarctic coasts. Some are being disturbed by tourists, airstrips and construction. Look for 🐧

🐟 Fishing		◠ Polar research centre
⚒ Coal		☠ Pollution
📷 Tourism		✲ Whales

A B C D E F G H J

THE ARCTIC

THE ARCTIC OCEAN IS covered by drifting ice up to 30 metres (98 feet) thick, which partially melts and disperses in the summer. Much of the surrounding land is tundra – plains and moorlands that are carpeted with moss and lichens, but permanently frozen beneath the surface. People have lived around the Arctic for thousands of years, hunting the mammals and fish that live in the ocean. This region has large deposits of oil, but the harsh climate makes it difficult to extract from the ground.

FISHFINGERS
Large numbers of cod, haddock, halibut and other fish live in the Arctic Ocean. Cod and haddock are taken to fish-processing factories in Greenland. Here they are frozen, canned or – in the case of cod – made into fishfingers, and exported to the markets of the USA and Europe. Look for ⌐

ARCTIC PEOPLES
Traditionally, the people of the Arctic survived by hunting animals. They used seal skin for boats and clothing and seal fat, (blubber) for fuel. Today, tools, clothes and buildings are made from modern materials. Rifles now replace harpoons and snow-mobiles are used for transport.

The northern lights can be seen over the Arctic at night.

Polar bears spend summers on the Arctic ice. They move further south in winter.

ICE-BREAKER
About half the Arctic Ocean is covered with ice in winter, but special ships called ice-breakers can still sail across it. In 1969, a large tanker, the *S.S. Manhattan,* penetrated the pack ice of the Northwest Passage (from eastern Canada to Alaska) for the first time.

GREENLAND
The first Europeans to explore and settle Greenland were Vikings, who arrived in about 986 AD. Greenland later came under Danish rule, and is now a self-governing part of Denmark.

The Arctic tern migrates every year between the Arctic and Antarctica.

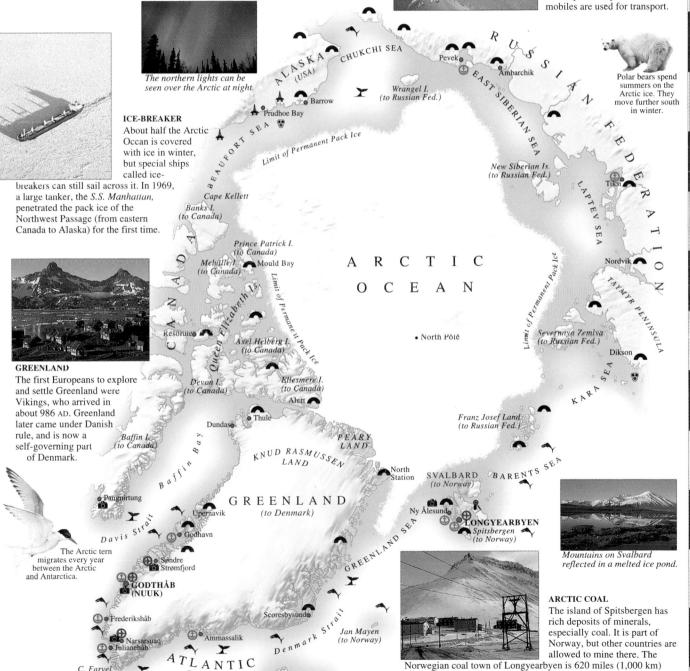

ALASKA (USA)
CHUKCHI SEA
RUSSIAN FEDERATION
Pevek
Ambarchik
EAST SIBERIAN SEA
Wrangel I. (to Russian Fed.)
Barrow
Prudhoe Bay
BEAUFORT SEA
Limit of Permanent Pack Ice
New Siberian Is. (to Russian Fed.)
LAPTEV SEA
Cape Kellett
Banks I. (to Canada)
Tiksi
Prince Patrick I. (to Canada)
Melville I. (to Canada)
Mould Bay
ARCTIC OCEAN
Nordvik
C A N A D A
Limit of Permanent Pack Ice
TAYMYR PENINSULA
Queen Elizabeth Is.
Axel Heiberg I. (to Canada)
North Pole
Severnaya Zemlya (to Russian Fed.)
KARA SEA
Resolute
Devon I. (to Canada)
Ellesmere I. (to Canada)
Dikson
Alert
Dundas
Thule
Franz Josef Land (to Russian Fed.)
Baffin I. (to Canada)
PEARY LAND
KNUD RASMUSSEN LAND
Baffin Bay
North Station
SVALBARD (to Norway)
BARENTS SEA
Pangnirtung
GREENLAND (to Denmark)
GREENLAND SEA
Ny Ålesund
LONGYEARBYEN
Spitsbergen (to Norway)
Upernavik
Davis Strait
Godhavn
Søndre Strømfjord
GODTHÅB (NUUK)
Scoresbysund
Denmark Strait
Jan Mayen (to Norway)
Frederikshåb
Narsarsuaq
Ammassalik
Julianehåb
C. Farvel
ATLANTIC OCEAN
ICELAND

0 250 500 750 1000
KM
0 100 200 300 400 500
MILES

Mountains on Svalbard reflected in a melted ice pond.

ARCTIC COAL
The island of Spitsbergen has rich deposits of minerals, especially coal. It is part of Norway, but other countries are allowed to mine there. The Norwegian coal town of Longyearbyen is 620 miles (1,000 km) from the mainland. It can be reached by sea for only eight months a year, making it difficult and expensive to ship coal out. Coal screes and long, severe winters make this a desolate place. Look for ⌐

THE ATLANTIC OCEAN

THE WORLD'S OCEANS cover almost three-quarters of the Earth's surface. Beneath the surface of the Atlantic Ocean lie vast, featureless plains and long chains of mountains called ridges. The Mid-Atlantic Ridge is one of the world's longest mountain chains; some of its peaks are so high that they pierce the surface as volcanic islands, such as the Azores. A huge rift valley 24-48 km (15-30 miles) wide runs down the ridge's centre. The deepest part of the Atlantic is 8 km (5 miles) below the surface. On average, the Atlantic has the warmest and saltiest waters of any ocean. Before regular shipping routes were established, the Atlantic isolated America from the prosperous countries of Europe, but today it is crossed by some of the world's most important trade routes. The North Atlantic has always been one of the world's richest fishing grounds, but it has been overfished, and fish stocks are now dangerously low.

Puffins breed on rocky islands, like the Faeroes.

FISHING
Catches of cod, herring and haddock in the North Atlantic have been severely reduced by over-fishing. Fishing fleets must now travel long distances and remain at sea for months at a time. The fish are processed on the fleet's factory ship to keep them fresh. Look for ⌁

WHALING
Whaling has been going on in the world's oceans for hundreds of years. But with the invention of the explosive harpoon, catches increased rapidly. Today some species of whales are threatened with extinction. Attempts are being made to ban whaling worldwide until numbers recover. Look for ⌁

"LAND OF ICE AND FIRE"
There are more than 100 volcanoes on Iceland. Many of them are still active. Beneath the island's harsh, rocky surface lie vast natural heat reserves. This energy is used to provide hot water and central heating for much of the population. Iceland's economy is based on fishing, which accounts for about 70 per cent of its exports.

TIDAL ENERGY
Electricity can be generated from the sea in areas where there is a big difference between high and low tide levels. A barrage, like this one at La Rance in France, has to be built across the estuary. Water passing backwards and forwards through the barrage drives the turbines. Look for ⌁

ICELAND
POP: 300,000

CAPE VERDE
POP: 400,000

Tomatoes and other fruit are grown in the warm climate of the Canary Islands.

NATO
The North Atlantic Treaty Organization (NATO) is an association of North American and European countries which was established to defend its members – principally against the former Soviet Union. Look for ⊞

British aircraft carrier

An extinct volcano on an island in the West Indies.

ARCTIC OCEAN

Greenland

GREENLAND SEA

ICELAND
Reykjavik
Denmark Strait

FAEROE ISLANDS
(to Denmark)

Rockall
(to UK)

Murmansk
Tallinn
Liepāja
BALTIC SEA

EUROPE

BLACK SEA

Port Said
Nile

NORTH SEA
Kristiansund
Ålesund
Bergen
Stavanger
Hangesund
Skagen
Esbjerg
Bremerhaven
Rotterdam
Boulogne
La Rance
Lorient

Aberdeen
Grimsby

Gibraltar
Casablanca
Safi

Porto

MEDITERRANEAN SEA
Livorno
Nimes
Marseille
A Coruña
Algiers Sfax

Madeira
(to Portugal)
Azores
(to Portugal)
Canary Islands
(to Spain)

AFRICA

Mid-Atlantic Ridge
North Equatorial
Atlantic Basin

Baffin Bay
Davis Strait

LABRADOR SEA

Farewell

Newfoundland
St John's
Grand Bank
Halifax

NORTH AMERICA

Hudson Bay

Bay of Fundy
Saint John
Portland
Gloucester
New York City
Baltimore

St Lawrence

New Orleans
Mississippi
Gulf of Mexico

Bermuda
(to UK)

SARGASSO SEA

West Indies

ATLANTIC

CAPE VERDE

TOURISM

A number of islands in the Atlantic, such as the Canaries and Madeira, are great tourist attractions, especially during winter in the Northern hemisphere. The Canaries are a chain of seven mountainous islands; some areas are green and lush, others volcanic. The volcanic lava produces dramatic black landscapes. Look for ⚲

SAILING

Areas of the Atlantic have become pleasure grounds. Sailing is one of the main activities, much of it in the warm seas of the Caribbean, but long distance races are increasingly popular, some of them transatlantic. Boats range from yachts sailed single-handed to ships like this tea clipper, sailed by large crews.

CABLES

Snaking across the ocean floor are cables carrying many forms of modern communication, such as telephone calls and fax messages. The first transatlantic cable was laid in 1866. The cables are laid by special ships, like this one in the North Atlantic.

Lobsters are caught in wickerwork lobster pots, baited with dead fish.

Massive icebergs drift among the pack ice, a threat to shipping in the Atlantic.

SALMON

The early years of an Atlantic salmon are spent in the river where it was born. Then it swims down river to the ocean. In the rich feeding grounds of the North Atlantic it rapidly gains weight. When ready to breed, the salmon's amazing homing device enables it to return to its native river. Here, on their long, hard journey upriver, salmon negotiate a waterfall. Few salmon survive this endurance test to breed a second time.

SARGASSO SEA

At the centre of three great North Atlantic currents lies the Sargasso Sea – an area of calm water, covered with *sargassum* weed. Sailors once believed their ships would be trapped by the weed, and sink.

Fish like these live amongst the sargassum weed

POLLUTION

There are very few laws to control the way the world's oceans are used. The North Atlantic is one of the busiest and most polluted. Ships discharge oil and chemicals and dump radio-active waste.

Some stretches of the northeast coast of America are so polluted that signs warn people not to swim. Plastic containers litter the world's coasts. International action to control this pollution is long overdue. Look for 💠

An isolated settlement on the Falkland Islands in the South Atlantic.

KEYBOX

Underwater wrecks: *Marine archaeology and location of wrecks was greatly advanced by the development of deep-sea diving equipment. Look for* ⚲

Pollution: *Oil rig blow-outs and spills from oil tankers along the coastlines and round the Gulf of Mexico are a major problem in the North Atlantic. Look for* 💠

Hurricane: *The warm Atlantic waters off the north coast of Brazil are the gathering grounds for hurricanes, which then sweep north-westward. Look for* 🌀

⚡	Alternative power
⚲	Tourism
▥	Military bases
✕	Whales
⚓	Fishing
⛴	Fishing ports
⛽	Oil
⬮	Gas

### Map labels

AFRICA
Niger
Congo
Libreville
Gulf of Guinea
São Tomé
Príncipe
Lagos
Guinea Basin
Angola Basin
Walvis Bay
Lüderitz
Port Nolloth
Cape Town
Cape of Good Hope
Cape Basin
ASCENSION ISLAND (to UK)
ST. HELENA (to UK)
TRISTAN DA CUNHA (to UK)
Gough Island (to UK)
Atlantic-Indian Ridge
Atlantic-Indian-Antarctic Basin
Mid-Atlantic Ridge

SOUTH AMERICA
ATLANTIC OCEAN
La Guaira
Georgetown
Cayenne
Cartagena
Panama City
Amazon
Fortaleza
Recife
Salvador
Rio de Janeiro
Mar del Plata
Bahía Blanca
Buenos Aires
Guyana Basin
Brazil Basin
Argentine Basin
Fernando de Noronha (to Brazil)
Trindade (to Brazil)
Cape Verde
Cape Verde Basin

FALKLAND ISLANDS (to UK)
SOUTH GEORGIA (to UK)
SOUTH SANDWICH ISLANDS (to UK)
South Orkney Is. (to UK)
South Shetland Is. (to UK)
SCOTIA SEA
WEDDELL SEA
ANTARCTICA

N
KM
MILES
0 50 100 150 200 250 300
0 50 100 150

Wild boar
Sus scrofa
Height: 1 m (3 ft)

Stag beetle
Lucanus cervus
Length: 8 cm (3 in)

European badger
Meles meles
Length: 1 m (3 ft)

EUROPE

EUROPE, THE SMALLEST CONTINENT after Australia, is less than half the size of North America and a quarter that of Asia. Yet it has a remarkable variety of climates, landforms and types of vegetation. Europe's main mountain ranges, including the Pyrenees and the Alps, roughly divide the continent north and south. They form a barrier that protects the south from the cold winds that blow from the north during winter. As a result, the south is much warmer and drier than the cool, wet, heavily-forested north. Europe has an irregular shape, with many interlocking fingers of land and sea. Because much of the land is close to the sea, coastal areas have fewer temperature extremes. Currents also affect the climate. Thanks to the powerful Gulf Stream, which brings immense amounts of warm water northwards from the Equator, even seas within the Arctic Circle stay ice-free throughout the year.

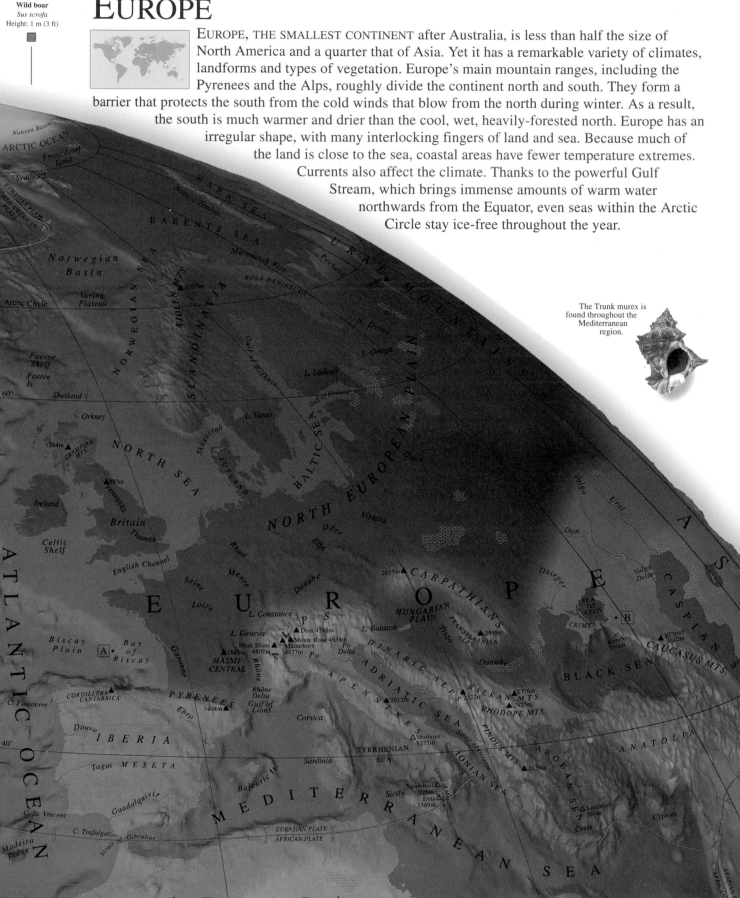

The Trunk murex is found throughout the Mediterranean region.

Nansen Basin
ARCTIC OCEAN
80°
Svalbard
Franz Josef Land
EURASIAN PLATE
NORTH AMERICAN PLATE
Norwegian Basin
Arctic Circle
Voring Plateau
Faeroe Shelf
Faeroe Is.
60°
Shetland
Orkney
Ireland
1344m GRAMPIAN MTS.
893m PENNINES
Britain
Thames
Celtic Shelf
English Channel
ATLANTIC OCEAN
Biscay Plain
[A]
Bay of Biscay
C. Finisterre
CORDILLERA CANTABRICA 2648m
PYRENEES
3404m
Ebro
Douro
IBERIA
Tagus MESETA
Guadalquivir
C. St. Vincent
Madeira Ridge
C. Trafalgar
Strait of Gibraltar
EURASIAN PLATE
AFRICAN PLATE
AFRICA

KARA SEA
BARENTS SEA
Novaya Zemlya
Murmansk Rise
Pechora
KOLA PENINSULA
URAL MOUNTAINS
2117m KJØLEN MTS.
N. Dvina
NORWEGIAN SEA
SCANDINAVIA
Gulf of Bothnia
L. Onega
L. Ladoga
L. Vaner
Gulf of Finland
NORTH SEA
JUTLAND
BALTIC SEA
Skagerrak
NORTH EUROPEAN PLAIN
Dvina
Oder
Vistula
Rhine
Elbe
Danube
Meuse
Seine
Loire
L. Constance
E U R O P E
A L P S
Dom 4545m
Mont Blanc 4807m
Monte Rosa 4634m
Matterhorn 4477m
1886m
MASSIF CENTRAL
L. Geneva
Garonne
Rhône
Rhône Delta
Gulf of Lions
Corsica
Sardinia
Balearic Is.
MEDITERRANEAN SEA
2655m CARPATHIANS
HUNGARIAN PLAIN
L. Balaton
Po Delta
Po
Danube
TRANSYLVANIAN ALPS
Tisza
DINARIC ALPS
ADRIATIC SEA
APENNINES
Vesuvius 1277m
TYRRHENIAN SEA
Sicily
Stromboli 926m
Etna 3369m
Strait of Messina
IONIAN SEA
Strait of Otranto
PINDUS MTS.
BALKAN MTS. 2376m
2522m
RHODOPE MTS. 2925m
2150m
AEGEAN SEA
Santorini 566m
Crete
Volga
Ural
Don
Dnieper
Volga Delta
A S I A
CASPIAN SEA
CRIMEA
SEA OF AZOV
Kerch Strait
[B]
El'brus 5642m
CAUCASUS MTS.
BLACK SEA
ANATOLIA
Cyprus
40°
ARABIAN PLATE
AFRICAN PLATE
Gulf of Sirte
0°
20°

Siberian tit
Parus cinctus
Length: 13 cm (5 in)

Green toad
Bufo viridis
Length: 10 cm (4 in)

Osprey
Pandion haliaetus
Wingspan: 1.6 m (5 ft)

BOGLANDS
Bogs cover many of northern
Europe's wettest areas. Mosses and
reeds are among the few plants that
grow in waterlogged soils. Wetlands
take thousands of years to develop
because plants grow so slowly there.

WAVE POWER
Waves can wear away the
shore, creating odd land-
forms. This seastack off the
Orkneys in the British Isles
is 135 m (450 ft) high.

Ammonites, fossil
relatives of today's
octopus, were once found
in Europe. They died out
65 million years ago.

PIONEERING BIRCH
Light-loving silver birches are
often the first trees to appear
on open land. Although quick-
growing, they are short-lived.
After a few years birches are
replaced by trees that can
survive shade, such as oaks.

English oak
Quercus robur
Height: 40 m (130 ft)

BARE MOUNTAIN
Ice, rain, wind and gravity strip
steep slopes of all soil. Rocks pile
up at the foot of peaks, where
plants can take root.

FJORDS
Glaciers have cut hundreds of narrow
inlets, or fjords, into Scandinavia's
Atlantic coastline. The water in the
inlet is calmer than in the open sea.

NEEDLELEAF FOREST
Cone-bearing trees such as
pine, larch and fir cover
Scandinavia. Most are
evergreen: they keep their
needle-like leaves even when
covered in snow for many
months of the year.

TREELESS TUNDRA
Arctic summers are so cool
that only the topmost layer of
frozen soil thaws. Only
shallow-rooted plants can
survive in the tundra.

Pine marten
Martes martes
Length: 52 cm (20 in)

ANCIENT WOODLANDS
Relics of Europe's ancient forests,
such as these oaks stunted by the
rain and wind, are found only in a
few valleys in southwest Britain.

This fossil of *Stauranderaster*,
a starfish once found in
this region, dates from
around 70 million
years ago.

DRY SOUTH
Crete is a mountainous
Mediterranean island
with hot dry summers.
Many plants survive the
summer as underground
bulbs, blooming briefly
in the wet spring.

YOUNG MOUNTAINS
The Alps are some of western Europe's highest
mountains. They are part of an almost
continuous belt that stretches from the Pyrenees
in the west to the Himalayas in Asia. The Alps
are still rising because of plate movements in
the Mediterranean region.

Sweet briar
Rosa rubiginosa
Height: 3 m (10 ft)

CROSS-SECTION THROUGH EUROPE

Massif Central
Bay of Biscay
Atlantic Ocean
Alps
Adriatic Sea
Dinaric Alps
Hungarian Plain
Transylvanian Alps
Black Sea
Crimea
Kerch Strait

3,000 (9,843)
0 Sea level
-4,500 (14,764)
Metres (feet)

A   **Length: 4,500 km (2,800 miles)**   B

KEY TO SYMBOLS

▲ *Mountain*
△ *Volcano*
Mangroves
Wetlands
Coral reef
*Plate margins showing
direction of movement*

KEY TO NATURAL VEGETATION

Tundra
Needleleaf forest
Broadleaf forest
Cold desert
Mountain
Mediterranean-type
Temperate grassland

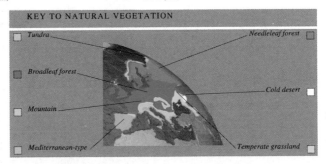

Spanish lynx
Felis lynx
Length: 1.3 m (4 ft)

SCANDINAVIA AND FINLAND

THE SCANDINAVIAN COUNTRIES of Norway, Sweden and Denmark and neighbouring Finland are situated around the Baltic Sea in northern Europe. During past ice ages, glaciers gouged and scoured the land, leaving deep fjords, lakes and valleys in their wake. Much of Norway and Sweden, and nearly two-thirds of Finland, is covered by dense forests of pine, spruce and birch trees. In the far north, winters are long and dark, and snow falls for about eight months of the year. Most Swedish people live in the central lowlands. Norway's economy depends on its shipbuilding, fishing and merchant fleets. Denmark is flat and low-lying, with abundant rainfall and excellent farmland. The Finnish people originally came from the east, via Russia, and consequently differ from the Scandinavians both in language and culture. All four countries have small populations, are highly industrialized and enjoy some of the highest standards of living in the world.

Meadow crops grown for livestock

Deep water enables ships to reach far inland

Rough upland grazing for sheep and goats

Fish farming of salmon in sheltered waters

Coastal fishing communities are declining

Cultivation limited to warm, south-facing slopes

Coastal islands form natural breakwaters

A NORWEGIAN FJORD

Norway is so mountainous that only three per cent of the land can be cultivated. Long inlets of sea, called fjords, cut into Norway's west coast. The best farmland is found around the head of the fjords and in the lowland areas around them. Over 70 per cent of Norway's population lives in cities, many of them in towns situated along the sheltered fjords.

The still waters of a Norwegian fjord.

NORWAY
POP: 4,382,000

FISHING

As Norway has so little farmland, fishing has always been a vital source of food. Today, about 95 per cent of the total catch is processed, about half made into fishmeal and oil. Fish-farming is on the increase, especially of salmon in the fjords. Look for

Fantoft Church, Bergen

Vast shoals of herring gather in the seas around Scandinavia

LAPLAND

Lapland is a land of tundra, forests and lakes. Here the *Samer,* or Lapps, still herd reindeer for their meat and milk. Development in the north now threatens their way of life.

STAVE CHURCHES

The wooden stave churches of Norway were built between AD 1000 and 1300. There were once 600 of them, but today only 25 are still standing. A stave church has a stone foundation with a wooden frame on top. The four wooden corner posts are called staves. Further wooden extensions can be added to the basic framework.

Lego building bricks were invented in Denmark.

SKIING

For thousands of years skiing has been the most efficient way of crossing deep snow on foot. This region is often thought to be the original home of skiing – in fact "ski" is the Norwegian word for a strip of wood. Long-distance cross-country skiing, or *langlaufen*, is a popular sport in Norway, Finland and Sweden.

SMÖRGÅSBORD

Smörgåsbord means "sandwich table" in Swedish. Other countries in this region have their own versions, but the idea is the same: a great spread of local delicacies, served cold on bread, which can include ingredients such as reindeer, fish, cheese and salad.

Scrambled egg
Prawn
Caviar
Asparagus
Smoked salmon

KEYBOX

Hydro-electric power *The region's mountainous terrain enables the majority of its electricity to be supplied by HEP. Look for*

Bridges: *Tunnels and bridges now link the Danish islands of Fyn and Sjaelland. Linking Denmark and Sweden is under discussion. Look for*

Cattle		Fishing	
Pigs		Fishing port	
Cereals		Mining	
Timber		Industrial centre	

COPENHAGEN

Copenhagen's fine natural harbour and its position at the main entrance to the Baltic Sea, helped it to become a major port and Denmark's capital city. The city's tiny shops, cobbled streets, museums and cafés attract over a million tourists each year.

Danish bacon for export

DENMARK
POP: 5,203,000

DANISH AGRICULTURE

Two-thirds of the total area of Denmark is used for farming. Denmark exports agricultural products all over the world. The main products are bacon, dairy products, cereals and beef. Cereals are widely grown, but mainly as fodder for pigs. Look for

*Map labels:*
Steinkjer, Hitra, Smøla, Vanadium, Trondheim, Coppe, Molde, Iron, Ålesund, Coppi, Røros, Nordfjord, L. Femunu, Sogne Fjord, Hermansverk, Gldma, Lillehamme, Bergen, Hardanger Fjord, Gjøvik, Hamar, L. Mjøsa, Honefoss, Oats, Haugesund, OSLO, Bokna Fjord, Drammen, Kongsberg, Stavanger, Porsgrunn, Dairy, Sandnes, Fredrikstad, Moss, Titanium, Otra, Dairy, Halden, Iron, Arendal, Dairy, Kristiansand, Oslo Fjord, Skagerrak, Uddevalla, Trollhättan, DENMARK, Göteborg, Hjørring, Borås, Frederikshavn, Ålborg, Varberg, Holstebro, Dairy, Rye, Randers, Halmstad, Ringkøbing, JUTLAND, Barley, Hälsingborg, Århus, Helsingør, Esbjerg, Horsens, COPENHAGEN, Hässleho, Ribe, Vejle, Malm, Åbenrå, Fyn, Odense, Slagelse, Sønderborg, Næstved, Sjaelland, Ystac, Nakskov, Barley, GERMANY, Nykøbing, Kattegat, Skagerrak

MIDNIGHT SUN
This may look like an ordinary sunset, but this photo of Bodø in Norway was taken at midnight. In the far north of this region, the sun never sets in mid-summer. The further north you travel, the longer is the period of midnight sun. In winter, in Lapland, the sun remains below the horizon for a week; in the far north, this period of darkness lasts two months.

Ladle

SAUNA BATHS
Some 1,000 years ago the Finns invented the steam bath, or *sauna*, as a way of cleansing and relaxing the body. The steam is produced by throwing water over hot stones. A plunge in an icy pool, or snowdrift, completes the process. The *sauna* has become a national institution.

Wooden bucket

FINLAND
POP: 5,059,000

TIMBER
Finland, Norway and Sweden are heavily forested. The timber is used in many ways, such as building, furniture and crafts. All three countries have large wood-pulp, paper and board industries. Finland and Sweden are now among the world's largest exporters of these products. This Swedish child's chair is cleverly designed to grow with the child. Look for ⌐

SWEDEN
POP: 8,813,000

SCANDINAVIAN DESIGN
Scandinavians have a highly developed sense of design which extends to everyday objects, such as stereo equipment, furniture and glass. Sweden and Finland are well known for their glassware, and the industry attracts many famous artists who create the new designs.

Glass fig from Finland
Glass pear from Finland
Glass aubergine from Sweden

Trolls are characters in Scandinavian folklore.

A forest bordering one of Finland's myriad lakes.

NORWEGIAN OIL
Since oil was discovered in the North Sea in the 1970s, Norway has become self-sufficient in natural gas and oil, which account for over half the country's export earnings. It is also a world leader in drilling platforms and tankers.

A classic Volvo saloon

CAR MANUFACTURE
For its size, Sweden has a large number of highly successful multi-national companies. Two examples are the motor manufacturers, Volvo and Saab-Scania, whose cars and trucks are widely exported. Volvo workers build cars in teams. The company pioneered this system to improve working conditions.

The carved prow of a Viking ship found in Norway.

Stockholm, Sweden's capital and an important seaport.

THE BRITISH ISLES

THE BRITISH ISLES CONSIST OF TWO large islands – Great Britain and Ireland – surrounded by many smaller ones. They are divided into two countries: the United Kingdom (UK), often known as Britain, and Ireland. At the end of the 18th century, the UK became the first country in the world to undergo an industrial revolution. It became the world's leading manufacturing and trading nation, and built up an empire that covered more than a quarter of the world. The UK's traditional industries, such as coal mining, textiles and car manufacturing, have declined in recent years, but service industries such as banking and insurance have been extremely successful. Ireland, which became independent from the UK in 1921, is still a mainly rural country and many Irish people make their living from farming. However, tourism and high-tech industries, such as computers and pharmaceuticals, are increasingly important. The UK and Ireland still have close trading links and many Irish people go to the UK to find work.

"THE TROUBLES"
When British Protestants settled in Ireland in the 17th century, they came into conflict with Irish Catholics, whose land they had seized. In 1921 the Protestant North refused to join the independent South. Catholics were discriminated against, in jobs and housing and violence erupted in the 1960s. British troops were sent to police the province.

AGRICULTURE AND INDUSTRY
Farming has always been Ireland's principal source of income. Dairy products, beef and potatoes are still important, but recently, the number of high-tech industries has increased.

Irish butter

OIL
Rich reserves of both oil and natural gas were found under the North Sea in the 1960s. By the late 1970s, natural gas was being piped to most homes, factories and businesses in the UK. Massive oil rigs were moored in the North Sea, and wells were dug by drilling into the ocean bed below the platforms. Oil rigs and onshore refineries brought employment to many areas, especially in eastern Scotland. But oil reserves are being steadily used up, and oil production is now in decline. Look for ▮

TARTAN TOURISM
Tourism is an important source of income for Scotland. People come to enjoy the beautiful highland scenery, and visit the ancient castles. For centuries, Scotland was dominated by struggles between rival families, known as clans. Today one of the most popular tourist souvenirs is tartan – textiles woven in the colours of the clans.

Tartan scarf

Scottish shortbread

Bright red letter boxes are a common sight on British streets.

FISHING
The waters of the north-east Atlantic are amongst the world's richest fishing grounds, well-stocked with mackerel, herring, cod, haddock and shellfish. The British Isles has many fishing ports, like this one in the north-east of England. But EU regulations designed to reduce catches and conserve fish stocks, are causing widespread discontent amongst fishermen. Look for ⚓

INDUSTRY

Many Japanese companies, car and electronics manufacturers in particular, are now based in the UK, attracted by a skilled labour force and access to European markets. Britain's traditional industries, such as textiles, steel and pottery have been joined by newer, high-tech industries. Look for ▮

AEROSPACE
UK firms design and build a wide range of civil and military aircraft. Perhaps the most famous is Concorde, a supersonic jet created in partnership with the French. Recently, the aerospace industry has been badly hit by world recession, and UK companies have had to develop products in other areas, such as electronics and telecommunications. Look for ✈

The supersonic jet, Concorde

A deep inlet of water – or loch – in the north of Scotland.

NORTH SEA

ATLANTIC OCEAN

Shetland

Lerwick

Orkney

Kirkwall

Stromness

Thurso

C. Wrath

Ullapool

Loch Shin

Loch Ness

Inverness Moray Firth

Elgin

Fraserburgh

Peterhead

Aberdeen

Dee

Barley Oats

Beef

Beef

Dundee

Firth of Forth

Perth

Edinburgh

SCOTLAND

Loch Lomond

Glasgow

Firth of Clyde

Greenock

Grangemouth

Arran

Kintyre

Jura

Islay

Oban

Mull

Fort William

Mallaig

Eigg

Muck

Rum

Canna

Coll

Tiree

Skye

North Minch

Harris

Little Minch

Lewis

Stornoway

Outer Hebrides

North Uist

South Uist

Benbecula

Barra

Beef

Beef

UNITED KINGDOM

SOUTHERN UPLANDS

GREAT BRITAIN

Tweed

Beef

Lough Foyle

LONDON

The Romans founded the town they called Londinium on the River Thames in AD 43. The UK's capital is now a huge, sprawling city with seven million inhabitants. London is the country's centre of finance, politics, law, and culture, and contains many famous historical buildings, shops, museums and theatres.

Big Ben

The Houses of Parliament, London

MULTICULTURAL BRITAIN

Since the 1960s, the UK has become an increasingly multicultural society. Large numbers of immigrants have come to the UK from former colonies in Africa, the Caribbean and Asia and have greatly enriched British culture with their own traditions.

HIGH FINANCE

The skyscrapers and office blocks that surround St. Paul's Cathedral in the City of London are home to one of the world's biggest financial centres. City companies specialize in banking and insurance, and lead the world in foreign currency deals. The City covers only a small area, but every day it is filled with more than half a million office workers.

Tea, served with milk, is Britain's national drink.

FARMING

About three-quarters of the land in the UK is used for farming. The crops vary from region to region and reflect the country's varied climate and soils. Barley, wheat, vegetables and sugar beet are the main crops in the east of the country, while beef and dairy farming is a speciality in the west.

SPORT

Many sports which are now played all over the world originated in the UK. Rugby, cricket and golf were all British inventions, while the rules of modern soccer were established on the sports fields of English schools.

Soccer ball

Cricket ball

Rugby ball

The rocky coast of Cornwall in southwest England.

Dublin's fine O'Connell bridge over the R. Liffey.

English beers are made from barley, malt and hops.

UNITED KINGDOM
Pop: 58,395,000

IRELAND
Pop: 3,462,000

KEYBOX

High-tech industry: Companies making scientific instruments, electronics and computers are based in southern England, Scotland and Ireland. Look for ▢

Tourism: Millions of visitors a year come to the UK to see palaces, castles, ancient monuments, cathedrals and museums. Look for ▦

Tunnel: The Channel Tunnel, linking England and France, is 50 km (31 miles) long. Passenger and freight trains use the tunnel. Look for ▣

Airport: Heathrow, 20 km (12 miles) from London, is the world's busiest international airport. It handles 58 million passengers a year. Look for ⊕

Cattle 🐂	Coal ⚒
Sheep 🐑	Industrial centre 🏭
Cereals 🌾	Oil refining ⛽
Market gardening 🌱	Aerospace industry ✈
Fishing port ⚓	Vehicle manufacture 🚗

N O R T H   S E A

ENGLISH CHANNEL

IRISH SEA

NORTHERN IRELAND

IRELAND

ENGLAND

WALES

SCOTLAND

PENNINES

CAMBRIAN MTS.

DARTMOOR

EXMOOR

COTSWOLDS

CHILTERNS

NORTH DOWNS

SOUTH DOWNS

MENDIP HILLS

MIDLANDS

EAST ANGLIA

THE FENS

ISLE OF MAN (to UK)

Channel Is.

ST. PETER PORT GUERNSEY (to UK)

ST. HELIER JERSEY (to UK)

Isles of Scilly

Strait of Dover

St. George's Channel

Bristol Channel

Cardigan Bay

Morecambe Bay

Solway Firth

The Wash

Lyme Bay

Donegal Bay

Galway Bay

Dingle Bay

Bantry Bay

Lough Neagh

Lough Corrib

Lough Ree

Lough Derg

Anglesey

Holy I.

Lundy

Isle of Wight

Big Ben

KM
MILES
0   25   50   75   100   150

N

59

SPAIN AND PORTUGAL

SPAIN AND PORTUGAL are located on the Iberian Peninsula, which is cut off from the rest of Europe by the Pyrenees. This isolation, combined with the region's closeness to Africa and the Atlantic Ocean, has shaped the history of the two countries. The Moors, an Islamic people from North Africa, occupied the peninsula in the 8th century AD, leaving an Islamic legacy that is still evident today. In 1492 the Moors were finally expelled from Catholic Spain. The oceangoing Spanish and Portuguese took the lead in exploring and colonizing the New World, and both nations acquired substantial overseas empires. During this era, Portugal was ruled by Spain from about 1580 to 1640. Eventually, both nations lost most of their colonies, and their once-great wealth and power declined. Spain was torn apart by a vicious civil war from 1936-39, and right-wing dictators ruled both Spain and Portugal for much of the 20th century. In the 1970s, both countries emerged as modern democracies, and have since experienced rapid economic growth, benefiting from their membership of the European Union. Today, their economies are dominated by tourism and agriculture, although Spanish industry is expanding rapidly.

The Cordillera Cantábrica in northwestern Spain.

PORTUGAL
POP: 9,884,000

FISHING

Portuguese sardine

The Portuguese have fished for cod off the eastern coast of Canada for over 500 years. Dried salt cod is still a common food today. Sardines from Portugal are considered the best in the world, and are exported from fish processing factories on the coast. Look for 🚢

GROWING CORKS

Spain and Portugal produce two-thirds of the world's cork. It is made from the outer bark of these evergreen oak trees. The bark is stripped off, seasoned, flattened, then laid out in sheets.

FORTIFIED WINES

Sherry *Port*

This region is famous for its fortified wines. They are made by adding extra alcohol to the wine during the fermentation process. Sherry is named after Jerez de la Frontera, while port comes from Porto. Look for ❀

KEYBOX

Forest products: Spain and Portugal are Europe's only source of eucalyptus, which is grown for its gum, resin, oil and wood. Look for 🌲

Fishing: Spanish fishing fleets are amongst the largest in Europe, concentrated around the northwest Atlantic coast. Look for 🐟

Vehicle manufacture: Spain ranks sixth in world car exports, specializing in small cars. Look for 🚐

🐑	Sheep	🚢	Fishing ports
🍋	Citrus fruit	⛏	Mining
🍇	Wine	🏭	Industrial centre
🫒	Vegetable oil	⚓	Tourism

A castle is visible on the wooded hills north of Lisbon.

LISBON

Portugal's great navigators and explorers set sail from Lisbon, on the mouth of the River Tagus. The city, which grew rich on global trade, was completely rebuilt after an earthquake destroyed two thirds of it in 1755.

Portugal exports large numbers of oysters caught in the Atlantic.

OLIVES

The deep fertile soils and warm climate of parts of Spain, especially Jaén in the southeast, are ideal for olive cultivation. Spain is one of the world's leading olive producers. Look for 🫒

IBERIAN INDUSTRY

Spain's industries are concentrated around the northern ports, such as Bilbao, and around the cities of Madrid and Barcelona. The main industries are shipbuilding, iron, steel and petrochemicals, although food-processing and textiles are also important. Spain is the fourth-largest steel exporter in the world. Look for 🏭

The Classical guitar is Spain's national instrument.

FISH DISHES

Paella is a classic Spanish dish from the Valencia region, where rice is grown. It consists of a variety of meat, fish, fresh vegetables and saffron-flavoured rice, simmered in a stock. Spaniards eat a lot of fish, and fish stew is another popular dish. Spain is also famous for its cured meats, especially ham, or *jamón serrano*.

ORANGES

Oranges were introduced to Spain by the Moors in about the 9th century AD. They are grown along the Mediterranean coast and are an important export. The best Spanish oranges come from Valencia. Oranges from Seville are used for making fine marmalade. Look for 🍊

Many tourists visit the beautiful Balearic Islands.

TOURISM

Fifty million visitors a year visit Spain's Mediterranean coast alone, and tourism accounts for 10 per cent of Spain's income. But large numbers of high-rise hotels have spoilt some stretches of the coastline, and popular beaches are very overcrowded. Look for 🏖️

FLAMENCO

Flamenco music and dance, developed by the Andalusian gypsies, are the major folk arts of Spain. Flamenco songs deal with the entire range of human emotion, from despair to ecstasy, and are performed with a passionate intensity. Dancers dress in traditional costume and accompany themselves on castanets and guitars.

Castanets

Flamenco dancer's fan and comb

SPAIN
POP: 39,664,000

Gibraltar has been a British colony since the 18th century.

THE ALHAMBRA

The Alhambra, at Granada in southern Spain, is a Moorish palace and fortress built during the 13th-14th centuries. It was the Moors' last stronghold in Spain. It is a beautiful example of Moorish architecture, famous for its delicately carved stone, brilliantly patterned mosaics and tiles, and alabaster fountains.

BULLFIGHTING

In Spain, bullfighting is a national sport. During a bullfight, brightly coloured capes are fluttered to tempt the bull to charge. When it charges, the matador sticks long, pointed barbs into the bull's shoulders. Once it is exhausted, the matador uses his sword to kill the bull, exposing himself to mortal danger.

CATHOLICISM

Like the Portuguese, the Spanish blend Roman Catholicism with customs and superstitions dating back to pre-Christian times. Their *fiestas* combine religious ceremonies with wine and dancing.

Map labels: Bay of Biscay, Santander, Iron, San Sebastián, Bilbao, Iron, BASQUE PROVINCES, Vitoria, Pamplona, Magnesium, Potassium, FRANCE, PYRENEES, ANDORRA, Roses, Girona, Costa Brava, Huesca, Potassium, CATALONIA, Terrassa, Sabadell, Badalona, Barcelona, Lleida, Reus, Tarragona, Golf de Sant Jordi, Burgos, Logroño, Soria, Ebro, Zaragoza, Mequinenza Res., Olives, Olives, Duero, Segovia, Gold, SIERRA DE GUADARRAMA, Guadalajara, Iron, Olives, Teruel, Castellón de la Plana, Olives, MADRID, Getafe, Fuenlabrada, Móstoles, Toledo, VALENCIA, Olives, Valencia, Júcar, Balearic Islands, Minorca, Mahón, Majorca, Palma de Mallorca, Ibiza, Ibiza, Formentera, Albacete, Ciudad Real, Uranium, Zinc, Lead, Olives, Segura, Olives, Benidorm, Alicante, Elche, Castanets, Murcia, Lead, SIERRA DE SEGURA, Olives, Zinc, Cartagena, Iron, Costa Blanca, MEDITERRANEAN SEA, Jaén, Olives, ANDALUSIA, Iron, Granada, SIERRA NEVADA, Almería, Motril, Costa del Sol, SPAIN, P A I N

Scale: 0 25 50 75 100 125 150 175 KM / 0 25 50 75 100 MILES

N (compass)

A B C D E F G H I J

FRANCE

FOR CENTURIES FRANCE has played a central role in European civilization. Reminders of its long history can be found throughout the land; prehistoric cave-dwellings, Roman amphitheatres, medieval cathedrals, castles, and the 17th- and 18th-century palaces of the powerful French monarchs. The French Revolution of 1789 swept away the monarchy and changed the face of France forever. The country survived the Napoleonic wars and occupation during World Wars I and II, and now has a thriving economy based on farming and industry. It is a land of varied scenery and strong regional traditions, the only country which belongs to both northern and southern Europe. Farming is still important, but many people have moved from the country to the cities. France still administers a number of overseas territories, all that remain of its once widespread empire. Today, France's population includes immigrants from its former colonies, especially Muslims from North Africa. France is one of the most enthusiastic members of the European Union.

PARIS
Paris, the capital of France, is the largest and most important city in the country. It lies on both banks of the River Seine. One of the world's great cities, Paris contains magnificent buildings, art treasures and elegant shops. The wrought-iron Eiffel Tower looms above the city, the symbol of Paris.

A cyclist in the *Tour de France*, the world's most famous cycle race.

FRANCE
POP: 57,800,000

AGRICULTURE
France is a mainly rural country producing a wide range of farm products. Some farms still use traditional methods but modern technology has transformed regions like the Paris Basin, where cereals are grown on a large scale. Look for ⚘

THE AIRBUS
Developing new aircraft is so costly that sometimes several countries form a company together to share the costs. One example is Airbus Industrie: the main factory is at Toulouse, but costs are shared by France, Germany, the UK and Spain. With successful aircraft already flying, Airbus Industrie is planning a jumbo jet. Look for ✈

KEYBOX

Market gardening: In the northwest the mild climate and sheltered conditions are ideal for growing early vegetables, called primeurs. Look for 🛒

Nuclear power: Lacking its own energy sources, France has developed its nuclear power industry. It now produces 70% of its electricity. Look for 🏭

Tourism: In the underdeveloped Mediterranean region tourism has been encouraged by the construction of attractive holiday resorts. Look for ⛱

Rail routes: France has Europe's largest rail network. Inter-city trains (TGVs), travel at speeds of up to 300 km (186 miles) per hour. Look for 🚆

⛉ Cheese	♜ Coal
🌾 Cereals	🏭 Industrial centre
🍓 Sugar beet	✈ Aerospace industry
🍇 Wine	🚗 Vehicle manufacturing
⬤ Mining	⛷ Skiing

CHATEAUS
France has many beautiful historic buildings. Along the banks of the River Loire and its tributaries are royal palaces, or chateaus, built by the royalty of France from the 15th-17th centuries. Chambord, originally a hunting lodge, has 440 rooms and 85 staircases. Fairytale palaces like these attract thousands of visitors each year.

Fields of sunflowers can be seen in many areas of France.

Head of garlic

Snail

Clove of garlic

Snails, served with butter and garlic, are a great French delicacy.

Camembert

CHEESE
France is famous for its cheese. Over 300 different varieties are made. Many, like Camembert, Roquefort and Brie, are world-famous and copied in many other countries. Each region has its traditional way of making and packaging its cheeses. Goat and sheep's milk is used as well as cow's. Look for ⛉

Brie

LE RUSTIQUE

The principality of Andorra is situated in the Pyrenees.

### Map labels
ENGLISH CHANNEL
Cherbourg
Le Havre
Channel Islands (to UK)
St. Lô
Caen
Wheat
NORMANDY
Wheat
Camembert
Iron
St. Malo
Île d'Ouessant
Brest
Wheat
St. Brieuc
TGV
Oats
Alençon
BRITTANY
Barley
Oats
Wheat
Rennes Laval
Le Mans
Quimper
Barley
Lorient
Vannes
Barley
Iron
Angers
Loire
Tours
Belle Île
St. Nazaire
Nantes
FR
ATLANTIC OCEAN
La Roche-sur-Yon
Wheat
Les Sables d'Olonne
Wheat
Poitiers
TGV
Wheat
La Rochelle
Charente
Wheat
Saintes
Angoulême
Barley
Dordogne
Bordeaux
Arcachon
Garonne
Agen
Maize
Mont-de-Marsan
Bayonne
Maize
Pau
Tarbes
Maize
PYRENEES
S

A B C D E F G H I J

WINE

When the Romans occupied France 2,000 years ago they planted vines. From these early beginnings, France became the centre of world wine making. The wine's quality depends on the region, soil and climate, and on the producer's skilful blending and fermentation. Champagne is produced in the area around Rheims. Look for 🍇

Bottle of Champagne

A circular poster display, a common sight in Paris.

CAFE LIFE

In the late 17th-century, when cafés first became fashionable in Paris, they were used as places to meet for a snack and to exchange news and gossip. The word café means "coffee" in French. Two centuries later, cafés have become popular throughout the world.

Perfume spray

FRENCH STYLE

The 14th-century French kings and their courts established a tradition of elegance and style which the French have maintained ever since. Paris is still the world's capital of "haute couture" – high fashion. French clothes designs, perfumes and cosmetics have a major influence on the world's fashion industry.

FRENCH FOOD

The French place enormous importance on food and wine. Food can be just as delicious in small, provincial restaurants as in Parisian ones. French cooks have created many great dishes which are widely imitated.

Fillet de Boeuf

French saloon car

MOTOR VEHICLES

France has the second largest vehicle industry in western Europe, producing about 3 million a year. Paris is the centre of production, although companies are encouraged to open factories in other cities. Look for 🚗

An Alpine peak in southeast France.

MONACO

Monaco is a tiny country situated on the Mediterranean coast. Its orchestra is larger than its army. Many people have settled in Monaco because of the lenient tax laws and the gambling facilities of Monte Carlo.

MONACO
POP: 31,000

Corsica
(to France)

The rugged landscape of the French island of Corsica.

ANDORRA
POP: 58,000

### Map labels

Strait of Dover, Dunkirk, Calais, Channel Tunnel, Boulogne, BELGIUM, Lille, Arras, Valenciennes, Wheat, Dieppe, Oats, Amiens, St. Quentin, Mézières, Laon, LUXEMBOURG, GERMANY, Rouen, Beauvais, Wheat, Wheat, Thionville, Iron, Metz, Verdun, Rheims, Châlons-sur-Marne, Marne, Bar-le-Duc, Nancy, Strasbourg, Évreux, Seine, Wheat, Wheat, PARIS, Versailles, Brie, Melun, Seine, Oats, Moselle, Épinal, Colmar, Boursin, Chartres, Troyes, Chaumont, Potassium, Mulhouse, VOSGES, Barley, Oats, Belfort, Vesoul, Wheat, Orléans, Auxerre, BURGUNDY, Dijon, Saône, Besançon, SWITZERLAND, Blois, Chambord, Doubs, JURA, Bourges, Nevers, Wheat, L. Geneva, FRANCE, Châteauroux, Rye, Moulins, Wheat, Bourg-en-Bresse, Annecy, ITALY, Uranium, Uranium, Vichy, Mâcon, Wheat, Barley, Lyon, Chambéry, ALPS, Limoges, Clermont-Ferrand, St. Étienne, Grenoble, MASSIF CENTRAL, Rye, Le Puy, Valence, Gap, Périgueux, Aurillac, Maize, Cahors, Tungsten, Mende, Rhône, Digne, Maize, Rodez, Tarn, Avignon, Maize, MONACO, MONTE CARLO, Nice, Montauban, Albi, Roquefort, Nîmes, Arles, Aix-en-Provence, Grasse, Canness, Côte d'Azur, Lead, Zinc, PROVENCE, Wheat, Toulouse, Gold, Silver, Montpellier, Marseille, Maize, Carcassonne, Wheat, Toulon, Îles d'Hyères, Foix, Maize, Perpignan, ANDORRA, ANDORRA LA VELLA, MEDITERRANEAN SEA, Corsica, Bastia, Ajaccio, Bonifacio

N

0 25 50 75 100 125 150 KM
0 25 50 75 100 MILES

THE LOW COUNTRIES

BELGIUM, THE NETHERLANDS and Luxembourg are the most densely populated countries in Europe. They are known as the "Low Countries" because much of the land is flat and low-lying. In the Netherlands, much of the land lies below sea level, and has been reclaimed from the sea over the centuries by ingenious technology. The marshy, drained soils are extremely fertile. All three countries enjoy high living standards, with well-developed industries and excellent rail, road and waterway communications with the rest of Europe. During the course of their history, the Low Countries have often been the battleground between warring nations, and both Belgium and Luxembourg only achieved independence in the 19th century. Belgium is still divided by language – Dutch is spoken in the north, while the Walloons in the south speak French. The northern Netherlands are mainly Protestant; the rest of the region is basically Roman Catholic. Today, the Low Countries are unswerving supporters of the European Union. The cities of Brussels, The Hague and Luxembourg are all headquarters of important European institutions.

FLOWERS

The Netherlands are Europe's largest producers of flowers, and spectacular fields of spring flowers in full bloom are a major tourist attraction. Cut flowers are flown daily from the Netherlands to cities all over the world. Cultivation of bulbs such as crocuses, hyacinths, daffodils and tulips is a speciality. They have been grown here since about 1600, when they were introduced from Turkey and the Middle East. Look for 🌷

Tulip

IMMIGRATION

Immigrants from the Netherlands' former colonies of Surinam, the Antilles and Indonesia have had a strong impact on Dutch life and culture. Indonesian restaurants are a common sight in Dutch cities, and *rijstafel* (rice surrounded by side dishes of egg, vegetables, meat and fish) is now a national dish.

Satay (barbecued meat)

Peanuts

Beef Rendang

Egg-fried rice

Prawns and garlic

Salad in peanut sauce

Pickled vegetables

DELFT TILE

Delft pottery has been made in the Netherlands since the 17th century. The technique of glazing pottery with tin, used in Delft, came to the Netherlands from the Middle East via Spain and Italy. This Delft tile is decorated with a windmill, a familiar sight in the Netherlands. There are about 1,000 windmills still standing today, dating mainly from the 18th and 19th centuries.

CITY OF CANALS

The Dutch capital, Amsterdam, is a city of islands, built on swampy land. It is criss-crossed by 160 canals. Many of the city's finest gabled houses date from the 16th-18th centuries, when merchants grew rich from trade and exploration. Amsterdam is not only the country's historic centre, it is also its second-largest port.

ROTTERDAM

Rotterdam is one of the world's largest ports, lying within a massive built-up and industrialized area called Randstad Holland. Rotterdam is situated near the mouth of the Rhine, which is an important trade route. Imported oil is refined locally; the port also handles minerals, grain, timber and coal.

FLOOD CONTROL

Much of the Netherlands lies below sea level, and is constantly at risk of flooding. Over the centuries, land has been painstakingly reclaimed from the sea. Barriers called dykes are built to keep the sea out and water is drained and pumped into canals. Originally the water was pumped out by windmills, but now electric pumps are used. Sluice-gates control the flow of excess water.

The rind of Dutch Edam cheese is coloured with anatto dye.

Both Belgium and the Netherlands are major beer exporters.

NETHERLANDS
POP: 15,612,000

### Map labels

GERMANY

DRENTHE

Delfzijl · Winschoten · Groningen · Assen · Emmen · Hoogeveen · Almelo · Hengelo · Enschede · Deventer · Zutphen · Apeldoorn · Amersfoort · Zwolle · IJssel · Meppel · Heerenveen · Drachten · Leeuwarden · Harlingen · Schiermonnikoog · Ameland · Terschelling · Vlieland · West Frisian Is. · WADDEN ZEE · IJSSELMEER · Flevoland · Lelystad · Harderwijk · Hilversum · Hoorn · Purmerend · Zaanstad · AMSTERDAM · Alkmaar · Den Helder · Texel · Velsen · IJmuiden · Haarlem · Leiden · The Hague · Alphen aan den Rijn

Wheat · Beef · Dairy

DAIRY PRODUCTS

More than one-third of Dutch farmland is used for dairy production. Dutch black and white Friesian cattle, which graze on the low-lying fertile land, are one of the finest dairy breeds in the world. The Netherlands exports more cheese than any other country. Cheese was originally made on a small scale in farmhouses, but today cheese-making is highly mechanized. Look for 🐄

HIGH TECHNOLOGY

All three countries have well-established electronics industries, making everything from razors to X-ray machines. Their position at the heart of Europe, good transport links, easy access to European markets and raw materials, as well as large pools of skilled labour, have all helped to make high technology industry a success.

LUXEMBOURG BANKING

Luxembourg is a centre of international banking and finance. It is the headquarters of the European Investment Bank, and more than 100 major banks are based there. Financial services are fast becoming more important than Luxembourg's traditional steel-manufacturing industries.

The picturesque fortress of Vianden overlooking the River Our in Luxembourg.

LUXEMBOURG
POP: 384,400

The medieval town hall at Leuven in Belgium.

COMMUNITY CAPITAL

The EU (European Union) was set up in 1957 to encourage free trade between member nations and administer shared economic, social and legal policies. There are 15 member nations. Brussels is the administrative capital of the EU, and Luxembourg is the headquarters of the Court of Justice and Investment Bank.

The EU flag is a symbol of unity in Europe

Belgium, especially Brussels, is famous for its rich chocolates.

DIAMONDS

Diamonds from Africa and Australia are cut, polished and sold in the cities of Antwerp and Amsterdam. Most of the diamonds are used in industry for sawing, drilling and grinding.

The medieval city of Bruges is famous for its canals and fine houses.

Flax, which is used to make linen, is grown on the flat plains of northern Belgium.

BELGIUM
POP: 10,042,000

KEYBOX

Gas: Offshore reserves in the North Sea are the fifth largest in the world. Gas is the main domestic fuel in the Netherlands.

Dams: The Netherlands's Delta Project is the world's largest water control project. Five dams prevent flooding and provide fresh water. Look for 🏛

Shipping canals: Most of Belgium's main inland industrial centres are linked with the North Sea ports and Antwerp by canals. Look for ‖

Market gardening

Flowers

Industrial centre

Cattle

Cereals

Sugar beet

GERMANY

BELGIUM

FRANCE

NETHERLANDS

LUXEMBOURG

Rotterdam • Dordrecht • Breda • Bergen op Zoom • Roosendaal • Middelburg • Flushing • Zeebrugge • Ostend • Veurne • Ieper • Torhout • Roeselare • Bruges • Kortrijk • Mouscron • Tournai • Ronse • Aalst • Ath • Ghent • Sint-Niklaas • Terneuzen • Antwerp • Mechelen • Turnhout • Baarle-Hertog (to Belgium) • Tilburg • Waalwijk • Oss • 's-Hertogenbosch • Eindhoven • Helmond • Weert • Venlo • Roermond • Maastricht • Heerlen • Genk • Hasselt • Tienen • Leuven • Nivelles • Brussels (Bruxelles) • Soignies • Mons • La Louvière • Charleroi • Gosselies • Namur • Dinant • Philippeville • Huy • Liège • Seraing • Herstal • Verviers • Eupen • Malmédy • St-Vith • Bastogne • Marche-en-Famenne • Neufchâteau • Arlon • Esch-sur-Alzette • LUXEMBOURG • Diekirch • Vianden • Nijmegen • Arnhem • Gouda • Delft • Hook van Holland • Europoort

Rhine • Maas • Lek • Scheldt • Westerschelde • Oosterschelde • Albert Canal • Meuse • Ourthe • Amblève • Lesse • Sûre • Our • Moselle • IJzer

Overflakkee • Delta Project

MILES
0 10 20 25 40 50 75
KM

N

GERMANY

SITUATED IN THE CENTRE OF EUROPE, Germany is now the continent's leading economic power. In the past it has been an area of great conflict; it was not until 1871 that a patchwork of independent states, who had fought bitterly for centuries, were united under Prussian leadership to form Germany. In this century Germany was shattered and the country divided between a Soviet-dominated communist East and a democratic West. The post-war years saw an amazing recovery in West Germany's economy. Natural advantages, such as a central position in Europe, large reserves of coal and iron, along with the construction of an efficient transport system and the determination to succeed, have all helped to create a dynamic economy. The East, on the other hand, lagged behind. In 1989, the Soviet Union began to disintegrate, and communism collapsed throughout Eastern Europe. The two halves of Germany were reunified in 1990, but problems soon became apparent. West Germans resented the huge amounts of money invested in the East to bring it up to their standards. East Germans became impatient with the slow pace of change. These resentments have led to violence against refugees, immigrants and "guest-workers", many of whom have lived in Germany for most of their lives.

CARS
Germany is Europe's largest vehicle producer, specializing in high-quality cars. American and Japanese car companies are based here, attracted by the skilled workforce. Look for

Brandenburg Gate

BERLIN
At the end of World War II, Berlin, Germany's capital city, was divided between the four victorious Allies. In 1961 the Berlin Wall was built to separate the Russian sector from the other three. In 1989 the wall came down: thousands of East Germans came through this Gate into the west.

AGRICULTURE
Germany produces all its own food, and is one of the world's main growers of sugar beet, barley and rye. Oats, rye and barley thrive in the mild, wet north, while wheat is grown in the warmer south. Look for

This decorated mug is called a stein, *and is used for beer.*

Green pastures and woodland on the flat, Baltic coast.

DRESDEN
Once Dresden was a beautiful old city, with many 18th-century buildings. But in World War II it was devastated by bombing. After extensive reconstruction, the city's historic buildings have now been restored to their former state.

Peppered salami

Salami

SAUSAGES
Sausages are Germany's favourite snack. There are many regional variations; Frankfurt has even given its name to the Frankfurter sausage. Germany also has over 200 varieties of bread.

A windmill in the fertile farmland of the northeast.

Many German towns have half-timbered buildings dating back to the Middle Ages.

OPTICAL SKILLS

Germany has a large number of optical instrument manufacturers, who make cameras, microscopes and telescopes. East Germany led the former Soviet bloc in this field. However, since reunification, many of these companies in the East have closed down as they were over-staffed and heavily subsidized, and now cannot compete without government support.

BROWN COAL

In eastern Germany, large amounts of lignite (brown coal) are mined from vast open pits. Lignite is used for generating electricity. When burnt, it causes severe pollution. Look for ⛏

PRECISION ENGINEERING

While heavy industry tends to be concentrated in north Germany, the south has become a centre for the manufacture of special steels, cutlery and precision instruments. This region lacks coal, so industry could not develop here until gas was piped in from the Netherlands. Look for 🗔

Flask, used in chemical experiments

CHEMICALS

Over half a million people are employed in Germany's chemical industry. Germany is the leading producer in Europe, and still dominates world markets, despite competition from the Far East. Raw materials for the chemical industry are transported along the River Rhine. Chemicals are widely used in industry to produce paints, detergents, cosmetics and medicines.

The Bavarian Alps are popular for winter sports.

BEER FESTIVALS

Many small Bavarian towns have annual beer festivals. Local people wear traditional costume, and spend several days drinking beer, dancing and singing to the accompaniment of brass bands.

BAVARIA

The Bavarian Alps rise behind the Catholic church of St. Koloman, near Hohenschwangau. Bavaria is mainly Catholic, with a strong regional identity. The beautiful scenery and historic towns all make Bavaria a popular tourist destination.

Beethoven, Germany's most famous composer, wrote many pieces for the piano.

RHINE BARGES

The River Rhine stretches from the North Sea deep into the German industrial heartland. Freight, such as coal, grain and timber, is often carried by barges like these. Many tourists also travel on the southern part of the Rhine to see the beautiful scenery, vineyards and castles on its banks.

KEYBOX

Shipbuilding: *Once a major industry in Germany's North Sea ports, shipbuilding is now in decline, and unemployment is growing. Look for* ⚓

Castles: *The Rhine trade route was protected by castles. Now they are a popular sight on tourist cruises. Look for* 🏰

Pollution: *The Rhine is polluted by industry, especially chemical works. Companies are beginning to find ways of cleaning up plants. Look for* ☣

Symbol	
🐄	Cattle
🌾	Cereals
🍠	Sugar beet
🍇	Wine
🌿	Hops

Symbol	
⚒	Mining
⬛	Coal
🏭	Industrial centre
🚗	Vehicle manufacture
🗔	High-tech industry

GERMANY
Scale 1:3,500,000

MILES
0 25 50 75
0 25 50 75 100 125 150 KM

N

BELGIUM
LUXEMBOURG
FRANCE
SWITZERLAND
AUSTRIA
CZECH REPUBLIC
RHINELAND
THURINGIA
BAVARIA
FRANCONIAN JURA
SWABIAN JURA
BAVARIAN ALPS
Thuringian Forest
Bohemian Forest
Black Forest

Görlitz
Bautzen
Dresden
Riesa
Colditz
Leipzig
Chemnitz
Zwickau
Gera
Plauen
Hof
Bayreuth
Jena
Erfurt
Gotha
Mühlhausen
Kassel
Fulda
Wartburg
Marburg
Giessen
Siegen
Hagen
Wuppertal
Remscheid
Bergisch Gladbach
Cologne
Bonn
Leverkusen
Düsseldorf
Krefeld
Mönchengladbach
Aachen
Trier
Saarbrücken
Kaiserslautern
Wiesbaden
Mainz
Frankfurt-im-Main
Offenbach
Darmstadt
Mannheim
Heidelberg
Heilbronn
Karlsruhe
Pforzheim
Stuttgart
Tübingen
Freiburg im-Breisgau
Konstanz
Friedrichshafen
Lindau
Garmisch-Partenkirchen
Hohenschwangau
Neuschwanstein
Linderhof
Rosenheim
Herrenchiemsee
Munich
Augsburg
Ingolstadt
Nuremberg
Erlangen
Würzburg
Schweinfurt
Bamberg
Regensburg
Landshut
Passau

Koblenz
Rheinfels
Kaub
Eltz
Schwangau
Chiemsee
Ammersee
Starnberger See

L. Constance

Rhine
Mosel
Main
Neckar
Danube
Inn
Ruhr
Eder
Fulda

Wheat
Barley
Dairy
Iron
Uranium
Copper
Potassium
Zinc
Lead

67

AUSTRIA AND SWITZERLAND

RUNNING THROUGH the middle of Austria and Switzerland are the Alps, the highest mountains in Europe. Both countries lie on Europe's main north-south trading routes, with access to the heart of Europe via the great Danube and Rhine waterways.

Switzerland was formed in the Middle Ages, when a number of Alpine communities united in defensive leagues against their more powerful neighbours. Modern Switzerland is a confederation of 23 separate provinces, called cantons. The country has three main languages – German, French and Italian. In contrast, Austria was once the centre of the Habsburg Empire, which had vast territories in Central Europe. When the Empire collapsed in 1918, Austria became an independent country. Austria has mineral resources, especially iron, and thriving industries. With few natural resources, Switzerland has concentrated instead on skilled, high-technology manufacturing.

Gold bar

BANKING
Switzerland is one of the world's main financial centres. People from all over the world put their money into Swiss bank accounts as the country is well-known for its political stability. Liechtenstein is also a major banking centre. Look for 🝙

DAIRY FARMING
Swiss dairy cattle spend winter in the Alpine valleys, and in summer are taken up to the Alpine pastures for grazing. The milk is used to make many varieties of cheese, such as Gruyère. Look for ♈

Porcelain teeth

FALSE TEETH
Liechtenstein is the headquarters of world dental manufacture. False teeth, filling materials and plastic for crown and bridge dental work are exported to more than 100 countries.

Liechtenstein is famous for its beautiful stamps.

The castle at Vaduz, the capital of Liechtenstein.

GENEVA
Switzerland has not been at war for 150 years and is therefore seen as a neutral meeting place. Many international organizations have their headquarters in the city of Geneva.

The Swiss consume more chocolate than any other nationality in the world.

KEYBOX

Hydro-electric power: The Swiss pioneered hydro-electricity. Today, Austria is an important producer, tapping the potential of the Danube. Look for ⊞

Climbing: Mountaineers first started climbing the Alps in the 19th century. Some of the peaks are still thought to be the world's toughest climbs. Look for ⛏

Tunnels: There are only a few road passes through the Alps, but railway routes through tunnels are helping to ease the traffic. Look for ⌒

Pollution: Tourism in the Alps, especially the heavy use of roads, is causing environmental problems. Look for ☣

🌾	Cereals	🕐	Watchmaking
🐂	Cattle	💉	Pharmaceuticals
🍇	Wine	🝙	Financial centre
🏭	Industrial centre	⛷	Skiing

SWITZERLAND
POP: 6,995,000

LIECHTENSTEIN
POP: 31,000

GERMANY

Schaffhausen
Büsingen (to Germany)
Frauenfeld
Sankt Gallen
Bregenz
Dornbirn
Basle
Rhine
Winterthur
Herisau
Appenzell
Feldkirch
Liestal
Dairy
Rye
Zurich
St. Anton
Landeck
Delémont
Olten
Aarau
Dairy
L. Zurich
Arlberg Tunnel
Solothurn
Dairy
Beef
Zug
VADUZ
La Chaux de Fonds
Biel
Aare
Rye
Lucerne
Schwyz
LIECHTENSTEIN
Glarus
L. Wallenstadt
Neuchâtel
L. Biel
Beef
L. Lucerne
L. Uri
Chur
BERN
Stans
Altdorf
Dairy
Yverdon
Fribourg
Thun
Sarnen
SWITZERLAND
Dairy
L. Neuchâtel
L. Brienz
Beef
Wheat
Interlaken
San Bernardino Tunnel
St. Moritz
Lausanne
Dairy
L. Thun
Mt. Eiger
St. Gotthard Tunnel
Dairy
Montreux
Gstaad
Jungfrau
BERNESE ALPS
Simplon Pass
Beef
L. Geneva
Sierre
Brig
Bellinzona
Locarno
Geneva
Sion
Rhône
Simplon Tunnel
L. Maggiore
Lugano
Martigny
Dairy
L. Lugano
Matterhorn
ITALY
Great St. Bernard Tunnel
FRANCE
ALPS
PENNINE ALPS
LEPONTINE ALPS
RHAETIAN ALPS

St. Bernard dogs were trained to rescue travellers lost in the Alps.

Rhône Valley offers route into the heart of the Alps

Bernese Alps

Brig

N

Simplon rail tunnel, built in 1906

Mount Eiger can be glimpsed through clouds.

ALPINE PASSES
Although the Alps are a formidable obstacle to communications, mountain passes have been used since prehistoric times. Since the 19th century, major engineering feats have made the Alps more accessible: bridges cross gorges and deep valleys and tunnels pass under the mountains.

Simplon Pass, built 1801-06, open to cars all year round

Heavily used trans-Alpine routes are congested and difficult to cross in winter

VIENNA

For many centuries, Austria was ruled by the Habsburg family. Their empire included Hungary; their capital was Vienna. The city contained many grand buildings and elegant palaces such as this one, the Schönbrunn Palace, which was the Habsburg family's summer residence. The Habsburg empire finally collapsed in 1918.

AUSTRIA
POP: 7,884,000

Cow bells help farmers to locate animals in remote Alpine pastures.

PHARMACEUTICALS

One of Switzerland's main industries is pharmaceuticals (making drugs and medicines). The industry has benefited from the Swiss emphasis on the importance of research and product development, the latest technology and a highly skilled workforce. Perfumes, cosmetics and drugs are all made in the Basle area. Look for ✏

WATCHMAKING

Watches and clocks have been made in Switzerland since the 16th century. Recently, however, Swiss companies have been under pressure from the Japanese and Americans who developed quartz technology. The Swiss have saved their industry by making certain of their more famous watches cheaper. Look for ☺

AUSTRIAN INDUSTRY

Hydro-electric power from the Austrian Alps is a major source of energy for heavy industry. Iron ore deposits around Linz and Donawitz fuel the Austrian steel industry. Some Austrian steel plants have been forced to close by lower world steel prices. Look for ⛏

Iron ore

The Abbey at Melk in Austria was built in the 18th century.

Edelweiss is a rare Alpine flower.

COFFEE AND CAKES

Sachertorte

The Ottoman Turks, who besieged Vienna in 1529 and 1683, first brought coffee to the city, and it was here that the first coffee-shop in Western Europe was opened. There are still many cafés in Vienna, where people drink coffee and eat Austria's famous chocolate cakes. *Sachertorte* is named after the Viennese pastry shop where it is made.

SKI CENTRE

The Alps are visited by over 100 million people each year. But ski-runs, improved roads and expanding resorts are all having a harmful effect on the environment. Huge numbers of trees have been cut down to make way for ski-runs, but these can provide routes for avalanches. Look for ⚑

AUSTRIAN TOURISM

Austria's tourist industry is booming due to the attractions of its beautiful scenery, historical towns, picturesque villages and winter sports facilities. Tourism is now one of Austria's most profitable industries. A quarter of Austria's tourists visit during the winter; many of the visitors come from nearby Germany.

SWISS FOLK TRADITIONS

Alpine accordion

Swiss folk traditions are very much alive; among the annual events are carnivals during Lent, cheese and wine-growers' festivals and celebrations marking the change of the seasons, such as the return of the cows from Alpine pasture. Colourful costumes and traditional musical instruments are used at these events.

CENTRAL EUROPE

IN 1989 THE COMMUNIST governments of Central Europe collapsed and the region entered a period of momentous change. All four countries of Central Europe only became independent states earlier this century. After World War II they were incorporated into the Soviet bloc and ruled by communist governments. These states started to industrialize rapidly, but they were heavily dependent on the former Soviet Union for their raw materials and markets. When communism collapsed in 1989, the new, democratically elected governments were faced with many problems: modernizing industry, huge foreign debts, soaring inflation, rising unemployment and terrible pollution. In 1993 the former state of Czechoslovakia was split into two countries, the Czech Republic and Slovakia.

Grudziądz, a medieval Polish town on the River Vistula.

POLAND
POP: 38,500,000

POLLUTION
The Czech Republic is Europe's most polluted country. The pollution comes from its own industry, but also from factories in Germany. Forests are dying because of acid rain, rivers are poisoned and the scarred landscapes will take decades to recover. Look for 💀

Wooden puppet

PUPPETS
Puppet shows are popular throughout Central Europe, but the former Czechoslovakia is acknowledged as the original home of European puppetry. Today, over a thousand Czech Republic and Slovak puppet companies perform plays.

GLASS
The Czech Republic's glass industry is centuries old. Glassware, such as this decanter and glasses, is often intricate and brightly coloured. The industry uses local supplies of sand to make the glass. Bohemian crystal is manufactured principally in the northwest around Karlovy Vary, and is also popular with the ever-increasing number of tourists.

PRAGUE
The Czech Republic's capital, Prague, has some of the most beautiful and well-preserved architecture in Europe. Since 1989, when the country was opened to tourists, thousands of people have flocked to the city Look for 📷

CZECH REPUBLIC
POP: 10,302,215

KEYBOX

Mining: Poland is one of the world's largest coal producers, but recently the industry has been affected by competition from abroad. Look for 🔨

Financial centre: In Hungary, the Budapest stock exchange opened in 1990, and many new banks have now opened in the city. Look for

Dam: The dam built by the Slovaks on the Danube at Gabčíkovo has caused a major dispute between Hungary and Slovakia. Look for 🏛

🌾 Cereals	🏭	Industrial centre
🥬 Sugar beet	🗑	Shipbuilding
🍓 Mixed fruit	📷	Tourism
🌲 Timber	🌱	Spas
⛑ Mining	💀	Pollution

HUNGARIAN INDUSTRY
Since the end of World War II Hungary has industrialized rapidly. It manufactures products such as aluminium, steel, electronic goods and vehicles, especially buses. But when the Soviet Union disintegrated, Hungarian manufacturers lost many of the traditional markets for their products – especially in heavy industry – and now face many problems. Look for 🏭

BEER
Some of Europe's finest beers and lagers are brewed in the Czech Republic. Pilsener lager originated in the town of Plzeň; Budweiser beer has been brewed at České Budějovice for over a century. Huge quantities of beer, the Budweiser beer in particular, are exported, principally to European countries such as Germany and the UK.

Beautifully painted eggs are sold in the Czech Republic and Slovakia at Easter.

HUNGARY
POP: 10,518,000

N

0	50	100	150	200	KM
0	25	50	75	100	MILES

Map labels: BALTIC, Słupsk, Koszalin, Pomeranian Bay, POMERANIA, Szczecin, Odra, Drawa, Pila, Gorzów Wielkopolski, Wheat, Rye, Warta, Poznań, POLAND, Zielona Góra, Bobr, Leszno, Wheat, Copper, Legnica, Wrocław, SILESIA, Wałbrzych, Barle, Liberec, Ústí nad Labem, Ohře, Labe, Jizera, Wheat, Hradec Králové, SUDETEN MTS, Karlovy Vary, Tin, Prague (Praha), Pardubice, Plzeň, CZECH REPUBLIC, L. Vltava, Tábor, Jihlava, Olomouc, Uranium, Zinc, Lead, Uranium, Blanice, Lužnice, České Budějovice, Jihlava, Brno, Wheat, MORAVIA, AUSTRIA, BRATISLAVA, SLOVENIA, Szombathely, Szentgotthárd, Rába, Zala, Zalaegerszeg, Nagykanizsa, CROATIA, Germany

SOLIDARITY

Many Polish people work in heavy industries, such as coalmining and shipbuilding. In 1980 discontent over poor working conditions led to a strike at this shipyard in Gdańsk, and to the birth of Solidarity, the Soviet bloc's first independent trade union. Solidarity has significantly influenced Polish politics.

Beechwood toy

TIMBER

Apart from the lowland area around the River Danube, the landscape of the Czech Republic and Slovakia is mountainous. Both countries have relatively small populations and much of the land is still covered with forest. Both countries have large timber industries. Some timber – mainly pine – is used to make furniture. Beech is often used for the manufacture of toys. Look for ⌐

RELIGION

For a thousand years, through invasions, wars, repression – and times when the country almost ceased to exist – the Polish people have found strength in their religious faith. Even during the last 40 years of communist government – which actively discouraged religion of any kind – 90 per cent of the population remained devout Catholics.

Wild boar, shown on this Polish stamp, are still found in the region.

PAPRIKA

The flat plains in Hungary are amongst the most fertile farming areas in Europe. Cereals, sugar beet and fruit are among the main crops. Sweet red peppers – from which paprika is made – are also grown. Paprika is a vital ingredient in many spicy Hungarian dishes

Morning mist rising over the western Carpathians.

BUDAPEST

Budapest, the Hungarian capital, was once two towns, Buda on the Danube's right bank, and Pest on the left. The town was very badly damaged during World War II, but many of its historic buildings have since been carefully restored. This vast, domed parliament building in Pest faces across the river to Buda.

Ernö Rubik, a Hungarian, invented this complex puzzle.

SPA BATHS

Hot thermal springs were used for medicinal purposes in ancient Greece and Rome. The Romans were the first to develop baths – like this one in Budapest where bathers enjoy a game of chess. Hungary now has 154 hot-spring baths, which are open to the public. The Czech Republic and Slovakia have 900 mineral springs and 58 health spas, which are reserved for medicinal purposes only. It is hoped that more foreigners will come to the region to use the thermal springs. Look for ⚓

Hungary's famous horses are bred on the Hungarian Plain.

SLOVAKIA
POP: 5,381,000

ITALY AND MALTA

AT VARIOUS TIMES in the past 2,000 years Italy has influenced the development of European civilization. From this narrow, boot-shaped peninsula the Romans established a vast empire throughout Europe and North Africa; Christianity was first adopted as an official religion by a Roman emperor, and Rome later became the centre of the Catholic Church. In the 14th century, an extraordinary flowering of the arts and sciences, known as the Renaissance, or "rebirth", started in Italy and transformed European thought and culture. Italy at this time was divided into independent city states, and was later ruled by foreign nations, including France and Austria. But in 1870, after centuries of foreign domination, Italy became an independent and unified country. Despite a lack of natural resources, and defeat in World War II, Italy has become a major industrial power. The country has long suffered from corruption and organized crime, but recent changes show promise of more political stability in the future.

Cappelletti (little hats)

Orecchioni (large ears)

Round tortellini (small pies)

PASTA

The Italian explorer, Marco Polo, is said to have brought the recipe for pasta to Italy when he returned from his great journey to China. Pasta is a type of dough made by adding water to wheat flour. It has become one of the world's most popular foods. It can be made into different shapes, and filled with meat or vegetables.

Masks like these are worn during the February carnival in Venice, which includes plays, masked balls and fireworks.

Pinnacles of the Dolomites in northeastern Italy.

VERONA

The ancient Romans were skilful engineers, and many of their remarkable buildings are still standing today. The foundations of much of Italy's road system was also built by the Romans. Verona is based on the Roman grid street plan. The town's ancient amphitheatre seats 22,000, and is still used.

Silk scarf

Suede shoe

DESIGN

Italians place great emphasis on design and produce beautiful looking products. This flair for design is particularly obvious in their cars and clothes. The fashion houses of Rome, Florence, Milan and Venice rival those of Paris, and Italian shoes and clothes are widely exported.

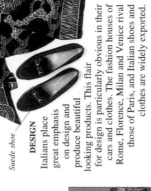

VENICE

This historic city is built on a number of islands in a shallow lagoon. Many buildings stand on wooden stilts driven into the mud. Venice's future is in the balance, threatened by flooding and pollution.

THE PO VALLEY

Between the Alps and the Apennines lies a huge triangular plain, drained by Italy's greatest river, the Po. The majority of the country's agriculture, population and industry is concentrated in this region. Its major cities, such as Milan and Turin, are important industrial and commercial centres.

The Alps

Turin

Milan

Farming of maize, wheat and rice

Po

Apennines

Genoa: major sea port and industrial centre

Alpine rivers supply water for HEP and irrigation.

Mountain passes link Italy to the rest of Europe

N

SAN MARINO
POP: 23,000

ITALY
POP: 57,956,000

SLOVENIA

AUSTRIA

SWITZERLAND

FRANCE

Trieste
Gulf of Venice
Udine
Maize
Piave
Belluno
Chioggia
Venice
Mestre
Treviso
Padua
Adige
Comacchio Lagoon
Ravenna
Cervia
Vicenza
Ferrara
Verona
Mantova
Bologna
Rimini
Riccione
Pesaro
SAN MARINO
Cremona
Parma
Reggio nell'Emilia
Modena
Po
Arno
Prato
Florence
Pistoia
Lucca
Pisa
Livorno
Viareggio
Marble
La Spezia
Arezzo
Siena
Perugia
Trasimeno
Ancona
Potenza
Wheat
San Benedetto del Tronto
Assisi
Pyrite
Elba
Mercury
Brescia
Bergamo
Monza
Milan
Novara
Piacenza
Alessandria
Turin
Asti
Savona
Genoa
Gulf of Genoa
Alassio
San Remo
Cuneo
Olive

A D R I A T I C

LIGURIAN SEA

T U S C A N Y

Maize
Wheat

MOTOR VEHICLES
Many Italian motor manufacturers are based around the cities of Milan and Turin. Italian engineers and designers have developed some of the finest cars in Europe, both high performance cars, and also cheaper, economical models. Look for 🚗

Model of Ferrari car

Sardinia, a large island in the Mediterranean.

A distant view of the snow-capped Apennines.

ROMAN CATHOLICS
Christianity is the world's most widespread religion. It is based on the life and teaching of Jesus Christ. Within Christianity there are different groups. Roman Catholicism, with its centre in Rome, is the largest group, with over a thousand million members. Catholics have a special reverence for Mary, the mother of Jesus.

VATICAN CITY
This walled city in the centre of Rome is the headquarters of the Roman Catholic Church and official residence of the Pope. It is the smallest independent state in the world, dominated by the great St. Peter's Basilica, seen here. The city has its own newspaper, coins, stamps, railway and radio stations.

Italians are passionate football supporters.

Italian national football shirt

AGRICULTURE
Agriculture is very important to the Italian economy. The main crops are olives, citrus fruits and wine. The best farming region is the Po Valley in the north. Southern Italy has always suffered from its hilly terrain and low rainfall, but due to irrigation and more modern farming methods, agriculture has improved since the 1950s.

KEYBOX

Wine: Italy is the world's largest wine producer. Recently, the wine industry has brought in rules for higher quality and better control. Look for 🍇

Oil refining: Italy is more dependent on imported fuel than any European country. Crude oil has to be imported and refined. Look for 🛢

Sightseeing: Millions of tourists visit Italy each year to see its historic towns, famous buildings and museums. Look for 📷

Icon	Label
🌾	Cereals
⋙	Rice
🍊	Citrus fruit
🫒	Vegetable oil
⛏	Mining
⚒	Industrial centre
🚗	Vehicle manufacture
✈	Tourism
☰	Archaeological sites
☢	Pollution

MALTA
Malta's position on the Mediterranean shipping routes explains its important role in the history of the region. The Romans, Arabs, French, Turks, Spanish and British have all colonized or fought over the island. In 1964 it became independent. Today, its main income comes from tourism and its port facilities.

VATICAN CITY POP: 1,000

MALTA POP: 370,000

Bottles of Chianti are often sold in a wicker casing, called a fiasco.

TYRRHENIAN SEA

ADRIATIC SEA

IONIAN SEA

MEDITERRANEAN SEA

Gulf of Taranto

Gulf of Squillace

Strait of Messina

Gulf of Gela

Gulf of Salerno

Bay of Naples

Gulf of Cagliari

Strait of Bonifacio

KM MILES

SARDINIA

SICILY

CALABRIA

MALTA

THE WESTERN BALKANS

THIS TROUBLED REGION of southeastern Europe consists of a wide variety of landscapes, religions, peoples and languages. The region was invaded many times, and from the 14th-19th centuries was occupied by the Turks. After World War II, both Albania and Yugoslavia were ruled by communist governments. When the communist leader, General Tito, died in 1980 the Yugoslav government became less centralized, and former republics now demanded their independence. Serbia, the largest and most powerful republic, resisted the break-up of Yugoslavia. In 1991, a bloody civil war broke out between Serbia and Croatia and, eventually, between Serbs and Muslims in Bosnia. Albania was isolated by its communist government from the rest of Europe and became economically backward. But the country has now shaken off its communist rulers and held democratic elections. The economy, however, is still in chaos.

The spectacular scenery of northern Slovenia.

SLOVENIA
POP: 2,016,000

CROATIA
POP: 4,801,000

Nugget of mercury ore

BOSNIA & HERZEGOVINA
POP: 4,446,000

Slovenia is a major producer of mercury, used in thermometers.

TOURISM
Many tourists used to visit former Yugoslavia, attracted by the country's beautiful scenery, warm climate and stunning coastline. By the late 1980s, an average of nine million visitors were coming to Yugoslavia every year. However, the violent civil war has now virtually put an end to the tourist industry. Look for 🖋

YUGO
This car, the Yugo, is manufactured in former Yugoslavia at Kragujevac. It was designed for foreign export, but the economic disruption caused by the civil war has dealt a death blow to this industry. Slovenia has had more success; French cars are made there under licence, and are sold to the domestic market. Look for 🚗

UNDER FIRE
The world looked on in horror as Dubrovnik, a beautiful city with an untouched centre dating back 1,000 years, came under Serbian attack in 1991. Sarajevo, the Bosnian capital, was another casualty; many of its historic mosques and churches were hit by shells. Other historic towns in Bosnia and Croatia have also suffered irreparable damage during the war.

FOLKLORE
Variations in national costume reflect the many different traditions and peoples living in this region. In Slovenia, for example, costumes show a strong Alpine influence – leather trousers and gathered *dirndl* skirts. Further south, the costumes look more oriental. The Dubrovnik region is famous for its costume of white dresses, embroidered blouses and waistcoats. Folk-music and dancing take place at religious festivals and on market-days, and are also laid on for tourist groups.

KEYBOX

Mining: Albania has some of the world's largest chromium reserves. Exports are hampered by outdated mining equipment and frequent strikes. Look for ⛏

Refugee centres: The war in former Yugoslavia has forced over a million people to leave their homes and seek asylum in nearby countries. Look for ⛺

🌾	Cereals	⚒	Coal
🚢	Mixed fruit	⚡	Hydro-electric power
🍇	Wine	🏭	Industrial centre
🚬	Tobacco	🚗	Vehicle manufacture
🐟	Fishing	🖋	Tourism

MARKETS
In peacetime, local markets in the region are packed with people and well-stocked with a wide range of produce from nearby farms. Large quantities of fruit and vegetables are grown in the mild, warm climate of the Croatian coast and in western Bosnia. Look for 🚢

0   50   100   150   KM

0   50   100   150   MILES

N

Walnuts flourish in the warm summers and well-drained soils of Yugoslavia.

IRON GATES
The Danube, the second-longest river in Europe, passes through Serbia on its journey from Germany to the Black Sea. As the river leaves the broad plains of Hungary, it is forced through this narrow gorge, called the Iron Gates. In 1972, Romania and Yugoslavia built a power station here to use the water to make electricity. Look for ⊞

CIVIL WAR
In 1990 Yugoslavia, crippled by an economic crisis, began to break up into independent countries. Serbia fiercely resisted this process, and fighting erupted in both Croatia and Bosnia. The Serbs began to force Bosnian Muslims out of their homes and settle there themselves, a policy which is called "ethnic cleansing".

LANGUAGE DIFFERENCES
The main language of the former Yugoslavia is Serbo-Croatian. It can be written in two different ways, using either the Roman or Cyrillic alphabet. Cyrillic is a Slavic alphabet created in the 9th century by two Greek brothers, who were Christians. Other languages used in this area include Slovenian and Macedonian.

YUGOSLAVIA
POP: 10,931,000

Postage stamp using Roman alphabet

Postage stamp using Cyrillic alphabet

There is very little farming in the mountains of Montenegro.

ALBANIA
There is little traffic in the central square in Albania's capital, Tirana: until recently, private cars were banned. Albania is now emerging from 50 years of isolation. Under communism, free speech and religion were forbidden. Even beards were not allowed. Although democratic elections have been held, the economy is in ruins and the government is unable to control the country. The Albanians are having great difficulty adjusting to the changes, and crime and vandalism are now serious problems.

MACEDONIA
POP: 2,093,000

ALBANIA
POP: 3,429,000

Grapes

Water-melon

Tomato

Potatoes

ALBANIAN AGRICULTURE
Although its economy is based on farming, Albania still has difficulties feeding its own population, which is the fastest-growing in Europe. The main crops are potatoes, maize, wheat, sugar beet, fruit and vegetables. Until recently, most of the land was owned and farmed by the state, but today it is farmed by individual families.

Mixed valley farming gives way to barren mountains in central Albania.

RELIGION
This beautiful church on the shores of Lake Ohrid dates back to the medieval period, when Macedonia followed the Eastern Orthodox church. Later, Bosnia, Montenegro and Serbia were occupied by the Ottoman Turks and became largely Muslim countries.

ROMANIA AND BULGARIA

ROMANIA AND BULGARIA ARE LOCATED in the southeast of Europe, on the shores of the Black Sea. The River Danube forms the border between the two countries, and the most fertile land in the region is found in the river's vast valley and delta. Forests of oak, pine and fir trees grow on the slopes of the Carpathian and Balkan Mountains.

Romania and Bulgaria were occupied by Romans, Bulgars, Hungarians and Turkish Ottomans, but this troubled history ended when they became independent countries in the late 19th and early 20th centuries. After two world wars, both countries became part of the Soviet communist bloc. Although they are no longer communist, economic reform has been slow, and unemployment, high prices and food shortages are still constant problems.

ROSE-OIL
Rose-petal

Used in perfume, rose-oil is literally worth its weight in gold. Central Bulgaria produces most of the world's supply. The world's largest rose gardens are at Kazanlŭk. Look for 🌹

THE PRESIDENTIAL PALACE
Under Romania's repressive communist leader, President Ceauşescu, food and energy supplies were rationed. Despite this, the President started a series of expensive building projects, such as this presidential palace in Bucharest. In 1989, the Romanian people rose up against communism, and executed their president.

TOBACCO
Bulgaria is the world's second largest exporter of cigarettes. Tobacco is grown in the fertile valleys of the River Maritsa. This woman is sorting tobacco leaves, ready for selling. Look for 🪈

YOGHURT
Yoghurt, made from the milk of cows, sheep or goats, is an important part of the Bulgarian diet. Many Bulgarians claim that eating yoghurt helps them live to a ripe old age.

Small farms in the wooded valleys of central Romania.

The Alexander Nevsky church in Sofia celebrates liberation from Turkish rule.

KEYBOX

Vehicle manufacture: Romanian factories make copies of French vehicles for export to China, Russia and many Western countries. Look for �

High-tech industry: Electronics earn Bulgaria foreign currency, although the computer industry is suffering from international competition. Look for 💻

Spas: Mineral springs and health treatments are provided by many spa resorts, which are a popular tourist attraction. Look for ⚘

Shipping canal: The Danube-Black Sea Canal enables ships to avoid the slow journey through the Danube Delta. Look for ⛴

🐂 Cattle	⛏ Mining
🌾 Cereals	⚒ Oil
🍇 Wine	◊ Gas
Tobacco	🏭 Industrial centre
🌹 Roses	Tourism

Bulgaria is the world's fourth largest wine exporter.

RILA MONASTERY
The walls of Rila monastery are decorated with no less than 1,200 superb wall-paintings. The monastery became a symbol of the Bulgarians' struggle to preserve the Christian faith during centuries of Turkish rule. The monastery was originally founded in 1335, and was rebuilt after it burnt to the ground in the 19th-century.

DRACULA
The story of Dracula is linked to Transylvania, and attracts many tourists to the region. Tales of the blood-sucking Count, complete with vampire bats, garlic cloves and wooden stakes, are thought to be based on Vlad the Impaler, a 15th-century prince who resisted Turkish rule. His name is explained by his habit of impaling his enemies on wooden stakes.

Count Dracula

ROMANIA
POP: 23,611,000

The heights of the Carpathian Mountains.

This rare ghost orchid grows in shady parts of Bulgarian forests.

INDUSTRY
These chimneys at Copşa Mică in Romania are belching out hydro-carbons, which pollute the air, water and soil. Romania's industrialization was not subject to pollution controls.

FARMING
The fertile lands of the Danube valley and the Black Sea plains are rich farming country: wheat, maize, potatoes and fruit are the main crops. Country traditions continue, especially in Romania, where many village scenes seem unchanged since medieval times.

POSTAGE STAMPS
The lettering on these Bulgarian postage stamps is in the Cyrillic alphabet. It dates back to the 9th-century AD, when Saints Cyril and Methodius devised the alphabet so that they could translate the Bible into Old Bulgarian. The Cyrillic alphabet is also used in the Russian Federation.

GYPSIES
Large numbers of gypsies (or Romanies) live in both Romania and Bulgaria. The gypsies are thought to have arrived from India, via the Middle East, in the 5th-century AD. Many gypsies still wander from place to place, trading goods for a living. Gypsies are often persecuted by their host countries, who find it hard to understand their different customs and way of life.

Traditional houses are preserved in rural Bulgaria.

BULGARIA
POP: 8,417,000

TOURISM
This region has experienced a great surge in package holidays over the last decade. International airports at Varna and Burgas serve visitors from western Europe, while Russian tourists cross the Black Sea by ferry. Many new resorts have been built, and the natural beauty of the coastline, with its sandy beaches, pine forests and old fishing villages, is often spoiled by ugly, high-rise developments. Look for ✍

GREECE

FROM THE EARLIEST TIMES, the life and economy of Greece has been shaped by its geography. It is a country of rugged mountains, isolated valleys, remote peninsulas and more than 1,400 scattered islands. The difficulty of travelling by land has turned Greece into a seafaring nation, which owns the second largest fleet of merchant ships in the world. Ninety per cent of its imports and exports are carried by sea rather than by road. Most people in Greece make their living from farming, but in recent years, tourism has become an important source of income. Tourists visit Greece not only for its warm, Mediterranean climate and beautiful landscape, but also for its ancient ruins. Many of these date from the 5th-century BC, when the country was the cultural centre of the western world, the birthplace of democracy, and home of great thinkers such as Socrates, Plato and Aristotle.

Greek Orthodox bishop

THE ORTHODOX CHURCH
Most Greek Christians belong to the Orthodox Church. This was founded in Constantinople (modern Istanbul) in the 4th-century AD. The Eastern Orthodox Church established there still flourishes in Greece, Eastern Europe and Russia.

Parsley
GREEK SALAD
Many Greek farms are small, growing just enough vegetables and fruit for the farmer's family. Lettuces, cucumbers, tomatoes, olives, herbs and cheese are the most common produce.

Aubergine
Cucumber
Beef tomato

ATHENS
Athens is famous for its Acropolis ("high place"), crowned by the Parthenon temple. Smog all too often obscures the Acropolis, and cars are banned from the city on certain days to reduce pollution.

The Parthenon temple (built 432 BC) was the centre of religious life in Classical Athens.

THE CORINTH CANAL
Athens is separated from the Ionian Sea by a narrow neck of land called the Isthmus of Corinth. In 1893 the Greeks cut a canal through the isthmus. It is 6.3 km (3.9 miles) long, but only just wide enough for a ship to squeeze between the cliffs on either side. Look for ⚏

Olives and cypresses grow throughout Greece.

KEYBOX

🏛	**Archaeological sites:** Remains from ancient Greece are found all over the country, attracting many visitors. Look for 🏛
🍇	**Sultanas and currants:** Greece is the world's largest exporter of these fruits. Small, black currants are named after the town of Corinth. Look for ❦
🏅	**The Olympic Games:** The event started in Olympia in 776 BC. Sports included running, wrestling, boxing, horse racing, javelin and discus. Look for 🏅

🍋	Citrus fruit	🐬	Fishing
🍇	Wine	⚓	Mining
🏺	Vegetable oil	🗼	Oil
❀	Cotton	🏭	Industrial centre
🚬	Tobacco	✎	Tourism

Tuning peg
Fretted fingerboard
Neck
String
Pegbox inlaid with mother-of-pearl
Soundhole
Body
Bridge

CLASSICAL MUSIC
The bouzouki is a stringed instrument, similar to a lute or a guitar, which is used in traditional Greek music. Folk dances, national costumes and music are still very popular at religious festivals such as Easter, and on special occasions such as weddings.

SACRED OIL
Olives have been grown in Greece for over two thousand years. In ancient times, the olive was sacred to Athena, the goddess of war, and olive wreaths were worn as a symbol of victory. Today, olives and olive oil are major exports. Look for 🫒

### Map labels

MACEDONIA
ALBANIA
GREECE
Vardar
Kilkis
L. Prespa
Florina
Edessa
Thessaloniki
L. Vegoritis
Kastoria
L. Kastorias
Veroia
Chromium
Kozani
Katerini
Thermaic Gulf
Aliakmon
Grevena
Pineios
PINDUS MOUNTAINS
Ioannina
Corfu
Igoumenitsa
Olives
Trikala
Larisa
Karditsa
Olives
Volos
IONIAN SEA
Arta
Chromium
Preveza
Lamia
Stylis
Lefkada
Loutra Aidipsou
Olives
Olives
Nickel
Astakos
L. Trichonida
Aluminium
Amfissa
Lefkada
Delphi
Olives
Acheloos
Mesolongi
Itea
Kefallonia
Lixouri
Argostoli
Gulf of Patrai
Patrai
Gulf of Corinth
Kyllini
Andravida
Corinth Canal
Zakynthos
PELOPONNESE
Corinth
Katakolo
Pyrgos
Marble
Mycenae
Zakynthos
Olympia
Epidaurus
Olives
Tripoli
Nafplio
Manganese
Olives
Leonidi
Olives
Olives
Kalamata
Sparti
Pilos
Olives
Gulf of Messini
Gytheio
Olives
Neapoli
Gulf of Laconia
Kythira

BULGARIA

THRACE

TURKEY

Drama

Serres

Xanthi

Komotini

Kavala

Alexandroupoli

Marble

Thasos

Samothraki

Olives

Polygyros

Singitic Gulf

Gulf of Kassandra

Limnos

Ayios Evstratios

A E G E A N   S E A

Sporades

Skiáthos

Evvoia

Skiros

Lesvos

Olives

Olives

Magnesite

Mytilini

Chios

Olives

Chios

Olives

Kymi

Olives

Olives

Chalkida

Marathon

ATHENS

Piraeus

Karystos

Andros

Lavrio

Tinos

Samos

Samos

Kéa

Mykonos

Ikaria

Kíthnos

Siros

Cyclades

Sérifos

Paros

Marble

Naxos

Kos

Kos

Sífnos

Amorgos

D o d e c a n e s e

Milos

Ios

Astipálaia

Thira

Rhodes

Rhodes

Olives

N

Monólithos

Rhodes

GREECE
POP: 10,386,000

0   25   50   75   100   125   KM

0   25   50   75   MILES

Karpathos

S E A   O F   C R E T E

Crete

Chania

Rethymno

Irakleio

Knossos

Agios Nikolaos

Olives

Olives

M E D I T E R R A N E A N   S E A

Greek doll wearing a traditional wedding dress.

Hand-painted pottery made in local workshops

TOURISM

Over 5 million tourists visit Greece every year, creating an enormous demand for goods and services. Hotels, restaurants and shops employ many people, while holiday purchases boost the Greek economy. Local workshops produce hand-crafted items such as pottery, leather bags and sandals for the tourist market.

A monastery perches on a vertical rock in central Greece.

FISHING

Fishing is an important part of the Greek economy, but the eastern Mediterranean has been over-fished: only mullet, squid, sardines and tunny are found in any quantity. Look for

The Mediterranean squid can grow to a length of 0.6 m (2 ft)

Sponges, found in the Mediterranean, are obtained by diving.

HILL-FARMING

Greece, with its mountainous landscape, has the largest number of small hill-farms in Europe. The soil is poor and many people are needed to work the land: nearly a third of the Greek labour force is employed in agriculture – more than anywhere else in Europe.

ADAPTABLE GOATS

Hardy goats are ideally suited to Greece's rugged landscape. They are tough and sure-footed, and able to survive on limited food resources. Goat's milk is used for making yoghurt and cheese. Goat skin is also made into leather and young goats (kids) are a great delicacy.

AΘHNA

Greek has its own alphabet, which dates back 2,500 years. This says "Athens".

A PLACE IN THE SUN

People have been coming to Greece for centuries to visit the remains of ancient Greek cities and temples. Today, many visitors come from northern European countries, especially Scandinavia, the UK and Germany. Thira, seen here, is just one of many popular island resorts. Look for

Olive trees grow in rows on the high, arid mountains of central Crete.

AN ISLAND LIFE

Tourism is more profitable than traditional pursuits such as farming and fishing. Today, yachts are beginning to outnumber fishing boats in local ports.

THE BALTIC STATES AND BELORUSSIA

THE THREE BALTIC STATES – Latvia, Lithuania and Estonia – made history in 1990-91 when they became the first republics to declare their independence from the Soviet Union. This was the end of a long series of invasions and occupations by the Vikings, Germans, Danes, Poles and Russians. A new era had begun, but many of the old problems – food shortages, pollution, weak economies – still remained. The region's flat landscape is well-drained by lakes and rivers and is ideal for farming. The main crops are grains, sugar beet and potatoes. In Belorussia heavy industry such as machine-building and metal-working is important, while the Baltic States manufacture electronics and consumer goods. Nearly half the population of the Baltic States are Russians who have moved there to work in industry. The Baltic Sea, although much of it is frozen in the winter months, gives access to the markets of northern Europe. Industrialization has left a terrible legacy. Summer resorts along the Baltic coast have been closed to visitors because of polluted seawater, and Belorussia was badly hit by the nuclear accident at Chernobyl in the Ukraine in 1986, when 70 per cent of the radioactive fall-out landed on its territory.

NEW CURRENCY
When the three Baltic States separated from the Soviet Union, they all stopped using the rouble and introduced their own currencies. Companies which had been owned and run by the communist state came under private ownership, and the Baltic States encouraged investment in these industries from abroad.

One of the many lakes of Lithuania.

KEYBOX

Cattle: The Baltic States were the centres of beef and dairy production for the former Soviet Union. Look for ▼	
Oil: The Baltic States used to obtain free oil by pipeline from the former Soviet Union. Now they depend on Estonia's oil shale deposits. Look for ▯	
Peat: This region has large supplies of peat – a fuel made from carbonized plant material found in bogs. Look for ▮	

🐖	Pigs	⛴	Fishing port
	Sugar beet	⛏	Mining
	Potatoes	🏭	Industrial centre
	Flax		Shipbuilding
	Timber	💻	High-tech industry

Spider, trapped in amber

BALTIC GOLD
Amber is the fossilized sap of ancient trees. The Baltic States produce two-thirds of the world's amber, most of it found along Lithuania's "amber coast". Amber has been collected and traded since prehistoric times. It is a precious stone, but is also valued for its medical properties. Even today it is used to treat rheumatism. Look for ◉

MINSK
Although Minsk was founded over 900 years ago, it has no historic buildings. The city was virtually destroyed by bombing during World War II, when half of Minsk's population is estimated to have been killed. After the war, the city was rebuilt, and became one of the industrial centres of the former Soviet Union.

NATIONAL DISH
Draniki is the national dish of Belorussia. It is made of grated potatoes fried in vegetable oil and served with sour cream. Potatoes are grown everywhere, and are one of Belorussia's main products. Large numbers of dairy cattle are kept on its extensive pastureland.

Sour cream

Beetroot, mixed with sour cream

Draniki

RUSSIAN FEDERATION (KALININGRAD OBLAST)

ESTONIA *POP: 1,572,000*

LITHUANIA *POP: 3,782,000*

K L M N O P R S T

Gulf of Finland

FLAX

Flax, from which linen is made, was one of the first plants ever cultivated. Mummies in ancient Egypt were wrapped in linen shrouds. Linen is made from flax fibres, which are separated from the plant, spun and woven. Flax is grown in the Baltic States, which export both cotton and linen textiles. The largest cotton mill in Europe is at Narva in Estonia. Look for ☒

Tiled rooftops in Tallinn's medieval centre.

Old-fashioned windmills can still be seen in the Baltic States.

TALLINN

Tallinn, Estonia's capital, is an important Baltic port, with regular ferries to Finland. In contrast to the modern port, the city centre has changed little since medieval times, with cobbled streets, ancient walls, turrets and gables.

RELIGION

The Hill of Crosses in Lithuania is a religious shrine where thousands of crosses have been put up to honour the dead. The Baltic peoples resisted the communist Soviet Union by remaining loyal to their own religions. Lithuania is Catholic, while Latvia and Estonia are Protestant.

LATVIA
POP: 2,643,000

Sprats are caught in the Baltic Sea, and are served with onions.

A LATVIAN IDENTITY

Only 52 per cent of the people of Latvia were born in the country. Russians, Belorussians and Ukrainians were resettled in Latvia when it was part of the Soviet Union. As a near minority in their own country, Latvians are acutely aware of their own national identity. They promote their language, national dress, dances and music – there are more than a million known Latvian folk songs.

RIGA

Situated on the Western Dvina, about 17 km (10.5 miles) inland from the Baltic Sea, Riga has been an important port since the 12th century. Although much of the old city has been destroyed by invasion and war, Riga still has a medieval heart – its oldest building dates back to the 13th century. Today, it is the industrial hub and main commercial port of the Baltic States.

HEAVY INDUSTRY

Many of the former Soviet Union's trains and railway carriages were manufactured in Latvia, the most industrialized of the Baltic States. Latvia also produces minibuses, trams, mopeds, washing machines and tape recorders. Look for ⬛

Russian paper and envelopes

BELORUSSIA
POP. 10,320,000

TIMBER

About one-third of this region is still covered with fir and pine forest, and timber is an important industry. Inland waterways are used to transport the wood, which is either made into wood-pulp for paper or used to make furniture and matches. Other former Soviet states also send their timber to the Baltic region for processing. Look for ⌐

Many mushrooms grow in the Belorussian forests. Picking mushrooms is a popular summer outing.

VODKA

Potatoes are one of the most important crops in Belorussia. They are exported to the Russian Federation where they are fermented and used to make the national drink, vodka. The name vodka comes from the Russian word *voda* which means "water". Cheap vodka has led to a high rate of alcoholism, which governments have tried to curb by heavily taxing alcohol.

Farmers collect hay in Belorussia.

N

0 25 50 75 100 125 150 175 KM

0 25 50 75 100 MILES

Rakvere, Kohtla-Järve, Narva, Dairy, Dairy, Dairy, L. Peipus, Tartu, Võrtsjärv, Dairy, Beef, Võru, Valga, Madona, Beef, L. Lubana, Ludza, Rēzekne, Krāslava, Daugavpils, L. Disna, Navapolatsk, Polatsk, Dairy, Vitsyebsk, Beef, Hlybokaye, Dairy, Lyepyel', L. Narach, Dairy, Orsha, Beef, Horki, Smarhon', Maladzyechna, Barysaw, Mahilyow, Zhodzina, Byarezina, MINSK, Dairy, Dairy, Dairy, Krychaw, Dairy, Bykhaw, Babruysk, Slutsk, Zhlobin, Beef, Salihorsk, Ptsich, Svyetlahorsk, Homyel, Luninyets, Rechytsa, Beef, Pripet, Kalinkavichy, Mazyr, Dnieper

RUSSIAN FEDERATION

BELORUSSIA (BELARUS)

UKRAINE

Western Dvina

EUROPEAN RUSSIA

THE RUSSIAN FEDERATION is the largest country in the world. Stretching across two continents – Europe in the west and Asia in the east – it is twice the size of the USA. The Ural Mountains form the division between the European and Asian parts of the country. The Russian Federation has fertile farmlands, vast mineral deposits and abundant timber, oil and other natural resources. Despite its size and natural wealth, Russia is currently in a state of political and economic turmoil. After centuries of rule by czars (emperors), the world's first communist government took power in Russia in 1917; five years later the country became the Union of Soviet Socialist Republics (USSR), which included many of the territories that were formerly parts of the Russian Empire. During 74 years of communist rule, the Soviet Union became an industrial and military superpower, but at an appalling cost to its people and environment. Economic problems led to liberal reforms beginning in the mid-1980s, but the reforms unleashed a whirlwind of change which led to the fall of the communist regime in December 1991. By then most of the non-Russian republics had declared independence. The new Russian Federation is now struggling to become a democracy.

MOSCOW

The city of Moscow was founded in the 12th century. At its centre is a fortified citadel called the *Kremlin*. Its stone walls enclose the grand palace of the czars, four cathedrals and a church. The *Kremlin* became – and is now – the country's seat of government.

St. Basil's, Moscow, built in the 16th century

RELIGION

Moscow is the spiritual centre of the Russian Orthodox church. For many decades, the Church was persecuted in Russia; today, churches are re-opening, and many Russian people are turning back to religion. Beautiful icons (religious images painted on wood), like this one, adorn the churches and people's homes.

САНКТ-ПЕТЕРБУРГ

The name "St. Petersburg", written in Russia's Cyrillic alphabet, which was devised by Christian missionaries in the 10th century.

ST. PETERSBURG

St. Petersburg, the capital of Russia from 1712-1918, was founded by *Czar Peter the Great* in 1703. It is built on 12 islands, linked by bridges, and has many elegant 18th-century buildings.

Northern Russia is covered with coniferous forest, called taiga.

RUSSIAN FEDERATION
POP: 150,638,000
(EUROPEAN RUSSIA)
POP: 108,950,000

Many wooden churches built in the 17th century still stand on small islands in Lake Onega.

KARA SEA
Novaya Zemlya
Baydarata Bay
Vaygach I.
Kara Strait
Kolguyev I.
BARENTS SEA
Chesha Bay
Mezen'
Pinega
WHITE SEA
KOLA PENINSULA
Murmansk
L. Umbozero
L. Pyaozero
L. Topozero
L. Segozero
L. Onega
L. Ladoga
Petrozavodsk
FINLAND
NORWAY
Gulf of Finland
St. Petersburg
ESTONIA
LATVIA
BELORUSSIA
Pskov
Novgorod
Neadl'
Smolensk
Dnieper
Brynsk
Kaluga
Tula
MOSCOW (MOSKVA)
Tver
Moscow-Volga Canal
Gzhel'
Vladimir
Ivanovo
Kostroma
Yaroslavl'
Rybinsk Res.
Volga
Cherepovets
Vologda
Gorodets
Nizhniy Novgorod
Kirov
Vetluga
Syktyvkar
Kama
Komi Res.
Potassium
Platinum
Uranium
Izhma
Pechora
Usa
Vorkuta
MOUNTAINS
RUSSIAN FEDERATION
Arkhangel'sk
Northern Dvina
Onega
Kem'
Iron
Nickel
Copper
Nickel
Iron
Phosphate
Aluminium
Aluminium
Oats
Rye
Barley
Wheat

82

Historic cathedrals and monasteries line the banks of the Volga at Yaroslavl'.

A scene from a Russian folk tale

LACQUERED BOX

Traditional Russian crafts have never been so popular – they have found a market in the West and earn Russia foreign currency. Lacquered boxes have been made in the Moscow region for the last four centuries. The papier mâché boxes are decorated with miniature paintings of folk stories, rural scenes, dances, forests and fairy tales, and are then lacquered.

FAST FOOD?

With the end of communism, foreign companies are investing in Russia and many joint ventures are being encouraged. For western countries, Russia provides a vast new market. Several western fast-food companies have opened restaurants in Moscow. They accept payment in roubles and are popular with local people, although queuing for four hours is not unknown.

BALLET

Ballet originally developed in western Europe, but in the late 19th century it was completely changed by the Russians. Inspired largely by one man, Diaghilev, Russian ballet became creative and exciting. The male dancer was more important, and more attention was paid to the music and the costumes. Russia's two most famous ballet companies are the Kirov and the Bolshoi. Both are a source of national pride.

A tutu, the costume worn by ballerinas

Ballet shoe

MiG fighter plane

MAKING WAVES

The manufacture and sale of weapons, such as this MiG fighter plane, has been badly hit by the end of the Cold War. At Nizhniy Novgorod, where nuclear submarines used to be built, many shipyard workers are now making a semi-automatic washing machine, called the "Wave". Large numbers of unsold machines fill the former shipyard's warehouses. Look for ✈

Enamelled chess-board

CHESS

Pottery from the town of Gzhel' near Moscow is collected by people all over the world. The patterns are painted by hand, using brushes made from squirrel hair. Cobalt-blue patterns are then enamelled on to a background of white. This chess-set, made in Gzhel', reflects the popularity of the game here – Russia has produced many of the world's grand masters of chess.

Chess piece

Model of a Lada hatchback

LADA

In 1965, the Russians signed a deal with the Italian car company, Fiat. A factory was built at Tol'yatti and is the largest car plant in the former Soviet Union. Ladas (based on the Fiat) are manufactured here, and some are exported to the West. Few Russians own a car, but the demand for imported western cars is growing. Look for 🚗

Fur hats with ear-flaps are essential in Russia's freezing winters.

MINERAL WEALTH

Mines are a common sight in Russia. There are large reserves of coal around Moscow. Nickel, copper, phosphates and cobalt are found in the far north. Iron, sulphur, copper, gold and nickel are mined in the south and southwest. Look for ⛏

Traditional hand-made wooden toy, in the form of a child and dancing bear.

KEYBOX

Reindeer: Nomads in the north herd reindeer, which are used to carry loads and for their meat, milk and skins. Look for ⚰

Hydro-electric power: Vast dams on the Dnieper and Volga rivers power electricity generators, which supply large cities and other republics. Look for ⚡

Vehicle manufacture: Cars are manufactured along the Volga. The truck plant at Naberezhnyye Chelny is the largest in the world. Look for 🚚

Pollution: Huge numbers of factories, which have grown without environmental controls, are polluting the region's rivers. Look for ☠

Cereals 🌾	Mining ⛏	
Sugar beet 🥬	Coal	
Citrus fruit	Industrial centre 🏭	
Tobacco	Aerospace industry ✈	

### Map labels

URAL
Vanadium
Iron
Nickel
Nickel
Perm'
Magnesium
Barley
Oats
Wheat
Izhevsk
Naberezhnyye Chelny
Copper
Orsk
Copper
Orenburg
Copper
Ufa
Copper
Nickel
Wheat
Vyatka
Wheat
Wheat
Yoshkar-Ola
Cheboksary
Wheat
Kazan
Rye
Ul'yanovsk
Tol'yatti
Samara
Maize
Saransk
Oats
Barley
Penza
Maize
Sulphur
Wheat
Balakovo
Wheat
Saratov
Maize
Volga
Tambov
Wheat
Volgograd
Volga
Kamyshin
Lipetsk
Iron
Maize
Don
Astrakhan
Volga-Don Canal
Elista
Maize
Kuma
Orël
Rye
Kursk
Iron
Voronezh
Wheat
Belgorod
Iron
Wheat
Rostov-na-Donu
Volga-Don Canal
Wheat
Kalmyunsk
Maize
Stavropol'
Nal'chik
Vladikavkaz
Groznyy
Makhachkala
Donets
Maize
Krasnodar
Wheat
Kuban
Maykop
Cherkessk
Sochi
CAUCASUS MTS.
GEORGIA
AZERBAIJAN
SEA OF AZOV
Kerch Strait
BLACK SEA
CASPIAN SEA
UKRAINE
KAZAKHSTAN

Scale

N

0 100 200 300 400 500 KM
0 50 100 150 200 250 300 MILES

UKRAINE, MOLDAVIA AND THE CAUCASIAN REPUBLICS

Cereals being harvested in the fertile fields of Ukraine

THE CAUCASUS MOUNTAINS run between the Black and Caspian Seas. Higher in places than the Alps, they form a natural barrier between the flat steppes of the Russian Federation to the north and the plateaux of Southwest Asia. The newly independent states to the south of the Russian Federation are rich in natural resources. Ukraine, the largest country in Europe, is dominated by a flat and fertile plain, where huge quantities of cereals are grown on large farms. Ukraine also possesses extensive coal and iron ore deposits and is heavily industrialized. Wine and fruit are produced in Moldavia and Georgia, where the climate is mild and the soil fertile. Mountainous Armenia is rich in minerals, while Azerbaijan has plentiful oil.

WINE

Georgian brandy

Moldavian wine

A quarter of the former Soviet Union's wine was produced in Moldavia, which is well known for its champagne. Vines also thrive on the warm, sunny hills of eastern Georgia, where wine and brandy are produced. Look for ❦

BORSCHT

Borscht, beetroot soup

Sour cream

Vegetable soups are the main food for many country people in cold regions throughout the world. Russia's famous beetroot soup, *borscht*, comes from Ukraine. There, the *borscht* also contains root vegetables, such as potatoes and carrots. *Borscht* is often served with savoury turnovers, called *piroshki*.

Piroshki, savoury pastries

CHERNOBYL

In 1986, a radiation leak at Chernobyl nuclear power station caused panic all over Europe. More than 100,000 people were evacuated from the area around the plant, where towns now stand desolate and empty. More than two million people still live, in fear and uncertainty, in the contaminated areas.

KEYBOX

Oil: There is a large oilfield under the delta of the River Kura in Azerbaijan. Offshore wells are also being dug in the Caspian Sea. Look for ⛏

Hydro-electric power: Dams on the River Dnieper supply water for crops and for electricity. The rivers of the Caucasus also provide electricity. Look for ⊞

High-tech: Electrical and electronic equipment, such as TVs and computers, are made in the Caucasian republics. Look for 💻

🌾	Cereals	⛑	Mining
🍇	Wine	⛏	Coal
🌿	Tea	🏭	Industrial centre
🌻	Sunflowers	⚓	Tourism
🐟	Fishing	☢	Nuclear pollution

BLACK SEA TOURISM

The Crimea attracts millions of visitors who cram onto the crowded beaches to enjoy the warm sun. Many visitors come for their health, rest and a regime of healthy eating, massage and exercise. Look for ⚓

MOLDAVIA
POP: 4,350,000

The barrier of the Caucasus Mountains blocks cold air from the north

Hardy crops, such as maize which can withstand frosts, are grown on lowlands

Black Sea

Tbilisi

Yerevan

Mountains force humid air to rise. It falls as rain in Georgia

Grapes and fruits grown in valleys

Baku

Cotton production along lower R. Kura

CASPIAN SEA

N →

THE CAUCASUS MOUNTAINS

Armenia, Azerbaijan and Georgia – the Caucasian Republics – are isolated from the Russian Federation by the Caucasus Mountains. The warm sub-tropical climate of the region allows an exotic range of crops to be grown. Georgia has a humid climate, so tea and citrus fruits are cultivated. In the drier east, the rivers running down from the mountains are used to water the fields.

Map labels: BELORUSSIA, POLAND, Chernihiv, Desna, Rye, Syr, Luts'k, Rye, Sluch, Korosten', Kiev Res., Rivne, Chernobyl, L'viv, Barley, Dniester, Zhytomyr, Barley, KIEV (KYIV), Dnieper, Sulphur, Wheat, Bila Tserkva, Ternopil', Khmel'nyts'kyy, Kremenchuk Res., Ivano-Frankivs'k, Wheat, Vinnytsya, Cherkasy, Barley, Kremenchuk, SLOVAKIA, CARPATHIANS, Kam"yanets'-Podil's'kyy, UKRA... , Chernivtsi, HUNGARY, Southern Bug, Kirovohrad, Wheat, Maize, Wheat, Kryvyy Rih, MOLDAVIA, Bălți, Wheat, Dubăsari, Maize, CHIŞINĂU (KISHINEV), Tiraspol, Maize, Wheat, Mykolaiv, ROMANIA, Tighina, Odesa, Kherson, Nov. Kakhovk., Maize, Bilhorod-Dnistrovs'kyy, Karkinit Gulf, Wheat, Reni, CR..., Yevpatoriya, Kalamit Gulf, Sevastopol', TURKEY, GEORGIA, ARMENIA, AZERBAIJAN, RUSSIAN FEDERATION

BLACK BREAD

Ukraine was known as the former Soviet Union's "breadbasket". Its broad flat steppes, with their fertile black earth, are intensively cultivated: wheat, buckwheat, potatoes, rye and flax are grown on vast farms. Much of Ukraine's countryside consists of endless fields of cereals, the view broken only by the occasional haystack.

Matrioshka dolls are hand-painted. Each is made from a single piece of wood.

UKRAINE
POP: 52,498,000

The Ukraine is the world's largest producer of buckwheat. Although it is ground up to make flour, buckwheat is not a true cereal.

KIEV

Kiev, founded in the 9th century, is the capital of Ukraine. St. Sophia's Cathedral, with its gilded domes, has been Kiev's most famous landmark since 1037. Kiev is situated on the banks of the River Dnieper, the republic's main waterway. It is within easy reach of the Black Sea ports, as well as being near Ukraine's industrial centre.

COAL

About a third of the former Soviet Union's coal came from the area around Donets'k in Ukraine, where there are about 40 deep mines. Miners working here are reasonably well-paid, but gas explosions and the frequent breakdown of equipment put them at risk. Death rates in these mines are 10 times higher than in mines in the USA. Look for

INDUSTRIAL HEARTLAND

Ukraine's Donbass region, with its rich reserves of coal, iron, manganese and other minerals, is a major industrial area. Heavy industry, such as iron and steel works, engineering and chemicals, still dominate the region, but today, cars, aircraft, televisions and computers are also manufactured here. Look for

CAUCASIAN CONFLICT

When the Caucasian republics were part of the Soviet Union, many different peoples were forced to live side by side. Since these countries became independent, many pent-up resentments have been unleashed. Within Muslim Azerbaijan, the Christian, mainly Armenian, region of Nagorno-Karabakh has caused great tension, and fighting has erupted.

TEA

Tea is a popular drink throughout the former Soviet Union, and over 90 per cent of the tea consumed here is grown in Georgia. Both black and green teas are grown on large tea plantations. Tea is served black and strong, with sugar or lemon. Look for

Decorated Black Sea fiddle, from Georgia.

SUNFLOWERS

Sunflowers are an important crop in southern Ukraine. The seeds, which can be eaten, contain oil and protein. Sunflower oil is used for cooking. The seeds are also used in the manufacture of margarine and soap, and are mixed with maize and peas for cattle feed. Look for

The snow-capped peaks of the Caucasus Mountains.

AZERBAIJAN
POP: 7,507,000

Caviar, served on toast

CAVIAR

The Russian sturgeon is a large fish, which can grow up to 7 m (23 ft) in length. Its eggs, called caviar, are an expensive delicacy. Sturgeon live in the Black and Caspian Seas and swim up rivers, such as the Dnieper, to breed in fresh water. Hydroelectric dams on these rivers have disrupted the sturgeons' routes, and polluted water is causing concern about falling numbers of fish. Look for

GEORGIA
POP: 5,478,000

TEXTILES

Georgia is famous for its silk and textiles. Brightly coloured and patterned cotton fabrics are woven with gold and silver thread. Worn by women as headscarves, these fabrics are seen throughout the Caucasus.

The Swallow's Nest Castle, high on a rock near Yalta.

ARMENIA
POP: 3,816,000

0 50 100 150 200 250 300 KM
0 50 100 150 MILES

### Map labels

RUSSIAN FEDERATION

Sumy
Barley
Wheat
Kharkiv
Poltava
Donets
Maize
Maize
Wheat
Kramators'k
Dnipropetrovs'k
Horlivka
Luhans'k
DONBASS
Donets'k
Makiyivka
Zaporizhzhya
Nikopol'
Maize
Kakhovka Res.
Maize
Mariupol'
Melitopol'
Berdyans'k
Maize
SEA OF AZOV
Kerch Strait
Kerch
CRIMEA
Feodosiya
Simferopol'
Yalta

BLACK SEA

RUSSIAN FEDERATION
CAUCASUS MTS.
Gagra
Sokhumi
Enguri
Och'amch'ire
GEORGIA
K'ut'aisi
P'ot'i
Bat'umi
Manganese
TBILISI (T'BILISI)
Rust'avi
Kura
TURKEY
Copper
Vanadzor
Gyumri
Maize
Gäncä
Mingdgevir Res.
Kura
Sumqayit
BAKU (BAKI)
AZERBAIJAN
L. Sevan
Sevan-Hrazdan
YEREVAN
Xankändi
NAGORNO-KARABAKH
Aras
Wheat
ARMENIA
AZERBAIJAN
Naxçıvan
Länkäran
IRAN
CASPIAN SEA
Quba

N

White-backed vulture
Gyps bengalensis
Wingspan: 2.2 m (7 ft)

Cheetah
Acinonyx jubatus
Length: 2.2 m (7 ft)

Aye-aye
Daubentonia madagascariensis
Length: 45 cm (18 in)

AFRICA

AFRICA IS THE SECOND largest continent after Asia, and the only one through which the Equator and both tropics run. It is also home to the world's longest river, the Nile. The climate and vegetation roughly mirror each other on either side of the Equator. In the extreme south, and along the Mediterranean coast in the north, hot dry summers are followed by mild wet winters. Similarly, the land around each tropic is hot and starved of rain, so great deserts have formed. Africa's immense tropical savannah grasslands are prone to drought, but around the Equator high rainfall has produced lush tropical rainforests. The volcanoes and strangely elongated lakes in the Great Rift Valley are evidence of cracks in the Earth's crust that threaten eventually to split Africa apart.

Burchell's zebra
Equus burchelli
Height: 1.2 m (4 ft)

■ HOT SAHARA
The inhospitable Sahara desert covers one-third of Africa. Temperatures can exceed 50°C (120°F).

Malachite is a copper-rich ore found in many parts of eastern Africa.

■ THUNDERING WATERFALL
The Zambezi River winds slowly through dry woodlands before reaching the Victoria Falls. Here it plummets 108 m (354 ft), creating so much noise and spray that local people call it "the smoke that thunders".

■ GREAT RIFT VALLEY
Cracks in the Earth's crust have made a valley 6,000 km (3,750 miles) long, and up to 90 km (55 miles) wide.

■ MISTY RAINFOREST
Tropical rainforests only grow where temperatures are always high, and rain is abundant. Here in central Africa, it rains every day – more than 2 m (7 ft) falls each year.

Umbrella thorn acacia
Acacia tortillis
Height: 18 m (60 ft)

The South African Turban shell looks like a headdress made of coiled cloth.

■ SERENGETI PLAIN
Savannah – grassland and open woodland – is home to huge herds of grazing animals, including wildebeest and zebra.

■ SAND DUNES IN THE NAMIB
The intensely hot Namib Desert forms a narrow strip down Africa's southwest coast. Rainfall is less than 15 cm (6 in) a year, but sea mists from the cold currents along the coast provide enough moisture for some plants and animals to survive.

Shells like this Black Mitre can be found in shallow water along the west African coast.

Gaboon viper
Bitis gabonica
Length: 2 m (7 ft)

■ ■ OKAVANGO DELTA
Not all rivers run to the sea. The Okavango River ends in a huge inland swamp that attracts thousands of water loving animals, such as hippopotamuses.

CROSS-SECTION THROUGH AFRICA

L. Victoria
Great Rift Valley (western)
Ruwenzori Mountains
Serengeti Plain
Great Rift Valley (eastern)
Atlantic Ocean
Congo Basin
Indian Ocean

3,000 (9,843)
Sea level
-4,500 (14,764)
Metres (feet)
A
Length: 4,500 km (2,800 miles)
B

■ SOUTHERN AFRICA
Rainfall is so low in southern Africa that for most of the year few plants show themselves above ground. But as soon as the rains come, a barren landscape is transformed, covered by a brilliant mass of flowers.

African elephant
Loxodonta africana
Height: 4 m (13 ft)

Desert scorpion
Androctonus australis
Length: 8 cm (3 in)

Mountain gorilla
Gorilla gorilla
Height: 1.8 m (6 ft)

BOTTLE TREES

Plants can resist drought by reducing their leaf-size and enlarging their stems to store water. Here in Madagascar's dry woodlands, huge-trunked baobabs, or "bottle trees", grow alongside spiny Dideria.

Black rhinoceros
Diceros bicornis
Length: 3.6 m (12 ft)

KEY TO SYMBOLS

▲ Mountain
△ Volcano
Mangroves
Wetlands
Coral reef
Plate margins with direction of movement

KEY TO NATURAL VEGETATION

Mediterranean-type
Hot desert
Tropical grassland
Tropical rainforest
Temperate grassland
Mountain
Dry woodland

NORTHWEST AFRICA

OVER THE CENTURIES, Northwest Africa has been invaded by many peoples. The entire north coast from the Red Sea to the Atlantic was once part of the Roman Empire. Later colonization by Italy, Great Britain, Turkey, Spain and France contributed to the culture of the countries, but it was the 7th-century Arab conquest which fundamentally changed the region. The conversion of the original peoples – the Berbers – to Islam, and the use of Arabic as a common language, gave these countries a sense of unity which remains today. In fact, the region is sometimes called the Maghreb, which means "west" in Arabic. In the northwest, the Atlas Mountains form a barrier between the wetter, cooler areas along the coast and the great Saharan Desert. This desert is the biggest on Earth, and is still growing. Water shortages and lack of land for farming are problems throughout the region, especially as the population of the Maghreb is increasing rapidly. In Algeria and Libya, however, the desert has revealed hidden riches – abundant oil and natural gas.

FEZ – AN ISLAMIC CITY
This view of the city of Fez in Morocco shows the flat-roofed houses that are traditional in this region. Seen from the narrow streets, the houses look blank and windowless, but this is because they are designed to face inwards on to central courtyards which are cool and private. Islamic cities may appear to be a chaotic maze of streets, but in fact they are laid out following guidelines set in the holy book of Islam, the *Koran*.

The Moroccans make a refreshing tea from the spearmint plant.

MOROCCO
POP: 28,913,000

WESTERN SAHARA
POP: 200,000

Morocco occupied the whole of Western Sahara in 1979.

BERBERS
Berbers were the original people of Northwest Africa. When the Arabs invaded, they were driven out of the fertile coastal areas. Many Berbers still live in remote villages or towns – such as here at Boumalne-Dadès – high in the Atlas Mountains, where their lifestyle and language have remained unchanged for centuries.

Couscous is the basic ingredient of many North African dishes. It is made of tiny pellets of flour, called semolina.

WESTERN SAHARA
Western Sahara is a sparsely populated desert area lying between Morocco and Mauritania. It was a Spanish colony until 1976, but is now fighting for independence from Morocco which claims two-thirds of the country, and the phosphates found there. This photo shows young members of the liberation movement.

The Ahaggar Mountains, Algeria, jut up in the middle of the Sahara.

KEYBOX

Mining: *Huge quantities of phosphates come from the sands of Western Sahara and Morocco. They are the vital raw material for fertilizers. Look for* 🪖

Gas: *Algeria has vast reserves of natural gas, much of it exported to Europe – some by pipeline to Italy across the Mediterranean Sea. Look for* ⚑

Archaeological sites: *Early civilizations, such as the Romans, built cities in the desert and along the coast of North Africa. Look for* ▥

🐑 Sheep		🚢 Fishing port	
🍊 Citrus fruit		🛢 Oil	
🌴 Dates		🏭 Industrial centre	
🍇 Wine		✒ Tourism	
🫒 Vegetable oil		🌴 Oases	

CARPETS AND RUGS
Hand-knotted carpets and rugs, with their distinctive bold patterns and deep pile, are made throughout the region. In Morocco the most important carpet factories are in Rabat and Fez. Craftworkers often work together in cooperatives to maintain high quality and to control prices.

Painted plate

Leather bag

TOURISM
Tourism is a vital source of foreign income for Morocco and Tunisia. When oil prices fell in the 1980s, tourism took the place of oil as the main source of foreign income. Modern hotels, built in traditional styles, have sprung up along the coast. Both countries produce handicrafts for tourists, such as leather and brassware. Look for ✒

THE TUAREG
The Tuareg are a nomadic tribe who inhabit a huge area of the Sahara. In the past they controlled the great camel caravans which crossed the desert to the Mediterranean, carrying slaves, ivory, gold and salt. Today, some Tuareg still follow the traditional desert way of life, but many have become settled farmers.

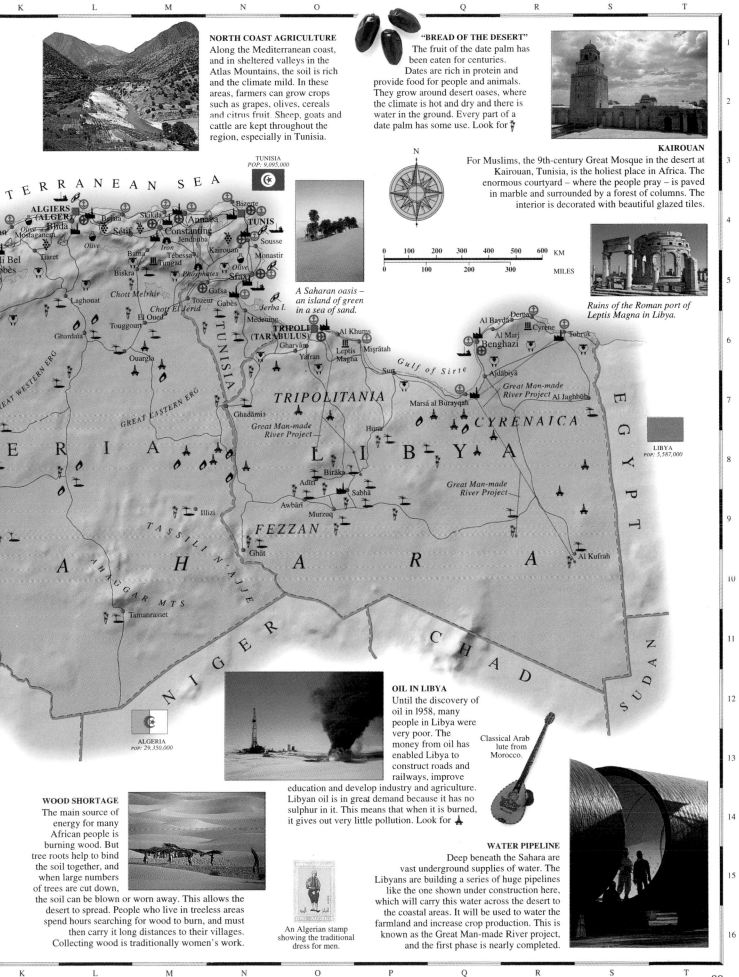

NORTH COAST AGRICULTURE
Along the Mediterranean coast, and in sheltered valleys in the Atlas Mountains, the soil is rich and the climate mild. In these areas, farmers can grow crops such as grapes, olives, cereals and citrus fruit. Sheep, goats and cattle are kept throughout the region, especially in Tunisia.

"BREAD OF THE DESERT"
The fruit of the date palm has been eaten for centuries. Dates are rich in protein and provide food for people and animals. They grow around desert oases, where the climate is hot and dry and there is water in the ground. Every part of a date palm has some use. Look for 🌴

KAIROUAN
For Muslims, the 9th-century Great Mosque in the desert at Kairouan, Tunisia, is the holiest place in Africa. The enormous courtyard – where the people pray – is paved in marble and surrounded by a forest of columns. The interior is decorated with beautiful glazed tiles.

Ruins of the Roman port of Leptis Magna in Libya.

A Saharan oasis – an island of green in a sea of sand.

TUNISIA
POP: 9,095,000

LIBYA
POP: 5,587,000

ALGERIA
POP: 29,350,000

An Algerian stamp showing the traditional dress for men.

Classical Arab lute from Morocco.

OIL IN LIBYA
Until the discovery of oil in 1958, many people in Libya were very poor. The money from oil has enabled Libya to construct roads and railways, improve education and develop industry and agriculture. Libyan oil is in great demand because it has no sulphur in it. This means that when it is burned, it gives out very little pollution. Look for ⛽

WOOD SHORTAGE
The main source of energy for many African people is burning wood. But tree roots help to bind the soil together, and when large numbers of trees are cut down, the soil can be blown or worn away. This allows the desert to spread. People who live in treeless areas spend hours searching for wood to burn, and must then carry it long distances to their villages. Collecting wood is traditionally women's work.

WATER PIPELINE
Deep beneath the Sahara are vast underground supplies of water. The Libyans are building a series of huge pipelines like the one shown under construction here, which will carry this water across the desert to the coastal areas. It will be used to water the farmland and increase crop production. This is known as the Great Man-made River project, and the first phase is nearly completed.

NORTHEAST AFRICA

WATERED AND FERTILIZED BY THE NILE, the longest river in the world, Egypt is a fertile strip running through the Sahara Desert. The first people settled there about 8,000 years ago and, by the time of the pharaohs, Egypt had become one of the world's first great civilizations. Today, Egypt is a relatively stable democracy, with a growing number of industries and control of the Suez Canal, one of the world's most important waterways. To the south are the highlands of Ethiopia and Eritrea. This area is fertile and well-watered in places, but recent droughts have made life precarious for the farmers and nomads who live there. The countries of Somalia, Sudan and Ethiopia have been beset by terrible problems, including drought, famine, religious conflicts and civil war. About half of Africa's 4.5 million refugees come from this area. In 1993, Eritrea gained independence from Ethiopia, after a civil war which lasted 30 years.

THE GIFT OF THE NILE
The River Nile floods in the summer, carrying rich mud from the highlands of Sudan and Ethiopia to the deserts of Egypt. This creates some of the most fertile land in the world. Nearly 99 per cent of the Egyptian population live along the banks of the Nile.

The ancient Egyptians used this reed-like plant, called *papyrus*, to make paper.

EGYPT
POP 59,713,000

TOURIST SOUVENIRS
Large numbers of "ancient Egyptian" *scarabs* (beetles) and other fake antiques are made locally and sold to tourists. City streets are lined with market stalls and the small workshops where these goods are made. Tourism has stimulated this informal economy.

Tomb dwelling in Cairo's City of the Dead

CAIRO
Cairo is the largest city in the Islamic world and is also one of the fastest-growing. Its current population is estimated at 9.5 million, but it is said to be increasing at a rate of 1,500 people a day. New arrivals live in squalid shanty towns on the outskirts of the city. The City of the Dead, a huge ancient cemetery outside Cairo, has now been occupied by the homeless.

SUEZ CANAL
Opened in 1869, the Suez Canal is one of the world's largest artificial waterways and a vital source of income for Egypt. It connects the Red Sea with the Mediterranean, offering a short cut from Europe through the Persian Gulf to India and the Far East. On average, 21,250 ships a year use the canal.

Coptic cross

THE COPTIC CHURCH
Although Ethiopia is surrounded by Islamic countries, about 40 per cent of its population is Christian. The isolated Ethiopian church developed into a unique branch of Christianity, called the Coptic Church.

Cotton jelaba

COTTON
Egypt produces about a third of the world's high-quality cotton. Textile industries, such as spinning, weaving and dyeing cotton are also important. Cotton is the coolest fabric to wear during hot summers. Egyptian men often wear a long-sleeved cotton garment, or *jelaba*. Look for 🪡

The gold death-mask of the Pharaoh Tutankhamun, c. 1352 BC

AGRICULTURE
Although there is fertile land in southern Ethiopia, farming methods are inefficient. The scratch plough is widely used, and – as its name implies – is only able to turn over the surface of the soil. After a few years, the goodness in the soil is used up, and crops will no longer grow.

TOURISM
Visitors from all over the world go to Egypt to see the pyramids and other ancient sites. Income from tourism helps to maintain these ancient sites. The Temple of Isis at Philae would have been flooded by the Aswān Dam, so it was moved, brick by brick, to another island. Look for 🏛

The Giza pyramids were built as tombs for the pharaohs.

### Map labels

MEDITERRANEAN SEA
ISRAEL
RED SEA
Gulf of Aqaba
Gulf of Suez
NUBIAN DESERT
LIBYAN DESERT
LIBYA
SINAI
EGYPT

Mursa Matrûh
Alexandria
El Mansûra
Port Said
Ismā'īlīya
Suez Canal
Suez
Ras Gharib
Tanta
CAIRO (EL QAHIRA)
Giza
Saqqara
Helwân
Beni Suef
El Faiyûm
El Minya
Asyût
Sohâg
Abydos
Qena
Bûr Safâga
Thebes
Valley of the Kings
Luxor
Idfu
Kom Ombo
Aswān
Philae
Aswān High Dam
L. Nasser
Wadi Halfa
Abu Simbel
Sulb Temple
Qaṭṭâra Depression
Nile

SOMALIA
POP: 9,077,000

DJIBOUTI
POP: 526,000

ERITREA
POP: 3,920,000

ETHIOPIA
POP: 51,000,000

SUDAN
POP: 27,061,000

SOMALIA
The Somalis overthrew their brutal dictator, President Barre, in 1991. A serious drought has since turned Somalia into a disaster area. Aid efforts have been blocked by a civil war between tribes, and millions of people are starving. Many Somalis have flocked to relief camps in search of food. Look for △

TEF
The most common food crop in Ethiopia is *tef* – a grain unique to this region. It is used to make *enjera*, a grey, unleavened bread which is eaten with meat and vegetables in a spicy sauce (*wat*). This is the Ethiopian national dish.

Unleavened bread, enjera
Vegetables in sauce, wat

Coffee, grown in the Ethiopian Highlands, is a valuable crop.

NOMADISM
For centuries this region has been populated by nomads, such as the Dinka of Sudan, who live by grazing their goats and camels on any available pastureland. They move from place to place according to the seasons and the weather conditions.

Djibouti is mainly arid desert, populated by nomads. Its busy port dominates the economy.

Donkeys are used throughout the region for pulling carts, and as beasts of burden.

Dates: Egypt is the world's largest date producer. Date stones dating to 4,500 BC have been found in Egypt. Look for 🌴

Dams: Both the Aswân High Dam, opened in 1970, and Sudanese dam projects control the Nile, providing irrigation and electricity. Look for

Aromatic oils: Frankincense is exported by Somalia. It is taken from trees by making cuts in the bark. It is used in incense and perfume. Look for

Cattle
Sheep
Coffee
Groundnuts
Cotton
Oil
Industrial centre
Archaeological sites
Refugee camps
Oases

KM
MILES
500
400
300
200
100
0
300
200
100
0

N

WEST AFRICA

THE LANDSCAPE OF WEST AFRICA ranges from the sand dunes of the Sahara, through the dry grasslands of the Sahel region, to the tropical rainforests in the south. There is just as much variety in the peoples of the region – more than 250 different tribes live in Nigeria alone. In the north, most people are Muslim, a legacy of the Arab traders who controlled the great caravan routes across the Sahara and brought the religion with them. It was from West Africa, particularly the coastal regions, that hundreds of thousands of Africans were transported to North and South America as slaves. Today many people in West Africa make their living from farming or herding animals. Crops such as coffee and cocoa are grown on large plantations. Like the logging industry, which is also a major source of earnings, these plantations are often owned by foreign multinational companies who take most of the profits out of the region. Recent discoveries of oil and minerals offered the promise of economic prosperity, but this has been prevented by falling world prices, huge foreign debts, corruption and civil wars.

Calabash (bowl) made from a vegetable called a gourd, then decorated.

MAURITANIA
POP: 2,399,000

SENEGAL
POP: 8,610,000

Kano mosque, built to serve the largely Islamic population in northern Nigeria.

GAMBIA
POP: 1,106,000

GUINEA-BISSAU
POP: 1,096,000

GUINEA
POP: 6,897,000

SIERRA LEONE
POP: 4,863,000

LIBERIA
POP: 3,136,000

IVORY COAST
POP: 14,891,000

DAKAR
Dakar, the capital of Senegal, is one of the main ports in West Africa. It lies on the Atlantic coast and has a fine natural harbour, large modern docks and ship repair facilities. It is the country's main industrial centre.

KEYBOX

Vegetable oil: The oil palm is widely grown throughout West Africa. Palm oil is used by people in the region and some is exported. Look for 🍶

Research centre: At a centre in Ibadan, Nigeria, new disease-resistant varieties of maize, cassava, and other crops have been bred. Look for 🔬

Film industry: Burkina has a large film industry, subsidized by the government, with studios in Ouagadougou and an annual film festival. Look for 🎥

Shipping registry: Many of the world's shipping countries register their ships in Liberia because of low taxes and lax employment rules. Look for ⚑

	Coffee		Forest products
	Cocoa		Fishing
	Ground nuts		Mining
	Cotton		Oil
	Timber		Industrial centre

TOURISM
Tourism in this region has expanded rapidly. In the Gambia, the number of visitors has risen from 300 in 1965 to over 100,000 a year in the 1990s. Most tourists stay along the Atlantic coast, but many also go on trips into the bush.

DEFORESTATION
The population of West Africa is growing rapidly. Vast areas of forest have been cut down, either for wood or to clear farmland to feed these extra people. This problem is particularly bad in the Ivory Coast, where little forest is left. Look for 🌲

Cocoa pod

Cocoa beans

Pulp

COCOA
The ancient Aztec people of Mexico were the first to make a drink called *chocolatl* from the seeds of the cacao tree – brought to West Africa by European colonizers. The region now produces over half the world's supply of cocoa beans. Look for 🍫

AFTER INDEPENDENCE
Since independence, some African countries have been plagued by many problems, such as unstable governments and foreign debts. Ivory Coast, however, is one of West Africa's most prosperous countries. Its last president built this cathedral when he had the capital moved to his family village at Yamoussoukro.

M N O P Q R S T

GROUNDNUTS
Groundnuts, or peanuts, grow on low, bushy plants and ripen in the ground – hence their name. They are grown throughout West Africa. Most of the crop is made into groundnut oil, which is used for cooking. Look for 🥜

MALI
POP: 11,124,000

BURKINA
POP: 10,628,000

MARKETS
Markets play a vital role, both for people living in towns and for farmers in the surrounding area. Here, women of the Dogon people in Mali display their wares at a market. In much of Africa women are responsible for growing crops, both for sale and as food for their families.

A deserted village at the bottom of dramatic rocky outcrops in Mali.

DESERT ON THE MARCH
The Sahara Desert is slowly spreading into the Sahel, helped by droughts, deforestation, and overuse of the land for farming. In 1973 the area was devastated by famine and 100,000 people died. Since then many schemes have been introduced to try and prevent the desert spreading any further.

A ceremonial figure. Many West African religious beliefs have spread to Central and South America.

A lone acacia tree in the desert area of Niger.

NIGER
POP: 9,386,000

NIGERIA
POP: 88,514,501

THE WODAABE
The Wodaabe are among the last nomads in Africa. They graze their herds in the borderlands between Niger and Nigeria. Every year they hold a festival at which the men compete for the title of "most beautiful and charming man." The judges are women. The men wear make-up which emphasizes their eyes and teeth.

GHANA
POP: 17,959,000

TOGO
POP: 4,264,000

BENIN
POP: 5,560,000

OIL IN NIGERIA
Nigeria's economy has been transformed by oil. Discovered in the 1950s, oil accounts for about 95 per cent of export earnings, and has paid for the development of new industries. Look for ⚓

RIVER NIGER
The Niger flows both north and south during its long journey to the Atlantic. Much of its course passes through the Sahel, where the persistent droughts have reduced water levels. In this region the river often evaporates completely during the dry season. As it reaches the wetter tropics in Nigeria, the amount of water increases, and farmers use large amounts of it for crops and livestock.

N

0 100 200 300 400 500 KM
0 50 100 150 200 250 300 MILES

**Map labels:**

ALGERIA
LIBYA
CHAD
CAMEROON

MALI
NIGER
NIGERIA
BURKINA
BENIN
GHANA
TOGO

ERG CHECH
AZAOUAD
ADRAR DES IFOGHAS
TALAK
TÉNÉRÉ
AÏR
PLATEAU DU MANGUENI
PLATEAU DU DJADO
SAHARA
SAHEL
COAST
Coast
JOS PLATEAU
Niger Delta
Bight of Benin

Timbuktu
Faguibine
L. Niangay
Gao
Mopti
Ouahigouya
Koudougou
OUAGADOUGOU
Bobo-Dioulasso
Fada-Ngourma
Dapaong
BENIN
Natitingou
Parakou
Kandi
Dolgutanga
Wa
Tamale
Kara
Sokodé
Abomey
GHANA
Sunyani
L. Volta
Atakpamé
Kumasi
Abengourou
Imbokro
Abidjan
Sekondi-Takoradi
Cape Coast
ACCRA
LOMÉ
PORTO-NOVO
Cotonou
Lagos
Ibadan
Abeokuta
Benin City
Onitsha
Owerri
Aba
Port Harcourt
Calabar
Enugu
Makurdi
Lokoja
Oshogbo
Ogbomosho
Ilorin
ABUJA
Minna
Kaduna
Zaria
Kano
Bauchi
Jos
Yola
Maiduguri
L. Chad
Nguru
Hadejia
Katsina
Gusau
Sokoto
Maradi
Kainji Res.
Niamey
Dosso
Tillabéry
Birni-n'Konni
Tahoua
Agadez
Zinder
Diffa
Nguigmi
Faguibine
Benue
Taraba
Gongola
Niger
Red Volta
Black Volta
White Volta
Oueme

Uranium
Manganese
Phosphates
Gum arabic
Iron
Tin
Gold
Rubber
Palm
Aluminium

CENTRAL AFRICA

MUCH OF THIS REGION IS COVERED in dense tropical rainforest, drained by the great Congo (Zaire) River and its tributaries. The climate is hot and humid. All the countries in the area have small populations – although some are increasing rapidly. French is the official language in many of the countries – a legacy from the days when they were French colonies. Zaire, the third largest country in Africa, has rich mineral deposits, but has declined economically since independence. In 1997 Zaire adopted the name Democratic Republic of the Congo. Chad has been torn apart by civil wars, and the Central African Republic has suffered from corrupt governments. Both countries are desperately poor. Equatorial Guinea has suffered so much from bad government that some 100,000 people have emigrated. Abundant minerals and oil have made Gabon the richest country in the region. Oil is also of major importance in the Congo, and both countries have relatively large city populations. Relatively prosperous, Cameroon is home to more than 200 different peoples.

HEALTH CLINIC

Traditional African medicine is still widely practised in this region, and western medicine has also been successfully used to cure or control many diseases. Medicines are often dispensed at village clinics like this one. But there are still major problems – many babies do not survive and there is a great shortage of doctors. In Chad, for example, over 40,000 people have to share one doctor.

A wooden figure from Cameroon, made to honour an ancestor.

LAKE CHAD

Lake Chad lies at the point where Chad, Cameroon, Niger and Nigeria meet. Due to a series of droughts, the rivers that feed the lake have shrunk and reduced it to a tenth of its former size. Fish from Lake Chad – such as this *tilapia* – are a major source of food for the people who live in the surrounding areas. But each year the fishermen must haul their boats further to reach the lake's receding water.

PYGMIES

Several groups of pygmies live scattered through the rainforests of Central Africa. They still survive mainly by hunting and gathering, but also trade with their neighbours and have learnt to speak their languages. Pygmies rarely reach a height of more than 125 cms (4 ft). This pygmy hut, made of banana fronds, is in a forest clearing in the Central African Republic.

Forested valleys and hills around Loubomo, Congo.

RELIGION

The main religion in this region is Christianity. But many Africans follow the traditional religions of their ancestors. They believe in many gods and spirits, who are often associated with natural forces or the elements, such as trees and thunder. This photo shows a ritual dance from Cameroon.

Dancer dressed as a leopard spirit

TRADITIONAL HOUSING

Traditional African houses vary from area to area, according to the building materials that are available locally. The walls of these houses in Cameroon are made of mud, and the roofs of straw. Building a house is one of the regular family tasks. As the family grows, so new houses are added to the group.

River flowing through dense rainforest in Cameroon.

CHAD
POP: 6,537,000

CENTRAL AFRICAN REPUBLIC
POP: 3,026,000

CAMEROON
POP: 13,651,000

L I B Y A

N I G E R

C H A D

S U D A N

C E N T R A L   A F R I C A N   R E P U B L I C

C A M E R O O N

NIGERIA

Faya

Mao

Bol
L. Chad

Bongor

N'DJAMENA
Kousseri

Guid

L. Lagdo

Garoua

Banyo

Bafoussam

Bamenda

Nkorsyumba

Ati

Biltine

Abéché

Am Timan

Mongo

Salamat

Sarh

Moundou
Lai
Erguig
Chari
Logone

Gore

Maroua

Ngaoundéré

Bouar

Bossangoa

Kaga-Bandoro

Ndélé

Birao

Bria

Bambari

Sibut

Bangassou

Obo

TIBESTI

Diamonds
Diamonds
Copper
Uranium
Chromium
Iron
Palm
Gold
Tin
Gold
Aluminium

ZAIRE POP: 45,142,000

DIAMONDS AND COBALT

Zaire is rich in a wide variety of minerals, particularly cobalt and diamonds used in industry. It is the world's largest producer of both. Cobalt is used in the manufacture of special steels – such as those required to withstand high temperatures – and for making magnets. Industrial diamonds are used for cutting and grinding hard surfaces. Look for ⬩

Alluvial diamond

ZAIRE'S LIFELINE

The River Congo (Zaire) sweeps in a huge arc through the region's rainforests on its route to the Atlantic Ocean. In Zaire the road and rail networks are in bad disrepair so the river acts as the country's principal lifeline. River boats transport people and goods, and act as markets, health clinics and bars.

EDUCATION

Since the 1960s, when many African countries achieved independence, improving education has been a major goal. But crowded classrooms, and lack of books and equipment are recurrent problems. Some countries, like Congo and Gabon, have compulsory education from six to sixteen, but few African children are able to continue beyond primary level. Here, children attend a village school in Cameroon.

Coconuts are one of the principal crops of the island state of São Tomé and Príncipe.

AGRICULTURE

The main crops in the region are cassava and yams, both root crops that grow in tropical and sub-tropical regions. Cassava is often grown in forest clearings, as shown here in Cameroon. It is turned into flour by pounding it to extract the sap. Yams are similar to potatoes, and can be mashed or boiled.

LIBREVILLE

Libreville, Gabon's capital, was founded in the mid-19th century as a settlement for freed French slaves. In fact, its name means "free town" in French. The city has expanded rapidly since the discovery of oil in the 1970s, and is now a major port.

TIMBER

Huge quantities of valuable hardwoods are cut down in the tropical rainforests of Gabon, and used for plywood and veneer. Eucalyptus trees require only seven years' growth before they can be cut down, and are increasingly grown for conversion into wood pulp. Most of the timber companies are foreign-owned, and take their profits out of the country.

Port-Gentil, Gabon's chief port, is on the Ogooué River.

EQUATORIAL GUINEA POP: 410,000

SAO TOME AND PRINCIPE POP: 136,000

GABON POP: 1,115,000

CONGO POP: 2,662,000

KEYBOX

Cotton: Chad is said to be the world's third poorest country. Attempts are being made to increase output of its main export, cotton. Look for 🌱

Oil: Cameroon, Gabon and Congo are all dependent on exporting oil. Zaire also has huge reserves which are, as yet, undeveloped. Look for 🛢

Bananas	Tobacco
Coffee	Forest products
Cocoa	Fishing port
Groundnuts	Mining
Vegetable oil	Industrial centre

CENTRAL EAST AFRICA

EAST AFRICA'S WEALTH lies in its land. Most people make their living from farming or cattle herding. Large areas covered with long grass, scrub and scattered trees, called savannah, provide grazing for domestic and wild animals alike. But some land, especially in Uganda and Zambia, cannot be used because of tsetse fly, which is dangerous to both animals and humans. Tea, coffee and tobacco are grown as cash crops throughout the area, especially in Kenya and Malawi. Uganda has great potential for farming, but for the last 20 years has been crippled by civil wars. Zambia, Rwanda, Burundi and Uganda all suffer from having no sea ports. Except in Kenya, industry everywhere is poorly developed. Only Zambia is rich in minerals. Burundi and Rwanda are densely populated, and Kenya now has the world's fastest growing population. After economic decline in the 1980s, Tanzania is slowly recovering.

THE SAMBURU
In Kenya's northern plateau region, tribes such as the Samburu continue to follow the traditional way of life of their ancestors. They live by grazing their herds of cattle, sheep and goats on the savannah. This *moran*, or warrior, wears numerous strings of beads, distinctive ivory earrings and always carries two spears and a knife.

PREDATORY FISH
Thirty years ago the Nile perch was introduced into Lake Victoria to increase fish production. Although the lake is vast, this fish now occupies every corner, and is killing off the original fish population. Look for

TRAINS
Countries with no coastline are very dependent on road and rail transport to link them to industrial centres and main ports. Although the African rail network is expanding, tracks are often poorly maintained. Here, people board a train at Kampala in Uganda.

POACHING
Africa's wildlife parks have helped preserve the animals, but poaching remains a major problem. Recently, in an attempt to save the elephants, a worldwide ban on the sale of ivory was imposed. But policing the parks is very costly; poachers are armed and dangerous. Here, in Tanzania, wardens are burning a poacher's hut.

AIDS
AIDS is a worldwide problem, but it is particularly widespread in Africa. Many people on the continent already suffer from diseases and malnutrition, which makes them more vulnerable to the illnesses associated with AIDS.

WILDLIFE RESERVES
Africa's great plains contain some of the world's most spectacular species of wildlife. All the countries in the region have set aside huge areas as national parks where animals are protected. Wildlife safaris attract thousands of tourists and provide countries with much needed foreign income. Look for

Tsetse fly carries a disease which can kill cattle and humans.

Copper bracelets

COPPER
There are huge desposits of copper in central Africa, centred around Ndola in Zambia. This region is often called the Copperbelt. Copper accounts for 90 per cent of Zambia's export earnings, but low prices in recent years and the discovery of cheaper substitutes have badly affected the industry. Supplies of copper are nearly used up, which could mean disaster for the Zambian economy. The Copperbelt now has improved transport links, such as the Tanzam Railway, which take the refined copper to various destinations. Look for

Vultures cluster in a lone tree on the Tanzanian grasslands.

KEYBOX

Coffee: *A valuable cash crop, coffee is grown in Uganda, Kenya, Tanzania and Rwanda. Kenya plans to triple production by the year 2000. Look for*

Market gardening: *Kenya has ideal conditions for growing vegetables and fruit, which are exported in large quantities, mainly to Europe. Look for*

Hydro-electric power: *The Kariba Dam on the Zambezi River, built by Zambia and Zimbabwe, supplies both nations with electricity. Look for*

Refugee camps: *Warfare in neighbouring countries has caused thousands of refugees to flee to temporary camps in the region. Look for*

⬇	Sugar cane	🌲	Forest products
🥥	Coconuts	🐬	Fishing
🌾	Tea	⛏	Mining
⚓	Cotton	🏭	Industrial centre
🍂	Tobacco		Wildlife reserves

AFRICAN VILLAGE
East African villages usually consist of a series of huts enclosed by thorn fences. This aerial photo shows a village belonging to the Masai tribe. A Masai man may have several wives. Each wife has her own huts, enclosed by a fence. The livestock is taken out to graze by day, and driven into the fenced enclosure at night.

N

| 0   100   200   300   400   500 | KM |
| 0   50   100   150   200   250   300 | MILES |

Z A

Solwezi

Col

West Lunga

Zambezi

Z A M B

Liuwa Plain

Kafue

A N G O L A

Kafue

KAFUE FLATS

Mongu

Zambezi

Choma

Sioma

Victoria Falls

Livingstone

NAMIBIA   BOTSWANA   ZIM

The Ruwenzori Mountains between Zaire and Uganda.

UGANDA
POP:19,278,000

RWANDA
POP: 7,500,000

BURUNDI
POP: 5,800,000

Southeast Sudan is administered by Kenya

SUDAN

ETHIOPIA

CHALBI DESERT

SOMALIA

Lokichokio

Mandera

Moyale

Kidepo

L. Turkana

Sibiloi

Arua

Albert Nile

Gulu

Pakwach

Moroto

Marsabit

Murchison Falls

Victoria Nile

L. Kyoga

Wajir

UGANDA

KENYA

Fort Portal

Kasese

L. Albert

Mbale

Kitale

Eldoret

Kakamega

Meru

Mt. Kenya

Tana

Garissa

Kampala

Jinja

Entebbe

Kisumu

Nakuru

Nyeri

Thika

Masaka

NAIROBI

Machakos

Queen Elizabeth

Mbarara

Bukoba

Musoma

Lake Victoria

Masai Mara

Kiunga Marine Reserve

Mgahinga

KIGALI

RWANDA

Butare

Mwanza

Serengeti

Amboseli

Tsavo

Galana

Malindi

BUJUMBURA

BURUNDI

Kagera

Ngorongoro

Kilimanjaro

Arusha

Moshi

L. Eyasi

L. Manyara

Mombasa

Kigoma

Shinyanga

Manyata

Singida

Tanga

Pemba I.

Tabora

TANZANIA

MASAI STEPPE

Pangani

Zanzibar

Zanzibar

DODOMA

Ruaha

Morogoro

Dar es Salaam

Sumbawanga

L. Rukwa

Iringa

Great Ruaha

Rufiji

Mafia I.

Tanzam Railway

Mikumi

Selous

Kilwa Masoko

Lindi

Mbala

Sumbu

Mbeya

Njombe

Songea

Mtwara

L. Mweru

Mwera Wantipa

Mansa

L. Bangweulu

Mpika

N. Luangwa

Mzuzu

L. Nyasa

Luangwa

MOZAMBIQUE

TANZANIA
POP: 31,698,000

Chingola

Mufulira

Kitwe

Ndola

Luanshya

Kasama

S. Luangwa

Lukusuzi

Nkhotakota

Lundazi

Kasungu

Chipata

MALAWI

Kabwe

Salima

LILONGWE

Copper

Zinc

Lead

LUSAKA

Kafue

Kariba Dam

L. Kariba

Lower Zambezi

Mwende

Zomba

Blantyre

Nsanje

MALAWI
POP: 11,552,000

ZAMBIA
POP: 9,623,000

Traditional East African bags, made from sisal, an important Kenyan and Tanzanian crop.

TEA CULTIVATION
East Africa's highlands are ideal for growing tea, especially in Kenya and Malawi. Most is grown on large plantations, often owned by foreign companies. In Kenya many Africans now grow tea on smallholdings. It is processed at co-operatively owned tea factories. Look for ✿

African dhows sailing off the coast of the island of Zanzibar.

KENYA
POP: 28,794,000

Cloves are one of Zanzibar's chief exports.

NAIROBI
Kenya's capital city now has more skyscrapers than many European cities. But so many people have come from the countryside to Nairobi to find work that the city's services, such as the water supply and drainage, have been strained to their limit.

N

Uganda: cattle grazed in dry lowlands

Semi-desert used by nomads for grazing cattle

Kampala

Nairobi

Nile

Poor soils, low rainfall, prone to tsetse fly

INDIAN OCEAN

Mombasa

Kilimanjaro

Dar esSalaam

Coastal lowlands: tropical crops

Highland areas: coffee and tea grown on fertile soils, with reliable rainfall

RIFT VALLEY
The Great Rift Valley stretches for over 9,600 km (6,000 miles) from Turkey to Mozambique, splitting into two arms in East Africa. In this region it contains lakes, swamps, ravines and volcanoes which in some cases reach heights of over 1,000 m (3,280 ft). On the well-watered, fertile slopes of the valley, crops like coffee and tea are grown. In the warm, damp coastlands, tropical crops such as sugar are cultivated.

SOUTHERN AFRICA

THE WEALTHIEST and most dominant country in this region is South Africa. Black African lands were gradually settled in the 19th century by Dutch colonists, their descendants – the Afrikaners – and the British. When vast deposits of gold and diamonds were discovered in the late 19th century, the country became rich. In 1948 the government introduced a system of "separate development", called apartheid, which separated people according to their colour, and gave political power to whites only. This policy led to isolation and sanctions from the rest of the world's nations, which only ended after the abolition of apartheid. The first democratic elections were held in 1994. After years of conflict, South Africa has now become a more integrated society. Most of the countries around South Africa rely on its industries for trade and work. After 30 years of unrest, Namibia has now won independence from South Africa. Mozambique and Angola are both struggling for survival after years of civil war. Zimbabwe has a relatively diverse economy, based on agriculture and its rich mineral resources.

The Ndebele people of the Transvaal often paint their houses in bright colours.

ANGOLA
POP: 11,440,000

The *ilimba* drum from Zimbabwe is made from the hard shell of a fruit called a gourd.

NAMIBIA
POP: 1,739,000

INDUSTRY
South Africa is the region's industrial leader. Johannesburg, the country's largest city, is seen here behind the huge mounds of earth excavated from the gold mines. Look for 🏭

URANIUM
Namibia is rich in copper, diamonds, tin and other minerals. Its mining industry accounts for 90 per cent of its export earnings. At Rössing, in the Namib Desert, uranium is extracted from a huge open-cast mine, and exported abroad. Look for ⚛

A lone thorn tree in the hot, sandy Namib Desert.

KEYBOX

Fishing: *Overfishing, by both foreign and local fleets, is a major threat to Namibia's once rich fishing grounds. Controls are in operation. Look for* 🐟

Oil: *Civil war in Angola has disrupted industry, but its oil reserves – the only major ones in the region – so far have been little affected. Look for* 🛢

Wildlife reserves: *Most of the region's countries have set aside large areas as wildlife parks, which are popular tourist attractions. Look for* 🦒

🐂	Cattle	🌱	Tea
🌾	Cereals	🚬	Tobacco
🍋	Citrus fruit	⛏	Mining
🍇	Wine	⚒	Coal
☕	Coffee	🏭	Industrial centre

BUSHMEN
Bushmen – or *San* – are one of the few groups of hunter-gatherers left in Africa. These tiny people can be traced far back into African history. Today some 1,000 bushmen still live in the harsh environment of the Kalahari Desert.

CAPE TOWN
Sprawled along the lower slopes of Table Mountain, and overlooking Table Bay, Cape Town has a spectacular setting. It is a busy port and the city where South Africa's parliament meets. Until the Suez Canal was opened, Cape Town lay on the main shipping route between Europe and Asia. Its harbour was often used by ships sheltering from the gales and stormy seas off the Cape of Good Hope.

Fresh maize

MAIZE
Maize is one of the main crops grown in this region. In the 1980s, the introduction of new kinds of seed and wider use of fertilizer greatly increased the production of maize. As most men work in industry, women cultivate the crops required to feed the family. Look for 🌾

DIAMONDS
Botswana was one of the world's poorest nations when it became independent. But since the discovery of diamonds in the Kalahari Desert, its economy has been transformed, and diamonds now make up 80 per cent of its exports. Look for ◆

THE SANGOMA
In most African tribal societies there is a person called a *sangoma* (sometimes known as a "witchdoctor"), who heals people, predicts the future and generally looks after the well-being of the people.

Acacias are a common sight on the savannah.

SUN CITY
The tourist resort of Sun City lies to the west of Johannesburg. Visitors from the region, and the rest of the world, are drawn to its luxury hotels, casino, game park and other attractions.

Poster for one of the political groups in Mozambique

MOZAMBIQUE
When Mozambique was abruptly given independence by Portugal in 1975, the country was unprepared for self-government. Continuous civil war for the last 20 years has left thousands dead, the economy in ruins, and many starving.

Lake Kariba is a huge, artificially constructed lake.

OSTRICH FARMS
Ostrich feathers were once in great demand as fashion accessories. Ostrich farmers grew rich, and were known as Feather Barons. Feathers are no longer fashionable, but ostriches are still farmed for their meat around Oudtshoorn, in South Africa.

"TOWNSHIPS"
The apartheid system meant that many black people were forced to live in "townships", often some distance from their work. The largest and best known is Soweto. People from Soweto – which means "South-Western Townships" – travel daily to work in Johannesburg.

Platinum is mined in northwestern South Africa

Platinum crystal

GOLD
Southern Africa has the richest deposits of valuable minerals in Africa. These miners are drilling for gold near Johannesburg, the area where gold was first discovered in 1886. This work is usually done by black Africans, but a mixed labour force will be more common in future. Gold from South Africa is often sold abroad in the form of coins called *Krugerrands*. Look for ●

LESOTHO'S WATER PROJECT
In contrast with surrounding areas, Lesotho's Maluti Mountains have plenty of water. A huge project is underway building dams and tunnels to transfer water and electricity to neighbouring South Africa.

Matsoku Dam
Maluti Mts.
Mashai Dam
Lengthy tunnels transfer water between dams
Katse Dam
Mohale Dam
SOUTH AFRICA
LESOTHO
Tsoelike Dam
Ntoahae Dam
Orange R.

ZIMBABWE
POP: 11,845,000

BOTSWANA
POP: 1,532,000

MOZAMBIQUE
POP: 15,300,000

SWAZILAND
POP: 882,000

LESOTHO
POP: 2,025,000

SOUTH AFRICA
POP: 43,715,000

99

THE INDIAN OCEAN

THE INDIAN OCEAN is the smallest of the world's oceans, but some 5,000 islands – many of them surrounded by coral reefs – are scattered across its area. Beneath its surface three great mountain ranges converge towards the ocean's centre – an area of strong seismic and volcanic activity. The ocean reaches its greatest depth – 7,440 m (24,400 ft) – in the Java Trench. Over 1,000 million people – about a fifth of the world's population – live in the countries around the Indian Ocean, representing an immense range of cultures and religions. Heavy monsoon rain and tropical storms cause flooding along the ocean's northern coasts. The world's largest oil-fields are located around the Persian Gulf.

Sugar cane

SUGAR

Sugar was first brought to Mauritius by the Dutch in the 1600s. Ninety per cent of the island's arable farmland is covered by sugar plantations. But today sugar has been replaced in importance by textiles, which now account for nearly half the island's exports. Look for ↓

KARACHI

In the mid-19th century a railway line was built along the Indus valley to Karachi, and it developed into a large port and industrial city. When Pakistan was created an independent nation in 1947, Karachi became the country's capital. It has now been replaced by the new city of Islamabad in the north.

FISHING

Large-scale fishing is far less developed in the Indian Ocean than in either the Atlantic or Pacific. Fishing is difficult because there are relatively few areas of shallow sea. Small-scale fishing, however, provides a valuable source of food. Many fishermen, like these Sri Lankans, use basic, often inefficient methods. Tuna is the most important catch in the area. Look for ↗

ISLANDS

The islands of the Indian Ocean include enormous ones like Madagascar, coral atolls like the Maldives, and volcanic islands like Réunion. All are threatened by rising sea levels which reduce the area of land available. Coral reefs are being eroded, leaving islands increasingly exposed to ocean tides and flooding.

MONSOON

Farmers in the lands around the Indian Ocean are wholly dependent on the coming of the monsoon rains. In May or June, the western arm of the monsoon sweeps in from the Arabian Sea, bringing torrential downpours which travel north through India. At the same time, the monsoon's eastern arm curves out of the Bay of Bengal, driving north as far as the Himalayan foothills. About 85 per cent of India's annual rainfall occurs during the monsoon periods.

Mangroves grow along many of the Indian Ocean's coasts.

COMOROS
POP: 676,000

The loggerhead turtle is one of the Indian Ocean's many endangered species.

TOURISM

The Indian Ocean islands are great tourist attractions. They welcome the money this brings, but the sheer number of visitors threatens to destroy the islands' environment. Look for ↖

Hotel complex on an island in Mauritius

Once thought extinct, the coelacanth has been found, alive and well, off southeast Africa.

MALDIVES
POP: 255,000

### Map labels

Port Said
Suez Canal
Suez
Nile
Kuwait City
Basra
Tigris
Euphrates
Manama
Persian Gulf
Râs al Ḥadd
Chāh Bahār
Gulf of Oman
Maṣīrah
ARABIA
Ṣalālah
Djibouti
Aden
Gulf of Aden
Socotra (to Yemen)
C. Xaafuun
RED SEA
Mombasa
Dar es Salaam
AFRICA
Mahajanga
MADAGASCAR
Antananarivo
C. Babaomby (to France)
MAYOTTE
Antsiranana
Grande Comore
MORONI
COMOROS
Aldabra Is. (to Seychelles)
SEYCHELLES
VICTORIA
Amirante Is. (to Seychelles)
Mascarene Plateau
Somali Basin
Carlsberg Ridge
ARABIAN SEA
Karachi
Indus
ASIA
HIMALAYAS
Ganges
Calcutta
Bombay
Vishakhapatnam
Madras
Cochin
C. Comorin
Laccadive Is. (to India)
MALE
MALDIVES
Maldive Ridge
BRITISH INDIAN OCEAN TERRITORY (to UK)
Diego Garcia
Sri Lanka
Trincomalee
Colombo
Dondra Head
Bay of Bengal
Andaman Is. (to India)
Nicobar Is. (to India)
ANDAMAN SEA
Rangoon
Irrawaddy
Mekong
Gulf of Thailand
George Town
Melaka
Strait of Malacca
Singapore
SOUTH CHINA SEA
Sumatra
Borneo
Java
JAVA SEA
Java Trench
COCOS IS. (to Australia)
CHRISTMAS I. (to Australia)
ASHMORE & CARTIER IS. (to Australia)
INDIAN
East Indian Ridge

STRAIT OF MALACCA

Since ancient times ships trading between the Indian and Pacific Oceans have passed through the shallow waters of the Strait of Malacca. This is the main route through the Indonesian archipelago. Ports like Melaka – seen here – have prospered from this trade.

DHOW

The Arab dhow has been one of the principal sailing boats in the Indian Ocean for over 4,000 years. Arabs used these sturdy craft on the trade routes from the Persian Gulf to China. Their cargoes included spices, cowrie shells, dates and slaves. Their large lateen, or triangular, sails make them easy to manoeuvre.

Mizzen mast

Furled lateen sail

Main mast

POLLUTION

The Indian Ocean is particularly at risk from oil pollution from tankers carrying oil from the Persian Gulf. The Persian Gulf itself is severely polluted by oil spills from ships, rigs and refineries. During the Gulf War of 1991, huge quantities of oil were released into the Gulf waters, causing appalling damage. Look for ⚓

SANCTUARY

Many species of whale breed in the Indian Ocean. In 1979 most of the Ocean was designated a whale sanctuary to protect them. The dugong – a marine mammal – is also threatened with extinction. Although it lives for up to 70 years, it matures late and produces few young in its lifetime. It is vegetarian, feeding exclusively on sea grasses.

Dugong

MADAGASCAR

This huge island off Africa's east coast is desperately poor. Most Madagascans make their living from farming, cattle herding or logging. In the last 25 years the population has doubled and the constant need for land and fuel has massively reduced the once extensive forests. The staple food is rice, the main exports are coffee and vanilla.

Vanilla pod

Vanilla seed

NAVAL BASES

The Indian Ocean is important to the major world powers as a link between the Atlantic and Pacific Oceans, and because it is the main route for tankers bringing oil from the Persian Gulf. The USA has a base on Diego Garcia. The French have a naval base on the island of Réunion. Look for ▦

KEYBOX

Shellfishing: An area near Karachi has been developed as a major shrimp nursery. It employs thousands of local workers. Look for 🦐

Industrial centre: Due to low labour costs and tax incentives, new industries, such as textiles, have been developed in Mauritius. Look for ⚒

Mining: Tin is dredged off the west coast of Thailand and east coast of Sumatra. Dredging can damage the seabed and mangroves. Look for ◔

Sugar cane	⚓	Gas
Coconuts	🌴	Tourism
Fishing	🐟	Underwater wrecks
Fishing port	⚓	Whales
Oil	⛴	Military bases

MILES / KM scale: 0 250 500 750 1000 / 0 500 1000 1500 2000KM

SEYCHELLES
POP: 75,000

MAURITIUS
POP: 1,140,000

MADAGASCAR
POP: 13,309,XXX

Huge ice floes drift north from Antarctica, becoming a major hazard to shipping.

## Map labels

AUSTRALIA

Fremantle, Cockburn Sound

INDIAN OCEAN

West Australia Basin

North West C.

C. Leeuwin

Broken Ridge

Southeast Indian Ridge

Ninety East Ridge

South Indian Basin

Mid-Indian Ridge

Amsterdam I. (to France)
St. Paul I. (to France)
Kerguelen Plateau
Kerguelen Is. (to France)
Heard I. Macdonald Is. (to Australia)

Crozet Basin
Crozet Is. (to France)
Prince Edward Is. (to South Africa)

ANTARCTICA

Atlantic-Indian Basin

Madagascar Basin
Madagascar Ridge

ANTANANARIVO
Fianarantsoa
Fianarantsoa
Tolian
Toliara

C. Vohimena

PORT LOUIS
MAURITIUS
Mascarenes
REUNION (to France)
Le Port

Limpopo
Beira
Durban
Cape Town
Simon's Town
C. of Good Hope

Huge baobab trees on the island of Madagascar.

Cedar of Lebanon
Cedrus libani
Height: 40 m (130 ft)

Common hamster
Cricetus cricetus
Length: 30 cm (12 in)

Waxwing
Bombycilla garrulus
Length: 18 cm (8 in)

NORTH AND WEST ASIA

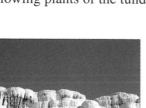

NORTH AND WEST ASIA contains some of the world's most inhospitable environments. In the south, the Arabian Peninsula is almost entirely a baking hot desert, where no plants can grow. To the north, a belt of rugged, snow-capped mountains and high plateaux cross the continent. The climate becomes drier and more extreme towards the centre of the continent. Dry hot summers contrast with bitterly cold winters. Cold deserts give way to treeless plains known as steppe, then to huge marshes, and to the world's largest needleleaf forest. In the extreme north, both land and sea are frozen for most of the year. Only in summer do the top layers of soil thaw briefly allowing plants of the tundra, such as moss and lichen, to cover the land.

■ **COLD FOREST**
Strong but flexible trunks and a tent-like shape help needleleaf trees to withstand the great weight of snow that covers them throughout the long winter.

Arabian oryx
Oryx leucoryx
Height: 1.2 m (4 ft)

HOT BATHS
These strange white terraces formed in the south-west of Asia in much the same way that a kettle "furs". Under-ground water heated by volcanic activity dissolves minerals in rocks. These are deposited when the water reaches the surface and cools.

■ **DROUGHT-TOLERANT TREES**
Plants growing near the Black Sea minimize water-loss during the long hot summers. Most have wax-covered leaves through which little water can escape.

Blue turquoise, a semi-precious stone mainly found in cold areas of north Asia.

■ **REGENERATING FOREST**
Juniper trees, unlike many plants, are able to withstand the acid soils of needleleaf forests. Here junipers cover the floor of a dense pine forest.

Baikal seal
Phoca sibirica
Length: 1.5 m (5 ft)
Only found in Lake Baikal

The fossilized head of *Gallimimus*, an ostrich-like dinosaur that once lived in Asia.

■ **VOLCANO**
There are more than 30 active volcanoes on the Kamchatka peninsula, on the Pacific Ocean's "Ring of Fire". Volcanic activity is due to the deep under-ground movements of the Eurasian plate.

■ **FROZEN RIVER**
The River Lena rises near Lake Baikal, the world's deepest and oldest freshwater lake. Like other Siberian rivers, it flows into the Arctic Ocean and is frozen over for eight or nine months of the year.

■ **SINAI'S ROCK "MUSHROOMS"**
In deserts, sand particles whipped along by high-speed winds create natural sculptures. Rock at the base of the "mushroom" has been more heavily eroded than rock above, leading to these unusual landforms.

Darkling beetle
Sternodes species
Length: 2 cm (1 in)

■ **HOT DESERTS**
The Arabian desert is one of the hottest and driest places in the world. Temperatures frequently reach 45°C (120°F), and very little rain falls.

□ **COLD WINTER DESERT**
Large parts of Central Asia are covered in deserts that are hot in summer, but very cold in winter. A river has been naturally dammed to form this lake, which is unusual in this dry region.

CROSS-SECTION THROUGH NORTH AND WEST ASIA

Arctic Ocean
Kara Sea
Ural Mts
Kirghiz Steppe
Aral Sea
Kara Kum
Iranian Plateau
Arabian Sea

1,500 (4,921)
0 Sea level
-3,000 (9,843)
Metres (feet)

A   *Length: 6,400 km (4,000 miles)*   B

Reindeer
Rangifer tarandus
Body length: 2.2 m (7 ft)

Pallas's cat
Felis manul
Length: 65 cm (26 in)

Grey wolf
Canis lupus
Length: 1.4 m (5 ft)

Siberian iris
Iris sibirica
Height: 1.2 m (4 ft)

The head of a fossilized *Benthosuchus*, which lived in Asia over 200 million years ago.

■ BROADLEAF DECIDUOUS FOREST

Broadleaf trees, such as oak, have larger wider leaves than needleleaf trees, such as pine. Broadleaf, or deciduous, trees shed all their leaves at once in the autumn; needleleaf, or evergreen, trees shed and replace their leaves all through the year.

ARCTIC OCEAN
North Pole
Lomonsov Ridge
Canada Basin
New Siberian Is.
EAST SIBERIAN SEA
BERING SEA
Limit of permanent ice sheet
Greenland
GREENLAND SEA
Franz Josef Land
Svalbard
Severnaya Zemlya
TAYMYR PENINSULA
LAPTEV SEA
Lena Delta
VERKHOYANSK RANGE
Probable plate margin
2959m
SEA OF OKHOTSK
Sakhalin
NORTH AMERICAN PLATE
EURASIAN PLATE
STANOVOY RANGE
2999m
Amur

NORWEGIAN SEA
BARENTS SEA
KARA SEA
Novaya Zemlya
1701m
CENTRAL SIBERIAN PLATEAU
SIBERIA
1894m
WEST SIBERIAN PLAIN
Ob
Yenisey
Angara
L. Baikal
Kerulen
Lena

ATLANTIC OCEAN
NORTH SEA
BALTIC SEA
EUROPE
URAL MOUNTAINS
Irtysh
4506m
ALTAI MTS.
DZUNGARIA
L. Zaysan
L. Alakol
Ili
TIEN SHAN
Pobeda Peak
7439m

KIRGHIZ STEPPE
Syr Darya
L. Balkhash
ARAL SEA
KYZYL KUM
Amu Darya
Lenin Peak 7134m
Communism Peak 7495m
7690m
HIMALAYAS
ASIA
EURASIAN PLATE
INDO-AUSTRALIAN PLATE
Tropic of Cancer

BLACK SEA
CAUCASUS MTS.
CASPIAN SEA
Karagiya Depression 132m
KARA KUM
HINDU KUSH
ANATOLIA
3734m
TAURUS MTS.
Cyprus
Euphrates
Tigris
ZAGROS MOUNTAINS
4548m
DASH-E-KAVIR
IRANIAN PLATEAU
DASHT-E-LUT
Indus
Ganges
INDIAN SUBCONTINENT
Bay of Bengal

MEDITERRANEAN SEA
EURASIAN PLATE
IRANIAN PLATE
AFRICAN PLATE
AFRICAN PLATE
SYRIAN DESERT
Dead Sea
SINAI DESERT
ARABIAN PLATE
Persian Gulf
Probable plate margin
IRANIAN PLATE
INDO-AUSTRALIAN PLATE
Gulf of Oman

RED SEA
ARABIAN PLATE
AFRICAN PLATE
AN NAFUD
ARABIAN PENINSULA
RUB' AL KHALI
ARABIAN SEA
Arabian Basin
Chagos-Laccadive Plateau
Sri Lanka

AFRICA
Gulf of Aden
Socotra
Ceylon Plain
Equator
INDIAN OCEAN

TURKEY AND CYPRUS

SITUATED PARTLY IN EUROPE and partly in Asia, Turkey is also balanced between modern Europe and its Islamic past. For 600 years, the Ottoman Turks ruled over a great empire covering a quarter of Europe, but by the early 20th century their empire had disappeared. In the 1920s, Mustapha Kemal (Atatürk) forcibly modernized Turkish society. Today, Turkey is becoming increasingly industrialized; textile and food-processing industries dominate the economy. In the central plateau, however, farmers and herders live as they have done for centuries, adapting their lives to the harsh environment. To the north, the Black Sea is rich in fish, and the fertile areas around its shores are well-suited to farming. The beautiful western and southern coasts are strewn with the remains of ancient Greek sites, and attract 1.5 million tourists to Turkey every year.

ISTANBUL
Istanbul is divided in two by a strait of water called the Bosporus. One part of the city is in Europe, the other in Asia. Its buildings are also a mix of East and West: grand mosques, graceful minarets and exotic bazaars rub shoulders with modern shops, offices and restaurants.

TURKEY
POP: 63,204,000

The harbour and castle of St. Peter at Bodrum.

STREET TRADERS
Large numbers of people from the countryside go to Turkey's cities to try to make a living. Many of them sell goods, food or drink on the streets or from makeshift market stalls. Others work as shoe-shiners, carrying their equipment in highly decorated brass cases.

A CLASSICAL LEGACY
The temple of Athena in Priene is one of Turkey's many ancient treasures. The Aegean coast was colonized by the ancient Greeks as early as 700 BC. Many people go to Turkey to visit the dramatic remains of Greek cities and temples. Look for ⁂

KEYBOX

Tobacco: Turkey is a major producer. Dark, Turkish tobacco is grown around the Black Sea and Aegean coasts. Look for ➤

Tourism: Coastal resorts are developing rapidly. Airports cater for growing numbers of visitors from northern Europe. Look for ✈

Dams: Ambitious dam-building programmes, especially in the south-east, are being used for hydro-electric power and for watering farmland. Look for ▦

Cereals		Cotton
Sugar beet		Fishing
Citrus fruit		Carpet-weaving
Wine		Industrial centre
Vegetable oil		Archaeological site

MOSQUE
Blue Mosque, Istanbul

Modern Turkey does not have a state religion. It was once an Islamic country, but earlier this century reforms limited the powers of the clerics and introduced civil law. Recently, however, there has been an Islamic revival and modern Turks are going back to many customs from their rich Islamic past.

ANKARA
Ankara has been the capital of Turkey since 1923. It is a planned, modern city with boulevards, parks and many high-rise flats. Until recently, the city suffered from terrible pollution, caused by people burning brown coal, or lignite, for heating. Now, clean natural gas is piped into the city from the Russian Federation.

Dried apricot
Almond
Hazelnut
Fig
Peach

This strange landscape is in Cappadocia, central Turkey.

AGRICULTURE
Turkey has a varied landscape and climate. This means that many different types of crop can be grown there and the Turks are able to produce all their own food. Cereals, sugar beet, grapes, nuts, cotton and tobacco are all major exports. Hazelnuts are grown along the shores of the Black Sea. Figs, peaches, olives and grapes are grown along the Mediterranean coast and in the coastal lowlands. Cereals are cultivated on the central plateau. Farms are still relatively small and only gradually being modernized, but despite this productivity is high.

Valuable Black Sea oyster beds are being destroyed by these whelks.

Veined rapa whelk

TURKISH FOOD

Typical Turkish food consists of fresh fruit, vegetables, meat and fish, flavoured with spices such as cinnamon and cumin. Lamb is the most common meat. It is often grilled on a skewer to make a kebab, or minced and made into spiced meatballs, served with rice or cracked wheat (*burgul*). Goat's yoghurt is eaten everywhere, often mixed with cucumber, garlic or mint to make a refreshing side-dish.

Burgul wheat
Tomato
Olive
Bay leaf
Yoghurt with cucumber
Lamb shish kebab

KILIMS

Knotted-pile carpets, called *kilims*, were first made many centuries ago by the Turks' nomadic ancestors. Each region of Turkey produces carpets with slightly different patterns and colours, although today chemical dyes are often used instead of the traditional vegetable colourings. Look for

Anchovies are caught in the Black Sea.

A 10th-century church on Lake Van in eastern Turkey.

RURAL LIFE

Life in the high plateaux of central Turkey is very hard. The winters are severe, and the landscape is desolate. Most people live as nomadic herders or small-scale farmers. Many people leave these areas to live in the overcrowded cities, or go to the rich countries of northern Europe as "guest workers".

Glazed tiles made in Iznik decorate many Turkish mosques.

Turkish coffee pot

Turkish delight

In 1983 the north of the island proclaimed itself the Turkish Republic of Northern Cyprus. It is only recognized by Turkey.

CYPRUS
POP: 742,000

Mohair comes from the Angora goat, native to central Turkey.

CYPRUS

Cyprus is the largest island in the east Mediterranean. Cypriots are a mixture of Greek and Turkish speakers. After independence in 1959, conflict between the two communities resulted in the United Nations sending a peace-keeping force, which still remains. Despite their presence, there was a Turkish invasion in 1974. Since then the island has been split into two parts.

WOMEN WORKERS

Although Turkish women are equal by law, traditions of male authority still persist, especially in the countryside. It is common to see old women doing back-breaking work in the fields, while their husbands look on. On the other hand, some Turkish women have succeeded in powerful jobs as politicians, judges, or bank directors.

COFFEE

Turkey, like other Middle Eastern countries, has a long tradition of coffee drinking. Turkish coffee is made by pounding the beans to a powder and then boiling this with sugar to make a strong, dark brew. Coffee houses are favourite meeting places, where people also smoke pipes, play cards and chat.

| | 50 | 100 | 150 | 200 | 250 | KM |
| 0 | 50 | | 100 | | 150 | MILES |

THE NEAR EAST

CAUGHT BETWEEN the two worlds of Europe and Asia, the Near East is bordered on the west by the fertile coasts of the Mediterranean Sea, and on the east by the arid deserts of Arabia. Some of the world's earliest civilizations were born here, while the history of all three of the world's great religions – Judaism, Christianity and Islam – is closely bound up with the region. Imperial conquerors and Christian and Muslim crusaders battled fiercely over this territory, and by the 17th century much of the region was part of the Turkish Ottoman empire. In 1918, the Near East came under the control of Britain and France; a dangerous mixture of religions and passionate nationalism plunged the area into conflict. Today, Lebanon is just beginning to emerge from a fierce civil war between Christians and Muslims. Israel, which became a Jewish state in 1948, has been involved in numerous wars with its neighbours and there is considerable unrest among its Palestinian population. Many Palestinian refugees, who have left Israel, are living in camps in Jordan and Lebanon. Despite these problems, the Near East continues to survive economically. Israel is highly industrialized and a world leader in advanced farming techniques. Syria has its own reserves of oil, and is gradually becoming more industrialized.

Carnation
Rose
Grapefruit
Orange
Lemon
Lime

FARMING
Although about half of Israel is desert, it is self-sufficient in most food, and actually exports agricultural produce, especially citrus fruits and flowers. Israeli farming uses advanced irrigation techniques and is highly mechanized. Many farms are run as *kibbutzim*; the land is owned by members, who share work and profits. Look for 🌾

JERUSALEM THE GOLDEN
The historic city of Jerusalem is held sacred by three major religions: Judaism, Christianity and Islam. Throughout its history, it has been the object of pilgrimage and religious crusades. For Jews, the Wailing Wall, seen here, is the most sacred site, while the Dome of the Rock is sacred to Muslims, reflecting divisions within Israel.

Skull-cap, yarmulke

JUDAISM
Judaism is one of the oldest religions in the world. Jews believe in one God, and the most devout (Orthodox) follow codes of behaviour based on laws contained in their holy book, the *Torah.* This is the first part of Old Testament and is written in Hebrew. Modern Hebrew is the language of Israel.

The Torah

Prayer shawl

UZI GUNS
Israel is a major arms producer, developing weapons for her own army, such as this Uzi gun, as well as medium-range missiles to deter Arab enemies. Military service in the Israel Defence Force (IDF) is compulsory for all Israeli citizens. Men must serve three years, unmarried women two years.

Lake Tiberias, known in the Bible as the Sea of Galilee.

WATER WARS
Throughout this region, water is in very short supply. Where water resources are shared (for example, Israel and Jordan share the Jordan River), disputes can occur. Israel leads the way in irrigation techniques. Fields are watered by drip irrigation – holes in pipes dispense exactly the right amount of water required, avoiding wastage.

DEAD SEA MUD
The Dead Sea, 400 m (1,300 ft) below sea level, is an enclosed salt lake. Salt levels are six times higher than in other seas, so no fish live in these waters. The Dead Sea is rich in minerals, some of which have medical properties.

Dead Sea mud is used as a skin conditioner, and cure for arthritis

Soap made from Dead Sea mud

KEYBOX

Cotton: Syria's most profitable cash crop is cotton. The area of land devoted to cotton has been expanded in recent years. Look for 🌿

Tourism: People come to this region from all over the world to visit archaeological sites, ancient cities, and holy places. Look for 📷

Refugee camps: Palestinian refugees have fled from Israel to Jordan and Lebanon. Many fled to Jordan from Kuwait after the 1991 Gulf War. Look for ⛺

🌾 Cereals	⛏ Mining
🍠 Sugar beet	⚒ Oil
🌿 Citrus fruit	🏭 Industrial centre
🫙 Vegetable oil	⚓ Tourism
🪈 Tobacco	🌾 Irrigated agriculture

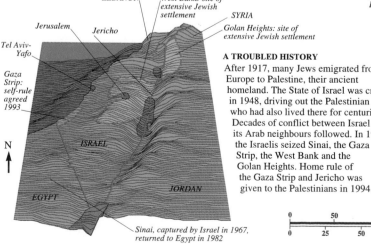

LEBANON
West Bank: site of extensive Jewish settlement
Jerusalem
Jericho
SYRIA
Golan Heights: site of extensive Jewish settlement
Tel Aviv-Yafo
Gaza Strip: self-rule agreed 1993
ISRAEL
JORDAN
EGYPT
N ↑
Sinai, captured by Israel in 1967, returned to Egypt in 1982

A TROUBLED HISTORY
After 1917, many Jews emigrated from Europe to Palestine, their ancient homeland. The State of Israel was created in 1948, driving out the Palestinian Arabs who had also lived there for centuries. Decades of conflict between Israel and its Arab neighbours followed. In 1967 the Israelis seized Sinai, the Gaza Strip, the West Bank and the Golan Heights. Home rule of the Gaza Strip and Jericho was given to the Palestinians in 1994.

SIN

Gulf of Suez

N

0	50	100	150	
KM
0	25	50	75	100
MILES

Krak des Chevaliers, in Syria, is a 12th-century crusader castle.

SYRIA
POP: 14,171,000

WAR-TORN LEBANON
Lebanon became independent in 1944. Christians, about 40 per cent of the population, held most of the wealth and power. The Muslim majority felt discriminated against. This grievance exploded into a bitter civil war in 1975. Agreements have now created a fragile peace.

The pomegranate fruit is grown in Israel.

LEBANON
POP: 3,082,000

ISRAEL
POP: 5,971,000

Golan Heights: Occupied by Israel

West Bank and Gaza Strip: Occupied by Israel under Palestinian administration

Hubble bubble tobacco pipe

HUBBLE BUBBLE
Throughout the Arab world, men enjoy spending their leisure hours in cafés, drinking tea or coffee, playing cards or backgammon, and smoking. Often they smoke pipes, called hubble bubbles, which draw the smoke into the mouth through water and a long tube. Tobacco is grown in Syria, and exported to other countries in the region. Look for

The Arabian *tibia*, one of the rich variety of shells found in the Red Sea.

DAMASCUS SOUK
Damascus, the capital of Syria, is one of the oldest cities in the world – its history goes back 4,000 years. At its centre, next to the main mosque, is a typical Middle Eastern *souk* (bazaar). Small winding covered streets are lined with stalls selling a wide range of produce. Behind the stalls are the workshops where craftsmen make their wares.

The hills and plateaux of Israel's Negev Desert.

JORDAN
POP: 4,234,000

ROSE-RED CITY
Petra, founded in about 400 BC, was the capital city of the Nabateans, a people from the Arabian peninsula who grew wealthy on the profits of the Arabian incense and spice trade. The city is located deep in a canyon, and its buildings are carved out of the soft pink limestone of the canyon walls. Large numbers of visitors come to Jordan to see ancient sites such as Petra and to enjoy the resorts and scuba-diving in the Red Sea.

BEDOUIN
The Bedouin are nomadic herders who live in dry regions of the Near East and Africa. They keep cattle, sheep and goats, which provide them with milk and meat and can be sold for food such as wheat, dates and coffee. The Bedouin move from place to place, following the wet and dry seasons, in search of grazing for their animals.

Wadi Rum in Jordan, where the desert meets sandstone hills.

THE MIDDLE EAST

THE WORLD'S first cities grew up about 5,500 years ago in the area between the Tigris and Euphrates rivers. The land in this region is dry, but these early people created ingenious irrigation techniques to direct the river water on to their fields of crops. In AD 570, the Prophet Mohammed, founder of the Islamic religion, was born in Mecca, in modern-day Saudi Arabia. Islam soon spread throughout the Middle East, where it is now the dominant religion, and into Africa. In recent years, the discovery of oil has brought great wealth to the countries around the Persian Gulf, and with it, rapid industrial and social change. Both Iran and Iraq earn huge revenues from oil, but they have been troubled by dictatorship and political unrest, as well as by a ten-year war. In 1991, the region was devastated by the Gulf War, which brought UN troops to the Middle East to fight against Iraq.

MIDDLE EASTERN FOOD

Pistachio nuts
Aduki beans
Green lentils
Red lentils
Dates
Chickpeas

Farming in the Arabian peninsula has been transformed by new irrigation methods. Saudi Arabia now exports wheat; the United Arab Emirates vegetables. Pulses such as lentils and chickpeas are the main food crops elsewhere.

BAGHDAD
Baghdad, Iraq's capital since 1918, has grown dramatically over the last 20 years, but was badly damaged during the Gulf War. The city has been rebuilt. Massive monuments to President Hussein once again adorn its streets.

For centuries Marsh Arabs have lived in the swampy delta of the Tigris and Euphrates.

ARAB DRESS
Kufiyah, *male headdress*
Khimar, *veil worn by women*

In summer, when temperatures in the Gulf reach 50° C (122° F), layers of loose robes and a head-dress are worn to make the heat bearable.

Hirz, *amulet charm case*
Aqaal, *used to secure headdress*

ISLAM
Mecca is Islam's holiest place and a centre of pilgrimage. Muslims believe in one God, *Allah*. They worship in mosques, and should pray five times a day, give alms, and fast for the month-long period of *Ramadan*.

MAKING THE DESERT BLOOM
Water is scarce all over this region, and is carefully managed. More than 60 per cent of the world's desalination plants are in the Arabian peninsula. They are used to extract the salt from sea water to make it drinkable. Look for ◊

Camels, known as "ships of the desert", can go for days without water, and are used to carry loads.

KEYBOX

Archaeological sites: *The ancient cities of the Middle East, such as Ur, date back to 3,500 BC. They are the oldest cities in the world. Look for* ▲

Dams: *A series of dams and barrages have been built along the Tigris and Euphrates to provide water for the dry plains of southern Iraq. Look for* ▥

Industrial centre: *Saudi Arabia's economy has been dominated by oil. It is seeking to widen its range of industries. Look for* 🏭

Symbol		Symbol	
🌾	Cereals	🛢	Oil
🌴	Dates	◊	Gas
🌾	Rice		Carpet-weaving
	Fishing	◊	Desalination plants

YEMEN
Unlike the rest of the Arabian peninsula, Yemen has enough rainfall to water its crops. Most crops are grown on mountain terraces in the highlands. The country is self-sufficient in barley, lentils, sorghum, maize and coffee. Look for ✿

The minaret of the Great Mosque at Sāmarrā', Iraq.

Yemen's capital, San'ā, dates back to the 7th century.

SYRIA
IRAQ POP: 21,882,000
JORDAN
EGYPT
An Nabk
Whea
Annah
Al Hadithah
Wādī Hawran
Wādī al Ghada
'Ar 'ar
Sakākah
Al Jawf
Gulf of Aqaba
Tabūk
AN NAFUD
Wheat
Wheat
Ha'il
SAUDI ARABIA POP: 18,171,000
Wheat
Wheat
NEJD
Buraydah
Yanbu al Bahr
Medina
Wheat
RED SEA
Mecca
Jedda
Ta' if
SAU
ARA
Al Buḥah
Wheat
ASIR
Khaybar
Barley
Abhā
Khamīs Mushayt
RUB
Najrān
Iīzān
Sa'dah
RAMLAT AS
Kamarān I.
Barley
Barley
Hajjah
Al Mahwit
Ma'rib
Hodeida
SAN'Ā
YE
Millet
HAD
Dhamār
Millet
Ibb
Ataq
Ta'izz
Al Bayda
Habban
Al Mukhā
Laḥij
Zinjibar
Aden
Bab el Mandeb

YEMEN POP: 14,361,000

KURDS

There are 25 million Kurds. They are one of the largest groups of stateless people in the world. Their homeland, Kurdistan, straddles three countries: Turkey, Iraq and Iran. Many Kurds were forced to leave this area by the Gulf War, and now live in refugee camps on the Iranian and Iraqi borders with Turkey.

Shahyad Monument

TEHRAN

The last Shah (king) of Iran used his great wealth to modernize the country by building dams, power stations, factories and roads. He ruled as a dictator, and the cities of Iran were filled with monuments in his name. Islamic fundamentalists overthrew the Shah in 1979.

TEXTILES

Iran is famous for its superb, hand-made carpets. They are produced by a combination of weaving and knotting the wool, often using patterns which are several hundred years old. They are coloured with vegetable dyes. Look for 🧶

Finely embroidered textiles, such as this saddlebag, are typically Kurdish.

The Zagros Mountains lie in the southwest of Iran.

OIL

The discovery of oil in the Persian Gulf region has brought enormous wealth to the Middle East. The region now supplies 30 per cent of the world's oil and Saudi Arabia is the world's largest single exporter. Pipelines cross the desert and huge tankers pick up oil from the coastal terminals, making the Gulf one of the world's busiest seaways. Look for ⚓

An oil pipeline snakes across the Arabian desert.

109

CENTRAL ASIA

THE CENTRAL ASIAN REPUBLICS lie on the ancient Silk Road between Asia and Europe, and their historic cities grew up along this route. Afghanistan controlled the route south into Pakistan and India, through the Khyber Pass in the Hindu Kush mountains. The hot, dry deserts of Central Asia and high, rugged mountain ranges of the Pamirs and Tien Shan were not suited to agriculture. For centuries people lived as nomads, herding sheep across the empty plains, or settled as merchants and traders in the Silk Road cities. When Central Asia became part of the communist Soviet Union, everything changed: local languages and the Islamic religion (which had come to the region from the Middle East in the 8th century) were restricted; irrigation schemes made farming the arid land possible; oil, gas and other minerals were exploited; industry was developed. Today, these newly-independent republics are returning to the languages, religion and traditions of their past. Afghanistan, independent since 1750, has recently suffered terrible conflict and economic collapse.

HORSEMEN OF THE STEPPES
The nomadic peoples of the steppes travel great distances on horseback, and horse fairs and races are important events in their calendar. Ashgabat in Turkmenistan is the main breeding centre for the Akhal-Teke, a much prized racehorse, able to maintain its speed in desert conditions.

Akhal-Teke racehorse

UZBEKISTAN
POP: 23,308,000

TURKMENISTAN
POP: 4,260,000

AGRICULTURE
Farming in this dry region depends on irrigation. The Karakum Canal is 1,100 km (683 miles) long – the longest canal in the world. It carries water from the Amu Darya towards the Caspian Sea, and waters vast areas of land. Draining the river, however, has also created desert landscapes.

Opium poppies are grown all over the region. They provide illegal money for many farmers, who supply the international drug trade.

SULPHUR
Turkmenistan's sulphur deposits are amongst the largest in the world. Sulphur is used in the manufacture of gunpowder, as well as in medicine, ointment and drugs. Turkmenistan also has large reserves of oil and gas, but has been slow to make money from its resources.

MARKETS
Towns such as Samarkand have changed little since the days of the Silk Road, and are still full of merchants and traders. Bazaars and street-side stalls sell local fruit and vegetables, herbs, spices, silk and cotton.

KEYBOX

Alternative energy: *Sunlight is used to generate power in Central Asia, providing a clean alternative to nuclear power. Look for* ⚡

Rail route: *The planned Trans-Asian Railway will connect Peking and Istanbul, via Central Asia and the Caspian Sea. Look for* 🚂

🐂	Cattle	⛏	Mining
🐑	Sheep	🛢	Oil
🍱	Mixed fruit	💧	Gas
🌿	Tobacco	〰	Carpet weaving
❀	Cotton	🏭	Industrial centre

Carrots were first grown for food in Afghanistan.

CARPETS
Carpets from Uzbekistan, Turkmenistan, northern Afghanistan and other parts of this region are world-famous. They are made by hand-knotting, and are woven from fine Karakul wool. They follow distinctive geometric patterns in a range of red, brown and maroon colours. Carpets are used as saddle-cloths, tent hangings and prayer mats. Look for 〰

KARAKUL SHEEP
Karakul sheep are bred for their distinctive curly fleece. They are especially important in Afghanistan. Nomadic people have herded sheep in this region for many centuries. Each summer they take their flocks up to the lush mountain pastures, and in winter they are herded down onto the plains. Look for 🐑

USTYURT PLATEAU

ARAL SEA

TURAN LOWLAND

Muynak•

L. Sarykamysh

Khodzheyli •Nukus

UZ

Sulphur

Zaliv Kara-Bogaz-Gol

Sulphur

Dashkhovuz• •Beruni
Urgench• Furtku

CASPIAN SEA

Krasnovodsk

Cheleken
Nebitdag

Kizyl-Arbat

TURKMENISTAN

Bezmein •ASHGABAT (ASHKHABAD)

Kizyl-Atrek

Mary

Tedzhen

I R A N

Kowl-e-Namaksār

Herā
A

Hāmūn-e-Ṣāber

Gowd-e-Zereh

ARAL TRAGEDY

Water from the Amu Darya is being diverted to irrigate cotton fields. Since reduced amounts of water are now flowing into the Aral Sea, it is shrinking, and is now only 60 per cent of its former size. Fishing villages that once stood on the sea coast are now stranded far inland, depriving villagers of their livelihood.

Estimated sea-level in year 2000
Sea-level in 1989
Kokaral
Sea-level in 1960
Exposed seabed becomes desert, 1960-89

The fishing village of Muynak is now over 48 km (30 miles) from the sea

Amu Darya

N

SAMARKAND

The Islamic religion reached this region in the 8th century AD. Today, after decades of suppression by the communists, Islam is once again widely followed. Most of the former Soviet Union's 60 million Muslims live in the Central Asian republics. New mosques are opened daily, and ancient religious buildings are being restored. The famous Registan Square at Samarkand is a magnificent monument to Islam, dating back to the 14th century.

The Tien Shan range of Central Asia reaches 7,439 m (24,460 ft).

WHITE GOLD

The annual cotton crop of Uzbekistan matches the entire output of the USA, but is of low quality. Cotton is so important that few other crops are grown. Look for

A road through the Khyber Pass links Afghanistan and Pakistan.

Velvet hats are worn in Uzbekistan.

Apricot
Water-melon
Peach

FRUITS OF THE DESERT

Many rivers rising in the high Pamirs and Tien Shan range flow across the desert. In spring, the rivers are swollen by melted snow from the mountains, which is rich in fertile mud. Their waters are channelled on to the fields to water crops such as water-melons, apricots and peaches, creating oases of green in the arid landscape. Look for

KABUL

The capital of Afghanistan occupies a strategic position, controlling the mountain passes to Pakistan. Large areas of Kabul were destroyed in the Afghan civil war, between the communist regime (defended by the Soviet Union), and Muslim tribes (*mojahedin*), which lasted from 1979 to 1989. The city's problems did not end with the withdrawal of Soviet troops: battles still rage on the outskirts of the city between various *mojahedin* groups, and everyday life continues to be completely disrupted by the fighting.

KM
MILES

RUSSIA AND KAZAKHSTAN

THE URAL MOUNTAINS FORM a natural barrier between the European and the Asian parts of Russia. Although over 77 per cent of the country lies in Asia, only 27 per cent of the population live here. Siberia dominates Russia east of the Urals, stretching to the Pacific Ocean and northwards into the Arctic. The climate is severe, parts of Siberia are colder in winter than the North Pole.

Siberia has huge deposits of gold, coal, diamonds, gas and oil, but workers had to be offered high wages and housing to work there. Today, both Russia and Kazakhstan have great economic potential, but are still coping with a legacy of severe industrial pollution.

HYDRO-ELECTRIC POWER

Siberia's rivers provide 80 per cent of Russia's hydro-electric power, fuelling industry throughout eastern Russia. Massive dams, such as this one on the River Angara, provide the power for the aluminium industry. Look for ⚏

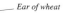
Ear of wheat

VIRGIN LANDS

In the 1950s, the Soviet Union tried to increase grain production. The empty steppes of Kazakhstan, known as the "Virgin Lands", were ploughed up to grow crops. Today, much of this farmland is reverting to steppe. Look for ♆

KEYBOX

Industrial centre: This region produces one-third of the former USSR's iron and steel. Timber processing is also very important. Look for 🏭

Pollution: Nearly 500 Soviet nuclear devices were detonated in Kazakhstan from 1949-1989. Many children in this area are malformed at birth. Look for ☢

Military bases: Russia's far East is a highly militarized area. The Russian Pacific fleet is based at Vladivostok. ICBM bases line the southeast border. Look for ✈

♆	Cereals	⛏	Coal
⅄	Timber	⚒	Oil
🐟	Fishing	◊	Gas
⬤	Mining	⚏	Hydro-electric power

KAZAKH HORSEMEN

The first inhabitants of the steppe were a nomadic people who travelled on horseback, herding their sheep with them. They slept in felt tents like these, called *yurts*. Their descendants, the Kazakhs, still place great value on horses and riding skills, and horse-racing is a popular sport. The Kazakh national drink is *kumiss* – fermented mare's milk. The traditional nomadic lifestyle of the steppe has gradually been replaced by large-scale agriculture and industry.

(map)

0 200 400 600 800 1000 KM
0 100 200 300 400 500 600 MILES

N

KAZAKHSTAN
POP: 17,575,000

Murmansk
Iron
L. Pyazero
FINLAND
KOLA PENINSULA
BARENTS SEA
Novaya Zemlya
Kem'
Arkhangel'sk
WHITE SEA
Kolguyev I.
KARA SEA
Belyy I.
ESTONIA
LATVIA
St. Petersburg
Pskov
Petrozavodsk
Novgorod
Rye
Nevel'
L. Onega
Onega
Mezen
Pechora
Uranum
Coal
Baydarata Bay
YAMAL PENINSULA
GYDA PENINSULA
BELORUSSIA
Smolensk
Aluminium
Cherepovets
Tver'
Oats
Vologda
Kotlas
Syktyvkar
Chromium
Coal
Vorkuta
Salekhard
Gulf of Ob
Nakhodka
MOSCOW
Kaluga
Bryansk
Tula
Orel
Yaroslavl'
Ivanovo
Vladimir
Oats
Uranum
Ob'
Pur
Taz
UKRAINE
Kursk
Ryazan
Lipetsk
Nizhniy Novgorod
Cheboksary
Kirov
Kama
Manganese
Platinum
WEST SIBERIAN PLAIN
Iron
Voronezh
Tambov
Penza
Saransk
Kazan'
Barley
Oats
Platinum
Serov
R
Maize
Wheat
Ul'yanovsk
Izhevsk
Perm
Nizhniy Tagil
SEA OF AZOV
Rostov-na-Donu
Saratov
Tol'yatti
Naberezhnyye Chelny
Yekaterinburg
Irtysh
Nizhnevartovsk
Krasnodar
Balakovo
Samara
Ufa
Oats
Tyumen'
Ob'
F vakh E
Sochi
Stavropol'
Volgograd
Sulphur
Gold
Copper
Kurgan
Ket'
BLACK SEA
Iron
Cherkessk
Elista
Ural'sk
Wheat
Orenburg
Copper
Magnitogorsk
Chelyabinsk
Kustanai
Petropavlovsk
Omsk
Itatka
ICBM Base
Tomsk
GEORGIA
Astrakhan
Iron
Ural
Wheat
Copper
Iron
Kokchetav
Oats
Achi
Vladikavkaz
Groznyy
Atyrau
Aktyubinsk
Emba
Chromium
Barley
Wheat
Wheat
Novosibirsk
Makhachkala
CASPIAN SEA
Fort Shevchenko
Aktau
KIRGHIZ STEPPE
Akmola
Barley
Pavlodar
Ob'
Novokuznetsk
Barnaul
KAZAKHSTAN
Aluminium
L.Tengiz
KAZAKH
Wheat
Aleysk
Air Base
Biysk
Iron
ARAL SEA
Manganese
Arkalyk
Copper
Karaganda
UPLANDS
Gold
Irtysh
Semipalatinsk
Ust' Kamenogorsk
Zine
UZBEKISTAN
Baykonur
Zhezkazgan
Chu
Wheat
Balkhash
Copper
L. Balkhash
L. Zaysan
Oats
Kzyl-Orda
Syr Darya
Shymkent
Zhambyl
Ili
Kapchagay
Taldy-Kurgan
CHINA
TURKMENISTAN
KYRGYZSTAN
ALMA-ATA (ALMATY)

SPACE CENTRE

The Russian space programme is based at Baykonur in Kazakhstan, where this Buran unmanned shuttle was launched in 1988. Russia's achievements in space technology started with the launch of the Sputnik satellite in 1957. Since then, Russia has been responsible for the first man in space, the first woman cosmonaut, and the first space walk. The Mir orbital station has now been in space for over five years.

SIBERIAN GOLD
The discovery of gold on the upper part of the River Lena in the 1840s led to a gold-rush. But conditions for 19th-century prospectors were terrible – they slept in flimsy huts in freezing temperatures, and many died. Today, the region has four major gold- fields as well as 800 diamond mines. Look for 🔨

A herd of reindeer graze on the tundra in northern Siberia.

A COLD CLIMATE
Siberian towns are built to withstand the region's harsh climate. Many houses are built on stilts, as frost damages normal foundations. Winters in the far north are extremely long – some towns do not see daylight for up to 47 days a year. Fruit and vegetables are grown locally in heated greenhouses.

Siberian huskies are used for pulling sledges and hunting.

The Kurile Islands are administered by the Russian Federation, but claimed by Japan.

The Kamchatka peninsula is a remote wilderness.

A child's toy wooden sledge from Siberia.

RUSSIAN FEDERATION
POP: 150,638,000
(SIBERIA)
POP: 40,250,000

TRIBESPEOPLE
The Chukchi people who live on the Kamchatka peninsula traditionally survive by hunting, reindeer herding and fishing. But the animals' natural habitats are slowly disappearing as forests are cut down for timber, and lakes and rivers are polluted by industrial waste. This is depriving the Chukchi hunters of their livelihood.

Fur hat

FUR
Hunters, trappers and fur-traders have been making a profitable living from Russia's animals since the 17th century. Siberia in particular has rich animal resources. The far East of the country has tigers and leopards, while the forests are home to the brown bear (often used as a symbol for Russia), sable, ermine, mink, lynx and foxes. Over-hunting has reduced the numbers of these animals in the wild, so most fur now comes from animals bred specially on fur farms.

INDUSTRIAL POLLUTION
Uncontrolled industrial growth has led to severe pollution problems in this region. The level of carbon emissions – caused by burning coal and oil – would not be acceptable in the West. Many children's illnesses in Russia are caused by contaminated air.

Russians heat water for tea in urns called samovars.

Lake Baikal contains 20 per cent of the world's fresh water.

Komodo dragon
Varanus komodoensis
Length: 3 m (10 ft)

Golden pheasant
Chrysolophus pictus
Length: 1 m (3 ft)

King cobra
Ophiophagus hannah
Length: 5.5 m (18 ft)

SOUTH AND EAST ASIA

THE WORLD'S 10 HIGHEST PEAKS, including Mount Everest, are all found in the Himalayas and other mountain ranges in the centre of this region. At these altitudes, monsoon rains fall as snow on mountain tops. The melted snow from the mountains feeds some of the largest rivers in the world, such as the Ganges and Irrawaddy, which have created huge deltas where they enter the sea. Fingers of land stretch into tropical seas and volcanic island chains border the continent. In tropical areas high rainfall and temperatures support vast areas of forest. Inland, a climate of extremes prevails, with baking hot summers and long harsh winters. Cold desert and grassy plains cover much of the interior.

■ ▲ VOLCANIC ROCK
This huge granite rock on Sri Lanka was formed in the mouth of a volcano. It is surrounded by forest.

Maidenhair tree
Gingko biloba
Height: 30 m (100 ft)

The Tiger cowrie is found on coral reefs.

■ ▲ YOUNG MOUNTAINS
Himalaya is the Nepalese word for "home of the snows". The range began to form about 40 million years ago – recent in the Earth's history.

■ △ ISLAND VOLCANOES
Plants are growing again on the scorched slopes of Bromo in Java, one of a chain of active volcanoes around the southeast Pacific.

■ TROPICAL RAINFOREST
Rainforests grow in layers: an understorey with creepers, and the main canopy through which tallest trees protrude.

Giant panda
Ailuropoda melanoleuca
Length: 1.5 m (5 ft)

■ HIDDEN CAVES
This maze of limestone caves along the Gulf of Thailand has been carved out by rainwater.

■ △ SACRED MOUNTAIN
Mount Fuji, Japan's highest peak, is surrounded by temperate broadleaf trees. Once an active volcano, Mount Fuji has not erupted for 300 years. The snow-capped summit is the rim of a volcanic crater.

The Royal cloak scallop shell is found in the waters of the Pacific Ocean.

⚠ MANGROVES IN SILHOUETTE
Mangroves grow along many coastlines, giving some protection during tropical storms.

Rafflesia
Rafflesia pricei
Width: 1 m (3 ft)

■ TROPICAL ISLAND
There are thousands of tiny coral islands in this region. Many are volcanic in origin, like this one in the South China Sea.

CROSS-SECTION THROUGH SOUTH AND EAST ASIA

8,848 (29,028)

Himalayas | *Plateau of Tibet* | *Daxue Shan* | *Great Plain of China* | *Yellow Sea* | *Korea*

Thar Desert | *Red Basin* | *Sea of Japan* | *Honshū*

Sea level 0

-4,500 (14,764)
Metres (feet)

A | *Length: 8,000 km (5,000 miles)* | B

■ COLD HIGH NEPAL
No trees are to be found above 3,000 m (10,000 ft) in the Himalayas, though dwarf shrubs and grasses can withstand the harsher conditions up to 4,500 m (15,000 ft). Higher still, the rock is bare, or covered in snow.

Wild yak
Bos grunniens
Length: 3 m (9 ft)

Chinese river dolphin
Lipotes vexillifer
Length: 2.4 m (8 ft)

Siberian tiger
Panthera tigris
Length: 2.4 m (8 ft)

Orang-utan
Pongo pygmaeus
Height: 1.5 m (5 ft)

AUTUMN ON HOKKAIDO
Hokkaidō is the most northerly of Japan's four islands. Its mountainous landscape is covered with broadleaf forests. The climate is moderated by the sea: winters are milder and rainfall is heavier than at the same latitude on the mainland.

KEY TO SYMBOLS

▲ Mountain
△ Volcano
⚜ Mangroves
Wetlands
Coral reef
Plate margins with direction of movement

KEY TO NATURAL VEGETATION

Cold desert
Mountain
Hot desert
Tropical rainforest
Needleleaf forest
Temperate grassland
Broadleaf forest
Temperate rainforest
Dry woodland

S I B E R I A

Arctic Circle

SEA OF OKHOTSK

NORTH AMERICAN PLATE
EURASIAN PLATE

Probable plate margin

Sakhalin

Kurile Is.

Hokkaidō

Kurile Trench

Kerulen

GREATER KHINGAN RANGE
▲1712m

MANCHURIAN PLAIN
L. Khanka

ALTAI MTS.
4506m

Turpan Depression
-154m
L. Bosten
Lop Nur

GOBI DESERT

Yellow R.

Amur

Sea of Japan

Honshū ▲Fuji 3776m
Japan Trench

40°

TIEN SHAN
7439m
Tarim

TAKLA MAKAN DESERT
7723m

QAIDAM BASIN
Qinghai Hu

KUNLUN MTS.

Yellow R.

Wei He
3767m ▲

GREAT PLAIN OF CHINA

YELLOW SEA

Korea
Korea Strait

Shikoku

Kyūshū
Unzen △ 1359m
▼9780m
PACIFIC PLATE
PHILIPPINE PLATE

HINDU KUSH
▲7690m
Indus
K2 8611m

PLATEAU OF TIBET

DAXUE SHAN

Jinsha

QIN LING

Huai He

Yangtze

EAST CHINA SEA

Ryukyu Is.

EURASIAN PLATE
PHILIPPINE PLATE

IRANIAN PLATE
INDO-AUSTRALIAN PLATE

Probable plate margin

THAR DESERT
Indus

H I M A L A Y A S
Manaslu 8156m
Dhaulagiri 8172m
Mt Everest 8848m
Kangchenjunga 8598m

7556m Red Basin

Dongting Hu

NAN LING
3164m ▲

Yuan
Gan He
Poyang Hu

Taiwan Strait

Taiwan

Tropic of Cancer

Rann of Kutch
Indus Delta

GANGES PLAIN
Ganges
Brahmaputra

Mali Hka

20°

Narmada

DECCAN PLATEAU

Gersuppa Falls 253m

Cauvery Falls 101m

Palk Strait

Godavari
Krishna

Bay of Bengal

Ganges Delta

Irrawaddy
Salween

Irrawaddy Delta

Andaman Is.

Nicobar Is.

ANDAMAN SEA

Gulf of Tonking

Mekong

Hainan

PACIFIC OCEAN

Philippine Basin

Pinatubo Mt 1759m

Philippines

Philippine Trench

-10057m

Yap Trench
▼-8527m

C. Comorin
Sri Lanka

Ceylon Plain

MALAY PENINSULA
Strait of Malacca
Isthmus of Kra
Gulf of Thailand
Tônlé Sap
Mekong Delta

SOUTH CHINA SEA
South China Basin

CELEBES SEA

Probable plate margin

Halmahera

Equator

Mid-Indian Ridge
Chagos Trench

Chagos-Laccadive Plateau

Ninety East Ridge
INDO-AUSTRALIAN PLATE
EURASIAN PLATE

Sumatra
Sunda Shelf

Borneo

Celebes

Moluccas

Seram

▲5030m
New Guinea

Mid-Indian Basin

Wharton Basin

Java Trench

J A V A   S E A

E A S T   I N D I E S

PACIFIC PLATE
INDO-AUSTRALIAN PLATE

MAOKE MTS.

INDIAN OCEAN

Krakatau △ 813m
Papandajan △ 2605m

Kelud △ 1731m
Bromo 2581m

Java
Tambora △ 2821m
Bali

Flores

Timor

ARAFURA SEA

80°   100°   120°   140°

60°

THE INDIAN SUBCONTINENT

SOUTH OF THE HIMALAYAS, the world's highest mountains, lies the Indian subcontinent. In the north of the region, the Buddhist kingdoms of Nepal and Bhutan cling to the slopes of the Himalayas. In the south, the island state of Sri Lanka hangs like a teardrop from the tip of India. The subcontinent has been invaded many times: the first invaders were fair-skinned, blue-eyed Aryan tribes, whose beliefs and customs form the basis of the Hindu religion. From the 16th century India was united and ruled by the Islamic Mogul emperors. Two centuries later it became a British colony. In 1947 India gained independence, but religious differences led to the creation of two countries – Hindu India and Muslim Pakistan. The eastern part of Pakistan later became Bangladesh. Today India is a thriving industrial power, but most people still live in villages and make their living from tiny farms. In spite of terrible poverty and a population of about 850 million people, India remains a relatively stable democracy.

PAKISTAN
POP: 138,672,000

The Thar Desert, a vast, arid region in India and Pakistan.

Sitar

MOOD MUSIC
Traditional Indian music is improvised. Its purpose is to create a mood, such as joy or sorrow. One of the main instruments is the *sitar*, which is played by plucking seven of the strings. Other strings, which are not plucked, vibrate to give the distinctive sound of Indian music.

PAKISTAN
This bus illustrates a big problem in Pakistan: over-population. Ninety-five per cent of the people are Muslim, and traditional Islam rejects contraception, so the birth-rate is high. Three million refugees, who fled the war in Afghanistan, have stretched resources further.

A MARBLE MEMORIAL
The Taj Mahal at Agra, in northern India, was built in the 17th century by the Mogul Emperor, Shah Jahan, as a tomb for his beloved wife. She was the mother of 14 children. Built of the finest white marble, the Taj Mahal is a supreme example of Islamic architecture and one of the world's most beautiful buildings.

KEYBOX

Aquaculture: This is a recent and highly successful industry in Bangladesh. Frogs' legs and shrimps are among the main products. Look for 🦐

Trekking: Every year some 250,000 trekkers visit Nepal, boosting its economy. But the extra visitors are damaging the environment. Look for 👟

Dams: Irrigation on a vast scale in the Indus Valley in Pakistan has sustained and increased the country's food production. Look for ▥

🌾	Cereals	⚓	Cotton
〰	Rice	♟	Mining
↓	Sugar cane	⛏	Coal
🌿	Tea	⬛	Industrial centre

INDUSTRY
After independence, India started to modernize, and is now one of the most industrialized countries in Asia. Factories make a wide range of goods, from cement to cars. Recently, the manufacture of goods such as machine tools and electronic equipment has increased. Local cotton is processed in mills like these in Ahmadabad. Look for ▪️

INDIAN FILMS
More films are produced in India than anywhere else in the world – including Hollywood. Bombay is the centre of the Indian film industry.

Jewellery, especially silver, is one of India's main exports.

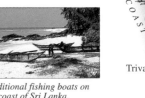

Traditional fishing boats on the coast of Sri Lanka.

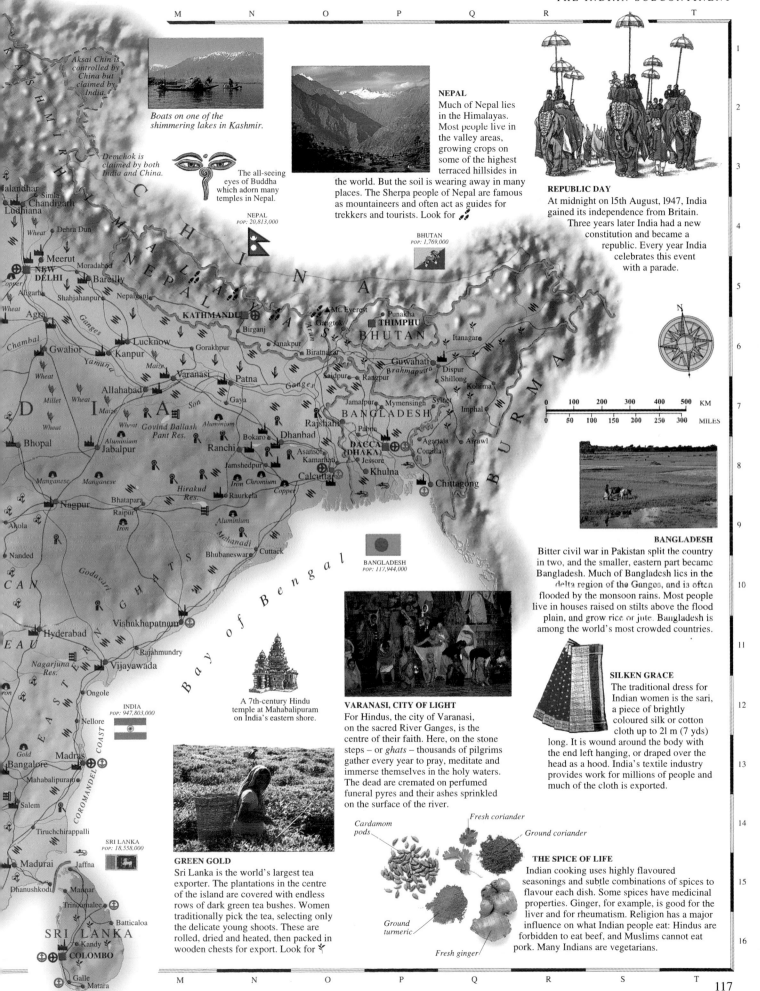

Aksai Chin is controlled by China but claimed by India.

Boats on one of the shimmering lakes in Kashmir.

Demchok is claimed by both India and China.

The all-seeing eyes of Buddha which adorn many temples in Nepal.

NEPAL

Much of Nepal lies in the Himalayas. Most people live in the valley areas, growing crops on some of the highest terraced hillsides in the world. But the soil is wearing away in many places. The Sherpa people of Nepal are famous as mountaineers and often act as guides for trekkers and tourists. Look for

NEPAL
POP: 20,813,000

BHUTAN
POP: 1,769,000

REPUBLIC DAY

At midnight on 15th August, 1947, India gained its independence from Britain. Three years later India had a new constitution and became a republic. Every year India celebrates this event with a parade.

KM
0   100   200   300   400   500
0   50   100   150   200   250   300
MILES

BANGLADESH

Bitter civil war in Pakistan split the country in two, and the smaller, eastern part became Bangladesh. Much of Bangladesh lies in the delta region of the Ganges, and is often flooded by the monsoon rains. Most people live in houses raised on stilts above the flood plain, and grow rice or jute. Bangladesh is among the world's most crowded countries.

BANGLADESH
POP: 117,944,000

SILKEN GRACE

The traditional dress for Indian women is the sari, a piece of brightly coloured silk or cotton cloth up to 2l m (7 yds) long. It is wound around the body with the end left hanging, or draped over the head as a hood. India's textile industry provides work for millions of people and much of the cloth is exported.

A 7th-century Hindu temple at Mahabalipuram on India's eastern shore.

INDIA
POP: 947,803,000

VARANASI, CITY OF LIGHT

For Hindus, the city of Varanasi, on the sacred River Ganges, is the centre of their faith. Here, on the stone steps – or *ghats* – thousands of pilgrims gather every year to pray, meditate and immerse themselves in the holy waters. The dead are cremated on perfumed funeral pyres and their ashes sprinkled on the surface of the river.

SRI LANKA
POP: 18,558,000

GREEN GOLD

Sri Lanka is the world's largest tea exporter. The plantations in the centre of the island are covered with endless rows of dark green tea bushes. Women traditionally pick the tea, selecting only the delicate young shoots. These are rolled, dried and heated, then packed in wooden chests for export. Look for

Cardamom pods

Fresh coriander

Ground coriander

Ground turmeric

Fresh ginger

THE SPICE OF LIFE

Indian cooking uses highly flavoured seasonings and subtle combinations of spices to flavour each dish. Some spices have medicinal properties. Ginger, for example, is good for the liver and for rheumatism. Religion has a major influence on what Indian people eat: Hindus are forbidden to eat beef, and Muslims cannot eat pork. Many Indians are vegetarians.

CHINA AND MONGOLIA

THE REMOTE MOUNTAINS, deserts and steppes of Mongolia and the northwestern part of China are harsh landscapes; temperatures are extreme, the terrain is rugged and distances between places are vast. Three large Autonomous Regions of China lie here – Inner Mongolia, Xinjiang and Tibet. Remote Tibet, situated on a high plateau and ringed by mountains, was invaded by China in 1950. The Chinese have systematically destroyed Tibet's traditional agricultural society and Buddhist monasteries. Most of China's ethnic minorities and Muslims (a legacy of Silk Road trade with the Middle East) are located in Inner Mongolia and Xinjiang. Roads and railways are being built to make these isolated areas accessible, and rich resources of coal are being exploited. Mongolia is a vast, isolated country. It became a communist republic in 1924, but has now re-established democracy. Most people still live by herding animals, although new industries have begun to develop.

Cylinder containing written prayer

In Tibet, written prayers are placed in prayer wheels. These small cylinders are rotated by hand.

MONGOLIAN STEPPES
About half the Mongolian population still live in the countryside, many as nomadic herders. Nomads live in *gers* – circular tents made of felt and canvas stretched over a wooden frame. They herd yak, sheep, goats, cattle and camels, and travel great distances on horseback.

The Tien Shan range in central Xinjiang.

KASHI MARKET
The city of Kashi is located in the far west of China. With its Muslim mosques, minarets and lively bazaar it is more like a city in the Middle East than China. Its Sunday market, the biggest in Asia, attracts up to 60,000 visitors. A vast array of goods are sold there: horses, camels, livestock, grains, spices and cloth.

KEYBOX

Timber: Forests in eastern Tibet have been cut down by the Chinese. Bare hillsides encourage soil erosion, flooding and landslides. Look for ⌐

Coal: Mongolia is a major exporter of coal to the Russian Federation. There are also open-cast mines in Xinjiang and Inner Mongolia. Look for ⚒

Pollution: Nuclear tests in Xinjiang have caused radiation fallout, pollution and many birth defects. Look for ☢

🐃	Cattle and yaks	⛏	Mining
🐑	Sheep	🛢	Oil
🌾	Cereals	🏭	Industrial centre
🍇	Mixed fruit	🏝	Oases

ADAPTABLE YAKS
Herders in Mongolia and Tibet keep yaks. They thrive at high altitudes, surviving extreme cold and even burrowing under snow for grass. Yaks provide milk, butter, meat, wool and leather. In Tibet, yak's butter is served with tea. Look for ☕

← N

Oases: winter and spring wheat, corn, rice and cotton are grown

Takla Makan Desert

Tarim

Lop Nur: saline lake

Passes through Tien Shan range

Turpan oasis: fruit and cotton are grown on irrigated land

SILK ROAD OASES
The oases of Xinjiang lie on the edge of the Takla Makan Desert, in the foothills of the Tien Shan range. They are watered by melted snow from the mountains, and sheltered by warm winds coming down the mountain slopes. Towns grew up next to the oases, which lie along the ancient Silk Road.

The high plateau of Tibet, known as "the roof of the world".

KAZAKHSTAN

L. Uvs
Ulaangom
L. Hyargas
Ölgiy
Hovd
Har Us L.
Uliasta
Altay
Wheat
Wheat
Yaks
Beef
Beef
Beef
Altay
ALTAI MTS.
Irtysh

KYRGYZSTAN

XINJIANG UIGHUR
Karamay
Yining
Kuytun
Shihezi
Ürümqi
Turpan
Hami
Maize
Iron
Beef
Beef
Beef
Wheat
Wheat
Wheat
Wheat

AUTONOMOUS

TIEN SHAN
Aksu
Korla
L. Bosten
Wheat
Wheat
Maize
Maize
Wheat

TAJIKISTAN

Kashi
Wheat

REGION

Tarim
Tarim Basin

Lop Nur

AFGHANISTAN

Shache
Wheat

KARAKORUM

Beef
Hotan
Wheat
Wheat

TAKLA MAKAN DESERT

CHI

Lenghu
Da Qaidam

PAKISTAN

Aksai Chin is controlled by China but claimed by India

ALTUN MTS.
Beef

KUNLUN MTS.

Golmud
Iron

INDIA

Demchok is claimed by both China and India

Gar
Yaks
Yaks
Yaks
Yaks

Tongtian He

TIBETAN

TANGGULA MTS.

AUTONOMOUS

GANGDISE RANGE
Tangra Yumco
Siling Co
Nam Co
Nagqu
Yaks
Lhasa
Nyingchi

Brahmaputra (Yarlung Zangbo)
Xigazê
Gyangze
Yamzho Yumco
Wheat
Wheat

REGION

HIMALAYAS

NEPAL
Nyalam
Mt. Everest
Yaks
Beef

BHUTAN
INDI

N O P Q R S T

NATIONAL GAMES
Horse-racing, archery and wrestling competitions are held all over Mongolia every July 11, the day of the national Nadam festival. Mongols are amongst the most accomplished riders in the world. They learn to ride as children, and some of the jockeys are only three years old.

MONGOLIA
POP: 2,560,000

STEEL CITY
Railways were built in the 1950s to transport coal and iron from the north of the country. Baotou is the centre of iron and steel production in Inner Mongolia. Look for

RUSSIAN FEDERATION

L. Hövsgöl
Moron — Beef
Yaks
Eglyn
HANGAYN NURUU
Beef
Tsetserleg — Yaks
Yaks
Tungsten
Arvayheer
Beef
Suhbaatar
Darhan — Copper
Erdenet — Gold
Wheat
ULAN BATOR (ULAANBAATAR)
Wheat
Tungsten
Orhon
Choybalsan
Kerulen
Wheat
Ondörhaan
Wheat
Saynshand
Uldz
Manzhouli
Hailar — Beef
Hulun Nur
Yakeshi
Zalantun
GREATER KHINGAN RANGE
Zinc
Lead
Beef
Ulanhot
Beef
Tongliao
INNER MONGOLIA
Xilinhot
Beef
Chifeng

MONGOLIA

GOBI DESERT

Erenhot
Beef
Wheat
Jining
Great Wall
EASTERN CHINA

Iron
Oats
Wheat
Hohhot
Baotou
Linhe — Wheat
Wheat
Dongsheng
Wuhai — Wheat
Wheat
ORDOS DESERT
Great Wall
Baidan Jaran Desert
Great Wall
Great Wall
Wheat
Wheat
Great Wall
Wheat

CHINA
POP: 1,252,188,000
(NORTHWEST CHINA)
POP: 43,099,600

NORTH KOREA

YELLOW SEA

SEA OF JAPAN

SOUTH KOREA

THIS MAP SHOWS THE NORTHWESTERN PART OF CHINA ONLY. THE REST OF CHINA IS SHOWN ON PP. 120-121.

Delingha
Qinghai Hu
Xining
Gonghe
QINGHAI
Yaks
BAYAN HAR MTS.
Yushu
Yaks
Mekong
Qamdo
Yaks
Salween
EASTERN CHINA
BURMA

A camel caravan crosses the Gobi Desert.

Lycium fruit
Dried fungus
Sliced deer antler
Gardenia fruit
Dried rhubarb

TRADITIONAL MEDICINE
Traditional Chinese medicine restores harmony between the body, mind and environment. Xining is a major export centre for traditional medicines such as caterpillar fungus, antlers, musk and rhubarb.

THE GREAT WALL
The Great Wall of China is 2,400 km (1,500 miles) long, and runs from the Chinese coast to Central Asia. Much of the present Great Wall was built in the early 15th century. It was intended to protect the Chinese against invasions by the nomadic Mongols to the north.

Scale: 0 100 200 300 400 KM / 250 500 750 MILES

Bactrian camels, with two humps, are used as pack animals in this region.

CHINA'S SORROW
The shallow, slow-moving Yellow River which rises in the high mountains of Tibet, brings fertile mud to the arid plains of northern China. However, build-up of muddy deposits on the river's bed has lifted the river-level above its banks, periodically causing terrible floods and famines.

POTALA PALACE
The spectacular Potala Palace in Lhasa, capital of Tibet, was built in the 17th century. It was the residence of the Dalai Lama, the head of the Buddhist faith in Tibet. When Tibet was invaded by China in 1950, Buddhism was brutally repressed by the Chinese. In 1959 there were over 6,000 monasteries in Tibet – by 1979 only five remained.

Loose tea leaves are compressed into hard blocks, easily carried by Tibetan nomads.

STAPLE FOODS
In contrast to the rest of China, rice is not the main food crop in the northern regions. Cereals, such as wheat, millet, oats, buckwheat and barley are grown on irrigated land or oases. Noodles and steamed buns (*mantou*) are the main bulk food of the north, served with spicy, barbecued meat. Look for

Wheat
Millet
Barley

CHINA AND KOREA

THE LANDSCAPE OF SOUTHEASTERN CHINA ranges from mountains and plateaux to wide river valleys and plains. One-fifth of all the people on Earth live in China – most of them in the eastern part of the country. For centuries, China was isolated from the rest of the world, ruled by powerful emperors and known to only a handful of traders. In the 19th century the European powers forced China to open its borders to trade, starting a period of rapid change. In 1949, after a long struggle between nationalists and communists, the People's Republic of China was established as a communist state. Taiwan became a separate country. The communist government has encouraged foreign investment, technological innovation and private enterprise, although calls for democracy have been suppressed. Korea has been dominated by its powerful Chinese and Japanese neighbours for many years. After World War II, Korea was divided in two. North Korea became one of the most isolated and repressive communist regimes in the world. South Korea transformed itself into a highly industrial economy.

PEKING OPERA
Traditional Chinese opera dates back 2,000 years and combines many different elements – songs, dance, mime and acrobatics. The stories are based on folktales. Make-up shows the characters' personalities – kind, loyal or wicked, for example.

Sesame oil
Dried mushroom

FOOD
Chinese food varies widely from region to region. Its most famous cuisine comes from the area around Canton, and uses a huge range of ingredients – it is said that the people from this region will "eat everything with wings except aeroplanes and everything with legs except the table". Chinese food has become popular all over the world.

Soy sauce
Dried prawn

INDUSTRY
Although China has extensive reserves of coal, iron ore and oil, its heavy industry is state-run, old-fashioned and inefficient. Seventy per cent of China's energy is provided by coal. About half China's coal comes from large, well-equipped mines; the rest is extracted from small local pits. These mines are notorious for their high accident rates. Look for 🔨

The Great Wild Goose pagoda at Xi'an was built in the 7th century AD. It formed part of a Buddhist monastery.

THIS MAP SHOWS THE SOUTH-EASTERN PART OF CHINA ONLY. THE REST OF CHINA IS SHOWN ON PP. 118-119.

KEYBOX

Hydro-electric power: *China's rivers have great potential; dams lakes and canals provide flood control and irrigation as well as electricity. Look for* ▥

Economic zones: *The Chinese government has set up special industrial zones, encouraging foreign investment through tax incentives. Look for* 🖐

Refugees: *Vietnamese refugees come to Hong Kong by boat. In 1991, there were over 61,000 Vietnamese in Hong Kong's detention camps. Look for* ⛺

Borders: *The most militarized border in the world divides Korea into communist North and democratic South. Look for* ⚔

⚘	Cereals	⬤	Mining
⚘	Rice	⚒	Coal
⚘	Tea	⚓	Oil
⚑	Timber	🏭	Industrial centre
⚓	Fishing	🗑	Shipbuilding

BABY BOOM
China's population is now over a billion, stretching resources such as land, food and education to the limit. Couples with only one child receive various benefits. If a second child is born, these benefits are withdrawn.

Tea, China's national drink, is grown on terraced hillsides in the south of the country.

AGRICULTURE
China feeds its vast population from only seven per cent of the world's farmland. In the fertile southern part of the country, the fields can yield three harvests every year – two crops of rice and a third crop of vegetables or cereals. Look for 🌾

RACIAL MINORITIES
This woman comes from the Hani people, one of the many different ethnic minorities who live in southwest China. Most minority groups live in remote, sparsely-inhabited regions. Many still follow traditional lifestyles based on herding, hunting, or growing food for their families.

MONGOLIA
WEST
WESTERN CHINA
Yumen
Great Wall
Yinchuan
Wuwei
NINGXIA HUI AUTONOMOUS REGION
Lanzhou
Wheat
Wheat
Wheat
C
Dadu He
Yalong
H
Mianyang
Litang
Jinsha
Chengdu
Maize
Leshan
Chongqing
Zigong
Xichang
Zunyi
Panzhihua
Aluminium
Copper
Dongchuan
Guiyang
Dali
Kunming
Maize
Hongshui He
BURMA
Gejiu
Maize
Tin
Maize
VIETNAM
Pingxiang
LAOS
Mekong

N

| 0 | 100 | 200 | 300 | 400 | 500 | 600 | KM |
| 0 | | 100 | 200 | | 300 | | MILES |

A jade vase. Jade is China's most precious stone.

THE DRAGON THRONE
The Hall of Supreme Harmony houses the Dragon Throne, seat of the former emperors of China. It is the largest building in Peking's Forbidden City, and dates back to the 15th century. Ordinary citizens were banned from this area, which was reserved for the Emperor and his courtiers. Today, the Forbidden City has been restored and opened to the public: it attracts millions of tourists every year.

北京

The word "Peking", written in Chinese. Each symbol stands for a word or an idea.

COMMUNISM
In the 1960s, China suffered a campaign of terror against artists, politicians and intellectuals. Although the regime is now more liberal, political messages displayed on walls are often the only way of challenging the government.

GINSENG
Korea exports this precious root, which is widely used in traditional Asian medicine. It is also popular in the West where it is thought to improve health and promote long life and vigour.

Ginseng roots are grown for 4-6 years, then steamed and dried.

Rice fields in South Korea. Rice thrives in the mild south.

NORTH KOREA
POP: 24,307,000

CHINA
POP: 1,252,188,000
(SOUTHEAST CHINA)
POP: 1,090,583,000

SOUTH KOREA
POP: 44,516,000

LAND OF MIRACLES
The Korean economy was devastated by World War II, but during the last 40 years South Korea has undergone an economic miracle. Today, it has a major shipbuilding industry and modern steelworks; cars, computers, televisions and videos pour off production lines. A quarter of all South Koreans live in the capital, Seoul, which has become one of the world's largest cities.

Playing table tennis is a national passion in China.

SHANGHAI
The port of Shanghai is the largest city in China. In the 19th century foreign countries, who were involved in trade with China, claimed sections of the city, establishing commercial buildings and warehouses, and giving central Shanghai the appearance of a European city. Today, Shanghai has become important as a centre of heavy industry.

The roofs of Wen-wu Temple, on Taiwan's Sun Moon Lake.

TAIWAN
POP: 20,800,000

THE LITTLE DRAGON
Taiwan is one of Asia's wealthiest economies. The country produces about 10 per cent of the world's computers, and also specializes in textiles and shoe-manufacturing. The Taiwanese refer to their country as the Republic of China, but China does not recognize the country under this name.

HONG KONG
The rocky island of Hong Kong became a British Crown Colony in the 19th century. In 1997 it will be returned to China, when it will become a "special administrative region". Hong Kong has the busiest container port in the world, and is a centre of trade, finance, manufacturing and tourism.

JAPAN

THE LAND OF THE RISING SUN, as Japan is sometimes called, was ruled for centuries by powerful warlords called *shōguns*, who discouraged any contact with the outside world. When traders from America and Europe arrived, Japan's isolation suddenly ended, the *shōgun* was overthrown and an emperor ruled the country. Over the next century, Japan transformed itself into one of the world's richest nations, a change in fortune all the more remarkable considering the country's geography. Japan consists of four main islands and 4,000 smaller islands. The majority of its 123 million people live closely packed together around the coast, since two-thirds of the land is mountainous and thickly forested. Japan has few natural resources and has to import most of its fuel and raw materials. The Japanese have concentrated on improving and adapting technology imported from abroad. Today, Japanese companies are world leaders in many areas of research and development, a success partly due to their management techniques which ensure a well paid and loyal workforce.

The Japanese are skilled at *bonsai* – the art of producing miniature trees and shrubs.

The Kurile Islands are administered by the Russian Federation, but claimed by Japan.

The Hidaka Mountains on the large island of Hokkaidō.

FOOD
The Japanese eat a lot of fish because there is not enough farmland to keep cattle for meat or dairy produce.

Lacquer dish

Rice

Seaweed

Marinated raw fish

SHIPBUILDING
A large number of the ships sailing the world today were made in Japan. Countries such as South Korea can now build ships more cheaply, however, and Japan's industry is declining. To remain competitive, Japanese shipbuilders are building specialized ships – such as cruise liners, and developing new products like oil-drilling platforms. Look for ⬩

JAPAN
POP: 126,320,000

RICE CULTIVATION
Rice is Japan's main food. Although only about 11 per cent of the land is suitable for farming, Japan produces enough rice for its own needs. The crop is intensively cultivated on small plots of land using fertilizers and sophisticated machinery, like this rice planter. The warm, wet summers in southern Japan are ideal for growing rice. Look for 〰

FISHING
Fish is a very popular food in Japan. Huge quantities are caught each year by the country's fishing fleet – the world's largest. One million tonnes of fish and shellfish are also bred every year in fish farms. These tuna are on sale in Tokyo's fish market. Look for ⚓

KABUKI THEATRE
There are two forms of traditional Japanese theatre: Noh and Kabuki. Noh is very old: the plays are based on myths of the gods and contain music and symbolic dancing. Kabuki theatres have plays based on stories of great heroes of the past. This photo shows a scene from a Kabuki play.

A miniature television, produced in Japan.

TRADITIONAL DRESS
Until the 19th century Japanese traditional dress varied greatly between the social classes. In the royal courts long-sleeved robes called *kimonos* were worn. Made of silk, these were wound round the body and tied with a sash. *Kimonos* are still worn on special occasions.

Silk kimono

Sea of Okhotsk

Iturup

Kurile Is.

Yekaterina Strait

Shikotan

Kunashir

Habomai Is.

Shikotan

La Pérouse Strait

Rebun-tō

Reshiri-tō

Wakkanai

Kitami

Abashiri

Nemuro

Kushiro

HOKKAIDŌ

Asahikawa

ISHIKARI MTS.

Obihiro

HIDAKA MTS.

Sapporo

Ishikari

Otaru

Ishikari Bay

Tomakomai

Uchiura Bay

Hakodate

Tsugaru Strait

Fukushima

Seikan Tunnel

Okushiri-tō

Aomori

Hachinohe

OU MTS.

Morioka

Akita

Yamagata

HONSHŪ

Sendai

Fukushima

Kōriyama

Utsunomiya

Mito

Hitachi

Iwaki

Kasumi Lagoon

Niigata

Nagano

Sado

Toyama Bay

Toyama

Kanazawa

ALPS

SEA OF JAPAN

JAPAN'S CAPITAL CITY

During the 500 years of its existence, Tokyo has survived fire, flood, earthquakes and destruction by war. Each disaster has required massive rebuilding. Earthquake-resistant materials and construction techniques, which enable a building to sway rather than fall, have allowed new skyscrapers to replace older buildings. But the danger of earthquakes remains, and there are plans to move the capital to a safer site further north.

VEHICLE INDUSTRY

Japanese vehicle manufacturers became world leaders in the 1980s thanks to their stylish designs, new technology and efficient production methods. Today, motor vehicles are the country's biggest export. Japanese vehicle manufacturers have also opened a number of factories overseas – in Europe, the USA and elsewhere. Countries in areas like eastern Europe can supply cheaper labour than in Japan. Look for 🚚

Japanese motorbike

RELIGION

There are two main religions in Japan – Buddhism and Shinto. People often follow both: it is common to be married with Shinto rituals, but buried with Buddhist. There are numerous Buddhist and Shinto shrines and temples in Japan. They were usually built of wood – and therefore vulnerable to fire – and temples like Ginkakuji in Kyōto have been rebuilt several times.

Mount Fuji is Japan's sacred mountain.

COMMUTING

Most Japanese people live in the cities, but few people can afford to live in the city centres, so most people have to commute to work. Trains are fast and efficient, but so overcrowded that special guards are employed to push commuters into the carriages.

A bottle of rice wine, or sake, Japan's national drink.

COMPUTERS

The Japanese excel at producing miniature electronic goods, such as computers and televisions. They have set such high standards that few countries can match them. A silicon "chip" able to hold 1,000 pages of newsprint in its memory is being developed.

SITE OF TOKYO

Built around Tokyo Bay, and hemmed in by mountains, Tokyo is unable to spread further inland or along the coast. The sprawling built-up region around Tokyo and Yokohama is the world's largest urban area, and is sometimes called a megalopolis. It has a population of over 27 million people, and accounts for 25 per cent of Japan's industrial production.

N

Rice and other crops grown in fertile volcanic soils and ideal climate

Tokyo Bay

Industrial and urban areas

Intensively cultivated lowlands due to shortage of farmland

To relieve overcrowding, developers build upwards, and into the sea on reclaimed land

SAGAMI SEA

Tokyo City

Yokohama

Mt. Fuji

The beautiful rocky coast of the Oki Islands, which lie in the Sea of Japan.

### Map labels

OCEAN

JAPANESE

Hakodate
Aomori
Sagami Sea
Izu Is.
Chiba
TOKYO
Kawasaki
Yokohama
Yokosuka
Mt. Fuji
Shizuoka
Hamamatsu
Okazaki
Nagoya
Gifu
Fukui
L. Biwa
Wakayama
Shingū
Mikasa Bay
Kyōto
Ōsaka
Kōbe
Himeji
Okayama
Kurashiki
Takamatsu
Tokushima
Wakayama
Kōchi
Matsuyama
Hiroshima
Tottori
Matsue
Hamada
Yamaguchi
Shimonoseki
Hagi
Kitakyūshū
Fukuoka
Saga
Beppu
Ōita
Kumamoto
Nagasaki
Saseho
Miyazaki
Nobeoka
Uwajima
Nakamura

Dōgo Oki Is.
Dōzen

Tsushima
Korea Strait
Gotō Is.
Ikí
Amakusa Is.
AMAKUSA SEA

CHUGOKU MTS
Inland Sea
SHIKOKU
KYŪSHŪ

Kagoshima
Ōsumi Strait
Ōsumi Is.
Tanega-shima
Yaku-shima

EAST CHINA SEA

RYUKYU IS.
Tokara Is.
Amami-ōshima
Amami Is.
Tokuno-shima
Okinoerabu-jima
Okinawa Is.
Okinawa
Naha

PACIFIC OCEAN

Scale

| 0 | 50 | 100 | 150 | 200 | 250 KM |
0 50 100 150 MILES

MAINLAND SOUTHEAST ASIA

MUCH OF THIS REGION is mountainous and covered with forest. Most of the people live in the great river valleys, plateaux or fertile plains. Farming is the main occupation, with rice the principal crop. Of the seven countries, only Thailand was not a British or French colony. Thais are deeply devoted to their royal family and Buddhist faith. The Federation of Malaysia includes 11 states on the mainland, joined in 1963 by Sabah and Sarawak in Borneo. This union of east and west has produced one of the world's most successful developing countries. Singapore, at first part of Malaysia, became a republic in 1965. The island controls the busy shipping routes between the Indian and Pacific Oceans. Cambodia, Laos and Vietnam have all suffered from many years of warfare. Cambodia's future is still uncertain, but the other two countries show signs of economic recovery. Burma has become increasingly isolated from the world by its repressive government.

BUDDHISM
Except for Malaysia, the main religion in this region is Buddhism. In Thailand and Burma, where almost all the people are Buddhists, every young man puts on the saffron robe, shaves his head and enters a monastery for several months.

Lacquer tray

Making lacquer ware is a traditional craft in Thailand.

VIETNAM
Rice is the principal crop in this country. As Vietnam is so mountainous, most people live in the two main river deltas. Two-thirds of the farmed land is devoted to growing rice. The wet-field, or *paddy*, is planted by women. Look for 〰

Durian fruit is grown throughout the region.

OPIUM
For the poor hill tribes of the remote "Golden Triangle" – the remote area where Burma, Laos and Thailand meet – growing opium poppies is one of the few sources of income. Useful painkillers can be made from the poppies, but so too are dangerous drugs, such as heroin and opium. The government is encouraging people in this area to grow other crops, such as flowers and tobacco.

Poppy seeds

Dried opium poppy

TIMBER
Thailand was once a major producer of teak, but so much of the country's forests have been cut down that commercial logging was banned in 1989 – until forests recover. Burma is now the world's principal teak exporter. Here, huge logs float down the Irrawaddy River. Look for ⅂

Boats on the Irrawaddy, the great river of Burma.

BURMA (MYANMAR) *pop: 47,502,000*

LAOS *pop: 5,015,000*

RUBIES
Several types of precious stone are mined in the northeast of Burma. The glowing red rubies from this region are considered the finest in the world. Many people in the East believe that wearing a ruby protects you from harm. Today Burma has a virtual monopoly over the ruby trade. Look for ⬥

Ruby   *Calcite*

FISHING
Fish is one of the main foods in this area. Thailand has a thriving fish canning industry. Fish farming in the inland lake of Tônlé Sap, Cambodia, is also successful. Here, in Burma, fish are caught from small huts built over the water. Look for ⌐

VIETNAM
POP: 70,900,000

The ancient temple (wat) of Angkor in Cambodia.

SINGAPORE
Singapore's modern container port and skyscrapers reflect its status as the financial and industrial centre of Southeast Asia. Over 25,000 vessels dock at Singapore each year; tourists pour into the island's airports; goods and people are carried into Malaysia and beyond by efficient transport systems. Shipbuilding and oil refining are among the main industries.

SINGAPORE
POP: 2,705,100

Orchids are grown in northern Thailand as an alternative to opium, and are widely exported.

CAMBODIA
POP: 9,660,000

WEST MALAYSIA
POP: 15,840,000

THAILAND
POP: 58,836,000

SOUTH CHINA SEA

Gulf of Thailand

Strait of Malacca

Strait of Singapore

Gulf of Martaban

ANDAMAN SEA

ELECTRONICS
Thailand and Malaysia are both industrializing rapidly. They have many factories where electronic products, like this pocket calculator, are assembled. Both countries now export a large number of manufactured goods. Malaysia makes its own car, the Proton; Thailand is a leading manufacturer of integrated circuits.

The Cameron High-lands, Malaysia.

Fruit of the oil palm

PALM OIL
The oil palm comes from West Africa, but has been successfully introduced into Malaysia and Indonesia. Palm oil and palm kernel oil, which are used in soap and as edible oils, are made from the fruit. Malaysia started production to lessen its dependence on the rubber crop – increasingly replaced by synthetic alternatives. Look for ⬤

ELEPHANTS
Compared to a tractor, a working elephant needs little fuel, does not rust and needs no spare parts. A tractor lasts for about six years, an elephant for 30, and it is less harmful to the environment. Elephants are used to move timber and to take tourists for rides in the forest.

Siamese cats originally came from Thailand – once called Siam.

Pineapple ring

PINEAPPLES
Thailand has become the world's biggest exporter of canned pineapple, 50 per cent of the product going to the USA. The pineapples are processed in factories where the skin is removed, the stem cut out and the fruit sliced into rings or chunks. Some of the largest factories in Thailand are owned by Japanese companies.

Pineapple fruit

FLOATING MARKET
Bangkok, Thailand's capital, is a noisy, hectic city, full of Buddhist temples – *wats* – and congested with traffic. The city was built on an island in the river, and the canals – or *klongs* – were once the city's streets. The few canals that remain are still used by flat boats – called *sampans* – to transport fresh fruit and vegetables from the countryside to the floating markets where the *sampans* act as shops.

KEYBOX

Mining: *Malaysia is the world's biggest producer of tin, but its resources are becoming depleted. Look for* ⛏

Dam: *A series of dams is planned on the Mekong to provide HEP and irrigation. All six countries involved must first reach agreement. Look for* 🏛

Tourism: *Over 3 million tourists visit Thailand each year, and tourism has become a major source of foreign currency. Look for* 📷

〰 Rice	🎣 Fishing
🥥 Coconuts	⛏ Coal
🌰 Vegetable oil	🛢 Gas
🌴 Timber	🏭 Industrial centre
🌲 Forest products	♜ Archaeological site

MARITIME SOUTHEAST ASIA

SCATTERED between the Indian and Pacific Oceans lies a huge crescent of mountainous tropical islands – the East Indies. The largest country in this region is Indonesia, which was ruled by the Dutch for nearly 350 years. Over half its 13,677 islands are still uninhabited. The island of Borneo is shared between Indonesia, the Malaysian enclaves of Sabah and Sarawak, and the Sultanate of Brunei. Indonesia's national motto, "Unity in diversity", ideally suits a country made up of 362 different peoples speaking over 250 dialects and languages. Indonesia's seizure of East Timor in 1975 has resulted in a long and bloody resistance by the islanders. Java, the main island, is so crowded that thousands of people have been moved to less populated islands. The Philippines, ruled for three centuries by Spain, then for 50 years by the USA, consists of over 7,000 islands. It is the only mainly Christian country in Asia. Much of the region is covered by forests, which contain some of the finest timber in the world.

COCONUTS

Indonesia and the Philippines are the world's major coconut growers. Every part of the tree has its uses, even the leaves. The kernel is dried to make copra from which a valuable oil is obtained. Look for 🥥

Kernel

STILT VILLAGES
Many of the villages in this region are built over water. The houses are made of local materials, like wood and bamboo, and built on stilts to protect them from vermin and flooding. For houses built on land, raised floors also provide shelter for the owner's animals which live underneath.

Helicopter

AIRCRAFT INDUSTRY
Indonesia has developed a thriving aircraft industry. About 12,000 workers assemble helicopters and aircraft at Bandung in Java. The factories are jointly owned by five international aircraft manufacturers. The first solely Indonesian-designed aircraft will soon be completed.

BRUNEI
The Sultanate of Brunei became rich when oil was discovered in 1929. This golden-domed mosque, built with the country's new-found wealth, towers above the capital, Bandar Seri Begawan. The small, predominantly Muslim, population pays no taxes, and enjoys free education and health care.

MALAYSIA
POP: 17,567,000
(EAST MALAYSIA:
SABAH AND SARAWAK)
POP: 3,360,000

RELIGION
Although about 90 per cent of Indonesians are Muslim, many of their religious ceremonies contain elements of other religions – like Hinduism and Buddhism – which blend with local traditions and beliefs. Recently, Islam has become more dominant. More girls now wear the Islamic headdress, like these pupils at a school in Sumatra.

Borobudur, the great 8th-century Buddhist temple on Java.

BRUNEI
POP: 288,000

Dense rainforest on Sumatra is home to elephants and tigers.

KEYBOX

Vegetable oil: Indonesia is now one of the world's major producers of palm oil. It has many uses, from hydraulic brake fluids to cooking oil. Look for 🍶

Research centre: Near Manila in the Philippines the Rice Research Institute has developed many of the world's modern high-yield types of rice. Look for 🔬

Pirates: Pirate attacks on vessels in the area are increasing, especially at night and in the busy shipping lanes of the Strait of Singapore. Look for ☠

〰 Rice		🐟 Fishing	
🥥 Coconuts		⛏ Mining	
Ⴈ Timber		⚓ Oil	
🌲 Forest products		🏭 Industrial centre	

JAKARTA

Situated on the island of Java, Indonesia's capital Jakarta has the largest population of any city in Southeast Asia – and is still growing rapidly. It was once the centre of the region's Dutch trading empire and many typical Dutch buildings still stand in the old part of the city. At night, skyscrapers glitter above the city's modern centre.

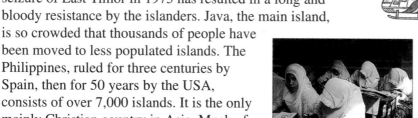

Banda Aceh
Rubber
Belawan
Medan
Simeulue
Pematangsiantar
L. Toba
Palm
Sibolga
Nias
Sumatra
Pini
Tanjungpinang
Pakambaru
Batu Is.
Siberut
Padang
Batanghari
Jambi
Lingga
Sipura
Singkep
North Pagai
Rubber
Bangka
South Pagai
Rubber
Tin
Pangkalpinang
Palembang
Karimata
BARISAN MTS.
Belitung
Tin
Bengkulu
Rubber
Palm
Enggano
Tanjungkarang
JAKARTA
Bogor
Cirebon
Sukabumi
Bandung
Semarang
Surabaya
Borobudur
Madura
Kangean
Bawean
Yogyakarta
Kediri
Malang
Jember
Banyuwangi
Java
Denpasar
Bali

SOUTH CHINA SEA
Kota Kinabalu
BANDAR SERI BEGAWAN
Miri
Kuala Belait
BRUNEI
Natuna
Natuna Is.
MALAYSIA (EAST)
Sibu
Sarikei
Kuching
SARAWAK
Borneo
Pontianak
Kapuas
MULLER MTS.
SCHWANER MTS.
Rubber
Mendawai
Barito
TAMABO RANGE
Rubber
Kualakapuas
Banjarmasin
JAVA SEA
INDIAN OCEAN

Strait of Singapore
Bintan
Anambas Is.

K L M N O P Q R S

PHILIPPINES
POP: 70,559,000

Luzon Strait

Laoag Aparri
Copper Tuguegarao
Vigan Ilagan
Gold
San Fernando
Baguio
Dagupan *Luzon*
Cabanatuan
Masinloc
Angeles MANILA
Lucena
Batangas Naga *Catanduanes*
Mindoro Legaspi
Masbate
Masbate
VISAYAN SEA Samar
Roxas *Leyte*
Panay Cadiz
Iloilo Tacloban
Bacolod Cebu
Negros *Bohol* Surigao
Copper *Cebu* *Nickel*
Dumaguete Butuan
Dipolog Cagayan de Oro
Iligan Bislig
Lanao
Zamboanga *Mindanao* Davao
General
Santos

Palawan

Puerto
Princesa

P H I L I P P I N E S

Mindoro Strait

Philippine Sea

Sulu Archipelago

Jolo
Jolo
Basilan
Tawitawi

alabac Strait
Banggi
Kudat
Ranau Sandakan
ABAH Lahad
Datu
Tawau
Rubber
Kayan

CELEBES SEA

Talaud Is.

Sangir

Sungir Is.

Manado

Gorontalo
Togian Is.

Gulf of
Tomini

Samarinda
Balikpapan Palu
Celebes
Iron
L. Towuti
Kendari *Wowoni*
Parepare *Nickel* *Muna*
Gulf of *Buton*
Bone
Ujung Pandang *Kabaena*
Selayar

O N E S I A

Makassar Strait

FLORES SEA

Lombok *Sumbawa*
Besar Raba
Sumbawa
Lesser Sunda Islands

Sumba

PACIFIC OCEAN

MOLUCCA SEA

Morotai

Halmahera

Gulf of
Weda
Nickel *Waigeo*
Sorong
Bacan
Moluccas *Misool*
Obi Gulf of Berau
Banggai Is.
Sula Is.
SERAM SEA
Seram
Buru *Seram*
Ambon
Banda Is.

BANDA SEA

Tukangbesi Is.

Damar
Wetar *Babar*
Alor *Leti Is.*
Dili
Flores
Ende *Timor*
Kupang
Roti

TIMOR SEA

Supiori Biak
Manokwari Biak
Yapen

Jayapura

I R I A N   J A Y A
M A O K E   M T S.
Copper *Gold*

ARAFURA SEA

Kai Is.

Aru Is.

Tanimbar Is. Dolak

Digul

Komoran

PAPUA NEW GUINEA

THE PHILIPPINES

Although the Philippines gained independence in 1946, the country has maintained close political and economic ties with its previous colonizer, the USA. English is widely spoken, especially in schools, and American products and customs are widespread, particularly around the huge US military bases near Manila, which were closed down in 1992.

Gong-chimes

A *bonang*, one of the instruments in a *gamelan* orchestra.

Batik cloth

BATIK

For over 1,000 years the art of *batik* has been practised in Indonesia, particularly in Java. Wax and dyes are used in a complex process to print colours and designs on to a variety of fabrics. Batik fabrics are often made into a garment called a *sarong*, which can be worn by both men and women.

Cinnamon
stick
Peppercorns
Nutmeg
Cloves

Spices from the Moluccas – known as the Spice Islands.

RICE TERRACES

Rice can be grown on lowland paddy fields, or on terraces cut into the mountainous slopes. Some of the terraces in the region are said to be over 2,000 years old. These remarkable structures help prevent soil erosion and use an ancient and complex system of sluices and canals to water the rice. Look for ≋

SHADOW PUPPETS

The shadow puppet shows of Indonesia, called *wayang,* are centuries old. The puppets are made from buffalo hide. Their faces are intricately carved to express their characters; the hero has a beautiful nose, the demon a short, ugly one. The puppet show is often accompanied by an orchestra, called a *gamelan*, which can contain up to 40 players.

TIMBER

Fine hardwoods, such as teak, grow in Indonesia's tropical rainforests. Now one of the world's major exporters of wood, especially plywood, Indonesia has built large-scale pulp and paper mills. Deforestation, especially here in Borneo, remains a major problem throughout the region. Look for ↑

Cowrie-shell
necklace

IRIAN JAYA

Irian Jaya – the western portion of New Guinea – is Indonesia's biggest province. Its densely forested and mountainous terrain has helped isolate it from Western influences. Many peoples in this region continue their local traditions, including the use of cowrie shells as a form of currency.

Planting rice at dusk in a rice paddy on Bali.

INDONESIA
POP: 208,660,000

0 100 200 300 400 500 600 KM
0 50 100 150 200 250 300 350 MILES

N

THE PACIFIC OCEAN

THE PACIFIC IS THE LARGEST and deepest of the world's oceans. It covers a greater area of the Earth's surface than all the land areas combined. At its deepest point – 11,033 m (36,197 ft) down in the Mariana Trench – it is deep enough to cover Mount Everest. More than half the world's population lives around the shores of the Pacific. The ocean's northern and western edges, known as the outer Pacific, are fringed with chains of islands, such as the Aleutians. The inner Pacific islands fall into three main groups: Melanesia, Micronesia and Polynesia. With the development of modern communications, trade and co-operation between countries surrounding the ocean – sometimes referred to as the "Pacific Rim" – is increasing. Countries such as Japan, Australia and New Zealand want the South Pacific made into a Nuclear-Free Zone, which would prevent all testing of nuclear weapons.

The Aleutians, a chain of volcanic islands in the Pacific.

MICRONESIA
POP: 101,000

NAURU
POP: 11,000

A coral atoll in French Polynesia.

PALAU
POP: 17,000

CONTAINER PORTS
Today, fruit, meat and many other goods are moved round the world in huge metal containers. Here, a ship waits to be unloaded at Kōbe, one of Japan's main container ports.

FISHING
Pacific Islanders fish mainly for food, although any surplus catch may be sold. Many fish are caught in the North Pacific by commercial shipping fleets operating far from their home bases. The biggest catches are made by Japan, Korea, Taiwan and the USA. The main fish caught is tuna. Look for 🐟

COCONUTS
The coconut palm is called "tree of life" by Pacific Islanders because it provides so many of their daily needs, such as food and building materials. Here the white "meat" of the coconut is dried to make copra, which is edible. Look for 🥥

Skipjack tuna

FIJI
Fiji is a group of volcanic islands surrounded by coral reefs. Although one of the few South Pacific islands to develop tourism, Fiji's economy is still dominated by the sugar cane crop – shown here being harvested. Recently, a number of tax-free factories have been set up which export a variety of products overseas; clothing, in particular, has proved very successful. Look for ⇩

SOLOMON ISLANDS
POP: 400,000

Tropical growth on an island in the Tonga group.

KEYBOX

Fishing: Since the first salmon farms were set up in 1982 around Chiloé Island, Chile, salmon farming has become a major industry. Look for 🐟

Mining: The South Pacific island of Nauru has become prosperous through the export of phosphates, used to make fertilizers. Look for ⬤

Pollution: Nuclear testing carried out by the USA and France has polluted certain islands in the South Pacific. Look for ☢

⇩	Sugar cane	🚢	Fishing ports
🥥	Coconuts	⚓	Tourism
🌴	Timber	⨈	Whales
🦐	Shellfishing	⫴	Military bases

VANUATU
POP: 173,000

FIJI
POP: 700,000

ISLANDS
The Pacific islands are scattered over a huge area, far from any industrial centre and from each other. Some of the islands are high and volcanic, others low coral atolls. They are home to over five million people whose one great shared resource is the sea. A huge variety of fish and shellfish are caught from small boats and by diving. In general, the soil of the islands is poor.

An outrigger canoe, the traditional craft of the Pacific Islanders.

— Outrigger float

— Wooden dugout hull

MARSHALL ISLANDS
POP: 48,000

Giant clam

UNITED STATES
POP: 263,563,000
HAWAII
POP: 1,160,000

KIRIBATI
POP: 66,000

NATURAL HAZARDS

The Pacific region is plagued by tropical storms, called typhoons. The area is also prone to tidal waves, or *tsunamis*, which are caused by a volcanic eruption or earthquake taking place underwater. A *tsunami* travels at great speed across the ocean, increasing to a huge size when it reaches shallow waters around the coast.

FARMING THE SEA

Aquaculture – or farming the sea for food – has gone on for centuries. China and Korea produce large quantities of seaweed each year; all kinds of shellfish are cultivated. The once plentiful Giant Clam, recently endangered due to over-fishing, can now be bred on farms. It is cultivated in the coastal waters of the South Pacific. Look for 🦪

MILITARY BASES

Powerful nations, such as the USA, are able to control and monitor vast expanses of ocean with their large navies. Fleets are stationed at strategic points, such as the USA's base at Guam. Its naval headquarters in the western Pacific is at Pearl Harbour on Hawaii, shown here. Look for ⫴

SURFING

Riding waves on a surf board is a popular sport. The world's major surf-sites are on coasts facing great expanses of ocean, where waves can grow and gather speed before they break on the seashore. The Pacific has many superb surfing areas, such as Hawaii.

GALAPAGOS ISLANDS

The British naturalist, Charles Darwin, used his observations of the plants and animals on the Galápagos Islands as evidence for his theory of evolution. The islands are still inhabited by species found nowhere else in the world, such as this giant tortoise.

Over 600 of these massive stone figures stand on Easter Island.

TOURISM

Despite improved air and sea links, tourism in the South Pacific islands is still relatively undeveloped. Islands lack modern facilities such as roads and hotels, and many suffer from a shortage of fresh water. Here a cruise ship anchors off Fiji. Look for ⚓

TONGA
POP: 101,000

WESTERN SAMOA
POP: 162,000

TUVALU
POP: 13,000

N

0	500	1000	1500	2000	2500	3000	KM
0		500		1000		1500	MILES

129

Koala
Phascolarctos cinereus
Length: 80 cm (31 in)

Funnel-web spider
Atrax robustus
Length: 3 cm (1 in)

Raggiana's bird of paradise
Paradisaea raggiana
Length: 1.4 m (4 ft)

OCEANIA

OCEANIA INCLUDES AUSTRALIA, New Zealand and numerous island groups in the Pacific. Australia – the smallest, flattest and driest continent – has been worn down by 3,000 million years of exposure to wind and rain. Away from Australia, along the edges of the continental plates, volcanic activity is common because the plates are still moving. These plate movements greatly affect New Guinea, the Pacific Islands and New Zealand. Elsewhere in the Pacific Ocean, thousands of tiny coral islands have grown on the tops of undersea volcanic mountains. Climates vary greatly across the region, from the wet tropical climates of the islands in the outer Pacific, to the hot, dry deserts of central Australia. Tropical rainforest can be found in northern Australia and on New Guinea.

Cider gum tree
Eucalyptus gunnii
Height: 25 m (76 ft)

Taipan
Oxyuranuus scutellatus
Length: 3.6 m (12 ft)

Giant white buttercup
Ranunculus lyalii
Size: 1 m (3 ft)

DESERT MOUNTAINS
For millions of years, erosion has scoured the centre of Australia. Mountains like Mount Olga have been reduced to stumps of sandstone.

SURF AND SAND
Powerful waves from the Tasman Sea wash the southeast coast of Australia, creating long, sandy beaches.

AUSTRALIA'S RAINFOREST
Over 600 different types of trees grow in the tropical rainforest on the Cape York Peninsula. Mists often hang over the forest.

TROPICAL GRASSLAND
Three great deserts dominate the centre of Australia. On the desert margins, some rain falls enabling scattered trees and grasses to grow.

DRY WOODLAND
Gum trees – otherwise known as Eucalyptus – abound in Australia. Many species are adapted to dry conditions, with leaves that hang straight down to avoid the full heat of the sun.

TEMPERATE RAINFOREST
Far from other land and surrounded by ocean, much of New Zealand has high rainfall and is warm all year round. These conditions encourage the unique plants of the temperate rainforest.

Black opal, a precious stone found in Australia.

△ **HOT NEW ZEALAND**
Steam rises from pools of sulphurous boiling water and mud, signs of volcanic activity along the plate margins. The heat comes from deep within the earth.

THE PINNACLES
Western Australia's weird limestone pinnacles stand out in the sandy desert. Rain and plant roots have shaped the pillars over the last 25,000 years.

CROSS-SECTION THROUGH AUSTRALIA AND OCEANIA

Exmouth Plateau
Great Victoria Desert
Flinders Ranges
Pacific Ocean
Indian Ocean
Mt. Bruce
Australian Alps
New Zealand
Tasman Sea

3,000 (9,843)
Sea level 0
-4,500 (14,764)
Metres (feet)

A

Length: 7,250 km (4,500 miles)

B

▲ **NEW ZEALAND'S ALPS**
Rising steeply from the coast, the Southern Alps cover 80 per cent of South Island. Glaciers moving down the mountains carved deep inlets – fjords – along the southwest coast.

Red kangaroo
Macropus rufus
Height: 2 m (6 ft)

Brown kiwi
Apteryx australis
Height: 35 cm (14 in)

Giant clam
Tridacna gigas
Shell: 1.5 m (5 ft)

Butterfly fish
Chaetodon auriga
Length: 20 cm (8 in)

PACIFIC OCEAN

Caroline Ridge

Melanesian
Basin

Gilbert Ridge

Equator

PHILIPPINE SEA

Philippine Basin

Philippine Trench

10057m

CELEBES SEA

Celebes Basin

Halmahera

Probable plate margin

Moluccas

Seram

JAVA SEA

EAST INDIES

Java

Bali

Sumba

Flores

Timor

EURASIAN PLATE

INDO-AUSTRALIAN PLATE

Yap Trench

8527m

BISMARCK SEA

Manam
1830m △

New Ireland

BISMARCK RANGE

Mt. Wilhelm
4506m ▲

New Britain

Mt. Ulawun
2335m △

New Britain Trench

8940m ▼

Solomon Islands

Mt. Bagana
1999m △

New Guinea

SOLOMON SEA

4036m △

OWEN STANLEY RANGE

Torres Strait

ARAFURA SEA

CAPE YORK PENINSULA

Great Barrier Reef

Coral Sea Basin

CORAL SEA

INDO-AUSTRALIAN PLATE

PACIFIC PLATE

Vanuatu

West Fiji Basin

Fiji

New Hebrides Trench

9175m

Probable plate margin

20°

New Caledonia

Tropic of Capricorn

South Fiji Basin

TIMOR SEA

ARNHEM LAND

Gulf of Carpentaria

Victoria

Flinders

North Australian Basin

KIMBERLEY PLATEAU

914m ▲

TANAMI DESERT

Lord Howe Seamounts

New Caledonia Basin

GREAT DIVIDING RANGE

A

Exmouth Plateau

GREAT SANDY DESERT

Mt. Bruce
122m ▲

L. Mackay

MACDONNELL RANGES
1510m ▲

SIMPSON DESERT

Great Artesian Basin

1615m ▲

Lord Howe Rise

North Island

GIBSON DESERT

Mt. Olga ▲
1069m

Uluru ▲
868m

AUSTRALIA

L. Eyre
16m

Darling

GREAT VICTORIA DESERT

L. Torrens

FLINDERS RANGES

Murray

L. Taupo

Ruapehu
2797m

40°

Perth Basin

Pinnacles Desert

NULLARBOR PLAIN

Great Australian Bight

Mt. Kosciusko
2230m
AUSTRALIAN ALPS

Bass Strait

New Zealand

TASMAN SEA

Probable plate margin

Sutherland Falls
580m

Mt. Cook
3764m

SOUTHERN ALPS

South Island

B

South Australian Basin

Tasmania

South Tasman Rise

INDO-AUSTRALIAN PLATE

PACIFIC PLATE

Macquarie Ridge

INDO-AUSTRALIAN PLATE
ANTARCTIC PLATE

Campbell Plateau

60°

SOUTHERN OCEAN

Hjort Trench

PACIFIC PLATE

ANTARCTIC PLATE

Antarctic Circle

Probable plate margin

South Indian Basin

ROSS SEA

ANTARCTICA

CORAL ISLAND
Coral grows in warm shallow seas.
Coral reefs surround many Pacific
islands, like this one in Fiji, and
form Australia's Great Barrier Reef.

The Southern triton
is common in
Australian waters.

Frilled lizard
Chlamydosaurus kingii
Length: 1 m (3 ft)

KEY TO SYMBOLS

▲ *Mountain*

△ *Volcano*

✲ *Mangroves*

▦ *Wetlands*

Coral reef

Plate margins with direction of movement

KEY TO NATURAL VEGETATION

☐ *Dry woodland*

☐ *Tropical grassland*

☐ *Hot desert*

☐ *Temperate grassland*

Tropical rainforest

Mediterranean-type

Temperate rainforest

AUSTRALIA AND PAPUA NEW GUINEA

AUSTRALIA IS A LAND OF EXTREMES. It is the world's smallest, flattest continent, with the lowest rainfall. The landscape ranges from rainforest along the north coast to arid desert – called the Outback – in the centre, to snowfields in the southeast. It is also one of the most urbanized countries; 70 per cent of the population live in towns and cities in the coastal regions, while much of the interior remains sparsely inhabited. Until two centuries ago this vast land was solely occupied by Aboriginal peoples, but in 1788 settlers from Britain established a colony on the southeast coast. Since then immigration, originally from Europe but now from Asia, has played a vital part in Australia's development. Australia is a wealthy and politically stable country with rich natural resources, steady population growth and increasingly strong trade links in the Pacific area, especially with Japan and the USA. Papua New Guinea, the eastern half of the mountainous island of New Guinea, was once an Australian colony, but became independent in 1975.

FLYING DOCTOR
In the Australian Outback, the nearest neighbour can live vast distances away. For a doctor to cover such huge areas by road would be impossible. About 60 years ago the Royal Flying Doctor Service was established. In an emergency a caller can contact the service by radio, 24 hours a day, and receive medical treatment within hours.

Quartz — Gold

MINING
Australia has large deposits of minerals such as gold, uranium, coal and diamonds. The mining of these minerals played an important part in the early development of the continent. Improved mining techniques have led to a resurgence in gold mining in Western Australia. Look for 🪙

THE GREAT OUTDOORS
Australia's climate is ideal for watersports and other outdoor activities. But Australians are increasingly aware of the danger of skin cancer due to the hole in the ozone layer above the Antarctic, and are learning to take precautions when in the sun.

Yam

Cassava

Cassava and yam are staple foods in Papua New Guinea.

KEYBOX

🐄	**Cattle:** Australia has about 24 million cattle and exports beef and veal to over 100 countries, especially Japan and the USA. Look for ▼
⛑	**Mining:** Papua New Guinea has recently become a major producer of gold, which is mined on the mainland and on the outlying islands. Look for 🪙
🦪	**Pearls:** Large South Sea pearls are cultivated in oysters in the waters along Australia's northwest coast. These are called "cultured" pearls. Look for 🦪

🐑 Sheep	⛴ Fishing ports
🌾 Cereals	⛏ Coal
🎋 Sugar cane	🏭 Industrial centre
🌲 Timber	✈ Major airstrips
🍇 Wine	⚓ Tourism

FIRST INHABITANTS
Aboriginal peoples believe they have occupied Australia since "before time began". Early Aboriginal societies survived by hunting and gathering. They had their own traditions of story telling, distinctive ceremonies and art styles. Today, 66 per cent of Aboriginal peoples live in towns. Here, 200 years after the first European settlement, activists march through Sydney demanding land rights. The government has introduced programmes to improve Aboriginal standards of living, education and employment.

The world's finest opals come from northern New South Wales.

WINE PRODUCTION
When Europeans began to settle in Australia, they brought with them skills such as wine-making. The British first began to grow grapes in South Australia, which now produces over half the country's wines and brandies. With the continued arrival of Europeans, other grapes were added, such as the famous French and German varieties. Grapes are now grown throughout the country, but notably in Western Australia in recent years. Australia is now producing vintages of international quality. Look for 🍇

### Map labels
TIMOR SEA
INDIAN OCEAN
Melville I.   Croker I.
Bathurst I.
Clarence Strait
DARWIN
ARN...
LA...
C. Londonderry   Joseph Bonaparte Gulf
Beef
Wyndham   Vic...
Beef
Collier Bay   Diamonds   KIMBERLEY PLATEAU   Beef
C. Leveque   KING LEOPOLD RANGES
Iron   Beef
Beef   Fitzroy   Halls Creek
Broome   NORT...
Copper
TERR...
Monte Bello Is.   Dampier   GREAT SANDY DESERT
Barrow I.   Port Hedland   Iron
North West C.   Iron   Manganese
HAMERSLEY RANGE   L. Mackay
Iron   L. Disappointment   MACDONNELL
L. Macleod   Ashburton   Iron
Gold   WESTERN
Carnarvon   Uluru
Murchison   GIBSON DESERT
Shark Bay   Gold
Dirk Hartog I.   Meekatharra   L. Carnegie   L. Wells
Gold   Gold
AUSTRALIA   GREAT VICTORIA DESERT
Mount Magnet   Nickel   AU...
Gold   Nickel
Geraldton   Gold
Zinc   L. Barlee   Nickel
L. Moore   Gold   Nickel
Oats   Kalgoorlie
Dairy   Wheat   NULLARBOR PLAIN
PERTH   Nickel
Fremantle   Gold   Gold
Rockingham   Dairy   Gold
C. Naturaliste   Dairy   Esperance   Great Australian Bight
Bunbury   Gold
Augusta   Barley   C. Pasley
C. Leeuwin
Albany

Lush, tropical rainforest in Queensland.

The Aboriginal peoples are skilled artists. This bark painting shows a crocodile.

MOUNTAIN BARRIERS

In highland areas of Papua New Guinea the mountain ranges have formed natural barriers between the different groups of people, helping to preserve a remarkable variety of cultures and languages. Over 700 different languages are still spoken there today.

PAPUA NEW GUINEA
POP: 4,100,000

PAPUA NEW GUINEA

Papua New Guinea's mountainous terrain and fast-flowing rivers make much of the country inaccessible by road. But an extensive network of airstrips have been built, and today almost every town and village has its airstrip. Look for ⊨

TOURISM

Two million tourists visit Australia each year, making tourism the country's fastest growing industry. The Great Barrier Reef is a major attraction, but the reef's fragile ecosystem is vulnerable to damage caused by divers and pollution. Look for ◮

Uluru (Ayers Rock) is a sacred site for some Aboriginal peoples.

Merino sheep are famous for their wool

SHEEP FARMING

Australia has about a sixth of the world's sheep – some 175 million of them. These produce a third of the world's wool, especially the fine quality used to make clothes. About 97 per cent of Australia's wool is exported, much of it to Japan, Western Europe and China. Look for ▼

SYDNEY

The concrete "sails" of the Sydney Opera House are a fitting emblem for one of the world's greatest sea-ports. Australia's largest city grew from the first European settlement on the continent, established by the British in 1788. Sydney will host the Olympic Games in the year 2000.

CULTURAL DIVERSITY

Immigration has been very important for the development of Australia. People from many different countries now live there, such as these Vietnamese schoolchildren who live in a Sydney suburb.

The red granite shoreline of eastern Tasmania.

AUSTRALIA
POP: 18,300,000

N

100 200 300 400 500 600 KM
0
0 100 200 300 MILES

133

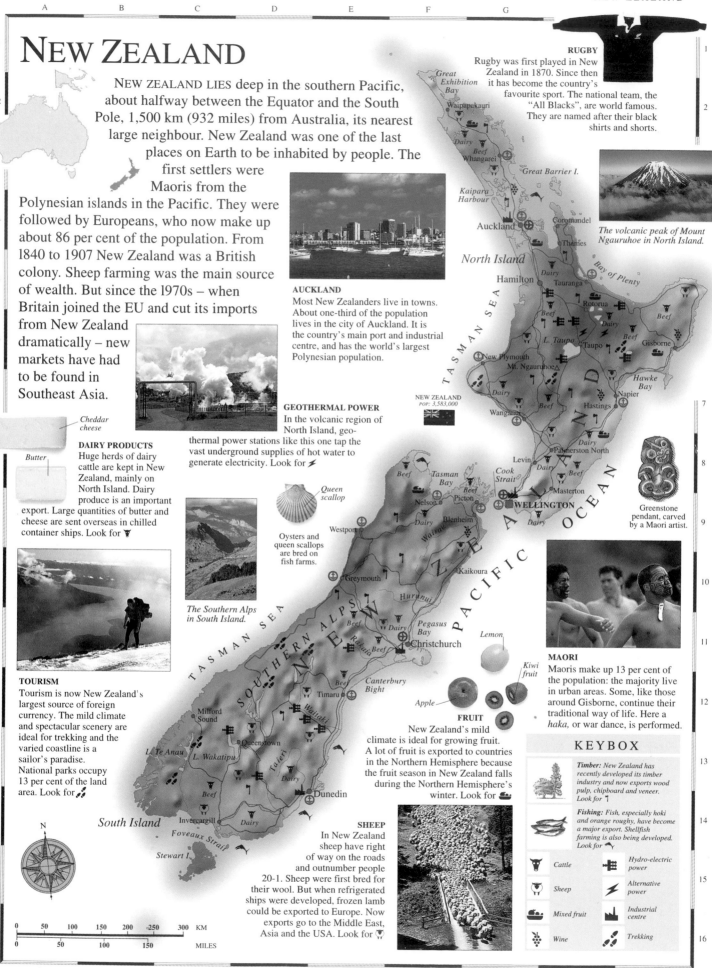

NEW ZEALAND

NEW ZEALAND LIES deep in the southern Pacific, about halfway between the Equator and the South Pole, 1,500 km (932 miles) from Australia, its nearest large neighbour. New Zealand was one of the last places on Earth to be inhabited by people. The first settlers were Maoris from the Polynesian islands in the Pacific. They were followed by Europeans, who now make up about 86 per cent of the population. From 1840 to 1907 New Zealand was a British colony. Sheep farming was the main source of wealth. But since the 1970s – when Britain joined the EU and cut its imports from New Zealand dramatically – new markets have had to be found in Southeast Asia.

RUGBY
Rugby was first played in New Zealand in 1870. Since then it has become the country's favourite sport. The national team, the "All Blacks", are world famous. They are named after their black shirts and shorts.

The volcanic peak of Mount Ngauruhoe in North Island.

AUCKLAND
Most New Zealanders live in towns. About one-third of the population lives in the city of Auckland. It is the country's main port and industrial centre, and has the world's largest Polynesian population.

NEW ZEALAND
POP: 3,583,000

Cheddar cheese

DAIRY PRODUCTS
Huge herds of dairy cattle are kept in New Zealand, mainly on North Island. Dairy produce is an important export. Large quantities of butter and cheese are sent overseas in chilled container ships. Look for ♥

Butter

GEOTHERMAL POWER
In the volcanic region of North Island, geo-thermal power stations like this one tap the vast underground supplies of hot water to generate electricity. Look for ⚡

Queen scallop

Oysters and queen scallops are bred on fish farms.

Greenstone pendant, carved by a Maori artist.

The Southern Alps in South Island.

MAORI
Maoris make up 13 per cent of the population: the majority live in urban areas. Some, like those around Gisborne, continue their traditional way of life. Here a *haka*, or war dance, is performed.

TOURISM
Tourism is now New Zealand's largest source of foreign currency. The mild climate and spectacular scenery are ideal for trekking and the varied coastline is a sailor's paradise. National parks occupy 13 per cent of the land area. Look for 👣

Lemon

Kiwi fruit

Apple

FRUIT
New Zealand's mild climate is ideal for growing fruit. A lot of fruit is exported to countries in the Northern Hemisphere because the fruit season in New Zealand falls during the Northern Hemisphere's winter. Look for 🍱

SHEEP
In New Zealand sheep have right of way on the roads and outnumber people 20-1. Sheep were first bred for their wool. But when refrigerated ships were developed, frozen lamb could be exported to Europe. Now exports go to the Middle East, Asia and the USA. Look for 🐑

KEYBOX

Timber: New Zealand has recently developed its timber industry and now exports wood pulp, chipboard and veneer. Look for ⫟

Fishing: Fish, especially hoki and orange roughy, have become a major export. Shellfish farming is also being developed. Look for ⌐

🐂 Cattle	Hydro-electric power
🐑 Sheep	⚡ Alternative power
Mixed fruit	Industrial centre
🍇 Wine	👣 Trekking

South Island

North Island

N

| 0 | 50 | 100 | 150 | 200 | 250 | 300 | KM |
| 0 | 50 | 100 | 150 | MILES |

Great Exhibition Bay
Waipapakauri
Dairy
Beef
Whangarei
Great Barrier I.
Kaipara Harbour
Auckland
Coromandel
Thames
Hamilton
Dairy
Tauranga
Bay of Plenty
Rotorua
Beef
Beef
Dairy
Beef
New Plymouth
Mt. Ngauruhoe
L. Taupo
Taupo
Gisborne
Dairy
Beef
Hastings
Hawke Bay
Napier
Wanganui
Beef
Palmerston North
Levin
Dairy
Beef
Masterton
WELLINGTON
Cook Strait
Tasman Bay
Nelson
Beef
Picton
Blenheim
Westport
Dairy
Wairau
Greymouth
Hurunui
Kaikoura
Beef
Dairy
Pegasus Bay
Beef
Christchurch
Rakaia
Beef
Canterbury Bight
Beef
Timaru
Waitaki
Milford Sound
Queenstown
L. Te Anau
L. Wakatipu
Taieri
Dairy
Beef
Dunedin
Invercargill
Dairy
Foveaux Strait
Stewart I.

TASMAN SEA
PACIFIC OCEAN
SOUTHERN ALPS
NEW ZEALAND

GLOSSARY

This list provides clear and simple meanings for certain geographical and technical terms used in this atlas.

Acid rain Rain which has been made poisonous by industrial pollution.

AIDS (Acquired Immune Deficiency Syndrome). A fatal condition spread by infected blood and certain body fluids.

Alliance A union of nations, which has been agreed by treaty for economic, political or military purposes

Alluvium Loose material, such as **silt**, sand and gravel, carried by rivers.

Alternative energy Sources of energy which can be renewed – such as solar or wind power. These forms of energy, unlike fossil fuel energy such as coal and oil, do not produce pollution.

Apartheid The policy, developed in South Africa, of separating peoples by race. Non-whites did not have the same democratic rights, and many public institutions were restricted to one race only.

Aquaculture Cultivation of fish and shellfish in lakes, **estuaries**, rivers or the sea.

Archipelago A group of islands.

Atoll A circular or horseshoe-shaped coral reef enclosing a shallow area of water.

Bilingual Speaking two languages.

Biotechnology The use of living organisms in the manufacture of food, drugs and other products. Yeast, for example, is used to make beer and bread.

Buddhism A religion that began in India in about 500 BC. It is based on the teachings of Buddha, who believed that good or evil deeds can be rewarded or punished in this life, or in other lives that will follow. Buddhists aim to achieve inner peace by living their lives according to the example set by Buddha.

Cash crop Agricultural produce grown for sale, often for foreign export, rather than to be consumed by the country or locality where it was grown.

Christianity A religion that began in the 1st century BC. Christians believe in one God and follow the teachings of Jesus Christ, whom they believe was the Son of God.

Civil war A war between rival groups of people who live in the same country.

Classical Art, architecture or literature which originated in the time of the ancient Greeks and Romans.

Colony A territory which belongs to another country. Also a group of people living separately within a country.

Communism An economic and political system of the 19th and 20th centuries in which farms, factories and the goods they produce are owned by the state.

Coniferous Trees or shrubs, like pine and fir, which have needles instead of leaves. Most are evergreen.

Conquistador The word is Spanish for "conqueror", and was applied to the Spanish explorers and invaders of Mexico and parts of South America in the 16th century.

Consumer goods Objects such as food, clothing, furniture, cars and televisions which are purchased by people for their personal and private use.

Continental plates The huge, interlocking plates which make up the Earth's surface. A plate margin is an area where two plates meet and is the point at which **earthquakes** occur most frequently.

Continental shelf The edge of a landmass which forms a shallow, raised shelf in the sea.

Cosmopolitan Influenced by foreign cultures.

Cottage industry The manufacture of products – often traditional ones like textiles or pottery – by people in their own homes.

Crude oil Oil in its original state, before chemicals and other oils have been removed by various processes in a refinery.

Crusades A series of wars from the 11th to 13th centuries when Christian European armies fought against non-Christian, often Islamic, armies for possession of the Holy Land, or Palestine.

Cultural heritage Anything handed down from a country's past, such as its traditions, art and architecture.

Currency The money of a particular country.

Deforestation The cutting of trees for timber or clearing of forest for farmland. The land is often left bare, leading to soil erosion and increasing the risk of flooding and landslides.

Democracy A political system in which everyone above a certain age has the right to vote for the election of his or her representative in the national and local government.

Desertification The creation of deserts either by changes in climate or by over-grazing, over-population, **deforestation** or over-cultivation.

Developing world Parts of the world which are still undergoing the process of industrialization.

Dictator A political leader who assumes absolute rule of a nation.

Earthquake A trembling or more violent movement of the ground caused by **seismic activity**. Earthquakes occur most frequently along **continental plate** margins.

Economy The organization of a country's finances, exports, imports, industry, agriculture and services.

Ecosystem A community of plants and animals dependent on each other and the habitat in which they live.

Electronics The use of electricity to produce signals that carry information and control devices, such as telephones or computers.

Emigrant A person who has moved from one country or region to settle in another country or region.

Empire A large group of countries ruled by one person – an emperor.

Equator An imaginary East-West line that circles the middle of the Earth at equal distance from the **Poles**. The Equator also marks the nearest point on the Earth's surface to the Sun, so has a consistently hot climate.

Estuary The mouth of a river, where the saltwater of the tide meets the freshwater of the river.

Ethnic diversity People of several different cultures living in the same region.

Ethnic minority A group of people who share a culture, and are outnumbered by others living in the same region.

European Union (EU) (or European Community, EC) A group of European countries linked together by treaty to promote trade, industry and agriculture within a **free-market economy**.

Exports Goods produced in a country but sold abroad.

Fauna Animals of a region.

Flora Plants of a region.

Foreign debt The money owed by one country to the government, banks or institutions of one or more other countries.

Foreign exchange Money brought into a country from abroad, usually by the sale of **exports**, by **service industries** or by tourism.

Free-market economy An economy which is regulated by the price of goods bought and sold freely in national and international markets.

Geothermal energy Electricity produced from hot rocks under the Earth's surface which heat water and produce steam which can then be used to generate electricity.

Geyser A fountain of hot water or steam that erupts periodically as a result of underground streams coming into contact with hot rocks.

Greenhouse effect A rise in the global temperature caused as heat, reflected and radiated from the Earth's surface, is trapped in the atmosphere by a build up of "greenhouse" gases, such as carbon dioxide. Also called "global warming".

Habitat A place or region where a certain animal or plant usually lives.

Heavy industry Industry that uses large amounts of energy and raw materials to produce heavy goods, such as machinery, ships or locomotives.

Hunter-gatherers People who do not grow their food, but obtain it by hunting it and gathering it from their environment. There are few hunter-gatherer groups left in the world today.

Hydro-electric power (HEP) Electricity produced by harnessing the force of falling water.

ICBM (Inter-continental Ballistic Missile) A missile, usually with a nuclear warhead, that can be fired from one continent to land in another.

Immigrant A person who has come to live in a country from another country or region.

Incentives Something that arouses or encourages people to greater efforts.

Inflation The rate at which a country's prices increase.

Informal economy An economy in which people buy and sell from each other, not through shops or markets.

Infrastructure The buildings, transport and communication links that enable goods to be produced and then moved about within a country.

Irrigation A system of watering dry areas. Water is carried or pumped to the area through pipes or channels.

Islam A religion revealed to the prophet Mohammed in the 7th century AD in the Middle East. Its followers, called Muslims (or Moslems), believe in one God, called Allah. The rules and beliefs of Islam are contained in its holy book, the Koran.

Islamic fundamentalist A person who strictly follows the rules and beliefs of Islam contained in the holy book, the Koran. See **Islam**.

Isthmus A narrow piece of land, connecting two larger bodies of land, surrounded on two sides by water.

Labour intensive An activity which requires large amounts of work or large numbers of workers to accomplish it.

Lent A period of time lasting 40 days observed by Christians during which they fast and prepare for the festival of Easter.

Lignite Woody or brown coal.

Living standards The quality of life in a country, usually measured by income, material possessions, and levels of education and health care.

Malnutrition A prolonged lack of adequate food.

Market gardening Farms and **smallholdings** growing fruit and vegetables for sale.

Megalopolis A very large or continuous urban area in which several large towns or cities have joined as their urban areas have spread.

Metropolis A major city, often the capital.

Militarized zone An area occupied by armed military forces.

Multi-national company A company which has branches, or factories, in several countries.

Nationalists Groups of people united in their wish for independence from a government or from foreign rule.

Neutral country A country which refrains from taking part in international conflicts.

Nomad A person who does not settle in one place for any length of time, but moves in search of hunting or grazing land.

Oil shale Flaky rock containing oil.

Pastoralist A person who makes a living from grazing livestock.

Peat Decomposed vegetation found in bogs. It can be dried and used as fuel.

Peninsula A strip of land surrounded on three sides by water.

Permafrost Permanently frozen ground. The surface thaws in summer but water cannot drain away through the frozen subsurface. Typical of **Subarctic** areas.

Pharmaceuticals The manufacture of medicinal drugs.

Plantation A large farm on which only one crop is usually grown.

Plate margin See **Continental plates.**

Polar regions The regions around the North and South Poles which are permanently frozen and where the temperature only rises above freezing point for a few months of the year.

Poles, the The term applied to the North and South Poles, the northernmost and southernmost points of the Earth's axis or rotation.

Prairie A Spanish/American term for a large area of grassland.

Privatization When state-owned activities and companies are taken over by private firms.

Protestant A member of one of the main Christian religions founded in the 16th century by those who did not agree with all aspects of the Roman Catholic Church. Protestantism became one of the main branches of **Christianity**.

Quota A maximum quantity imposed on the number of goods produced, imported or exported by a country.

Rainforest Dense forest found in hot and humid equatorial regions; often called tropical rainforest.

Raw materials Substances in a natural or unrefined state used in the manufacture of goods, like cotton for textiles and bauxite for aluminium.

Refugees People who flee their own country or region because of political, religious or racial persecution.

Republic The form of government in a country that has no monarch. The head of state is usually a president, like the President of the USA.

Reservation An area of land set aside for occupation by specific people, plants or animals.

Revenue Money paid to a government, like taxes.

Roman Catholic A Christian who accepts the Pope as his or her spiritual leader.

Rural In, or belonging to, the countryside.

Savannah Tropical grasslands where an annual dry season prevents the growth of most trees.

Seismic activity Tremors and shocks in the Earth's crust usually caused by the movement of plates along a fault.

Service industry An industry that supplies services, such as banking, rather than producing manufactured goods.

Shanty town An area in or around a city where people live in temporary shacks, usually without basic facilities such as running water.

Silt Small particles, finer than sand, often carried by water and deposited on river banks, at river mouths and harbours. See also **alluvium.**

Smallholding A plot of agricultural land smaller than a farm.

Socialism Political system whereby the economy is owned and controlled by the state and not by private companies or individuals.

Soviet bloc All those countries which were ruled directly or indirectly by the communist government of the former USSR.

Staple crop The main crop grown in a region.

Staple food The basic part of a diet, such as rice or bread.

Steppes An extensive, grass-covered and virtually treeless plain, such as those found in Siberia.

Stock Exchange A place where people buy and sell government bonds, **currency**, stocks and financial shares in large private companies.

Strategic Carefully planned or well placed from a military point of view.

Subarctic The climate in **polar** regions, characterized by extremely cold temperatures and long winters.

Technological The application of science through the use of machines.

Temperate The mild, variable climate found in areas between the **tropics** and cold **polar** regions.

Tropic of Cancer, Capricorn Two imaginary lines of latitude drawn on the Earth's surface above and below the Equator. The hottest parts of the world are between these two lines.

Tropics, the An area between the **Equator** and the **tropics of Cancer and Capricorn** that has heavy rainfall and high temperatures and lacks any clear seasonal variation.

Tundra Vegetation found in areas within the Arctic Circle, such as dwarf bushes, very short grasses, mosses and lichens.

United Nations (UN) An association of countries established to work together to prevent wars, and to supply aid, advice and research on an international basis.

Urban area Town, city or extensive built-up area.

West, the Those countries in Europe and North America with **free-market economies** and **democratic** governments.

Western The economic, cultural and political values shared by countries belonging to **the west.**

Dorling Kindersley would like to thank the following for their help supplying objects for photography: Catherine Lucas, Clare Carolin, Dina Adkins, Clive Webster; Russian Connections for supplying the *draniki* on p.5 and p.80; Mexicolore, London, for skeleton and *sarape* on p.38; Fiat Auto SpA for Fiat Tempra on p.47; Uruguayan Embassy for scarf on p.49; Rosenthal Studio Haus Ltd., London, for glass fruit on p.57; Heal's, London, for child's chair on p.57; Minans Restaurant, London, for *rijstafel* on p.64; Philips Consumer Electronics, London, for television on p.65; BMW (GB) Ltd., Bracknell, for car on p.66; Leica UK, London, for camera on p.67; Watches of Switzerland Ltd., London, for watch on p.69; Hannah Kodicek for puppet on p.70; Henry Marchant Ltd., London for Bohemian glass on p.70 and ballet costume on p.83; Exico Ltd., London, for wooden duck on p.71; The Greek Shop, London, for doll on p.79; Soccer Scene, London for football shirt on p.73 and rugby shirt on p.134; Gucci, London, for shoes and scarf on p. 72; Embassy of Latvia for currency on p.80; Embassy of Lithuania for currency on p.80; The Russian Shop, London, for chess set, child's toy, lacquered box on p.83, Georgian scarf and Russian dolls on cover and p.85, *samovar* and doll on p.112 and mink hat on p.113; Liberty's, London, for rug on p.88; African Centre, London, for African sculptures on p.93, cover and p.94; Sofra Restaurant, London, for coffee pot and dish on cover and p.123; Covent Garden Oriental Carpets for carpet and saddle cloth on p.110; Ranger Arms Co. Ltd. for gun on p.106; Sandra Schneider for *yarmulke*, prayer book, shawl, etc. on p.106; Saree Emporium, London, for saris on p.117; East West Herb Shop, London, for herbal medicines on p.119; Chuntex (UK) Ltd. for computer monitor on p.121; Tourism Authority of Thailand for lacquer work on p.124.

Map symbols designed by: Kenny Laurenson

Other help supplied by: Crispian Martin St. Valery, Alastair Owens, Janet Oswald, Rosemary Cowan, Jane Lewis, Judy Chamberlain, Michael Capon and George Heritage.

Antarctic terrain supplied by Mullard Space Science Laboratory, University College London, using data from the radar altimeter aboard the European Space Agency's ERS-1 satellite

PICTURE CREDITS:
Heather Angel: 86cl. B. and C. Alexander: 25tl, 25tr, 51cl. Max Alexander: 63cr. P. and G. Bowater: 69bcb. Chris Branfield: front cover cl. Duncan Brown: 117bl. J Allan Cash: front cover bl, 31tr, 36tc, 38cl, 42cl, 42bc, 44bc, 49tcr, 56cr, 56bcl, 57bc, 57bl, 57br, 58tr, 60bl, 61c, 61bl, 61bc, 62cl, 71c, 74ct, 76c, 76bc, 78br, 92 c, 93br, 94bl, 100bc, 104ct, 104cl, 105bc, 108bl, 108hr, 109tr, 109bcr, 110br, 114tcr, 117ct, 120cbr, 123c, 127c. Cephas: 49ctr. Mark Chapman: 93cl. J.R.Chapman: 88cr, 88br, 96tr, 116cr, 117tl. Oliver Crimmon: 96ctr. Ann Clarke: 49bc. John Cleare/Mountain Camera: 40bcl. Stephanie Colasanti: 106cr. Bruce Coleman: 65bl, 18tr; Gene Ahrens 26cb, 27tl, 27cr; Alain Compost 126cr, 126bl; Gerald Cubitt 13bl, 94bl, 99bc, 99cb, 114ct, 114ctr, 114cbl, 126cr; Francisco J.Erize 50cl; M. P. L. Fogden 35tc; Jeff Foott Productions 20ct; Christer Fredriksson 86cttr; Dr. Charles Henneghien 93tc; Hans Gerd Heyer 121cbr; Udo Hirsch 129cbr; Johnny Johnson 50cr;

Herbert Kranawetter 75br; O. Langrand 95tl; Wayne Lankinen 30bcl; Thor Larsen 51bc; Leonard Lee Rue 21cbr; Luiz C. Marigo 13cbl, 40ctr; Larry Mulvehill/Black Star 120cl; John Murray 114cl, 128cbl; Orion Press 122cr; Charlie Ott 20tl; Dieter and Mary Plage 40ctl; Dr. Eckhart Pott 38c; Dr. Sandro Prato 73cl, 128cb; Fritz Prenzel 128cb, 28br; Hans Reinhard 50bl, 71bc; N.Tomalin 35tr; Konrad Wothe 101tl; Jonathan T. Wright 32c, 83tl; J. Zwanepoel 65cl. Colorific: Linda Bartlett 75c; Steve Benbow 75bc; Marcus Brooke 102ctl; David Burnett/Contact Press 33ctr; Paul Conklin 32cl; John Dominis 74cl; Enrico Ferorelli 33ct; Frank Hermann 94tr; Anthony Joyce 133bl; Sarah Meltzoff/Black Star 137tr; Christopher Morris/Blackstar 75tr; Peter Nacke/Picture Group 84clb; Lehtikuva Ov 14cb; Reza/Black Star 15tl; Malcolm Sanders 133tl; Michael St. Maur Sheil 99c; Peter Turnley/Blackstar 84tr. Comstock: 72ct. Steven J. Cooling 99ct, 134cbl. Lupe Cubna: 48tc. James Davis/Worldwide: 24bc, 46br, 52bl, 53cr, 69bl, 89ct, 107bl; WVF/Maarten Udema 112cl. Ecoscene: Peter Hulme back cover cr, 55cl. Lynn Edelman: 45bc. For Eigeland: 96cl. Environmental Picture Library: 92 tr, 102ctr. Robert Estall: 23bc. Chris Fairclough: 90c, 106c, 116cl, 117c; P. George 117tc. Sydney Freelance: 132bl. Ronald Grant Archive: 116bl. Sonia Halliday: Sue Taylor 107br. R. Hanbury Tennison: 77cbr. Robert Harding: front cover cr, 11tr, 13tr, 14cr, 15tc, 23cb, 26cr, 27bcl, 35cr, 39cb, 39bl, 45cl, 46ctr, 46tr, 49cr, 52cl, 56tcr, 56cl, 56c, 61c, 63cbr, 65tl, 65bl, 68tr, 68cl, 68br, 76cl, 78cl, 79tr, 80cr, 89tr, 89tcr, 90br, 91bl, 93bc, 98cbl, 100tc, 111bc, 116br, 117bcr, 125tcl, 125cr, 125bcl, 125cb, 125bc, 125br, 127tcr; Mohamed Amin 108cl; Bildagentur Schuster/Eckhardt 66cl, 66tr, 67cl, 78cbr; Bildagentur Schuster/Scholz 85tr; Graham Birch 126tr; C.E.Clark 99cr; C Delu 95ctl; F.Dubes 63bc; Alan L.Durand 85cbr; Explorer/J. P. Nacivet 62c; Robert Fererck 45tc; Fournie 124cr; Robert Francis 13cl, 39c, 39bcr; Lee Frost 78c; James Green 79bcr; Ian Griffiths 94cr, 133tcr; Gavin Heller 43bl, 115tl; Michael Jenner 104cb, 107cr; Paolo Koch 126ccr; David Lomax 42cr, 43tc; Claude Martine 63cb; Photri 10tr, 100tr, 28tr; Chris Rennie 39cr, 77tr, 77ct, 110cl; Rolf Richardson 77bc; Sassoon 124tc; M. Short 79cb, 105cb, 105bl; Julia Thorne 51br; David Tokeley 116ct; Adina Tovy 29bl; Vaduz 68cr; A. C.Waltham 34c, 34bcr; Elizabeth Weiland 119tl; G. M.Wilkins 99tl; Adam Woolfitt 53cl, 64tr, 64c, 75tc, 102ct, 104br. Paul Harris: 24ct, 24cb, 25br, 83cl, 83br, 113tr, 113cb, 113bcr, 118tcr, 119cl, 122c. J. Henderson: 79cb. John Heseltine: 59tr. Leila Hilland: 133tr. Jimmy Holmes /Himalayan Images: 118c, 118cl, 119c, 122cl, 123tl. Pippa Hurst: 88cl. Hutchison Library: 24cl, 43br, 92bl, 95cl, 107cl, 81tr, 13tcl; Robert Aberman 104bl; John Egan 79cr; Sarah Errington 100cr, 112bc; J.G.Fuller 129tc; John Hatt 102tbr; Richard House 47ctl; Victoria Ivleva 81c; Joan Klatchko 104cr, 104bl; Michael Macintyre 121ctr, 129tr; Stephen Pern 49cr; R. Reeve 52ctr; Bernard Regent 130ctl; Kirsten Rodgers 44tcr; Prue Rankin Smith 42tr; Andrei Solomonov 85ct; Trevor Page 10ltr; Michael Macintyre 121ctr; A. Hyman: 110c. ICCE: S. M. Andrews 86ctl, 89bl. Image Bank: 9ccl; Peter Hendrie, 85bc; H.J.Aders 50ct; Gio Barto 88tr; Vladimir Birgos 81tcl; Ira Block 22cr; David Brownell 35tcr; P. and G. Bowater 33cl; Edward W. Bower 28cl; Luis Castaneda 29bc; Gerard Champlong 34cl; Gary S. Chapman 42bcr; S. Costa 47bc; Melchior Di Giacomo 15bl, 43c; Wendy Dison 119bl; Tom Owen Edwards 51cbl, 75cr; Grant V. Faint 69tc, 121cbl; David W. Hamilton 60br; David Hiser 114ctr; Don Klumpp 74c; Steve Krongard 11tr; Patti McConville 37tr; Fong Siu Nang 120bc; Nick Nicholson 129br; Albert Normandin 22bcr; Francisco Onatanon 61bl; John R. Ramey 35bl; Guido Alberto Rossi front cover bl, 43tr, 43ct, 100bcl; Steve Satushek 23tl, 36cbl, 12cb; Erik Leigh Simmons 31bc; John Lewis Stage 47tr; Peter Turner 28cr; Frank Wing 120tr; Hans Wolf 67br. Images: 14cl, 21bl; Andris Apse 130cbr; Horizon 127br. Impact: B. Babanov/Vika 113tcl; A. Bradshaw/Visions 113bc; Piers Cavendish 94ct, 97ctr; Rupert Conant 71tr; Anita Corbin 126c; John Denham 66tl; Colin Jones 28bl; Mike McQueen 114br; M. Milivojevic 70bl; Paul O'Driscoll 99tcr. Ann Jousiffe: 89br.

Kaleidoscope: Victor Englebert 93cbr. Frank Lane: D.Hoadley 12 tr; W. Wisniewski 53bl, 102cbr. Anthony Lambert: 77cr. Nicki Liddiard: 58cr. Life File: 48bl; Sue Davies 29c, 44tr; Juliet Highet 79br; Eddy Tan 60tr; Sergei Verein 113bl. Catherine Lucas: 96c. Magnum: Abbas 45tcr; Eve Arnold 90bl; Bruno Barbey 92cl, 109cr, 123cl, 124bl; Rene Burri 34bl; M. Franck 91tr; S. Franklin 90ctr, 108tr; Thomas Hoepker 66cr, 67cr; David Hurn/J.Hillelson 89cb; Hiroji Kubota 119cbr; Fred Mayer 102cr; Gideon Mendel 92e; Eli Reed 107tl; Marc Riboud 102bl, 109bc; Dennis Stock 26c, 28br; Kryn Taconis/John Hillelson 22br; Chris Steele-Perkins 91br, 98c; Dennis Stock 53tr. Military and Research Services/Todd Shipyards: 101tcl. Tim Motion: 60c, 62tr. National Maritime Museum: 101br. Natural History Photographic Agency: ANT 13ct; Anthony Bannister 86bcl; Stephen Krasemann 128tr; Dr. Ivan Polunin 114cbr; John Shaw 13ct. Nature Photographers: Peter Craig Cooper 98cbr; Mark Pidgeon 87bl; Roger Tidman 97tl. New Zealand Tourist Office: 134cr. Nissan: 58hr. Oxford Scientific Films: I. Bernard 40cbr; Tony Bomford 49bcr; Len E.Lauber 118c; Terry McCarthy 34c; Larry Ulrich 20tc; Konrad Wothe 40cr. Panos: 46cbr; Heidi Bradner 70ct; Matthew Boysons 52cr; Alain le Garsmeur 119tr. Philips CED Publicity: 65tcr. Pictor: back cover tl, 12ctr, 13cr, 14c, 22bl, 23tr, 28c, 31br, 32br, 33cbl, 47cr, 48tr, 55ctr, 59cl, 86cb, 86bcr, 90tr, 98bc, 101bc, 102cbl, 124c, 129ctr, 130bl. John Pilkington: 111tcr. Pirelli Cables: 53br. Planet Earth Pictures: 20tr, 20cl; Yuri Shibnev 102tr, 103tr; John Eastcott/Yva Momatiuk 13tc; William M. Smithey Jr. 21cbl. Philip Powell: front cover cbl. Quadrant: 47cr. Donna Rispoli 127c. Science Photo Library: Martin Bond 9ccr; David Parker 9 cr; Ray Ellis 13br; Simon Frazer 55cr; John Heseltine 55cb; Michael Martin 55tcl; Novosti Press Agency 112ct. South American Pictures: 44cr, 45bl, 49tcr. Spectrum: 55ctl, 55br, Jean Paul Nacivet 55tr. Frank Spooner: Tordai 38c. John Massey Stewart: 81tl. Still Pictures: 25tc; Doug Armand 100tr; Mark Edwards 88bc; Jim Kingshott 74br; Thia Konig 37ctr; Bob Evans 45cr; David Hanson 36bl, 37cbl, 71br; David Hiser 21cb, 51ct, 128br; Ernst Hohne 67bl; Gary Irving 30bc, 30bcr; Geoff Johnson 111tr; H. Richard Johnson 11tr; Chris Kapolka 130cr; Oldrich Karasek 70c; Mitch Kezan 96cl; Jim Kingshott 74br; Thia Konig 37ctr; Ken Wilson 133bc; Ina Strading: 81ct. Survival Anglia: 82c; Ross Bray 107bc; Andrew Park 16bc; Ken Biggs 12tcr; Allan Bramley 130ct; Doug Boult 24c; Michael Buselle 59bc; Julian Calder 111c, 121tl; Mike Caldwell 74bl; John Callahan 12lbc; Hubert Camille 62tr; Bryn Campbell 52tc; Paul Chesley 121cr, 130ctr, 134br; Paul Damien 33tl; Nicholas De Vore 40cb; Doris De Witt 28tr; Sepp Dietrich 71cb; Richard Elliot 134cb; John Garrett 132 cl; Margaret Gowan 120bl; David Hanson 36bl, 37cbl, 71br; David Hiser 21cb, 51ct, 128br; Ernst Hohne 67bl; Gary Irving 30bc, 30bcr; Geoff Johnson 111tr; H. Richard Johnson 11tr; Chris Kapolka 130cr; Oldrich Karasek 70c; Mitch Kezan 96cl; Jim Kingshott 74br; Thia Konig 37ctr; Peter Lamberti 11cbr; John Lawlor 37tl; Alan Levenson 121tr; Lukasseck 34cb; Angus Mackaillop 15cbl; Mike McQueen 55cl; Roger Mear 50br; Lawrence Migdale 59cr; Ian Murphy 59br, 64bl; Donald Nausbaum 41bl; Nicholas Parfitt 86cbr,96br; Tom Raymond 29cr; Mitch Reardon 2c,133cb; Steven Rothfeld 14br; David Schultz 33tr; Mark Segal 30c; Hugh Sitton 90cl, 100ctr, 104tr; Adam Smith 47cl, P. and K. Smith 36cr; Robin Smith 131bl; Bill Staley 21ctr; Alena Vikova 72tr; Charlie Waite 59bl, 73tr; Ken Wilson 133bc. Ina Strading: 81ct. Survival Anglia: 82c; Ross Bray 107bc; Andrew Park 16bc; Ken Biggs 12tcr; Allan Telegraph Colour Library: 58cl, 99tr; J. C. Davies 72cbr; N. MacIntyre 122br; J. C. Meauxsonne 53tcl; P.Wadey 121tr. Travel Photo International: 71ct, 120cbl. Tony Waltham: 9cl. Alan Watson: 40ct. Chris Whitwell: 119tc, 124tr. David Woodfall: 81bc. World Wildlife Fund: 40bcr; John Newby 93cr; Mauri Rautkari 94bcl. Zefa: 20ctl, 29cbr, 51ctl, 66bl, 70c, 73br, 80cr, 81tr, 94br, 106ctr; P. W. Bading 22tr; Jim Brandenburg 31tl; Damm front cover ce, 97cr; P. Fera 57tr, 109br; K. Goebel 27bcr, 108ct; Jens Herrman 91cbr; Hunter 121cbr; Janicek 105cr; Minden 96bl; Sonak 84bl; Steenmans 83tr.

INDEX

Throughout the Atlas, population figures have been taken from the latest official estimates.

HOW TO USE THE GRID

Page number 42
Grid reference A1

Grid references in the Index help you to find places on the map. For example, if you look up Nairobi in the Index, you will see the reference 97 O5. The first number, 97, is the page number of the map on which Nairobi appears. Find the letters and numbers which border the page, and trace a line across from the letter and down from the number. This directs you to the exact grid square in which Nairobi is located.

The numbers that appear after the names are the page numbers, followed by the grid references.

There are two sorts of factbox in the index. Countries that are more important economically or politically in their area have a larger factbox.

In the factboxes, many statistics are not yet available for the new states of the world. When we have been unable to find the correct figure, N/A is given, which stands for not available.

Population density
This is the total population divided by the land area of a country.

Average life expectancy
This is the average life expectancy at birth, barring war or natural disasters.

Literacy
This is the percentage of people over the age of 15 years who can read and write a simple sentence. Where figures for male (m) and female (f) have not been available, we have used an average (av.).

Death penalty
The countries with Yes use the death penalty regularly. Some of the states with No still have a law permitting the death penalty but do not use it.

Percentage of urban population
This is the percentage of the total population who live in towns or cities.

Calories consumed daily
The recommended daily number for a healthy life is about 2500 calories; the inhabitants of some countries consume far more than others.

The following abbreviations have been used in the index:

anc. = ancient name
Arch. = Archipelago
C. = Cape
E. = East
Ft. = Fort
I. = Island
Is. = Islands
L. = Lake
Mt. = Mountain
Mts. = Mountains
N. = North
N.P. = National Park
Pen. = Peninsula
prev. = previously
Pt. = Point
Res. = Reservoir
R. = River
S. = South
St. = Saint
var. = variant name
W. = West

A

A Coruña (var. La Coruña) Spain 52 J8, 60 G3
Aachen Germany 67 C11
Aalst Belgium 65 F14
Aarau Switzerland 68 F9
Aare *River* Switzerland 68 E9
Aba Nigeria 93 O13
Ābādān Iran 109 L7
Abajo Mountains *Mountain range* Utah, USA 35 K5
Abakan Russian Federation 112 J11
Abashiri Japan 122 M3
Abaya, L. *Lake* Ethiopia 91 J16
Abéché Chad 94 K7
Abengourou Ivory Coast 93 K12
Åbenrå Denmark 56 H16
Abeokuta Nigeria 93 N12
Aberdare Range *Mountain range* Kenya 97 O5
Aberdeen Scotland, UK 52 K7, 58 J8
Aberdeen South Dakota, USA 33 N6
Aberdeen Washington, USA 36 G7
Aberystwyth Wales, UK 59 G14
Abhā Saudi Arabia 108 H13
Abidjan Ivory Coast 93 K13
Abilene Texas, USA 35 P10
Abitibi, L. *Lake* Ontario/Quebec, Canada 25 K11
Abomey Benin 93 M12
Abu Dhabi (var. Abū Ẓabī) United Arab Emirates 109 N11
Abu Simbel *Archaeological site* Egypt 90 F9
Abū Ẓabī *see* Abu Dhabi
Abuja Nigeria 93 O11
Abydos *Archaeological site* Egypt 90 G8
Abyssinia *see* Ethiopia
Acapulco Mexico 39 M14
Accra Ghana 93 L13
Acheloos *River* Greece 78 H7
Achinsk Russian Federation 112 J10
Acklins I. *Island* Bahamas 43 M5
Aconcagua *Mountain* Argentina 41
Ad Dafrah *Desert region* United Arab Emirates 109 N12
Ad Dahna *Desert region* Saudi Arabia 109 L10
Ad Dammām Saudi Arabia 109 M9
Ad Dawḥah *see* Doha
Ad-Diwaniyah Iraq 109 K5
Adak I. *Island* Aleutian Is. Alaska, USA 22 A6
Adamawa Highlands *Physical region* Cameroon 87
Adana Turkey 105 M10
Adapazari Turkey 104 I5
Adare, C. *Cape* Victoria Land, Antarctica 50 E12
Addis Ababa Ethiopia 91 J15
Adelaide South Australia, Australia 133 L13
Aden Yemen 100 E7, 108 I16
Aden, Gulf of *Sea feature* Arabia/E Africa 87, 91 N14, 100 E7, 103, 114
Adige *River* Italy 72 I7
Adirı Libya 89 O8
Adirondack Mts. *Mountain range* New York, USA 27 L7
Adiyaman Turkey 105 O9
Admiralty Is. *Island group* Papua New Guinea 133 N1
Adrar Algeria 88 J8
Adrar des Ifôghas *Mountain range* Mali 93 M6
Adrian Michigan, USA 31 O10
Adriatic Sea S Europe 54, 72 K10, 74 I9
Adwa Ethiopia 91 J13
Adycha *River* Russian Federation 113 N6
Aegean Sea Greece/Turkey 54, 79 M7, 104 F7
Ağri (var. Karaköse) Turkey 105 R6
Afghanistan *Country* C Asia 110-111

Afghanistan 110-111

a Dari, Pashto • ⬤ Afghani • ▮ 25 • ⬤ 42 • ⬤ £7.03 • ✦ (m) 44% (f) 14% • ♀ 8 • ✦ 5148 • ✦ Yes • ⬚ 18% • ¶ 2022

Africa *Continent* 8, 11, 12, 13, 15, 87, 103
African Plate *Physical feature* 8, 20, 41, 54, 87, 103
'Afrīn *River* Syria/Turkey 107 N2
Afyon Turkey 104 J8
Agadez Niger 93 P7
Agadir Morocco 88 G6
Agartala India 117 P8
Agatti I. *Island* Aleutian Is. Alaska, USA 22 A4
Agen France 62 J13
Agios Nikolaos Crete, Greece 79 N16
Agra India 117 K5
Agri *River* Italy 73 M14
Agrigento Sicily 73 J18
Aguarico *River* Ecuador 44 D8
Aguascalientes Mexico 39 L10
Agulhas Basin *Sea feature* Atlantic/Indian Ocean 87
Agulhas, C. *Cape* South Africa 87, 98 J16
Agulhas current *Ocean current* Indian Ocean 12
Agulhas Ridge *Sea feature* Atlantic Ocean 87
Ahaggar *Mountain range* Algeria 87, 89 L11
Ahmadabad India 116 I8
Ahvāz Iran 109 M6
Aïr *Mountain range* Niger 93 P7
Aix-en-Provence France 63 O13
Aizawl India 117 Q8
Ajaccio Corsica 63 S16

Ajdābiyā Libya 89 Q7
Ajmer India 116 J6
Akanthou Cyprus 105 L12
Akhisar Turkey 104 H7
Akimiski I. *Island* Canada 24 J8
Akita Japan 122 K7
Akmola (var. Akmolinsk, Tselinograd) Kazakhstan 122 G11
Akmolinsk *see* Akmola
Akola India 117 K9
Akpatok I. *Island* Canada 25 N3
Akron Ohio, USA 31 Q10
Aksai Chin *Disputed region* China/India 16, 117 L1, 118 J2
Aksaray Turkey 105 L8
Akseki Turkey 104 J10
Aksu China 118 F7
Aksum Ethiopia 91 J13
Aktau (var. Shevchenko) Kazakhstan 112 D10
Aktyubinsk (var. Aqtöbe) Kazakhstan 112 E10
Akyab *see* Sittwe
Al 'Amārah Iraq 109 L6
Al 'Aqabah (var. Aqaba) Jordan 107 L14
Al Azraq Jordan 107 N10
Al Bāḩah Saudi Arabia 108 H12
Al Başrah Iraq 109 L7
Al Baydā Libya 89 R6
Al Baydā' Yemen 108 I16
Al Buraymī Oman 109 O11
Al Ghaydah Yemen 109 L16
Al Hoceima Morocco 88 J4
Al Hillah Iraq 109 K5
Al Hudaydah *see* Hodeida
Al Hufūf Saudi Arabia 109 L10
Al Ḩadīthah Iraq 109 J4
Al Ḩasakah Syria 107 R2
Al Jaghbūb Libya 89 S7
Al Jawf Saudi Arabia 108 I6
Al Jubayl Saudi Arabia 109 L9
Al-Juf *see* El Djouf
Al Karak Jordan 107 M11
Al Khābūrah Oman 109 O11
Al Khums Libya 89 O6
Al Kufrah Libya 89 S10
Al Kūt Iraq 109 L5
Al Kuwayt *see* Kuwait City
Al Lādhiqīyah (var. Latakia) Syria 107 M4
Al Madīnah *see* Medina
Al Mafraq Jordan 107 M9
Al Mawit Yemen 108 I15
Al Manāmah *see* Manama
Al Marj Libya 89 Q6
Al Mukallā Yemen 109 K16
Al Mukhā (var. Mocha) Yemen 108 H16
Al Qunayṭirah Syria 107 M8
Al Qurnah Iraq 109 L6
Alabama *River* Alabama, USA 29 K8
Alabama *State* USA 29
Alajuela Costa Rica 42 E13
Alakol', L. *Lake* Kazakhstan 103
Alamogordo New Mexico, USA 35 M10
Åland Is. *Island group* Finland 57 M11
Alanya Turkey 105 K10
Alapaha *River* Georgia, USA 29 N9
Alaska *State* USA 22, 51
Alaska, Gulf of *Sea feature* Alaska, USA 10, 20, 22 G9, 129 L3
Alaska Peninsula *Physical feature* 20
Alaska Range *Mountain range* Alaska, USA 10, 20, 22 F7
Alassio Italy 72 C9
Alazani *River* Azerbaijan/Georgia 85 Q12
Alba Iulia Romania 76 I6
Albacete Spain 61 M10
Albania *Country* SE Europe 75

Albania 75

a Albanian • ⬤ Lek • ▮ 121 • ⬤ 73 • ⬤ £0.22 • ✦ (av.) 15% • ⬚ 35%

Albany Georgia, USA 29 M9
Albany New York, USA 26-27
Albany Oregon, USA 36 G9
Albany Western Australia, Australia 132 G14
Albany *River* Ontario, Canada 24 J9
Albatross Plateau *Sea feature* Pacific Ocean 129 O7
Albert Canal *Waterway* Belgium 65 I14
Albert, L. *Lake* Uganda/Zaire 87, 97 L3, 95 P12
Albert Lea Minnesota, USA 30 H8
Albert Nile *River* Uganda 97 M2
Alberta *Province* Canada 23
Albertville *see* Kalemie
Albi France 63 L13
Albina Surinam 44 O6
Ålborg Denmark 56 H14
Albuquerque New Mexico, USA 35 L8
Albury New South Wales, Australia 133 N14
Alcántara Res. *Reservoir* Spain 60 H9
Aldabra Is. *Island group* Seychelles, Indian Ocean 100 F8
Aldan *River* Russian Federation 113 N9
Aleg Mauritania 92 G7
Aleksinac Serbia, Yugoslavia 75 O8
Alençon France 62 J6
Aleppo *see* Ḩalab
Alert *Research centre* Canada 51 O11
Alessandria Italy 72 D7
Ålesund Norway 52 L7, 56 H8
Aleutian Basin *Sea feature* Bering Sea 103
Aleutian Is. *Island group* Alaska, USA 22 B6, 128 J4
Aleutian Trench *Sea feature* Pacific Ocean 20, 128 J4

Alexander Arch. *Island group* Alaska, USA 22 H11
Alexandretta *see* Iskenderun
Alexandria (var. El Iskandarīya) Egypt 90 F6
Alexandria Louisiana, USA 28 H8
Alexandria Romania 77 L10
Alexandria Virginia, USA 29 R3
Alexandroupoli Greece 79 N2
Aleysk Air Base *Military centre* Russian Federation 112 I11
Algeciras Spain 60 I15
Alger *see* Algiers
Algeria *Country* N Africa 88-89

Algeria 88-89

a Arabic • ⬤ Dinai • ▮ 11 • ⬤ 66 • ⬤ £0.64 • ✦ (m) 70% (f) 45% • ♀ 74 • ✦ 43 • ✦ Yes • ⬚ 52% • ¶ 2866

Alghero Sardinia 73 G13
Algiers (var. Alger; anc. Icosium) Algeria 52 K9, 89 L4
Aliakmon *River* Greece 78 I4
Alicante Spain 61 N11
Alice Springs Northern Territory, Australia 133 K9
Alicudi *Island* Lipari Is., Sicily 73 K16
Aligarh India 117 K5
Alkmaar Netherlands 64 H8
Allahabad India 117 M7
Allegheny Mts. *Mountain range* West Virginia, USA 29 Q3
Allentown Pennsylvania, USA 27 K12
Allier *River* France 63 M11
Alma-Ata (var. Almaty) Kazakhstan 112 G13
Almalyk Uzbekistan 111 K9
Almaty *see* Alma-Ata
Almelo Netherlands 64 M9
Almería Spain 61 L14
Alor *Island* Indonesia 127 N15
Alor Setar Malaysia 125 I17
Alotau Papua New Guinea 133 O4
Alpena Michigan, USA 31 O6
Alphen aan den Rijn Netherlands 64 H10
Alps *Mountain range* C Europe 8, 11, 54, 63 P11, 68 G14, 72 D6
Altai Mts. *Mountain range* Asia 103, 105, 118 I5
Altamura Italy 73 N13
Altay Mongolia 118 I5
Altdorf Switzerland 68 G10
Altiplano *Physical region* Bolivia 41
Alton Illinois, USA 31 I13
Altoona Pennsylvania, USA 26 I12
Altun Ha *Archaeological site* Belize 42 C6
Altun Mts. *Mountain range* China 118 H9
Alturas California, USA 37 I12
Alytus Lithuania 80 I10
Am Timan Chad 94 K8
Amakusa Is. *Island group* Japan 123 C15
Amakusa Sea Japan 123 B15
Amami Is. *Island group* Japan 123 B19
Amami-ōshima *Island* Amami Is., Japan 123 B18
Amarapura Burma 124 G7
Amarillo Texas, USA 35 O8
Amasya Turkey 105 M5
Amazon *River* S America 41, 44 G9, 46 H7, 53 F12
Amazon Basin *Physical region* Brazil 11, 41
Amazonia *Physical region* S America 44 G8, 46 C8
Ambarchik Russian Federation 51 R5, 113 O4
Ambato Ecuador 44 C9
Amblève *River* Belgium 65 K16
Ambon Ambon, Indonesia 127 O13
Amboseli *National park* Kenya 97 P6
Ambre, Cap d' *see* Bobaomby, C.
Ambriz Angola 98 G4
Ameland *Island* West Frisian Is. Netherlands 64 K6
American Samoa *Dependent territory* Polynesia, Pacific Ocean 129 V5
Amersfoort Netherlands 64 J10
Amery Ice Shelf *Coastal feature* Indian Ocean Coast, Antarctica 50 G8
Ames Iowa, USA 33 Q9
Amfissa Greece 78 I8
Amga *River* Russian Federation 113 N9
Amherst Burma 125 G11
Amiens France 63 L3
Amirante Is. *Island group* Seychelles 100 F9
Amistad Res. *Reservoir* Mexico/Texas, USA 35 O13
Amlia I. *Island* Aleutian Is., Alaska, USA 22 B7
Amman (var. Rabbah Ammon; anc. Philadelphia) Jordan 107 M10
Ammassalik Greenland 51 N15
Ammersee *Lake* Germany 67 I16
Amol Iran 109 O4
Amorgos *Island* Cyclades, Greece 79 O12
Amritsar India 116 J3
Amstelveen Netherlands 64 I10
Amsterdam Netherlands 64 I9
Amsterdam New York, USA 27 L9
Amsterdam I. *Island* Indian Ocean 101 I13
Amstetten Austria 69 P5
Amu Darya *River* C Asia 103, 111 L8
Amundsen Gulf *Sea feature* Northwest Territories, Canada 23 I2
Amundsen-Scott *Research centre* Antarctica 50 E9
Amundsen Sea Pacific Ocean, Antarctica 50 C10

a Language (official or most commonly spoken) • ⬤ Currency • ▮ Population density per square kilometre • ⬤ Average life expectancy • ⬤ Price of 1 dozen hen's eggs • ✦ Literacy • ♀ Number of TVs per 1,000 people • ✦ Number of people per doctor • ✦ Death penalty • ⬚ Percentage of urban-based population • ¶ Average number of calories consumed daily per person

137

Amur (var. Heilong Jiang) *River* China/Russian Federation 103, 113 O11, 115, 121 O1
An Nabk Saudi Arabia 108 H5
An Nafūd *Desert region* Saudi Arabia 103, 108 I6
An-Najaf Iraq 109 K5
An Nāşirīyah Iraq 109 L6
Anabar *River* Russian Federation 113 L6
Anaconda Montana, USA 32 G6
Anadyr' Air Base *Military centre* Russian Federation 113 Q3
Anambas Is. *Island group* Indonesia 126 F10
Anamur Turkey 105 K11
Anatolia *Region* Turkey 54, 103
Anchorage Alaska, USA 22 G8
Ancona Italy 52 L8, 72 J9
Ancyra *see* Ankara
Andalusia *Region* Spain 60-61
Andaman Is. *Island group* India, Indian Ocean 100 K7, 115
Andaman Sea Indian Ocean 100 K7, 115, 125 F12
Andautonia *see* Zagreb
Anderson Indiana, USA 31 N12
Andes *Mountain range* S America 11, 41, 44 E7, 48 H8
Andizhan Uzbekistan 111 P6
Andorra *Country* SW Europe 63

Andorra 63

ⓐ Catalan · ⬛ Franc and Peseta · ♦ 108 · ♥ 77 · ◓ £1.12 · ❤ (m) 100% (f) 100% · ⌂ 95%

Andorra la Vella Andorra 63 L16
Andravida Greece 78 H9
Andros *Island* Cyclades, Greece 79 M9
Andros I. *Island* Bahamas 43 K3
Angara *River* Russian Federation 103, 113 K10
Angarsk Russian Federation 113 L11
Ángel de la Guarda I. *Island* Mexico 38 G4
Angel Falls *Waterfall* Venezuela 41
Angeles Luzon, Philippines 127 L4
Ångerman *River* Sweden 57 L8
Angers France 62 I7
Angkor Wat *Archaeological site* Cambodia 125 L13
Anglesey *Island* Wales, UK 59 G13
Angol Chile 49 G12
Angola *Country* Southern Africa 98

Angola 98

ⓐ Portuguese · ⬛ Kwanza · ♦ 8 · ♥ 46 · ◓ £1.63 · ❤ (m) 55% (f) 28% · ⌂ 28%

Angola Basin *Sea feature* Atlantic Ocean 53 K13, 87
Angora *see* Ankara
Angoulême France 62 J10
Angren Uzbekistan 111 O6
Anguilla *Dependent territory* West Indies 43 S9
Ankang China 121 K10
Ankara (prev. Angora; anc. Ancyra) Turkey 105 K6
Ann Arbor Michigan, USA 31 O9
Annaba Algeria 89 M4
'Annah Iraq 108 J4
Annam *see* Vietnam
Annapolis Maryland, USA 29 S3
Annecy France 63 P9
Anshan China 121 O6
Antakiyah *see* Antakya
Antakya (var. Antakiyah; anc. Antioch) Turkey 105 N11
Antalya Turkey 104 J10
Antananarivo Madagascar 101 E11
Antarctic Circumpolar current *Ocean current* Southern Ocean 12
Antarctic Plate *Physical feature* 8, 41, 87, 131
Antarctica *Continent* 8, 11, 12, 13, 41, 50, 131
Anticosti, Île d' *Island* Quebec, Canada 25 Q9
Antigua Antigua & Barbuda 43 T11
Antigua and Barbuda *Country* West Indies 43 T10

Antigua and Barbuda 43

ⓐ English · ⬛ Dollar · ♦ 182 · ♥ 74 · ◓ £1.29 · ❤ (m) 90% (f) 88% · ⌂ 31%

Antioch *see* Antakya
Antipodes Is. *Island group* New Zealand, Pacific Ocean 128 J13
Antofagasta Chile 48 F6, 129 R10
Antsirañana (prev. Diégo-Suarez) Madagascar 100 F10
Antwerp (var. Anvers) Belgium 65 G13
Antwerp I. *see* Anvers I.
Anvers (prev. Antwerp I.) *Island* Pacific Ocean, Antarctica 50 B8
Anvers *see* Antwerp
Anzio Italy 73 I12
Aomori Japan 122 K6
Aosta Italy 72 B6
Aparri Luzon, Philippines 127 L2
Apatin Serbia, Yugoslavia 75 L3
Apeldoorn Netherlands 64 K10
Apennines *Mountain range* Italy 54, 72 I10
Aphrodisias *Archaeological site* Turkey 104 H9
Apia Western Samoa, Pacific Ocean 128 J9
Appalachian Mts. *Mountain range* USA 10, 20, 26 I13, 29 P4

Appenzell Switzerland 68 H9
Appleton Wisconsin, USA 31 K7
Apure *River* Venezuela 44 H5
Aqaba *see* Al 'Aqabah
Aqaba, Gulf of *Sea feature* SW Asia 90 H7, 107 L14, 108 G6
Aqtöbe *see* Aktyubinsk
Ar-Ramadi Iraq 109 K4
Ar Raqqah Syria 107 P3
Ar Riyāḍ *see* Riyadh
Ar Rustāq Oman 109 O12
Arabian Basin *Sea feature* Arabian Sea 103, 114-115
Arabian Desert *Desert region* SW Asia 11
Arabian Peninsula *Peninsula* SW Asia 87, 103
Arabian Plate *Physical feature* 8, 54, 87, 103, 115
Arabian Sea Arabia/India 100 G6,103, 109 N15, 114-115, 116 H10
Aracaju Brazil 46 N10
Arad Romania 76 G5
Arafura Sea Australia/Indonesia 131, 133 K4, 127 S13, 128 G9
Araguaia *River* Brazil 41, 46 J10
Arāk Iran 109 M5
Aral Sea *Lake* Kazakhstan/Uzbekistan 103, 110 I3, 112 E11
Aram *see* Syria
Aranđelovac Serbia, Yugoslavia 75 N6
'Ar'ar Saudi Arabia 108 I5
'Ar'ar, Wādī *Seasonal watercourse* Iraq/Saudi Arabia 108 J5
Aras *River* Azerbaijan/Iran 85 S14
Arauca Colombia 44 G6
Arauca *River* Colombia/Venezuela 44 G5
Arcachon France 62 I12
Arda *River* Bulgaria/Greece 77 K15
Ardabīl Iran 109 M2
Ardennes *Physical region* Belgium 65 K17
Arendal Norway 56 I12
Arequipa Peru 45 G15
Arezzo Italy 72 H10
Argentina *Country* S America 48-49

Argentina 48-49

ⓐ Spanish · ⬛ Peso · ♦ 12 · ♥ 71 · ◓ £0.67 · ❤ (m) 94% (f) 95% · ⌨ 222 · ✚ 328 · ✱ No · ⌂ 86% · ⅰ 3113

Argentine Basin *Sea feature* Atlantic Ocean 53 G15
Argentino, L. *Lake* Argentina 49 I18
Argeş *River* Romania 77 M10
Arghandāb *River* Afghanistan 111 M13
Argostoli Kefallonia, Greece 78 F9
Århus Denmark 56 I15
Arica Chile 48 F3
Arizona *State* USA 34-35
Arkalyk Kazakhstan 112 F11
Arkansas *River* USA 20, 28 I5, 33 N13, 35 O5
Arkansas *State* USA 28
Arkansas City Kansas, USA 33 P13
Arkhangel'sk Russian Federation 82 J7
Arlberg Tunnel *Tunnel* Austria 68 I9
Arles France 63 N13
Arlon Belgium 65 K19
Armenia Colombia 44 E6
Armenia *Country* SW Asia 85

Armenia 85

ⓐ Armenian · ⬛ Dram · ♦ 113 · ♥ 73 · ◓ £2.12 · ❤ N/A · ⌂ 68%

Armidale New South Wales, Australia 133 O12
Arnhem Netherlands 65 K11
Arnhem Land *Physical region* Northern Territory, Australia 131, 132 J5
Arnhem, C. *Cape* Northern Territory, Australia 133 L5
Arno *River* Italy 72 F9
Arran *Island* Scotland, UK 58 G10
Arras France 63 L2
Arta Greece 78 G6
Artesia New Mexico, USA 35 M10
Artigas Uruguay 48 M8
Artvin Turkey 105 Q4
Aru Is. *Island group* Indonesia 127 Q14
Arua Uganda 97 L2
Aruba *Dependent territory* Caribbean Sea 43 N13
Arun *River* India/Nepal 117 O6
Arusha Tanzania 97 O7
Aruwimi *River* Zaire 95 M12
Arvayheer Mongolia 119 L6
Arvidsjaur Sweden 57 M6
Aş Şalt Jordan 107 M10
As Sulaymānīyah Iraq 109 L3
As Suwaydā' Syria 107 N8
Asahikawa Japan 122 L3
Asansol India 117 O8
Ascension I. *Dependent territory* Atlantic Ocean 53 J12
Asela Ethiopia 91 J15
Ashburton *River* Western Australia, Australia 132 F9
Asheville North Carolina, USA 29 O5
Ashgabat (prev. Ashkhabad) Turkmenistan 110 I8
Ashkhabad *see* Ashgabat
Ashland Oregon, USA 37 H11
Ashmore & Cartier Is. *Dependent territory* Indian Ocean 100 N10

Ashtabula Ohio, USA 31 Q9
Asia *Continent* 8, 10, 11, 12, 15, 20, 87, 103, 130
Asir *Province* Saudi Arabia 108 I12
Asmara Eritrea 91 I13
Aspen Colorado, USA 35 L4
Assab Eritrea 91 L13
Assad, L. (var. Buḩayrat al Asad) *Lake* Syria 107 P3
Assen Netherlands 64 M7
Assisi Italy 72 I10
Astakós Greece 78 G8
Asti Italy 72 C7
Astipálaia *Island* Dodecanese, Greece 79 O12
Astoria Oregon, USA 36 G7
Astrakhan Russian Federation 83 G15
Asunción Paraguay 48 M6
Aswān Egypt 90 G9
Aswān High Dam *Dam* Egypt 90 G9
Asyût Egypt 90 F8
At Ţafīlah Jordan 107 M11
Atacama Desert *Desert region* Chile 12, 22, 41, 48 G5
Atakpamé Togo 93 M12
Ataq Yemen 108 J16
Atar Mauritania 92 H5
Atatürk Barrage *Dam* Turkey 105 O9
Atbara Sudan 91 H11
Atbara *River* Sudan 91 H12
Ath Belgium 65 E15
Athabasca Alberta, Canada 23 L13
Athabasca *River* Canada 23 L12
Athabasca, L. *Lake* Alberta/Saskatchewan Canada 20, 23 L11
Athens Georgia, USA 29 N7
Athens Greece 79 K9
Athlone Ireland 59 C12
Ati Chad 94 J7
Atka I. *Island* Aleutian Is. Alaska, USA 22 B7
Atlanta Georgia, USA 29 M7
Atlantic City New Jersey, USA 27 L14
Atlantic-Indian-Antarctic Basin *Sea feature* Atlantic Ocean 53 M16
Atlantic-Indian Basin *Sea feature* Indian Ocean 101 E15
Atlantic Indian Ridge *Sea feature* Atlantic Ocean 53 M15
Atlantic Ocean 8, 10, 13, 20, 41, 52-53, 54, 86-87, 103
Atlas Mts. *Mountain range* Morocco 88 I6
Atlixco Mexico 39 N12
Attapu Laos 125 N12
Attawapiskat Ontario, Canada 24 J8
Attawapiskat *River* Ontario, Canada 24 I8
Atter, L. *Lake* Austria 69 O6
Attu I. *Island* Aleutian Is. Alaska, USA 22 A4
Atyrau (prev. Gur'yev) Kazakhstan 112 D10
Auburn New York, USA 26 J8
Auch France 63 K14
Auckland New Zealand 134 G4
Auckland Is. *Island group* New Zealand, Pacific Ocean 128 I13
Augrabies Falls N.P. *National park* South Africa 98 I13
Augsburg Germany 67 I15
Augusta Georgia, USA 29 O8
Augusta Maine, USA 27 P6
Augusta Sicily 73 L18
Augusta Western Australia, Australia 132 F13
Aurillac France 63 L11
Aurora Colorado, USA 35 M4
Aurora Illinois, USA 31 L10
Austin Minnesota, USA 30 H8
Austin Texas, USA 35 Q12
Austral Ridge *Sea feature* Pacific Ocean 129 L11
Australia *Country* Oceania 132-133

Australia 132-133

ⓐ English · ⬛ Dollar · ♦ 2 · ♥ 77 · ◓ £0.87 · ❤ (m) 99% (f) 99% · ⌨ 486 · ✚ 438 · ✱ No · ⌂ 85% · ⅰ 3216

Australia *Continent* 8, 11, 12, 15, 131
Australian Alps *Mountain range* Australia 11, 131
Australian Capital Territory *Territory* (prev. Federal Capital Territory) Australia 133
Australian Desert *Desert region* Australia 11
Austria *Country* C Europe 68-69

Austria 68-69

ⓐ German · ⬛ Schilling · ♦ 93 · ♥ 76 · ◓ £1.88 · ❤ (m) 99% (f) 99% · ⌨ 481 · ✚ 336 · ✱ No · ⌂ 58% · ⅰ 3495

Auxerre France 63 M7
Aveiro Portugal 60 F7
Avignon France 63 O13
Ávila Spain 60 I7
Avilés Spain 60 I3
Awasa Ethiopia 91 J16
Awash Ethiopia 91 K15
Awash *River* Ethiopia 91 K14
Awbārī Libya 89 O9
Axel Heiberg I. *Island* Northwest Territories, Canada 20, 23 N3, 51 O10
Axios *see* Vardar
Ayacucho Peru 45 E13
Aydarkul', L. *Lake* Kazakhstan/Uzbekistan 111 M6
Aydin Turkey 104 G9
Ayers Rock *see* Uluru

Ayios Evstratios *Island* Greece 79 M6
Ayon Is. *Island group* Russian Federation 113 O3
Ayr Scotland, UK 58 G10
Ayutthaya Thailand 125 J12
Ayvacik Barrage *Dam* Turkey 105 M5
Ayvalik Turkey 104 G7
Aẕ Ẕahrān *see* Dhahran
Az Zarqā' Jordan 107 M9
Az Zubayr Iraq 109 L7
Azaouâd *Physical region* Mali 93 L7
Azerbaijan *Country* SW Asia 85

Azerbaijan 85

ⓐ Azerbaijani · ⬛ Ruble · ♦ 83 · ♥ 71 · ◓ £0.66 · ❤ (av.) 99% · ⌂ 53%

Azores *Island group* Atlantic Ocean 8, 52 I9
Azov, Sea of (var. Azovs'ke More) Russian Federation/Ukraine 54, 83 C13, 85 L9
Azovs'ke More *see* Azov, Sea of
Azul Argentina 49 M11

B

Ba'abda Lebanon 107 M7
Baalbek Lebanon 107 M6
Bab el Mandeb *Channel* Yemen 108 H16
Babahoyo Ecuador 44 C9
Babar *Island* Indonesia 127 P15
Babruysk (var. Bobruysk) Belorussia 81 M13
Babylon *Archaeological site* Iraq 109 K5
Bacan *Island* Indonesia 127 O11
Bacău Romania 77 M4
Bačka Topola Serbia, Yugoslavia 75 M3
Bacolod Negros, Philippines 127 M6
Bad Ischl Austria 69 O7
Badain Jaran Desert *Desert region* China 119 L8
Badajoz Spain 60 H10
Badalona Spain 61 Q6
Baden Austria 69 S5
Badgastein Austria 69 N8
Bādiyat ash Shām *see* Syrian Desert
Badlands *Physical region* North Dakota, USA 33 L5
Bafatá Guinea-Bissau 92 G9
Baffin *Region* Northwest Territories, Canada 23 P6
Baffin Bay *Sea feature* Canada/Greenland 10, 20, 23 P4, 51 N12, 52 F6
Baffin I. *Island* Northwest Territories, Canada 10, 20, 23 Q5, 51 M12
Bafia Cameroon 94 F10
Bafoussam Cameroon 94 F10
Bagana, Mt. *Volcano* Solomon Is. Pacific Ocean 131
Baghdad Iraq 109 K4
Baghlān Afghanistan 111 N10
Baguio Luzon, Philippines 127 L3
Bahamas *Country* West Indies 43

Bahamas 43

ⓐ English · ⬛ Dollar · ♦ 26 · ♥ 69 · ◓ £0.79 · ❤ (m) 90% (f) 89% · ⌂ 75%

Bahamas *Island group* West Indies 20, 41
Bahawalpur Pakistan 116 I4
Bahía Blanca Argentina 49 L12, 53 F14
Bahir Dar Ethiopia 91 I14
Bahr el Azraq *see* Blue Nile
Bahr el Jebel *see* White Nile
Bahrain (anc. Tylos) *Country* SW Asia 109

Bahrain 109

ⓐ Arabic · ⬛ Dinar · ♦ 762 · ♥ 69 · ◓ £0.96 · ❤ (m) 82% (f) 69% · ⌂ 83%

Bahrat Lut *see* Dead Sea
Baia Mare Romania 76 I2
Baidoa *see* Baydhabo
Baikal, L. *Lake* Russian Federation 103, 113 L11
Baile Atha Cliath *see* Dublin
Băile Herculane Romania 76 H8
Bairiki Tarawa Kiribati, Pacific Ocean 128 I8
Baja Hungary 71 L15
Baja California *Peninsula* Mexico 20, 38 G5, 41
Baker City Oregon, USA 36 K9
Baker I. *Dependent territory* Polynesia, Pacific Ocean 128 J8
Bakersfield California, USA 37 K17
Bakhtārān (var. Kermanshah) Iran 109 L4
Baki *see* Baku
Baku (var. Bakı) Azerbaijan 85 T13
Balabac Strait *Channel* Borneo/Philippines 127 K7
Balakovo Russian Federation 83 I12
Balaton, L. *Lake* Hungary 54, 71 K14
Balbina Res. *Reservoir* Brazil 46 F7
Balearic Islands *Island group* Spain 54, 61
Bali *Island* Indonesia/SE Asia 115, 126 J16, 131
Balikesir Turkey 104 H6
Balikpapan Borneo, Indonesia 127 K12
Balkan Mts. *Mountain range* SE Europe 54, 76 J13, 75 P9
Balkhash, L. *Lake* Kazakhstan 103, 112 G12

Ballarat Victoria, Australia 133 M14
Balleny Is. *Island group* Pacific Ocean, Antarctica 50 F12
Balsas *River* Mexico 39 M12
Baltic Sea N Europe
52 M7, 54-55, 57 M13, 70 J1, 80 G4, 103
Baltimore Maryland, USA 29 S3
Baltimore Virginia, USA 52 D9
Baltiysk Russian Federation 80 E9
Bamako Mali 92 I9
Bambari Central African Republic 94 K10
Bamenda Cameroon 94 E10
Ban Houayxay Laos 124 J9
Banda Is. *Island group* Indonesia 127 P13
Banda Sea SE Asia 127 N13, 128 F9
Bandar-e Abbās Iran 109 O9
Bandar-e Büshehr Iran 109 M8
Bandar Seri Begawan (var. Brunei Town) Brunei 126 J4
Bandirma Turkey 104 H6
Bandon Oregon, USA 36 F10
Bandundu (prev. Banningville) Zaire 95 I14
Bandung Java, Indonesia 126 G15
Bangalore India 117 K13
Bangassou Central African Republic 94 L10
Banggai Is. *Island group* Indonesia 127 N12
Banggi *Island* Malaysia 127 K8
Bangka Indonesia 126 G12
Bangkok (var. Krung Thep) Thailand 125 J12
Bangladesh (prev. East Pakistan) *Country* S Asia 117

Bangladesh 117

a Bengali · 🗣 Taka · ♦ 812 · ● 52 · 🥚 £0.68 ·
🗣 (m) 47% (f) 22% · 🖵 5 · ✚ 6219 · 💀 Yes ·
🏚 16% · 🍽 2021

Bangor Maine, USA 27 Q6
Bangor Northern Ireland, UK 59 F11
Bangui Central African Republic 94 J10
Bangweulu, L. *Lake* Zambia 97 L12
Banhine N.P. *National park* Mozambique 99 N10
Bani *River* Mali 92 J9
Banja Luka Bosnia and Herzegovina 74 J5
Banjarmasin Borneo, Indonesia 126 J13
Banjul (prev. Bathurst) Gambia 92 F9
Banks I. *Island* Northwest Territories, Canada 20, 23 L5, 51 N8
Banks L. *Lake* Washington, USA 36 J6
Banningville *see* Bandundu
Banská Bystrica Slovakia 71 L11
Bantry Bay *Sea feature* Ireland 59 A14
Banyo Cameroon 94 F10
Banyuwangi Java, Indonesia 126 J15
Baoji China 121 K9
Baotou China 119 N8
Bar Montenegro, Yugoslavia 75 L10
Bar-le-Duc France 63 N5
Baranavichy (var. Baranovichi) Belorussia 80 J13
Baranovichi *see* Baranavichy
Barbados *Country* West Indies 43 T14

Barbados 43

a English · 🗣 Dollar · ♦ 600 · ● 75 · 🥚 £1.65 ·
🗣 (m) 99% (f) 99% · 🏚 45%

Barbados *Island* West Indies 41
Barbuda *Island* Antigua & Barbuda 43 T10
Barcelona Spain 61 Q6
Barcelona Venezuela 44 J4
Bareilly India 117 L5
Barents Sea Arctic Ocean 51 R12, 54, 82 L5, 103
Bari Italy 73 N13
Barinas Venezuela 44 G5
Barisan Mts. *Mountain range* Sumatra, Indonesia 126 E12
Barito *River* Borneo, Indonesia 126 J11
Bârlad Romania 77 N5
Barlee, L. *Lake* Western Australia, Australia 132 G12
Barnaul Russian Federation 112 I11
Barnstaple England, UK 59 G16
Baroda *see* Vadodara
Barquisimeto Venezuela 44 H4
Barra *Island* Scotland, UK 58 E8
Barranquilla Colombia 44 E4
Barreiras Brazil 47 K11
Barreiro Portugal 60 F10
Barrie Ontario, Canada 25 K14
Barrow Alaska, USA 22 H4
Barrow *River* Ireland 59 D13
Barrow I. *Island* Western Australia, Australia 132 E12
Barstow California, USA 37 M18
Bartang *River* Tajikistan 111 P8
Bartica Guyana 44 M6
Barysaw (var. Borisov) Belorussia 81 M11
Basel *see* Basle
Basilan *Island* Philippines 127 M8
Basle (var. Basel) Switzerland 68 F8
Basque Provinces *Region* Spain 61 L4
Basra Iraq 100 E4
Bass Strait *Channel* Australia 131, 133 N15
Basse-Terre Guadeloupe 43 S12
Basse Terre *Island* Guadeloupe 43 S12
Bassein Burma 124 E10
Basseterre St Kitts & Nevis 43 S10
Bastia Corsica 63 S14
Bastogne Belgium 65 K18

Basutoland *see* Lesotho
Bata Equatorial Guinea 95 E11
Batangas Luzon, Philippines 127 L4
Batanghari *River* Sumatra, Indonesia 126 E12
Batavia New York, USA 26 I8
Batavia *see* Jakarta
Bătdâmbâng Cambodia 125 K13
Bath England, UK 59 I16
Bathurst I. *Island* Northern Territory, Australia 132 I5
Bathurst I. *Island* Northwest Territories, Canada 23 M1
Bathurst New Brunswick, Canada 25 P11
Bathurst *see* Banjul
Batman Turkey 105 Q8
Batna Algeria 89 M4
Baton Rouge Louisiana, USA 28 I9
Batticaloa Sri Lanka 117 L16
Battle Creek Michigan, USA 31 N9
Batu Is. *Island group* Indonesia 126 D11
Bat'umi Georgia 85 O13
Bauchi Nigeria 93 P11
Bautzen Germany 67 N11
Bavaria *Region* Germany 67 J9
Bavarian Alps *Mountain range* Austria/Germany 67 J17
Bawean *Island* Indonesia 126 I14
Bay City Michigan, USA 31 O8
Bayamo Cuba 43 K6
Bayan Har Mts. (var. Bayan Har Shan) *Mountain range* China 119 K11
Bayan Har Shan *see* Bayan Har Mts.
Baydarata Bay *Sea feature* Russian Federation 82 O6, 112 I6
Baydhabo (var. Baidoa) Somalia 91 M17
Baykonur Kazakhstan 112 F11
Bayonne France 62 H14
Bayram-Ali Turkmenistan 111 K9
Bayreuth Germany 67 J13
Beagle Channel *Channel* Argentina 49 L20
Bear Is. *Island group* Russian Federation 113 O4
Bear L. *Lake* Idaho/Utah, USA 34 J2
Beaufort Sea Arctic Ocean 10, 20, 22 J6, 51 N7
Beaufort West South Africa 98 J15
Beaumont Texas, USA 35 T12
Beauvais France 63 L4
Beaver I. *Island* Michigan, USA 31 M5
Bečej Serbia, Yugoslavia 75 M4
Béchar Algeria 88 J6
Bedford Indiana, USA 31 M13
Be'er Sheva' *see* Beersheba
Beersheba (var. Be'er Sheva') Israel 107 L11
Bei'an China 121 P3
Beijing *see* Peking
Beira Mozambique 99 O9, 101 D11
Beirut (var. Beyrouth; anc. Berytus) Lebanon 107 M7
Beja Portugal 60 G12
Bejaïa Algeria 89 L4
Belarus *see* Belorussia
Belawan Sumatra, Indonesia 126 D9
Belaya Tserkov *see* Bila Tserkva
Belcher Islands *Island group* Canada 25 K5
Beledweyne Somalia 91 M16
Belém Brazil 46 J7
Belfast Northern Ireland UK 59 F11
Belfort France 63 P6
Belgaum India 116 I11
Belgian Congo *see* Zaire
Belgium *Country* W Europe 65

Belgium 65

a Dutch, French · 🗣 Franc · ♦ 304 · ● 76 · 🥚 £1.25 · 🗣 (m) 99% (f) 99% · 🖵 452 · ✚ 309 · 💀 No · 🏚 97% · 🍽 3902

Belgorod Russian Federation 83 E12
Belgorod-Dnestrovskiy *see* Bilhorod-Dnistrovs'kyy
Belgrade (var. Beograd) Serbia, Yugoslavia 75 N5
Belgrano II *Research centre* Antarctica 50 D7
Beli Drim *River* Serbia, Yugoslavia 75 N9
Beli Timok *River* Serbia, Yugoslavia 75 P8
Belice *River* Sicily 73 I18
Belitung Indonesia 126 G13
Belize *Country* C America 42

Belize 42

a English · 🗣 Dollar · ♦ 8 · ● 68 · 🥚 £0.92 ·
🗣 (m) 93% (f) 93% · 🏚 50%

Belize *River* Belize 42 C6
Belize City Belize 42 C6
Belle Fourche *River* Wyoming, USA 33 K7
Belle Île *Island* France 62 G8
Belle Isle *Island* Newfoundland, Canada 25 R7
Belle Isle, Strait of *Channel* Newfoundland, Canada 25 R8
Bellevue Washington, USA 36 H6
Bellingham Washington, USA 36 H5
Bellingshausen Plain *Sea feature* Pacific Ocean 20
Bellingshausen Sea Pacific Ocean, Antarctica 50 B9
Bellinzona Switzerland 68 H12
Bello Colombia 44 E6
Belluno Italy 72 H6
Belmopan Belize 42 C6
Belo Horizonte Brazil 47 L13
Beloit Wisconsin, USA 31 K9

Belorussia (var. Belarus) *Country* NE Europe 80-81

Belorussia 80-81

a Belorussian · 🗣 Ruble · ♦ 50 · ● 73 · 🥚 £2.31 ·
🗣 (m) 99% (f) 99% · 🖵 268 · ✚ 246 · 💀 Yes ·
🏚 66% · 🍽 N/A

Belyy Is. *Island group* Russian Federation 112 I5
Bemidji Minnesota, USA 30 G3
Benares *see* Varanasi
Bend Oregon, USA 36 I9
Bendery *see* Tighina
Bendigo Victoria, Australia 133 M14
Benevento Italy 73 L13
Bengal, Bay of *Sea feature* India/SE Asia 103, 100 J6, 115, 117 P9, 124 D9
Benghazi Libya 89 Q6
Bengkulu Sumatra, Indonesia 126 E13
Benguela Angola 98 G6
Benguela current *Ocean current* S Atlantic Ocean 12
Beni *River* Bolivia 45 H13
Beni Mellal Morocco 88 I6
Beni Suef Egypt 90 F7
Benidorm Spain 61 O11
Benin (prev. Dahomey) *Country* W Africa 93

Benin 93

a French · 🗣 Franc · ♦ 44 · ● 51 · 🥚 £0.86 ·
🗣 (m) 32% (f) 16% · 🏚 38%

Benin, Bight of *Sea feature* W Africa 93 N13
Benin City Nigeria 93 O12
Bennington Vermont, USA 27 M9
Benton Harbor Michigan, USA 31 M10
Benue *River* Cameroon/Nigeria 87, 93 P12
Beograd *see* Belgrade
Beppu Japan 123 D14
Berat Albania 75 M13
Berau, Gulf of *Sea feature* Irian Jaya, Indonesia 126 Q12
Berbera Somalia 91 M14
Berbérati Central African Republic 95 H11
Berbice *River* Guyana 44 M7
Berdyans'k Ukraine 85 L8
Beretty ő *River* Hungary/Romania 71 N14
Bereza *see* Byaroza
Bergama *see* Pergamon
Bergamo Italy 72 E6
Bergen Norway 52 K7, 56 H10
Bergen *see* Mons
Bergen op Zoom Netherlands 65 G12
Bergisch Gladbach Germany 67 E11
Bering Sea Pacific Ocean 10, 20, 22 C7, 103, 113 R5, 128 J3
Bering Strait *Channel* Arctic Ocean/Pacific Ocean 20, 22 E4, 103, 128 J2
Berlin Germany 66 L9
Bermejo *River* Argentina/Bolivia 48 K5
Bermuda *Dependent territory* Atlantic Ocean 52 F9
Bermuda *Island* Atlantic Ocean 20
Bermuda Rise *Sea feature* Atlantic Ocean 20
Bern Germany 66 E9
Bernese Alps *Mountain range* Switzerland 68 F12
Beroea *see* Halab
Berry Is. *Island group* Bahamas 43 K2
Bertoua Cameroon 94 G10
Beruni Uzbekistan 110 J5
Berytus *see* Beirut
Besançon France 63 O7
Beskid Mts. *Mountain range* C Europe 71 L9
Bethel Alaska, USA 22 E7
Bethlehem West Bank 107 L10
Beykoz Turkey 104 J9
Beyrouth *see* Beirut
Beyşehir Turkey 104 J9
Beyşehir, L. *Lake* Turkey 104 J9
Bezmein Turkmenistan 110 H8
Bhamo Burma 124 H6
Bhatapara India 117 M9
Bhavnagar India 116 I8
Bhopal India 117 K8
Bhubaneswar India 117 N9
Bhumiphol Res. *Reservoir* Thailand 124 H10
Bhutan *Country* S Asia 117

Bhutan 117

a Dzongkha · 🗣 Ngultrum · ♦ 31 · ● 49 · 🥚 £0.56 · 🗣 (m) 51% (f) 25% · 🏚 5%

Biak *Island* Indonesia 127 R11
Białystok Poland 71 O4
Bicuari N.P. *National park* Angola 98 G7
Biddeford Maine, USA 27 O8
Biel Switzerland 68 E9
Biel, L. *Lake* Switzerland 68 E10
Bielefeld Germany 66 F10
Bielsko-Biała Poland 71 L9
Bien Hoa Vietnam 125 L14
Big Spring Texas, USA 35 O11
Bighorn *River* Montana/Wyoming, USA 32 J6
Bighorn Mts. *Mountain range* Wyoming, USA 32 J7
Bihać Bosnia and Herzegovina 74 I5
Bijagós Archipelago *Island group* Guinea-Bissau 92 F10
Bijelo Polje Montenegro, Yugoslavia 75 M9

Bikini *Island* Marshall Islands, Pacific Ocean 128 I7
Bila Tserkva (var. Belaya Tserkov) Ukraine 84 I5
Bilbao Spain 61 L3
Bilecik Turkey 104 I6
Bilhorod-Dnistrovs'kyy (var. Belgorod-Dnestrovskiy) Ukraine 84 I8
Billings Montana, USA 32 I6
Biloxi Mississippi, USA 28 J9
Biltine Chad 94 K7
Bindura Zimbabwe 99 M8
Binghamton New York, USA 27 K10
Bingöl Turkey 105 Q7
Bintan *Island* Indonesia 126 F11
Bío-Bío *River* Chile 49 H12
Birāk *Oasis* Libya 89 O8
Birao Central African Republic 94 L8
Biratnagar Nepal 117 O6
Birganj Nepal 117 N6
Birkenhead England, UK 59 H13
Birmingham Alabama, USA 29 L7
Birmingham England, UK 59 I14
Birni n'Konni Niger 93 O9
Biscay, Bay of *Sea feature* Spain 54, 61 L3
Biscay Plain *Sea feature* Atlantic Ocean 54
Bishkek (prev. Frunze) Kyrgyzstan 111 Q4
Bisho South Africa 99 L15
Bishop California, USA 37 K15
Biskra Algeria 89 L5
Bislig Mindanao, Philippines 127 N7
Bismarck North Dakota, USA 33 M5
Bismarck Arch. *Island group* Papua New Guinea 133 O1
Bismarck Range *Mountain range* Papua New Guinea 131, 133 N2
Bismarck Sea Papua New Guinea 131, 132 O1
Bissau Guinea-Bissau 92 F10
Bistriţa Romania 76 J3
Bitlis Turkey 105 R8
Bitola Macedonia 75 O13
Bitterroot Range *Mountain range* Idaho/Montana 32 G6
Biysk Russian Federation 112 I11
Bizerte Tunisia 89 N4
Bjelovar Croatia 74 J3
Black Forest (var. Schwarzwald) *Physical region* Germany 67 F15
Black Hills *Mountain range* South Dakota/Wyoming, USA 33 L7
Black R. (var. Song Da) *River* China/Vietnam 124 I2
Black R. *River* Arkansas/Missouri, USA 28 J4
Black Rock Desert *Desert region* Nevada, USA 20, 34 F1
Black Sea (var. Chernoye More, Kara Deniz) Asia/Europe 52 N8, 54, 77 P11, 85 M11, 103, 105 N4
Black Volta *River* West Africa 87, 93 K10
Blackpool England, UK 59 H12
Blackwater *River* Ireland 59 C14
Blagoveshchensk Russian Federation 113 O11
Blanca, Bahía *Sea feature* Argentina 49 L12
Blanca, Costa *Coastal region* Spain 61 O11
Blanco, Cape *see* Nouadhibou, Râs
Blanice *River* Czech Republic 70 H10
Blantyre Malawi 99 O15
Blenheim New Zealand 134 G9
Blida Algeria 89 L4
Bloemfontein South Africa 99 K13
Blois France 63 K7
Bloomington Illinois, USA 31 K12
Bloomington Indiana, USA 31 M13
Bloomington Minnesota, USA 30 H6
Blue Mesa Dam *Dam* Colorado, USA 35 L5
Blue Mountains *Mountain range* Oregon/Washington, USA 36 K9
Blue Nile (var. Bahr el Azraq) *River* Ethiopia/Sudan 87, 91 H13
Blue Nile *River* 87
Bluefields Nicaragua 42 E11
Bo Sierra Leone 92 H12
Bo Hai *Sea feature* China 121 N7
Boa Vista Brazil 46 F6
Boaco Nicaragua 42 D10
Bobaomby, C. (var. Cap d' Ambre) *Cape* Madagascar 100 O9
Bobo-Dioulasso Burkina 93 K10
Bóbr *River* Poland 70 G9
Bobruysk *see* Babruysk
Bocas del Toro Panama 42 F14
Bochum Germany 66 E10
Bodensee *see* Constance, L.
Bodø Norway 57 L4
Bodrum Turkey 104 G9
Boende Zaire 95 K12
Bogor Java, Indonesia 126 G14
Bogotá (prev. Santa Fe) Colombia 44 E6
Bohemian Forest (var. Böhmerwald) *Physical region* Czech Republic/Germany 67 L14
Böhmerwald *see* Bohemian Forest
Bohol *Island* Philippines 127 M6
Boise Idaho, USA 32 F8
Bokaro India 117 N8
Bokna Fjord *Coastal feature* Norway 56 H11
Bol Chad 94 H7
Bolgatanga Ghana 93 L10
Bolivia *Country* S America 45

Bolivia 45

a Aymara, Quechua, Spanish · 🗣 Boliviano · ♦ 7 · ● 60 · 🥚 £0.52 · 🗣 (m) 85% (f) 70% · 🖵 163 · ✚ 2100 · 💀 No · 🏚 51% · 🍽 1916

Bologna Italy 72 G8

a Language (official or most commonly spoken) · 🗣 Currency · ● Population density per square kilometre · ● Average life expectancy · 🥚 Price of 1 dozen hen's eggs · 🗣 Literacy · 🖵 Number of TVs per 1,000 people ·
✚ Number of people per doctor · 💀 Death penalty · 🏚 Percentage of urban-based population · 🍽 Average number of calories consumed daily per person

139

C

Carlyle L. *Lake* Illinois, USA 31 K14
Carmen I. *Island* Mexico 38 H7
Carnarvon Western Australia, Australia 132 E10
Carnegie, L. *Lake* Western Australia, Australia 132 H10
Carolina Brazil 46 K9
Caroline Is. *Island group* Federated States of Micronesia, Pacific Ocean 128 H8
Caroline Ridge *Sea feature* Pacific Ocean 131
Carpathians *Mountain range* E Europe 54, 71 I 10, 77 L4, 84 E6
Carpentaria, Gulf of *Sea feature* Northern Territory/Queensland, Australia 131, 133 L6
Carson City Nevada, USA 34 E3
Cartagena Colombia 44 E4, 53 D11
Cartagena Spain 61 N12
Cartago Costa Rica 42 E13
Cartwright Newfoundland, Canada 25 R6
Casa Grande Arizona, USA 34 I10
Casablanca Morocco 52 K9, 88 H5
Cascade Range *Mountain range* USA 20, 36 I8
Caseyr, C. *Cape* Somalia 87
Casper Wyoming, USA 33 K9
Caspian Sea *Lake* Asia/Europe 54-55, 83 G16, 85 T13, 103, 109 N2, 110 F7, 112 C10
Castellón de la Plana Spain 61 O8
Castelo Branco Portugal 60 G9
Castries St Lucia 43 T13
Castro Chile 49 G15
Cat I. *Island* Bahamas 43 L3
Catalonia *Region* Spain 61 P6
Catamarca Argentina 48 I8
Catanduanes *Island* Philippines 127 M4
Catania Sicily 73 L18
Catanzaro Italy 73 N16
Catskill Mts. *Mountain range* New York, USA 27 L10
Cauca *River* Colombia 44 E5
Caucasus Mts. *Mountain range* Europe/Asia 54, 83 E16, 85 P11, 103
Cauquenes Chile 48 G12
Cauvery Falls *Waterfall* India 115
Cavally *River* Ivory Coast 92 I13
Caxito Angola 98 G4
Cayenne French Guiana 44 P7, 53 F11
Cayman Brac *Island* Cayman Islands 42 I6
Cayman Islands *Dependent territory* Caribbean Sea 42 H6
Ceará Plain *Sea feature* Atlantic Ocean 41
Cebu Cebu, Philippines 127 M6
Cebu *Island* Philippines 127 M6
Cedar *River* Iowa, USA 33 Q8
Cedar Rapids Iowa, USA 33 R9
Cedros I. *Island* Mexico 38 F5
Cefalù Sicily 73 K17
Celaya Mexico 39 M11
Celebes (var. Sulawesi) *Island* Indonesia 115, 127 L12, 131
Celebes Basin *Sea feature* SE Asia 131
Celebes Sea SE Asia 115, 127 M9, 128 F8, 131
Celje Slovenia 74 H2
Celle Germany 66 H9
Celtic Shelf *Sea Feature* Atlantic Ocean 54
Central African Republic *Country* C Africa 94 95

Central African Republic (C.A.R.) 94-95

ⓐ French · 🌐 Franc · ♦ 5 · ♥ 49 · ◯ £4.30 · 🐛 (m) 52% (f) 25% · 🏠 47%

Central America *Region* 20, 41
Central Arizona Project *Irrigation project* Arizona, USA 34 I9
Centralia Illinois, USA 31 K14
Central Siberian Plateau *Physical region* Russian Federation 103, 113 L6
Cerralvo I. *Island* Mexico 38 I8
Cerro Bonete *Mountain* Chile 41
Cerro de Pasco Peru 44 D12
Cēsis Latvia 80 J5
České Budějovice Czech Republic 70 H10
Česma *River* Croatia 74 I3
Cetatea *see* Bucharest
Ceuta *Spanish enclave* NW Africa 88 I4
Cévennes *Mountain range* France 63 M13
Ceyhan *River* Turkey 105 N9
Ceylon *see* Sri Lanka
Ceylon Plain *Sea feature* Indian Ocean 103, 115
Chad *Country* C Africa 94

Chad 94

ⓐ Arabic, French · 🌐 Franc · ♦ 5 · ♥ 48 · ◯ £2.15 · 🐛 (m) 42% (f) 18% · 🏠 30%

Chad, L. *Lake* C Africa 87, 93 R9, 94 H7
Chagai Hills *Mountain range* Pakistan 116 F4
Chagos-Laccadive Plateau *Sea feature* Indian Ocean 103, 115
Chagos Trench *Sea feature* Indian Ocean 115
Chāh Bahār Iran 100 G5, 109 Q11
Chaitén Chile 49 H15
Chalbi Desert *Desert region* Kenya 97 P2
Chalcis *see* Chalkida
Chalkida (var. Chalcis) Greece 79 K8
Châlons-sur-Marne France 63 N5
Chambal *River* India 117 K6
Chambéry France 63 O10
Chambord France 63 K7
Champaign Illinois, USA 31 L12
Champasak Laos 125 M12

Champlain, L. *Lake* New York/Vermont, USA 27 M6
Chañaral Chile 48 G7
Chandigarh India 117 K4
Changchun China 121 P5
Changsha China 121 L15
Changzhi China 121 L8
Chania Crete, Greece 79 L15
Channel Islands *Island group* UK 59 H18, 62 G4
Channel-Port-aux-Basques Newfoundland, Canada 25 R10
Chanthaburi Thailand 125 K13
Chapala, L. *Lake* Mexico 39 L11
Chardzhev (prev. Chardzhou) Turkmenistan 111 K8
Chardzhou *see* Chardzhev
Charente *River* France 62 I10
Chari *River* Chad 94 H8
Chariton *River* Iowa/Missouri, USA 33 R10
Charleroi Belgium 65 G16
Charles, Cape *Cape* Virgina, USA 29 S5
Charleston South Carolina, USA 29 P8
Charleston West Virginia, USA 29 P3
Charleville Queensland, Australia 133 N10
Charlotte North Carolina, USA 29 P6
Charlotte Amalie *Virgin Islands (US)* 43 R9
Charlottesville Virginia, USA 29 Q4
Charlottetown Prince Edward Island, Canada 25 Q11
Chartres France 63 K5
Chashma Barrage *Dam* Pakistan 116 I2
Châteauroux France 63 K8
Chatham Is. *Island group* New Zealand, Pacific Ocean 128 J12
Chattahoochee *River* Alabama/Georgia, USA 29 M7
Chattanooga Tennessee, USA 29 M6
Chauk Burma 124 F8
Chaumont France 63 N6
Cheboksary Russian Federation 83 I11
Cheboygan Michigan, USA 31 N5
Cheju South Korea 121 P9
Chelan, L. *Lake* Washington, USA 36 I6
Cheleken Turkmenistan 110 F6
Chelm Poland 71 P7
Chelyabinsk Russian Federation 112 G9
Chelyuskin, C. *Cape* Russian Federation 113 L4
Chemnitz Germany 67 L11
Chenab *River* India/Pakistan 116 J3
Chengdu China 120 J10
Chequamegon Bay *Physical feature* Wisconsin, USA 30 J4
Cherbourg France 62 H4
Cherepovets Russian Federation 82 H9
Cherkasy Ukraine 84 J5
Cherkessk Russian Federation 83 E15
Chernigov *see* Chernihiv
Chernihiv Ukraine 84 I3
Chernivtsi (var. Chernivtsi) Ukraine 84 F6
Chernobyl Ukraine 84 I4
Chernovtsy *see* Chernivtsi
Chernoye More *see* Black Sea
Chernyakhovsk Russian Federation 80 G10
Chesapeake Bay *Maryland/Virginia, USA* 29 S4
Chesha Bay *Sea feature* Russian Federation 82 L6
Chester England, UK 59 H13
Chesterfield Inlet *Sea feature* Northwest Territories, Canada 23 O9
Chesuncook L. *Lake* Maine, USA 27 P4
Chetumal Mexico 39 T12
Cheyenne Wyoming, USA 33 K10
Cheyenne *River* South Dakota/Wyoming, USA 33 M7
Chi-lung Taiwan 121 O13
Chiang Jiang *see* Yangtze
Chiang Mai Thailand 124 I9
Chiang Rai Thailand 124 I9
Chiba Japan 123 L11
Chibougamau Quebec, Canada 25 L10
Chicago Illinois, USA 31 L12
Chichén Itzá *Archaeological site* Mexico 39 T11
Chiclayo Peru 45 C11
Chico California, USA 37 H13
Chicoutimi Quebec, Canada 25 N11
Chidley, C. *Cape* Quebec, Canada 25 O2
Chiemsee *Lake* Germany 67 K16
Chifeng (var. Ulanhad) China 119 Q6
Chihuahua Mexico 39 K5
Chile *Country* S America 48-49

Chile 48-49

ⓐ Spanish · 🌐 Peso · ♦ 18 · ♥ 72 · ◯ £0.67 · 🐛 (m) 94% (f) 93% · 🖥 205 · ♣ 2383 · 🐍 Yes · 🏠 86% · 🍴 2581

Chile Basin *Sea feature* Pacific Ocean 41, 129 P12
Chile Chico Chile 49 I16
Chile Rise *Sea feature* Pacific Ocean 41
Chillán Chile 49 G12
Chillicothe Ohio, USA 31 P13
Chiloé I. *Island* Chile 41, 49 G15, 129 Q13
Chilpancingo Mexico 39 N13
Chimbay Uzbekistan 110 J9
Chimborazo *Mountain* Ecuador 41
Chimbote Peru 45 C12, 129 Q9
Chimkent *see* Shymkent
Chimoio Mozambique 99 N9
Chin Hills *Mountain range* Burma/India 124 E7

China *Country* E Asia 9, 118-119, 120-121

China 118-121

ⓐ Mandarin · 🌐 Yuan · ♦ 123 · ♥ 70 · ◯ £0.37 · 🐛 (m) 84% (f) 62% · 🖥 31 · ♣ 1077 · 🐍 Yes · 🏠 33% · 🍴 2639

China Lake Naval Weapons Center *Military centre* California, USA 37 I17
Chinandega Nicaragua 42 C10
Chindwin *River* Burma/India 124 F6
Chingola Zambia 97 K13
Chinhoyi (var. Sinoia) Zimbabwe 99 M8
Chioggia Italy 72 H7
Chios Chios, Greece 79 O8
Chios *Island* Greece 79 O8
Chipata Zambia 97 M13
Chippewa, L. *Lake* Wisconsin, USA 30 J5
Chirchik Uzbekistan 111 N6
Chiriquí, Gulf of *Sea feature* Panama 42 E15
Chişinău (var. Kishinev) Moldavia 84 H8
Chita ICBM Base *Military centre* Russian Federation 113 M11
Chitré Panama 42 G15
Chittagong Bangladesh 117 P8
Chitungwiza Zimbabwe 99 M8
Chobe *River* Botswana/Namibia 99 K8
Chobe N.P. *National park* Botswana 99 K8
Chojnice Poland 71 K3
Cholula *Archaeological site* Mexico 39 N12
Choluteca Honduras 42 C9
Choma Zambia 96 J16
Chon Buri Thailand 125 J13
Ch'ŏngjin North Korea 121 Q5
Chongqing China 120 J11
Chott El Jerid *Physical region* Algeria 87 M6
Choybalsan Mongolia 119 O4
Christchurch New Zealand 134 H11
Christiania *see* Oslo
Christianstad Virgin Islands 43 R10
Christmas I. *Dependent territory* Indian Ocean 100 M10
Chu *River* Kazakhstan/Kyrgyzstan 112 F12
Chubut *River* Argentina 49 I15
Chūgoku Mountains *Mountain range* Japan 123 E12
Chukchi Sea Arctic Ocean 51 P5, 113 P2
Chumphon Thailand 125 H14
Chuquicamata Chile 48 G5
Chur Switzerland 68 I10
Churchill Manitoba, Canada 23 O11
Churchill *River* Manitoba, Canada 23 O11
Churchill Falls Newfoundland, Canada 25 P7
Cienfuegos Cuba 42 I4
Cincinnati Ohio, USA 31 O13
Cirebon Java, Indonesia 126 H15
Citlaltépetl, Mt. *Mountain* Mexico 20
Ciudad Bolívar Venezuela 44 J5
Ciudad del Este Paraguay 48 O6
Ciudad Guayana Venezuela 44 K5
Ciudad Juárez Mexico 39 K3
Ciudad Madero Mexico 39 O10
Ciudad Obregón Mexico 38 I5
Ciudad Real Spain 61 K10
Ciudad Victoria Mexico 39 N9
Čiovo *Island* Croatia 74 I8
Civitavecchia Italy 73 H11
Clair Eagle L. *Lake* California, USA 37 H12
Claremont New Hampshire, USA 27 N8
Clarence Strait *Channel* Northern Territory, Australia 132 I5
Clarenville Newfoundland, Canada 25 T9
Clarion Facture Zone *Sea feature* Pacific Ocean 129 M7
Clarksville Tennessee, USA 29 L4
Clearwater Florida, USA 29 N13
Clermont Queensland, Australia 133 O9
Clermont-Ferrand France 63 M10
Cleveland Ohio, USA 31 P10
Clipperton Fracture Zone *Sea feature* Pacific Ocean 129 M7
Clipperton I. *Dependent territory* C. America, Pacific Ocean 129 O7
Cloncurry Queensland, Australia 133 M8
Clovis New Mexico, USA 35 N9
Cluj-Napoca Romania 76 I4
Clyde *River* Scotland, UK 58 H10
Coast Ranges *Mountain range* N America 10, 20, 37 G13
Coatzacoalcos Mexico 39 Q13
Cobán Guatemala 42 B7
Cobija Bolivia 45 I15
Cochabamba Bolivia 45 I15
Cochin India 100 I17, 116 J15
Cochrane Chile 49 I17
Cochrane Ontario, Canada 24 J11
Cockburn Sound Australia 101 M12
Coco *River* Honduras 42 E9
Cocos Is. *Dependent territory* Indian Ocean 100 L10
Cocos Plate *Physical feature* 8, 20, 41
Cocos Ridge *Sea feature* Pacific Ocean 41, 129 P8
Cody Wyoming, USA 32 I7
Coeur d'Alene Idaho, USA 32 F4
Coiba I. *Island* Panama 42 F15
Coihaique Chile 49 H16
Coimbatore India 116 J14
Coimbra Portugal 60 F8
Colbeck, C. *Cape* Pacific Ocean Coast, Antarctica 50 D11
Colchester England, UK 59 L15
Colditz *Castle* Germany 67 L11
Colhué Huapí, L. *Lake* Argentina 49 J16
Colima Mexico 39 K12
Colima *Volcano* Mexico 20

China *Country* E Asia 9, 118-119, 120-121

Coll *Island* Scotland, UK 58 F8
Collier Bay *Sea feature* Western Australia, Australia 132 H6
Colmar France 63 P6
Cologne (var. Köln) Germany 67 E11
Colombia *Country* S America 44

Colombia 44

ⓐ Spanish · 🌐 Peso · ♦ 32 · ♥ 69 · ◯ £0 54 · 🐛 (m) 88% (f) 86% · 🖥 115 · ♣ 1102 · 🐍 No · 🏠 70% · 🍴 2598

Colombian Basin *Sea feature* Caribbean Sea 41
Colombo Sri Lanka 100 I7, 117 K16
Colombus Nebraska, USA 33 O10
Colón Argentina 48 M9
Colón Panama 42 G14
Colonia Uruguay 48 N10
Colonsay *Island* Scotland, UK 58 F9
Colorado *River* Argentina 49 K13
Colorado *River* Mexico/USA 20, 35 K5, 37 O18, 38 G1, 41, 129 N5
Colorado *State* USA 35
Colorado Plateau *Physical region* Arizona, USA 34 I7
Colorado Project *Irrigation project* Colorado, USA 34 H10
Colorado Springs Colorado, USA 35 M5
Columbia Missouri, USA 33 R11
Columbia South Carolina, USA 29 P7
Columbia *River* Canada/USA 20, 23 K14, 36 K5, 129 N4
Columbine, C. *Cape* South Africa 98 I15
Columbus Georgia, USA 29 M8
Columbus Indiana, USA 31 N13
Columbus Mississippi, USA 29 K7
Columbus Ohio, USA 31 P12
Colville *River* Alaska, USA 22 H5
Comacchio Lagoon *Lake* Italy 72 H8
Comayagua Honduras 42 C8
Comilla Bangladesh 117 P8
Communism Peak (var. Pik Kommunizma, prev. Mt. Stalin) *Peak* Tajikistan 103
Como, L. *Lake* Italy 72 E6
Comodoro Rivadavia Argentina 49 K16
Comorin, C. *Cape* India 100 I7, 115
Comoros *Country* Indian Ocean 100 E10

Comoros 100

ⓐ Arabic, French · 🌐 Franc · ♦ 221 · ♥ 56 · ◯ £1.19 · 🐛 (m) 56% (f) 40% · 🏠 28%

Comoros Is. *Island group* Indian Ocean 87
Conakry Guinea 92 G11
Concepción Chile 49 G12, 129 Q12
Concepción Paraguay 48 M5
Conchas L. *Lake* New Mexico, USA 35 M10
Conchos *River* Mexico 38 J5
Concord California, USA 37 H14
Concord New Hampshire, USA 27 N8
Concordia Argentina 48 M9
Congo *Country* C Africa 95

Congo 95

ⓐ French · 🌐 Franc · ♦ 7 · ♥ 52 · ◯ £1.13 · 🐛 (m) 70% (f) 44% · 🏠 41%

Congo (var. Zaire) *River* C Africa 11, 53 M12, 87, 95, J12, 98 G2, 95 I13
Congo Basin *Physical region* Congo/Zaire 11, 87
Connecticut *River* USA 27 N7
Connecticut *State* USA 27
Constance, L. (var. Bodensee) *Lake* C Europe 54, 67 G17, 68 H8
Constantine Algeria 89 M4
Constantinople *see* Istanbul
Constanţa Romania 77 P9
Contwoyto L. *Lake* Northwest Territories, Canada 23 M9
Coober Pedy South Australia, Australia 133 K11
Cook Islands *Dependent territory* Polynesia, Pacific Ocean 129 K10
Cook, Mt. *Mountain* South I. New Zealand 131
Cook Strait *Channel* New Zealand 128 I12, 131, 134 G8
Cooktown Queensland, Australia 133 N6
Cooper Creek *River* Queensland/South Australia, Australia 133 K11
Coos Bay Oregon, USA 36 F10
Copán *Archaeological site* Honduras 42 C8
Copenhagen Denmark 56 J15
Copiapó Chile 48 G7
Coppermine Northwest Territories, Canada 23 L8
Coppermine *River* Northwest Territories, Canada 23 L8
Copşa Mică Romania 76 J6
Coquilhatville *see* Mbandaka
Coquimbo Chile 48 G8
Corabia Romania 76 J10
Coral Sea Pacific Ocean 128 H10, 131, 133 O4
Coral Sea Basin *Sea feature* Pacific Ocean 131
Coral Sea Is. *Dependent territory* Pacific Ocean 128 H10
Cordillera Cantábrica *Mountain range* Spain 54, 60 I4
Córdoba Argentina 48 J9
Córdoba Spain 60 J12
Cordova Alaska, USA 22 G9
Corfu Corfu, Greece 78 F5

ⓐ Language (official or most commonly spoken) · 🌐 Currency · ♦ Population density per square kilometre · ♥ Average life expectancy · ◯ Price of 1 dozen hen's eggs · 🐛 Literacy · 🖥 Number of TVs per 1,000 people · ♣ Number of people per doctor · 🐍 Death penalty · 🏠 Percentage of urban-based population · 🍴 Average number of calories consumed per person

141

Durango Mexico 39 K8
Durazno Uruguay 48 N10
Durban South Africa 99 M14, 101 C12
Durham North Carolina, USA 29 Q5
Durrës Albania 75 L12
Dushanbe (prev. Stalinabad) Tajikistan 111 N8
Düsseldorf Germany 67 D11
Dutch East Indies *see* Indonesia
Dutch Guiana *see* Surinam
Dutch Harbor Unalaska I. Aleutian Is. Alaska, USA 22 C8
Dvina *see* Dvina, Northern *or* Dvina, Western
Dvina, Northern *River* Russian Federation 54, 80 J10
Dvina, Western (var. Daugava) *River* NE Europe 54, 80 I6, 81 M8
Dzhalal-Abad Kyrgyzstan 111 P6
Dzhambul *see* Zhambyl
Dzhezkazgan *see* Zhezkazgan
Dzhizak Uzbekistan 111 M7
Dzhugdzhur Range *Mountain range* Russian Federation 113 O9
Dzungaria *Mountain range* China/Kazakhstan 103

E

Eagle L. *Lake* California, USA 37 I12
Eagle L. *Lake* Maine, USA 27 P3
Eagle Mountain L. *Lake* Texas, USA 35 Q10
Eagle Pass Texas, USA 35 P14
East African Plateau *Physical feature* Kenya/Uganda 87
East Anglia *Region* England, UK 59 M14
East C. *Cape* Papua New Guinea 133 P14
East China Sea China 115, 121 O12, 123 B17, 128 F6
East Frisian Is. *Island group* Germany 66 E7
East Greenland current *Ocean current* Atlantic Ocean 12
East Indies (var. Indonesia) *Island group* SE Asia 115, 131
East Liverpool Ohio, USA 31 Q11
East London South Africa 99 L15
East Pacific Ridge *Sea feature* Pacific Ocean 41
East Pacific Rise *Sea feature* Pacific Ocean 129 O9
East Pakistan *see* Bangladesh
East St. Louis Illinois, USA 30 J14
East Siberian Sea Arctic Ocean 51 R6, 103, 113 O3
Easter I. *Island* Polynesia, Pacific Ocean 129 O10
Eastern Ghats *Mountain range* India 117 L11
Eastmain *River* Quebec, Canada 25 M8
Eastport Maine, USA 27 R5
Eau Claire Wisconsin, USA 30 I6
Eblana *see* Dublin
Ebolowa Cameroon 95 F11
Ebro *River* Spain 54, 61 M5
Ecuador *Country* S America 44

Ecuador 44

ⓐ Spanish • 🐚 Sucre • ♦ 38 • ♥ 66 • ◔ £0.31 • 🕮 (m) 88% (f) 84% • 🏠 56%

Ed Damazin Sudan 91 H14
Ed Damer Sudan 91 H11
Ed Dueim Sudan 91 G13
Ede Netherlands 64 K10
Edéa Cameroon 95 F11
Eder *River* Germany 67 G11
Edessa Greece 78 I3
Edinburgh Scotland, UK 58 I10
Edirne Turkey 104 G4
Edmonds Washington, USA 36 H6
Edmonton Alberta, Canada 23 L13
Edward, L. *Lake* Uganda/Zaire 95 O12, 97 K4
Edwards Air Base *Military centre* California, USA 37 L18
Edwards Plateau *Physical region* Texas, USA 35 P12
Eforie-Nord Romania 77 P9
Egadi Is. *Island group* Sicily 73 H17
Egiyn *River* Mongolia/Russian Federation 119 L4
Eğridir, L. *Lake* Turkey 104 J8
Egypt *Country* NE Africa 90

Egypt 90

ⓐ Arabic • 🐚 Pound • ♦ 53 • ♥ 61 • ◔ £0.52 • 🕮 (m) 63% (f) 34% • 🖵 109 • ✚ 5092 • 🕊 Yes • 🏠 47% • 🍴 3336

Eiger, Mt. *Mountain* Switzerland 68 F11
Eigg *Island* Scotland, UK 58 F8
Eindhoven Netherlands 65 J13
Eire *see* Ireland
Eisenstadt Austria 69 S5
El Aaiun (var. Laâyoune) Western Sahara 88 F7
El Faiyûm Egypt 90 F7
El Fasher Sudan 91 D13
El Ferrol Spain 60 G3
El Iskandarîya *see* Alexandria
El Jerid, Chott *Salt lake* Tunisia 89 M5
El Juf *see* El Djouf
El Khartûm *see* Khartoum
El Mansûra Egypt 90 F6

El Minya Egypt 90 F7
El Obeid Sudan 91 F13
El Oued Algeria 89 M6
El Paso Texas, USA 35 L11
El Qâhira *see* Cairo
El Salvador *Country* C America 42

El Salvador 42

ⓐ Spanish • 🐚 Colon • ♦ 256 • ♥ 64 • ◔ £0.59 • 🕮 (m) 76% (f) 70% • 🏠 44%

El Suweis *see* Suez
Elat Israel 107 L14
Elâziğ Turkey 105 P8
Elba *Island* Italy 72 F10
Elbasan Albania 75 M12
Elbe *River* Germany 54, 66 I8
Elbe *see* Laba
Elbert, Mt. *Mountain* Colorado, USA 20
Elbląg Poland 71 L2
El'brus *Mountain* Russian Federation 54
Elburz Mts. *Mountain range* Iran 109 N4
Elche Spain 61 N11
Eldoret Kenya 97 O4
Elephant Butte Res. *Reservoir* New Mexico, USA 35 L10
Elephant I. *Island* South Shetland Is. Antarctica 50 B6
Eleuthera *Island* Bahamas 43 L2
Elgin Scotland, UK 58 I7
Elisabethville *see* Lubumbashi
Elista Russian Federation 83 F14
Elk Poland 71 N3
Elko Nevada, USA 34 H2
Ellensburg Washington, USA 36 I7
Ellesmere I. *Island* Northwest Territories, Canada 20, 23 N1, 51 O11
Ellsworth Mountains *Mountain range* Antarctica 50 C9
Elmira New York, USA 26 J10
Eltz *Castle* Germany 67 E12
Elwell, L. *Lake* Montana, USA 32 I4
Ely Nevada, USA 34 H4
Elyria Ohio, USA 31 P10
Emba *River* Kazakhstan 112 E10
Emden Germany 66 E7
Emerson (Trimmu) Barrage *Dam* Pakistan 116 I3
Emmen Netherlands 64 N8
Emona *see* Ljubljana
Emperor Seamounts *Sea feature* Pacific Ocean 128 I5
Emporia Kansas, USA 33 P12
Empty Quarter *see* Rub 'al Khali
Ems *River* Germany 66 E9
En Nahud Sudan 91 E13
Encarnación Paraguay 48 N7
Ende Flores, Indonesia 127 M15
Enderby Land *Region* Antarctica 50 G7
Enewetak *Island* Marshall Islands, Pacific Ocean 128 H7
Enggano *Island* Indonesia 126 E14
England *Country* UK 59
English Channel France/UK 54, 59 J17, 62 I3
Enguri *River* Azerbaijan/Georgia 85 O11
Enid Oklahoma, USA 33 O14
Enna Sicily 73 K18
Enns *River* Austria 69 P7
Enriquillo, L. *Lake* Dominican Republic 43 N8
Enschede Netherlands 64 N10
Ensenada Mexico 38 F2
Entebbe Uganda 97 M4
Enugu Nigeria 93 O12
Ephesus *Archaeological site* Turkey 104 G8
Epidaurus *Archaeological site* Greece 78 J10
Épinal France 63 P6
Equatorial Current *Ocean current* Pacific Ocean 12
Equatorial Guinea *Country* C Africa 95

Equatorial Guinea 95

ⓐ Spanish • 🐚 Franc • ♦ 15 • ♥ 47 • ◔ £2.15 • 🕮 (m) 64% (f) 37% • 🏠 27%

Er Rachidia Morocco 88 I6
Er Roseires Dam *Dam* Sudan 91 H14
Erdenet Mongolia 119 L4
Ereğli Turkey 105 L9
Erenhot China 119 O6
Erfurt Germany 67 I11
Erie Pennsylvania, USA 26 G10
Erie, L. *Lake* Canada/USA 20, 24 J15, 26 G9, 31 P9
Erie Canal *Waterway* New York, USA 26 I8
Eritrea *Country* E Africa 91

Eritrea 91

ⓐ Amharic • 🐚 Birr • ♦ 37 • ♥ 48 • ◔ N/A • 🕮 (av.) 71% • 🏠 N/A

Erivan *see* Yerevan
Erlangen Germany 67 I13
Ernakulam India 116 J14
Erne, Lough *Lake* Northern Ireland, UK 59 D11
Ertix He *see* Irtysh
Erzincan Turkey 105 P6
Erzurum Turkey 105 Q6
Es Semara *see* Smara
Esbjerg Denmark 52 L7, 56 H15

Escanaba Michigan, USA 31 L5
Esch-sur-Alzette Luxembourg 65 L19
Escuintla Guatemala 42 A8
Eşfahān Iran 109 N6
Eskimo Pt. Northwest Territories, Canada 23 O10
Eskişehir Turkey 104 J6
Esla Res. *Reservoir* Spain 60 I6
Esmeraldas Ecuador 44 C8
Esperance Western Australia, Australia 132 H13
Espinho Portugal 60 F7
Espíritu Santo I. *Island* Mexico 38 I10
Esquel Argentina 49 H15
Essaouira Morocco 88 G6
Essen Germany 66 E10
Essequibo *River* Guyana 44 M7
Estelí Nicaragua 42 D10
Estevan Saskatchewan, Canada 23 N15
Estonia (var. Estonskaya SSR) *Country* NE Europe 80-81

Estonia 80-81

ⓐ Estonian • 🐚 Kroon • ♦ 35 • ♥ 48 • ◔ £0.38 • 🕮 (m) 99% (f) 99% • 🏠 71%

Estonskaya SSR *see* Estonia
Ethiopia (var. Abyssinia) *Country* E Africa 91

Ethiopia 91

ⓐ Amharic • 🐚 Birr • ♦ 48 • ♥ 48 • ◔ £0.50 • 🕮 (av.) 29% • 🖵 2 • ✚ 38539 • 🕊 Yes • 🏠 13% • 🍴 1667

Ethiopian Highlands *Mountain range* Ethiopia 87, 91 J15
Etna *Volcano* Sicily
Etosha N.P. *National park* Namibia 98 I19
Etosha Pan *Salt basin* Namibia 98 H8
Euboea *see* Evvoia
Eugene Oregon, USA 36 G9
Eupen Belgium 65 L15
Euphrates *River* SW Asia 100 E4, 103, 105 O10, 107 R5, 109 K6
Eurasian Plate *Physical feature* 8, 20, 54, 87, 103, 115, 131
Eureka California, USA 37 F12
Europe *Continent* 8, 10, 11, 12, 13, 15, 20, 103
Europoort Netherlands 64 H11
Evanston Illinois, USA 31 L10
Evansville Indiana, USA 31 L14
Everard, L. *Lake* South Australia, Australia 133 K12
Everest, Mt. (var. Qomolangma Feng) *Mountain* China/Nepal 115, 117 O5
Everett Washington, USA 36 H6
Everglades, The *Swamp region* Florida, USA 20, 29 N14
Évora Portugal 60 G11
Évreux France 63 K5
Evvoia (var. Euboea) *Island* Greece 79 K7
Exeter England, UK 59 G16
Exmoor *Physical region* England, UK 59 G16
Exmouth Plateau *Sea feature* Indian Ocean 131
Eyasi, L. *Lake* Tanzania 97 N7
Eyre, L. *Lake* South Australia, Australia 131, 133 L11

F

Fada-Ngourma Burkina 93 M10
Faeroe Islands *Dependent territory* Atlantic Ocean 52 J7
Faeroe Islands *Island group* Atlantic Ocean 54
Faeroe Shelf *Sea feature* Atlantic Ocean 54
Faguibine, L. *Lake* Mali 93 K7
Fairbanks Alaska, USA 22 H7
Fairmont Minnesota, USA 30 G8
Faisalabad Pakistan 116 I3
Falkland Escarpment *Sea feature* Atlantic Ocean 41
Falkland Is. *Dependent territory* Atlantic Ocean 53 F15
Falkland Is. *Island group* Atlantic Ocean 41
Fall River Massachusetts, USA 27 O11
Falmouth England, UK 59 E17
Falun Sweden 57 L11
Famagusta Cyprus 105 L12
Faradje Zaire 95 O11
Farafangana Madagascar 101 E11
Farewell, Cape Greenland 52 H7
Fargo North Dakota, USA 33 O5
Faribault Minnesota, USA 30 H7
Farmington New Mexico, USA 35 K6
Faro Portugal 60 G13
Faro Yukon Territory, Canada 22 I9
Fårö *Island* Sweden 57 M13
Farvel, Cape (var. Kap Farvel) *Cape* Greenland 51 M16
Fax *River* Sweden 57 K8
Faya *see* Faya Largeau
Faya Largeau *see* Faya
Faya (var. Faya Largeau) Chad 94 J5
Fayetteville Arkansas, USA 28 H3
Fayetteville North Carolina, USA 29 Q6
Fdérik Mauritania 92 H4
Fear, Cape *Cape* North Carolina, USA 29 Q8
Federal Capital Territory *see* Australian Capital Territory
Fehmarn *Island* Germany 66 J6
Feira de Santana Brazil 47 N11
Felbertauern Tunnel *Tunnel* Austria 69 M8

Feldkirch Austria 68 I9
Felixstowe England, UK 59 M15
Femund, L. *Lake* Norway 56 J9
Fens, The *Physical region* England, UK 59 K14
Feodosiya Ukraine 85 K10
Fergana Uzbekistan 111 P6
Fergus Falls Minnesota, USA 30 F5
Fernando de Noronha I. *Island* Atlantic Ocean 53 I12
Fernando Póo *Island* Equatorial Guinea 87
Ferrara Italy 72 H8
Fethiye Turkey 105 H10
Feuilles, Rivière aux *River* Quebec, Canada 25 M4
Fez Morocco 88 I5
Fezzan *Physical region* Libya 89 O9
Fianarantsoa Madagascar 101 E11
Fier Albania 75 L13
Figueira de Foz Portugal 60 F8
Figuig Morocco 88 J6
Fiji *Country* Melanesia, Pacific Ocean 128 J10

Fiji 128

ⓐ English • 🐚 Dollar • ♦ 41 • ♥ 65 • ◔ £1.17 • 🕮 (m) 90% (f) 84% • 🏠 39%

Fiji *Island group* Melanesia, Pacific Ocean 131
Filadelphia Paraguay 48 L4
Filchner Ice Shelf *Coastal feature* Atlantic Ocean Coast, Antarctica 50 D8
Filicudi *Island* Lipari Is. Sicily 73 K16
Fimbul Ice Shelf *Coastal feature* Atlantic Ocean Coast, Antarctica 50 E6
Findlay Ohio, USA 31 O11
Finger Lakes *Physical feature* New York, USA 26 J9
Finisterre, C. *Coastal feature* Spain 54
Finland *Country* N Europe 57

Finland 57

ⓐ Finnish, Swedish • 🐚 Markka • ♦ 16 • ♥ 76 • ◔ £1.54 • 🕮 (m) 99% (f) 99% • 🖵 497 • ✚ 515 • 🕊 No • 🏠 60% • 🍴 3253

Finland, Gulf of *Sea feature* Baltic Sea 54, 57 O12, 81 K1, 82 E7
Firenze *see* Florence, Italy
Firth of Clyde *Sea feature* Scotland, UK 58 G10
Firth of Forth *Sea feature* Scotland, UK 58 I9
Fish *River* Namibia 98 I13
Fishguard Wales, UK 59 F15
Fitzroy *River* Western Australia, Australia 132 H7
Flagstaff Arizona, USA 34 I7
Flaming Gorge Dam *Dam* Utah, USA 35 K3
Flaming Gorge Res. *Reservoir* Utah/Wyoming, USA 32 I10
Flathead L. *Lake* Montana, USA 32 G4
Flin Flon Manitoba, Canada 23 N13
Flinders I. *Island* Queensland, Australia 131, 133 M7
Flinders I. *Island* Tasmania, Australia 133 N15
Flinders Ranges *Mountain range* South Australia, Australia 131, 133 L12
Flint Michigan, USA 31 O8
Flint *River* Florida/Georgia 29 M9
Florence (var. Firenze) Italy 72 G9
Florence Alabama, USA 29 K5
Florence South Carolina, USA 29 P7
Florencia Colombia 44 E8
Flores Guatemala 42 B6
Flores *Island* Indonesia 115, 131, 127 M15
Flores Sea Indonesia 127 L14
Florianópolis Brazil 47 J15
Florida Uruguay 48 N10
Florida *State* USA 29 N11
Florida Keys *Island group* Florida, USA 29 O16
Florida, Straits of *Channel* Cuba/USA 29 P15
Florina Greece 78 I4
Flushing (var. Vlissingen) Netherlands 65 E13
Fly *River* Papua New Guinea 133 M3
Foča Bosnia and Herzegovina 75 L8
Focşani Romania 77 N6
Foggia Italy 73 M12
Föhr *Island* North Frisian Is. Germany 66 G5
Foix France 63 L15
Fond du Lac Wisconsin, USA 31 K8
Fongafale Tuvalu, Pacific Ocean 128 J9
Forlì Italy 72 H8
Formentera *Island* Balearic Islands 61 P11
Formosa Argentina 48 M6
Fort Bliss Military Reservation *Military centre* New Mexico, USA 35 L11
Fort Collins Colorado, USA 35 M3
Fort-de-France Martinique 43 T13
Fort Dodge Iowa, USA 33 Q8
Fort-Foureau *see* Kousseri
Fort Lamy *see* N'Djamena
Fort Lauderdale Florida, USA 29 O15
Fort McMurray Alberta, Canada 23 L12
Fort McPherson Northwest Territories, Canada 22 J7
Fort Myers Florida, USA 29 N14
Fort Nelson British Columbia, Canada 23 J11
Fort Peck L. *Lake* Montana, USA 32 J4
Fort Portal Uganda 97 L4
Fort Resolution Northwest Territories, Canada 23 L10
Fort Shevchenko Kazakhstan 112 D10
Fort Simpson Northwest Territories, Canada 23 K10
Fort Smith Arkansas, USA 28 H4
Fort Smith Northwest Territories, Canada 23 L11

ⓐ Language (official or most commonly spoken) • 🐚 Currency • ♦ Population density per square kilometre • ♥ Average life expectancy • ◔ Price of 1 dozen hen's eggs • 🕮 Literacy • 🖵 Number of TVs per 1,000 people • ✚ Number of people per doctor • 🕊 Death penalty • 🏠 Percentage of urban-based population • 🍴 Average number of calories consumed daily per person

143

Greenville Liberia 92 I13
Greenville Mississippi, USA 28 I6
Greenville South Carolina, USA 29 O6
Greifswald Germany 66 L6
Grenada *Country* Caribbean Sea 43 S15

Grenada 43

a English · **☒** Dollar · **♦** 268 · **♥** 70 · **◷** £3.10 · **☕** (av.) 90% · **⌂** 34%

Grenadines, The *Island group* St Vincent & The Grenadines 43 S14
Grenoble France 63 O11
Grevena Greece 78 H4
Greymouth New Zealand 134 E10
Grim, C. *Cape* Tasmania, Australia 133 M15
Grimsby England, UK 52 K8, 59 K13
Grodno *see* Hrodna
Groningen Netherlands 64 M6
Groote Eylandt *Island* Northern Territory, Australia 133 L5
Grootfontein Namibia 98 I9
Grosseto Italy 72 G10
Groznyy Russian Federation 83 F16
Grudziądz Poland 71 L3
Gstaad Switzerland 68 E11
Guacanayabo, Gulf of *Sea feature* Cuba 42 J6
Guadalajara Mexico 39 L11
Guadalajara Spain 61 L8
Guadalcanal *Island* Solomon Islands, Pacific Ocean 128 I9
Guadalquivir *River* Spain 54, 60 I12
Guadalupe Mexico 39 L9
Guadarrama, Sierra de *Mountain range* Spain 61 K7
Guadeloupe *Dependent territory* Caribbean Sea 43 S11
Guadiana *River* Portugal/Spain 60 G11
Gualeguaychu Argentina 48 M9
Guallatiri *Volcano* Chile 41
Guam *Dependent territory* Micronesia, Pacific Ocean 128 G7
Guanare Venezuela 44 H5
Guangxi Zhuang Autonomous Region China 121 K14
Guangzhou *see* Canton
Guantánamo Cuba 43 L6
Guantánamo Bay *Sea feature* Cuba 43 L7
Guarda Portugal 60 H8
Guatemala *Country* C America 42

Guatemala 42

a Spanish · **☒** Quetzal · **♦** 87 · **♥** 64 · **◷** £0.51 · **☕** (m) 63% (f) 47% · **⌂** 39%

Guatemala Basin *Sea feature* Pacific Ocean 41
Guatemala City Guatemala 42 B8
Guaviare *River* Colombia/Venezuela 44 F7
Guayaquil Ecuador 44 C9, 129 Q8
Guayaquil, Gulf of *Sea feature* Ecuador/Peru 44 B9
Guaymas Mexico 38 H5
Guddu Barrage *Dam* Pakistan 116 H4
Guernsey *Dependent territory* W Europe 59 H18
Guiana Highlands *Mountain range* South America 41
Guider Cameroon 94 G8
Guilin China 121 K13
Guinea *Country* W Africa 92

Guinea 92

a French · **☒** Franc · **♦** 24 · **♥** 44 · **◷** £1.21 · **☕** (m) 35% (f) 13% · **⌘** 7 · **⌂** 10300 · **☠** Yes · **⌂** 26% · **⸖** 2132

Guinea, Gulf of *Sea feature* C Africa 53 L11, 87, 95 E11
Guinea Basin *Sea feature* Gulf of Guinea, Atlantic Ocean 53 K12, 87
Guinea-Bissau (prev. Portuguese Guinea) *Country* W Africa 92

Guinea-Bissau 92

a Portuguese · **☒** Peso · **♦** 36 · **♥** 41 · **◷** £1.53 · **☕** (m) 50% (f) 24% · **⌂** 20%

Guiyang China 120 J12
Gujranwala Pakistan 116 J3
Gujrat Pakistan 116 J3
Gulf Stream current *Ocean current* Atlantic Ocean 12
Gulf, The *see* Persian Gulf
Gulfport Mississippi, USA 28 J9
Gulja *see* Yining
Gulu Uganda 97 M2
Gümüşhane Turkey 105 P5
Gur'yev *see* Atyrau
Gusau Nigeria 93 O10
Gusev Russian Federation 80 G10
Guwahati India 117 P6
Guyana (prev. British Guiana) *Country* S America 44

Guyana 44

a English · **☒** Dollar · **♦** 4 · **♥** 65 · **◷** £2.11 · **☕** (m) 97% (f) 95% · **⌂** 35%

Guyana Basin *Sea feature* Atlantic Ocean 53 G11
Gwalior India 117 K6
Gwelo *see* Gweru
Gweru (prev. Gwelo) Zimbabwe 99 M9
Gyandzha *see* Gäncä
Gyangzê China 118 I13
Gyda Peninsula *Physical feature* Russian Federation 112 I6
Győr Hungary 71 K13
Gytheio Greece 78 I12
Gyumri (var. Kumayri; var. Leninakan) Armenia 85 P13
Gzhel' Russian Federation 82 G10

H

Ha Giang Vietnam 124 M7
Haapsalu Estonia 80 I2
Haarlem Netherlands 64 H9
Ḥabbān Yemen 108 J16
Habomai Is. *Island group* Japan 122 O2
Hachinohe Japan 122 L6
Hachiōji Japan 123 K11
Hadejia *River* Nigeria 93 Q9
Haeju North Korea 121 P7
Hagen Germany 67 E11
Hagi Japan 123 D13
Hague, The Netherlands 64 G10
Hai Phong Vietnam 124 N8
Haifa (var. Hefa) Israel 107 L8
Haikou China 121 K15
Ḥā'il Saudi Arabia 108 I8
Hailar China 119 P3
Hainan *Island* China 115, 121 K16
Hainburg Austria 69 T4
Haines Alaska, USA 22 I10
Haines Junction Yukon Territory, Canada 22 I19
Haiti *Country* Caribbean Sea 43

Haiti 43

a French, Creole · **☒** Gourde · **♦** 240 · **♥** 54 · **◷** £0.55 · **☕** (m) 59% (f) 47% · **⌂** 28%

Ḥajjah Yemen 108 H15
Hakkâri Turkey 105 S8
Hakodate Japan 122 K5, 128 G5
Halden Norway 56 J12
Ḥalab (var. Aleppo; anc. Beroea) Syria 107 N3
Halcarnassus Turkey 104 G9
Halifax Nova Scotia, Canada 25 Q13, 52 F8
Halle Germany 66 K10
Hallein Austria 69 N7
Halley *Research centre* Antarctica 50 D7
Halls Creek Western Australia, Australia 132 I7
Halmahera *Island* Indonesia 115, 131, 127 P10
Halmstad Sweden 56 I14
Hälsingborg Sweden 56 J15
Hamada Japan 123 D12
Hamadān Iran 109 M4
Ḥamāh Syria 107 N5
Hamamatsu Japan 123 J12
Hamar Norway 56 J10
Hamburg Germany 66 H7
Hämeenlinna Finland 57 O10
Hamersley Range *Mountain range* Western Australia, Australia 132 F9
Hamhŭng North Korea 121 P6
Hami (var. Kumul) China 118 J7
Hamilton New Zealand 134 G5
Hamilton Ontario, Canada 25 K14
Hamm Germany 66 F10
Ḥammār, L. al *Lake* Iraq 109 L6
Hammerfest Norway 57 O1
Hāmūn-e-Ṣāberī *Salt pan* Afghanistan/Iran 110 J14
Handan China 121 M8
Hangayn Nuruu *Mountain range* Mongolia 119 K4
Hangzhou China 121 O11
Hannover *see* Hanover
Hanoi Vietnam 124 M8
Hanover (var. Hannover) Germany 66 H9
Har Us L. *Lake* Mongolia 118 J5
Ḥaraḍ Saudi Arabia 109 L10
Harare (prev. Salisbury) Zimbabwe 99 M8
Harbin China 121 P4
Hardanger Fjord *Sea feature* Norway 56 H10
Harderwijk Netherlands 64 J10
Harer Ethiopia 91 L14
Hargeysa Somalia 91 M14
Harīrūd *River* C Asia 111 L11
Harlan County L. *Lake* Nebraska, USA 33 N11
Harlingen Netherlands 64 J7
Harney L. *Lake* Oregon, USA 36 K10
Härnösand Sweden 57 M9
Harper Liberia 92 I13
Harris *Island* Scotland, UK 58 F7
Harrisburg Pennsylvania, USA 26 J13
Harrisonburg Pennsylvania, USA 27 M11
Harry S. Truman Res. *Reservoir* Missouri, USA 33 U12
Harstad Norway 57 M3
Hartford Connecticut, USA 27 M11
Hasselt Belgium 65 J14
Hässleholm Sweden 56 J15
Hastings England, UK 59 L17
Hastings Nebraska, USA 33 O10
Hastings New Zealand 134 H7
Hat Yai Thailand 125 I16
Hatteras, Cape *Cape* North Carolina, USA 20, 29 S6

Hatteras Plain *Sea feature* Atlantic Ocean 20
Hattiesburg Mississippi, USA 28 J8
Haugesund Norway 52 K7, 56 H11
Havana (var. La Habana) Cuba 42 H3
Havre Montana, USA 32 I4
Havre-Saint-Pierre Quebec, Canada 25 P9
Hawaii *Island* Pacific Ocean 12
Hawaii *State* USA, Pacific Ocean 129 L6
Hawaiian Is. *Island group* Polynesia, Pacific Ocean 8, 129 K7
Hawke Bay *Sea feature* New Zealand 134 I7
Ḥawrān, Wadi *Seasonal watercourse* Iraq 108 J4
Hay River Northwest Territories, Canada 23 L10
Hayes *River* Manitoba, Canada 23 P12
Hays Kansas, USA 33 N13
Hazleton Pennsylvania, USA 27 K12
Heads, The *Cape* Oregon, USA 36 F10
Heard and MacDonald Islands *Dependent territory see* Heard I, MacDonald Is
Heard I. *Island* Indian Ocean 50 I7, 101 H15
Heathrow *Airport* England, UK 59 K16
Heerenveen Netherlands 64 K7
Heerlen Netherlands 65 K15
Hefa *see* Haifa
Hefei China 121 N10
Heidelberg Germany 67 F14
Heilbronn Germany 67 G14
Heilong Jiang *see* Amur
Hejaz *Region* Saudi Arabia 108 H9
Helena Montana, USA 32 H5
Helgoland Bay (var. Helgoländer Bucht) *Sea feature* Germany 66 G6
Helgoländer Bucht *see* Helgoland Bay
Helmand *River* Afghanistan/Iran 111 L12
Helmond Netherlands 65 K12
Helsingør Denmark 56 J15
Helsinki Finland 57 O11
Helwân Egypt 90 F7
Henderson Nevada, USA 34 H7
Hengelo Netherlands 64 N10
Henrietta Maria, C. *Cape* Canada 24 J6
Henzada Burma 124 F10
Herāt Afghanistan 110 J12
Herisau Switzerland 68 H8
Herlen Gol *see* Kerulen
Hermansverk Norway 56 I9
Hermit Is. *Island group* Papua New Guinea 133 N1
Hermosillo Mexico 38 H4
Herrenchiemsee *Castle* Germany 67 K16
Herstal Belgium 65 K15
Hialeah Florida, USA 29 O15
Hibbing Minnesota, USA 30 H3
Hidaka Mts. *Mountain range* Japan 122 L4
Hidalgo del Parral Mexico 39 K6
Hierosolyma *see* Jerusalem
Hiiumaa *Island* Estonia 80 H2
Hildesheim Germany 66 H9
Hillsboro Oregon, USA 36 H8
Hilversum Netherlands 64 J10
Himalayas *Mountain range* S Asia 8, 11, 103, 115, 117 M5, 118 H14
Ḥimş Syria 107 N5
Hindu Kush *Mountain range* 103, 111 O10, 115
Hinnøya *Island* Norway 57 L3
Hirakud Res. *Reservoir* India 117 M9
Hirfanli Barrage *Dam* Turkey 105 L7
Hiroshima Japan 123 E13
Hispania *see* Spain
Hispaniola *Island* Caribbean Sea 20, 41
Hit Iraq 108 J4
Hitachi Japan 122 L10
Hitra *Island* Norway 56 I7
Hjørring Denmark 56 H13
Hjort Trench *Sea feature* 131
Hlybokaye (var. Glubokoye) Belorussia 81 J9
Ho Chi Minh City (prev. Saigon) Vietnam 125 N14
Hobart Tasmania, Australia 133 N16
Hobbs New Mexico, USA 35 N10
Hodeida (var. Al Hudaydah) Yemen 108 H15
Hoek van Holland Netherlands 65 G11
Hof Germany 67 J12
Hohe Tauern *Mountain range* Austria 69 N8
Hohenschwangau *Castle* Germany 67 I17
Hohhot China 119 O7
Hokkaidō *Island* Japan 115, 122 L3
Holguín Cuba 43 K6
Holland Michigan, USA 31 M9
Hollywood California, USA 37 K18
Hollywood Florida, USA 29 O15
Holon Israel 107 L10
Holstebro Denmark 56 H14
Holy I. *Island* Wales, UK 59 G13
Holyhead Wales, UK 59 G13
Home Counties *Region* England, UK 59 K16
Homer Alaska, USA 22 F8
Homyel' (var. Gomel) Belorussia 81 O14
Honduras *Country* C America 42

Honduras 42

a Spanish · **☒** Lempira · **♦** 47 · **♥** 65 · **◷** £0.56 · **☕** (m) 75% (f) 70% · **⌂** 44%

Honduras, Gulf of *Sea feature* C America 42 C7
Hønefoss Norway 56 I11
Hong Gai Vietnam 124 N8
Hong Kong *Dependent territory* SE China 121 M14 128 E7
Hongshui He *River* China 120 J13
Hongze Hu *Lake* China 121 N9
Honiara Guadalcanal Solomon Islands, Pacific Ocean 128 I9

Honolulu Oahu Hawaiian Islands, Pacific Ocean 129 K6
Honshū *Island* Japan 115, 122 J9
Hoogeveen Netherlands 64 M8
Hoorn Netherlands 64 I8
Hoover Dam *Dam* Arizona/Nevada, USA 34 H7
Hopa Turkey 105 Q4
Hopedale Newfoundland, Canada 25 P5
Hopkinsville Kentucky, USA 29 L3
Horki (var. Gorki) Belorussia 81 O11
Horlivka (var. Gorlovka) Ukraine 85 M6
Hormuz, Strait of *Channel* Iran/Oman 109 O10
Horn of Africa *Physical region* Somalia 91 O14
Horn, Cape *Cape* Chile 49 L20, 56 F16, 129 Q14
Horsens Denmark 56 I15
Hot Springs Arkansas, USA 28 H5
Hotan China 118 F9
Houlton Maine, USA 27 Q3
Houston Texas, USA 35 S13
Hovd Mongolia 118 I5
Hövsgöl, L. *Lake* Mongolia 119 L3
Howland I. *Dependent territory* Polynesia, Pacific Ocean 128 J8
Hradec Králové Czech Republic 70 I8
Hrodna (var. Grodno) Belorussia 80 I12
Hron *River* Slovakia 71 L11
Hrvatska *see* Croatia
Huai He *River* China 115
Huainan China 121 N10
Huambo (var. Nova Lisboa) Angola 98 H6
Huancayo Peru 45 E13
Huang He *see* Yellow R.
Huánuco Peru 45 D12
Huascarán *Mountain* Peru 41
Huddersfield England, UK 59 J13
Huddinge Sweden 57 L12
Hudiksvall Sweden 57 L10
Hudson *River* New York, USA 27 M10
Hudson Bay *Sea feature* Canada 10, 20, 23 P10, 24 I5, 52 D7
Hudson-Mohawk Gap *Physical feature* New York/Vermont, USA 27 M9
Hudson Strait *Channel* Canada 20, 23 R8, 25 M2
Hue Vietnam 125 N11
Huehuetenango Guatemala 42 A7
Huelva Spain 60 H13
Huesca Spain 61 N5
Hughenden Queensland, Australia 133 N8
Hulun Nur *Lake* China 119 P4
Humber *River* England, UK 59 K13
Humboldt *River* Nevada, USA 34 H2
Hūn Libya 89 P7
Hungarian Plain *Physical region* Hungary 54, 71 L14
Hungary *Country* C Europe 70-71

Hungary 70-71

a Hungarian · **☒** Forint · **♦** 114 · **♥** 71 · **◷** £0.44 · **☕** (m) 99% (f) 99% · **⌘** 410 · **✚** 330 · **☠** No · **⌂** 61% · **⸖** 3644

Huntington West Virginia, USA 29 O3
Huntington Beach California, USA 37 L19
Huntsville Alabama, USA 29 L6
Huron Ohio, USA 31 P10
Huron, Lake *Lake* Canada/USA 20, 24 J13, 31 O6
Hurunui *River* New Zealand 134 F10
Hüsum Germany 66 G6
Hutchinson Kansas, USA 33 O12
Huy Belgium 65 J16
Hvar *Island* Croatia 74 J8
Hwange (prev. Wankie) Zimbabwe 99 L8
Hwange N.P. *National park* Zimbabwe 99 L9
Hyargas, L. *Lake* Mongolia 118 J4
Hyderabad India 117 K11
Hyderabad Pakistan 116 H6
Hyères, Îles d' *Island* France 63 P14
Hyparis *see* Southern Bug
Hyvinkää Finland 57 O11

I

Ialomiţa *River* Romania 77 N9
Iaşi Romania 77 N5
Ibadan Nigeria 93 N12
Ibagué Colombia 44 E7
Ibar *River* Serbia, Yugoslavia 75 N9
Ibarra Ecuador 44 C8
Ibb Yemen 108 I16
Iberian Pen. *Physical region* SW Europe 54
Ibiza Ibiza, Balearic Islands, Spain 61 P10
Ibiza *Island* Balearic Islands, Spain 61 P10
Ibotirama Brazil 47 L11
Ibrī Oman 109 O12
Ica Peru 45 E14
Iceland *Country* Atlantic Ocean 51, 52 J7

Iceland 52

a Icelandic · **☒** Krona · **♦** 3 · **♥** 78 · **◷** £2.72 · **☕** (m) 100% (f) 100% · **⌘** 320 · **✚** 376 · **☠** No · **⌂** 91% · **⸖** 3611

Iceland *Island* Atlantic Ocean 8, 10, 20, 103
Icosium *see* Algiers
Idaho *State* USA 32
Idaho Falls Idaho, USA 32 H8
Idfu Egypt 90 G8
Ieper Belgium 65 C15
Iglesias Sardinia 73 C15
Igoumenitsa Greece 78 F5

a Language (official or most commonly spoken) · **☒** Currency · **♦** Population density per square kilometre · **♥** Average life expectancy · **◷** Price of 1 dozen hen's eggs · **☕** Literacy · **⌘** Number of TVs per 1,000 people · **✚** Number of people per doctor · **☠** Death penalty · **⌂** Percentage of urban-based population · **⸖** Average number of calories consumed daily per person

145

Kampuchea *see* Cambodia
Kam'yanets'-Podil's'kyy (var. Kamenets-Podol'skiy) Ukraine 84 G6
Kananga (prev. Luluabourg) Zaire 95 K15
Kanazawa Japan 122 H10
Kanchanaburi Thailand 125 I12
Kandahar *see* Qandahār
Kandi Benin 93 N10
Kandla India 116 H7
Kandy Sri Lanka 117 L16
Kangaroo I. *Island* South Australia, Australia 133 L14
Kangchenjunga *Mountain* China 115
Kangean *Island* Indonesia 126 J14
Kanggye North Korea 121 P6
Kangnŭng South Korea 121 Q7
Kanjiža Serbia, Yugoslavia 75 M3
Kankakee Illinois, USA 31 L11
Kankan Guinea 92 I10
Kano Nigeria 93 P10
Kanpur India 117 L6
Kansas *State* USA 33
Kansas City Kansas, USA 33 Q11
Kansas City Missouri, USA 33 Q11
Kansk Russian Federation 113 K10
Kao-hsiung Taiwan 121 O14
Kaolack Senegal 92 F8
Kap Farvel *see* Farvel, Cape
Kapchagay Kazakhstan 112 H13
Kapfenberg Austria 69 Q7
Kapos *River* Hungary 71 K15
Kapuas *River* Borneo, Indonesia 126 I11
Kara Togo 93 M11
Kara-Balta Kyrgyzstan 111 Q4
Kara-Bogaz-Gol, Zaliv *Bay* Turkmenistan 110 F5
Kara Deniz *see* Black Sea
Kara Kum *Desert region* Turkmenistan 11, 103
Kara Sea Russian Federation 51 S11, 54, 82 O5, 103, 112 I5
Kara Strait *Channel* Russian Federation 82 N6
Karabük Turkey 105 K5
Karachi Pakistan 100 H5, 116 G6
Karaganda (var. Qaraghandy) Kazakhstan 112 G11
Karaginskiy Is. *Island Group* Russian Federation 113 Q5
Karagiya Depression *Physical region* Asia 103
Karaj Iran 109 N4
Karakaya Barrage *Dam* Turkey 105 P8
Karakinit Gulf *Sea feature* Ukraine 84 I9
Karakorum Mts. *Mountain range* C Asia 118 E9
Karaköse *see* Ağri
Karakum Canal *Waterway* Turkmenistan 111 K9
Karaman Turkey 105 K9
Karamay China 118 H5
Karasburg Namibia 98 I13
Karasjok Norway 57 O2
Karbala Iraq 109 K5
Karditsa Greece 78 I6
Karimata *Island* Indonesia 126 H12
Karisimbi, Mt. *Volcano* Zaire 87
Karlovac Croatia 74 H4
Karlovy Vary Czech Republic 70 G8
Karlskrona Sweden 57 K15
Karlsruhe Germany 67 F14
Karlstad Sweden 57 K12
Karpathos *Island* Dodecanese, Greece 79 Q15
Kars Turkey 105 R5
Karshi Uzbekistan 111 L18
Karymskaya Sopka *Volcano* Siberia 103
Karystos Greece 79 L9
Kasai *River* Angola/Zaire 95 J14
Kasama Zambia 97 M11
Kasese Uganda 97 L4
Kāshān Iran 109 N5
Kashgar *see* Kashi
Kashi (var. Kashgar) China 118 E8
Kashmir *Region* S Asia 117 K2
Kaskaskia *River* Illinois, USA 31 K13
Kasongo Zaire 95 N14
Kassala Sudan 91 I12
Kassandra, Gulf of *Sea feature* Greece 79 K4
Kassel Germany 67 H11
Kastamonu Turkey 105 L5
Kastoria Greece 78 H3
Kastorias, L. *Lake* Greece 78 H3
Kasumi Lagoon *Coastal feature* Japan 122 L10
Kasungu *National park* Malawi 97 M13
Kasur Pakistan 116 J3
Katakolo Greece 78 H10
Katar *see* Qatar
Katavi *National park* Tanzania 97 M9
Katerini Greece 78 I4
Katha Burma 124 G6
Kathmandu Nepal 117 N5
Katowice Poland 71 L9
Katsberg Tunnel *Tunnel* Austria 69 O9
Katsina Nigeria 93 P9
Kattegat *Channel* Denmark/Sweden 56 I14
Kaub *Castle* Germany 67 E12
Kaufmann Peak *see* Lenin Peak
Kaunas Lithuania 80 I9
Kavadarci Macedonia 75 O12
Kavala Greece 79 L2
Kawa *Archaeological site* Sudan 91 F11
Kawasaki Japan 123 K11
Kayan *River* Borneo, Indonesia 127 K10
Kayes Mali 92 H8
Kayseri Turkey 105 M8
Kazakh Uplands *Physical region* Kazakhstan 112 H11

Kazakhstan *Country* C Asia 112

Kazakhstan 112

a Kazakh · 🏛 Afghani · ♦ 6 · ♥ 69 · ⊙ N/A · 📖 N/A · 🏠 58%

Kazan' Russian Federation 83 J11
Kazanlŭk Bulgaria 77 L13
Kéa *Island* Cyclades, Greece 79 L10
Keban Barrage *Dam* Turkey 105 O7
Kecskemét Hungary 71 M14
Kédainiai Lithuania 80 I9
Kediri Java, Indonesia 126 I15
Keetmanshoop Namibia 98 I12
Kefallonia *Island* Ionian Is. Greece 78 G8
Kegon Falls *Waterfall* Japan 115
Kelang Malaysia 125 I19
Kelkit *River* Turkey 105 P6
Kellett, Cape *Cape* Canada 51 N8
Kelmé Lithuania 80 H8
Kelud *Volcano* Java, Indonesia 115
Kem' Russian Federation 82 I6
Kemerovo Russian Federation 112 I10
Kemi Finland 57 O6
Kemi *River* Finland 57 O5
Kemijärvi Finland 57 P5
Kenai Alaska, USA 22 G8
Kendari Celebes, Indonesia 127 M13
Kenema Sierra Leone 92 H12
Kenge Zaire 95 J14
Kénitra Morocco 88 I5
Kennebec *River* Maine, USA 27 P5
Kennedy Space Center Florida, USA 29 O12
Kennewick Washington, USA 36 K8
Kenora Ontario, Canada 24 F9
Kenosha Wisconsin, USA 31 L9
Kentucky *River* Kentucky, USA 29 N3
Kentucky *State* USA 29
Kenya *Country* E Africa 97

Kenya 97

a Swahili · 🏛 Shilling · ♦ 44 · ♥ 59 · ⊙ £0.46 · 📖 (m) 81% (f) 59% · ♀ 9 · ♣ 6552 · ♥ Yes · 🏠 24% · 📺 2163

Kenya, Mt. *National park* Kenya 97 P5
Kerch Ukraine 85 L9
Kerch Strait (var. Kerchens'ka Protoka) *Channel* Russian Federation/Ukraine 54, 83 C14, 85 L9
Kerchens'ka Protoka *see* Kerch Strait
Kerguelen *Island group* Indian Ocean 101 H14
Kerguelen I. *Island* Indian Ocean, Antarctica 50 I7
Kerguelen Plateau *Sea feature* Indian Ocean 101 H14
Kermadec Is. *Island group* Polynesia, Pacific Ocean 128 J11
Kermadec Trench *Sea feature* Pacific Ocean 128 J11
Kermān Iran 109 P8
Kermanshah *see* Bakhtarān
Kerulen (var. Herlen Gol) *River* Mongolia/China 103, 114, 119 N4
Ket' *River* Russian Federation 112 I10
Ketchikan Alaska, USA 22 I12
Kewanee Illinois, USA 30 J11
Keweenaw Bay *Physical feature* Michigan, USA 31 L4
Key West Florida, USA 29 N16
Khabarovsk Russian Federation 113 P11
Khambhat, Gulf of *Sea feature* India 116 I9
Khamis Mushayt Saudi Arabia 108 I13
Khān Yūnis Gaza Strip 107 K11
Khānaqīn Iraq 109 L4
Khanka, Lake *Lake* 115
Khankendy *see* Xankändi
Kharkiv (var. Kharkov) Ukraine 85 L5
Kharkov *see* Kharkiv
Khartoum (var. El Khartûm) Sudan 91 G12
Khartoum North Sudan 91 G12
Khasab Oman 109 O10
Khashm el Girba Dam Sudan 91 I12
Khaskovo Bulgaria 77 L14
Khatanga *River* Russian Federation 113 K6
Khaybar Saudi Arabia 108 I13
Kherson Ukraine 84 J8
Khmel'nyts'kyy Ukraine 84 G5
Khodzheyli Uzbekistan 110 I5
Khon Kaen Thailand 125 K11
Khorog Tajikistan 111 P9
Khorramshahr Iran 109 L7
Khouribga Morocco 88 H5
Khudzhand (prev. Leninabad) Tajikistan 111 O7
Khulna Bangladesh 117 P8
Khyber Pass *Physical feature* Afghanistan/Pakistan 111 O12
Kičevo Macedonia 75 N12
Kidepo *National park* Uganda 97 N2
Kiel Germany 66 H6
Kiel Canal *Waterway* Germany 66 G6
Kielce Poland 71 M7
Kieta Bougainville, Papua New Guinea 133 Q2
Kiev (var. Kiyiv) Ukraine 84 I4
Kiev Res. *Reservoir* Ukraine 84 I4
Kiffa Mauritania 92 H7
Kigali Rwanda 97 L6
Kigoma Tanzania 97 L8
Kikwit Zaire 95 J14
Kilimanjaro *National park* Kenya/Tanzania 97 P6

Kilimanjaro *Volcano* Tanzania 87
Kilis Turkey 105 N10
Kilkis Greece 78 J2
Killarney Ireland 59 B14
Kilwa Masoko Tanzania 97 Q10
Kimberley South Africa 99 K13
Kimberley *Physical region* Western Australia, Australia 131, 132 I6
Kimito Finland 57 N11
Kindu Zaire 95 M13
King I. *Island* Tasmania, Australia 133 M15
King Leopold Ranges *Mountain range* Western Australia, Australia 132 H7
King William I. *Island* Northwest Territories, Canada 23 N7
King's Lynn England, UK 59 L14
Kingman Reef *Dependent territory* Polynesia, Pacific Ocean 129 J7
Kingston Jamaica 42 J8
Kingston New York, USA 27 L10
Kingston Ontario, Canada 25 L14
Kingston-upon-Hull England, UK 59 K13
Kingstown St Vincent & The Grenadines 43 T14
Kinshasa (prev. Léopoldville) Zaire 95 H14
Kintyre *Peninsula* Scotland, UK 58 F10
Kirghiz Range *Mountain range* Kazakhstan/Kyrgyzstan 111 P5
Kirghiz Steppe *Physical Region* Kazakhstan 103, 112 F10
Kiribati *Country* Micronesia/Polynesia, Pacific Ocean 128 J8

Kiribati 128

a English, I Kiribati · 🏛 Dollar · ♦ 100 · ♥ 56 · ⊙ £2.45 · 📖 (av.) 10% · 🏠 36%

Kirikkale Turkey 105 L6
Kirinyaga *Volcano* Kenya 87
Kiritimati (var. Christmas Island) *Dependent territory* Pacific Ocean 128 L8
Kirkenes Norway 57 P2
Kirklareli Turkey 104 G4
Kirksville Missouri, USA 33 R10
Kirkuk Iraq 109 K3
Kirkwall Orkney Scotland, UK 58 J6
Kirov Russian Federation 82 J10
Kirovabad *see* Gäncä
Kirovakan *see* Vanadzor
Kirovohrad (var. Yelyzavethrad) Ukraine 84 J6
Kiruna Sweden 57 N4
Kirşehir Turkey 105 L7
Kisangani (prev. Stanleyville) Zaire 95 M12
Kishinev *see* Chişinău
Kiska I. *Island* Aleutian Is. Alaska, USA 22 A5
Kismaayo Somalia 91 L18
Kisumu Kenya 97 N4
Kitakyūshū Japan 123 C13
Kitale Kenya 97 N4
Kitami Japan 122 M3
Kitchener Ontario, Canada 25 K14
Kithnos *Island* Cyclades, Greece 79 L11
Kitikmeot *Region* Northwest Territories, Canada 23 M7
Kitimat British Columbia, Canada 23 I12
Kitwe Zambia 97 K13
Kitzbühel Austria 69 M8
Kiunga Marine Reserve *Nature reserve* Kenya 97 R6
Kivu, L. *Lake* Rwanda/Zaire 95 O13, 97 L6
Kiyiv *see* Kiev
Kizilirmak *River* Turkey 105 M7
Kizyl-Arbat Turkmenistan 110 H7
Kizyl-Atrek Turkmenistan 110 G8
Kjølen Mts. *Mountain range* Norway/Sweden 54, 57 K6
Klagenfurt Austria 69 P9
Klaipėda Lithuania 80 G8
Klamath Falls Oregon, USA 37 H11
Klerksdorp South Africa 99 K12
Ključ Bosnia and Herzegovina 74 I6
Klosterneuburg Austria 69 S4
Kluane L. *Lake* Yukon Territory, Canada 22 H9
Klyuchevskaya Sopka *Volcano* Siberia 103
Knin Croatia 74 I6
Knittelfeld Austria 69 Q8
Knossos *Archaeological site* Crete, Greece 79 M16
Knoxville Tennessee, USA 29 N5
Knud Rasmussen Land *Physical region* Greenland 51 O12
Ko Phangan *see* Phangan I.
Ko Phuket *see* Phuket I.
Ko Samui *see* Samui I.
Kōbe Japan 15, 123 G12, 128 G5
Koblenz Germany 67 E12
Kobryn Belorussia 80 I14
Kočani Macedonia 75 P11
Kōchi Japan 123 F13
Kodiak Kodiak I. Alaska, USA 22 F9
Kodiak I. *Island* Alaska, USA 20, 22 F9
Kohima India 117 Q7
Kohtla-Järve Estonia 81 L2
Kokand Uzbekistan 111 O6
Kokchetav (var. Kökshetau) Kazakhstan 112 G10
Kokkola Finland 57 N8
Kokomo Indiana, USA 31 M11
Kokshaal-Tau Mts. *Mountain range* China/Kyrgyzstan 111 S5
Kökshetau *see* Kokchetav
Kola Peninsula *Physical feature* Russian Federation 54, 82 J6
Kolda Senegal 92 G9
Kolguyev I. *Island* Russian Federation 82 M6
Kolka Latvia 80 H4

Köln *see* Cologne
Kolonia *see* Palikir
Kolubara *River* Serbia, Yugoslavia 75 M6
Kolwezi Zaire 95 M17
Kolyma *River* Russian Federation 113 O5
Kolyma Range *Mountain range* Russian Federation 113 N13
Kom Ombo *Archaeological site* Egypt 90 G9
Kommunizma, Pik *see* Communism Peak
Komoé *River* Ivory Coast 93 K11
Komoran *Island* Indonesia 127 T15
Komotiní Greece 79 N2
Komsomol'sk-na-Amure Russian Federation 113 P10
Kongolo Zaire 95 N14
Kongsberg Norway 56 I11
Königsberg *see* Kaliningrad
Konjic Bosnia and Herzegovina 75 K7
Konstanz Germany 67 G16
Konya Turkey 105 K9
Kopaonik *Mountain range* Serbia, Yugoslavia 75 N8
Koper Slovenia 74 F3
Koprivnica Croatia 74 J2
Korarnikhon Tajikistan 111 N8
Korčula *Island* Croatia 74 I9
Korçë Albania 75 N13
Korčulanski Kanal *Channel* Croatia 74 I8
Korea *Region* E Asia 115
Korea Bay *Sea feature* Korea/China 121 O7
Korea Strait *Channel* Korea/Japan 115, 121 Q9, 123 B13
Korhogo Ivory Coast 92 J11
Kōriyama Japan 122 K9
Korkodon *River* Russian Federation 113 P5
Korla China 118 G6
Kornat *Island* Croatia 74 H7
Koror Palau, Pacific Ocean 128 G8
Körös *River* Hungary 71 M14
Korosten' Ukraine 84 H4
Kortrijk (var. Courtrai) Belgium 65 D15
Koryak Range *Mountain range* Russian Federation 113 Q4
Kos Kos, Greece 79 Q12
Kos *Island* Dodecanese, Greece 79 Q12
Kosciusko, Mt. *Mountain* Australia 131
Košice Slovakia 71 N11
Kossou, L. de *Lake* Ivory Coast 92 J12
Kosti Sudan 91 G13
Kostroma Russian Federation 82 H9
Koszalin Poland 70 J2
Kota India 116 I6
Kota Baharu Malaysia 125 J17
Kota Kinabalu Borneo, Malaysia 126 J8
Kotka Finland 57 P11
Kotlas Russian Federation 82 J9
Kotto *River* Central African Republic/Zaire 94 L9
Kotzebue Alaska, USA 22 G5
Kotzebue Sound *Sea feature* Alaska, USA 22 F4
Koudougou Burkina 93 L9
Kourou French Guiana 44 P6
Kousseri (prev. Fort-Foureau) Cameroon 94 H7
Kouvola Finland 57 P11
Kowl-e-Namaksār *Salt pan* Afghanistan/Iran 110 J12
Kowloon Hong Kong 121 M14
Kozani Greece 78 I4
Kra, Isthmus of *Physical region* Thailand 115, 125 H15
Krācheh Cambodia 125 M13
Kragujevac Serbia, Yugoslavia 75 N7
Krak des Chevaliers *Syria* 107 M5
Krakatau *Volcano* Indonesia 9, 114
Kraków (var. Cracow) Poland 71 M9
Kralendijk Netherlands Antilles 43 O14
Kraljevo Serbia, Yugoslavia 75 N7
Kramators'k Ukraine 85 L6
Kranj Slovenia 74 G2
Krāslava Latvia 81 L6
Krasnoarmeysk Russian Federation 82 H13
Krasnodar Russian Federation 83 D14
Krasnovodsk Turkmenistan 110 F6
Krasnoyarsk Russian Federation 112 J10
Krefeld Germany 67 D11
Kremenchuk Ukraine 84 J6
Kremenchuk Res. *Reservoir* Ukraine 84 J5
Krems Austria 69 Q4
Kretinga Lithuania 80 G7
Kribi Cameroon 95 E11
Krichev *see* Krychaw
Krishna *River* India 115, 116 J11
Kristiansand Norway 56 H12
Kristianstad Sweden 57 K15
Kristiansund Norway 52 L7
Krivoy Rog *see* Kryvyy Rih
Krk *Island* Croatia 74 G4
Krka *River* Croatia 74 I6
Krŏng Kaôh Kŏng Cambodia 125 K14
Kruger N.P. *National park* South Africa 99 M11
Krung Thep *see* Bangkok
Kruševac Serbia, Yugoslavia 75 O8
Krychaw (var. Krichev) Belorussia 81 O12
Krym *see* Crimea
Kryvyy Rih (var. Krivoy Rog) Ukraine 84 J7
Krzna *River* Belorussia/Poland 71 O5
Kuala Belait Brunei 126 J9
Kuala Lumpur Malaysia 125 J19
Kuala Terengganu Malaysia 125 K18
Kualakapuas Borneo, Indonesia 126 J13
Kuantan Malaysia 125 K18
Kuba *see* Quba
Kuban *River* Russian Federation 83 E14
Kuching Borneo, Malaysia 126 H10
Kudat Borneo, Malaysia 127 K8
Kufstein Austria 69 M7
Kuito Angola 98 H6

a Language (official or most commonly spoken) · 🏛 Currency · ♦ Population density per square kilometre · ♥ Average life expectancy · ⊙ Price of 1 dozen hen's eggs · 📖 Literacy · 📺 Number of TVs per 1,000 people · ♣ Number of people per doctor · ♥ Death penalty · 🏠 Percentage of urban-based population · ♀ Average number of calories consumed daily per person

147

Londinium *see* London
London (anc. Londinium) England, UK 14, 59 K16
London Ontario, Canada 24 J15
Londonderry Northern Ireland, UK 58 E10
Londonderry, C. *Cape* Western Australia, Australia 132 H5
Londrina Brazil 47 I14
Long Beach California, USA 37 K19, 129 N5
Long Branch New Jersey, USA 27 L13
Long I. *Island* Bahamas 43 L4
Long I. *Island* New York, USA 27 N12
Long Xuyen Vietnam 125 N13
Longeau Queensland, Australia 133 N9
Longmont Colorado, USA 35 M4
Longreach Queensland, Australia 133 N9
Longview Washington, USA 36 H8
Longyearbyen Svalbard, Arctic Ocean 51 Q13
Lop Nur *Lake* China 115, 118 I8
Lopatka, C. *Cape* Russian Federation 113 R8
Lord Howe I. *Island* Australia, Pacific Ocean 128 I11
Lord Howe Rise *Sea feature* Pacific Ocean 128 I12, 131
Lord Howe Seamounts *Sea feature* Pacific Ocean 131
Lorengau Admiralty Is. Papua New Guinea 133 O1
Lorient France 52 K8, 62 G7
Los Alamos New Mexico, USA 35 L7
Los Angeles California, USA 14, 37 K18
Los Angeles Chile 49 G12
Los Mochis Mexico 38 I7
Lošinj *Island* Croatia 74 G5
Lot *River* France 63 K12
Lötschberg Tunnel *Tunnel* Switzerland 68 F11
Louang Namtha Laos 124 J8
Louang Phrabang Laos 124 K9
Loubomo Congo 95 G14
Louga Senegal 92 F8
Louise, L. *Lake* Alberta, Canada 23 L14
Louisiade Archipelago *Island group* Papua New Guinea 133 P4
Louisiana *State* USA 28
Louisville Kentucky, USA 29 M3
Lourenço Marques *see* Maputo
Loutra Aidipsou Greece 78 J7
Louvain *see* Leuven
Lovech Bulgaria 77 K12
Lowell Massachusetts, USA 27 O9
Lower Red L. *Lake* Minnesota, USA 30 G3
Lower Tunguska *River* Russian Federation 113 L9
Lower Zambezi *National park* Zambia 97 L14
Loznica Serbia, Yugoslavia 75 L6
Lualaba *River* Zaire 95 M13
Luanda (prev. Loanda) Angola 98 G4
Luang Lagoon *Coastal feature* Thailand 125 I16
Luangwa *River* Zambia 97 M12
Luangwa, N. *National park* Zambia 97 M12
Luangwa, S. *National park* Zambia 97 M13
Luanshya Zambia 97 K13
Lubana, L. *Lake* Latvia 81 K6
Lubango Angola 98 G7
Lubbock Texas, USA 35 O9
Lübeck Germany 66 I7
Lublin Poland 71 O7
Lubumbashi (prev. Elisabethville) Zaire 95 N17
Lucapa Angola 98 J4
Lucca Italy 72 F9
Lucena Luzon, Philippines 127 L4
Lučenec Slovakia 71 L12
Lucerne (var. Luzern) Switzerland 68 G10
Lucerne, L. of *Lake* Switzerland 68 G10
Lucknow India 117 L6
Lüderitz Namibia 53 M14, 98 H12
Ludhiana India 117 K1
Ludza Latvia 81 L7
Luena Angola 98 I5
Lugano Switzerland 68 H12
Lugano, L. *Lake* Italy/Switzerland 68 H12
Lugansk *see* Luhans'k
Lugenda *River* Mozambique 99 O6
Lugo Spain 60 G3
Luhans'k (var. Lugansk; prev. Voroshilovgrad) Ukraine 85 M6
Luik *see* Liège
Luke Air Force Range *Military centre* Arizona, USA 34 H10
Lukusuzi *National park* Zambia 97 M13
Lule *River* Sweden 57 M4
Luleå Sweden 57 N6
Lulonga *River* Zaire 95 J12
Lulua *River* Angola/Zaire 95 L16
Luluabourg *see* Kananga
Lumbala N'guimbo Angola 98 J6
Lumphat Cambodia 125 N13
Lundazi Zambia 97 N13
Lundy *Island* England, UK 59 F16
Lüneburg Germany 66 I8
Luninyets Belorussia 81 K14
Luoyang China 121 L9
Lusaka Zambia 97 K15
Lusambo Zaire 95 L14
Luton England, UK 59 K15
Luts'k Ukraine 84 F4
Lutzow-Holm Bay *Sea feature* Indian Ocean Coast, Antarctica 50 G6
Luxembourg *Country* W Europe 65

Luxembourg 65

ⓐ French, German, Litzebuergish · 🕭 Franc · ♦ 146 · ♥ 75 · ⌂ £1.67 · 🖷 (m) 100% (f) 100% · 🖵 255 · ✚ 529 · ☠ No · 🏚 84% · ╟ 3902

Luxembourg Luxembourg 65 L19

Luxor Egypt 90 G8
Luzern *see* Lucerne
Luzon *Island* Philippines 127 M3
Luzon Strait *Channel* Philippines 127 L1
Lužnice *River* Czech Republic 70 H10
L'viv (var. L'vov) Ukraine 84 F5
Lyepyel' (var. Lepel') Belorussia 81 M10
Lyme Bay *Sea feature* England, UK 59 H17
Lynchburg Virginia, USA 29 Q4
Lynn Massachusetts, USA 27 O9
Lynn Lake Manitoba, Canada 23 N12
Lyon France 63 N10

M

Ma'ān Jordan 107 M12
Maarianhamina Finland 57 M11
Maas *River* Germany/Netherlands 65 L12
Maastricht Netherlands 65 K15
Mabaruma Guyana 44 L5
Macao *Dependent territory* SE China 121 M14
Macao Macao, SE China 121 M14
Macapá Brazil 46 I7
Macdonald Is. *Island group* Indian Ocean 101 H15
Macdonnell Ranges *Mountain range* Northern Territory, Australia 131, 132 J9
Macedonia (var. Makedonija) *Country* SE Europe 75

Macedonia 75

ⓐ Macedonian · 🕭 Denar · ♦ 79 · ♥ 72 · ⌂ N/A · 🖷 (av.) 93% · 🏚 54%

Maceió Brazil 46 O10
Machakos Kenya 97 P5
Machala Ecuador 44 B9
Machu Picchu *Archaeological site* Peru 45 F13
Mackay Queensland, Australia 133 O8
Mackay, L. *Lake* Northern Territory/Western Australia, Australia 131, 132 I9
Mackenzie *River* Northwest Territories, Canada 10, 20, 23 K7
Mackenzie *River basin* N America 11
Mackenzie Bay *Sea feature* Indian Ocean Coast, Antarctica 50 I5
Mackenzie Bay *Sea feature* Northwest territories/Yukon Territory, Canada 22 J6
Mackenzie King I. *Island* Northwest Territories, Canada 23 L4
Mackenzie Mts. *Mountain range* Northwest Territories, Canada 22 J9
Mackinac, Strait of *Channel* Michigan, USA 31 N5
Macleod, L. *Lake* Western Australia, Australia 132 E9
Macomb Illinois, USA 30 J12
Mâcon France 63 N9
Macon Georgia, USA 29 N8
Macoraba *see* Mecca
Macquarie I *Island* Pacific Ocean 128 I13
Macquarie Ridge *Sea feature* Pacific Ocean 128 I13, 131
Madagascar *Country* Indian Ocean 100

Madagascar 100

ⓐ French, Malagasy · 🕭 Franc · ♦ 21 · ♥ 51 · ⌂ £1.09 · 🖷 (m) 88% (f) 73% · 🏚 24%

Madagascar *Island* Indian Ocean 87
Madagascar Basin *Sea feature* Indian Ocean 87, 101 F11
Madagascar Ridge *Sea feature* Indian Ocean 87, 101 E12
Madang Papua New Guinea 133 N2
Madeira *Island* Atlantic Ocean 52 J9
Madeira *Island group* Atlantic Ocean 87
Madeira *River* Bolivia/Brazil 41, 46 F8
Madeira Ridge *Sea feature* Atlantic Ocean 54, 87
Madeleine, Îles de la (var. Magdalen Is.) *Island group* Quebec, Canada 26 Q10
Madison Wisconsin, USA 31 K8
Madona Latvia 81 K6
Madras India 100 I7, 117 L13
Madre de Dios *River* Bolivia/Peru 45 H13
Madrid Spain 61 K8
Madura *Island* Indonesia 126 I16
Madurai India 117 K15
Mae Khlong (var. Meklong) *River* Thailand 125 H12
Maebashi Japan 122 J10
Mafeteng Lesotho 99 L14
Mafia I. *Island* Tanzania 97 Q10
Magadan Russian Federation 113 P7
Magdalen Is. *see* Madeleine, Îles de la
Magdalena *River* Colombia 41, 44 E5
Magdeburg Germany 66 J9
Magellan, Strait of *Channel* Chile 41, 49 I20
Magerøy *Island* Norway 57 P1
Maggiore, L. *Lake* Italy/Switzerland 68 G12, 72 D6
Magnitogorsk Russian Federation 112 F9
Mahabalipuram India 117 L13
Mahajanga Madagascar 100 E10
Mahalapye Botswana 99 L10
Mahanadi *River* India 117 N9
Mahé *Island* Seychelles 100 F9
Mahilyow (var. Mogilev) Belorussia 81 N11
Mahón Minorca, Spain 61 S8

Mai-Ndombe, L *Lake* Zaire 95 J13
Maiduguri Nigeria 93 R10
Main *River* Germany 67 G13
Maine *State* USA 27 P4
Mainz Germany 67 F13
Maitland New South Wales, Australia 133 P12
Majorca (var. Mallorca) *Island* Balearic Islands, Spain 61 R8
Majuro Marshall Islands, Pacific Ocean 128 I8
Makarikari *see* Makgadikgadi Pans
Makassar *see* Ujung Pandang
Makassar Strait *Channel* Borneo/Celebes, Indonesia 127 K13
Makedonija *see* Macedonia
Makeni Sierra Leone 92 H11
Makeyevka *see* Makiyivka
Makgadikgadi Pans (var. Makarikari, Soa Salt Pan) *Salt basin* Botswana 99 K9
Makhachkala Russian Federation 83 F16
Makiyivka (var. Makeyevka) Ukraine 85 M7
Makkah *see* Mecca
Makkovik Newfoundland, Canada 25 Q6
Makokou Gabon 95 G12
Makran *Physical region* Pakistan 116 F5
Makurdi Nigeria 93 P12
Malabar Coast *Coastal region* India 116 I14
Malabo Equatorial Guinea 95 E11
Malacca *see* Melaka
Malacca, Strait of *Channel* SE Asia 100 L8, 115, 130
Maladzyechna (var. Molodechno) Belorussia 81 K11
Málaga Spain 60 J14
Malakal Sudan 91 G15
Malang Java, Indonesia 126 I15
Malanje Angola 98 H4
Malatya Turkey 105 O8
Malawi *Country* C Africa 97

Malawi 97

ⓐ English · 🕭 Kwacha · ♦ 93 · ♥ 46 · ⌂ £0.68 · 🖷 (m) 34% (f) 12% · 🏚 12%

Malay Pen. *Peninsula* SE Asia 115
Malaya *see* Malaysia
Malaysia (prev. Malaya) *Country* SE Asia 125

Malaysia 125

ⓐ Malay · 🕭 Ringgit · ♦ 56 · ♥ 70 · ⌂ £0.65 · 🖷 (m) 87% (f) 70% · ✚ 148 · ☠ 2708 · ☠ Yes · 🏚 43% · ╟ 2774

Malaysia (East) Borneo, SE Asia 126
Maldive Ridge *Sea feature* Indian Ocean 100 H9
Maldives *Country* Indian Ocean 100 I8

Maldives 100

ⓐ Divehi · 🕭 Rufiyya · ♦ 737 · ♥ 62 · ⌂ £1.33 · 🖷 (m) 91% (f) 92% · 🏚 30%

Male Maldives 100 I8
Malheur L. *Lake* Oregon, USA 36 K10
Mali (prev. French Sudan) *Country* W Africa 92-93

Mali 92-93

ⓐ French · 🕭 Franc · ♦ 7 · ♥ 48 · ⌂ £1.41 · 🖷 (m) 41% (f) 24% · 🏚 19%

Mali Hka *River* Burma 115
Malindi Kenya 97 Q7
Malines *see* Mechelen
Mallaig Scotland, UK 58 G8
Mallorca *see* Majorca
Malmédy Belgium 65 L16
Malmö Sweden 56 J15
Malta (var. Melita) *Country* Europe 73

Malta 73

ⓐ Maltese, English · 🕭 Lira · ♦ 1113 · ♥ 74 · ⌂ £0.78 · 🖷 (m) 96% (f) 96% · 🏚 87%

Maltahöhe Namibia 98 H11
Maluku *see* Moluccas
Mamberamo *River* Indonesia 127 S12
Mamoré *River* Bolivia 45 J14
Mamry, L. *Lake* Poland 71 N3
Man *Ivory Coast* 92 I12
Man, Isle of *Dependent territory* W Europe 59 G12
Manado Celebes, Indonesia 127 N10
Managua Nicaragua 42 D9
Managua, L. *Lake* Nicaragua 42 D10
Manam *Volcano* New Guinea 131
Manama (var. Al Manamah) Bahrain 100 F5, 109 M9
Manaslu *Mountain* China 115
Manaus Brazil 46 F8
Manchester England, UK 59 I13
Manchester New Hampshire, USA 27 N9
Manchuria *Region* China 121 P4
Manchurian Plain *Physical region* China 115
Mandalay Burma 124 H7
Mandera Kenya 97 R2
Mangalia Romania 77 P10
Mangalore India 116 I13
Mangla Res. *Reservoir* India/Pakistan 116 J2

Manguéni, Plateau du *Physical region* Niger 93 R5
Manhattan Kansas, USA 33 P11
Manicouagan Res. *Reservoir* Quebec, Canada 25 N9
Manila Philippines 15, 127 L4, 128 F7
Manisa Turkey 104 G8
Manistee Michigan, USA 31 M7
Manistee *River* Michigan, USA 31 M7
Manitoba *Province* Canada 23
Manitoba, L. *Lake* Manitoba, Canada 20
Manitowoc Wisconsin, USA 31 L7
Manizales Colombia 44 D6
Mankato Minnesota, USA 30 H7
Mannar Sri Lanka 117 K15
Mannheim Germany 67 F13
Mannu *River* Sardinia 73 D15
Manokwari Irian Jaya, Indonesia 127 Q11
Manono Zaire 95 N15
Mansa Zambia 97 K12
Mansel I. *Island* Canada 25 K2
Mansfield Ohio, USA 31 P11
Manta Ecuador 44 B9
Mantova (var. Mantua) Italy 72 F7
Mantua *see* Mantova
Manyara *National park* Tanzania 97 O7
Manyara, L. *Lake* Tanzania 97 O7
Manzanillo Mexico 39 K12
Manzhouli China 119 P3
Manzini Swaziland 99 M12
Mao Chad 94 H7
Maoke Mts. New Guinea 115
Maputo (prev. Lourenço Marques) Mozambique 99 N12
Mar Chiquita, L. *Salt lake* Argentina 48 K8
Mar del Plata Argentina 49 N12, 53 F14
Maracaibo Venezuela 44 G4
Maracaibo, L. *Sea feature* Venezuela 41, 44 G5
Maracay Venezuela 44 I4
Maradi Niger 93 O9
Maramba *see* Livingstone
Maranhão Res. *Reservoir* Portugal 60 G10
Marañón *River* Peru 41, 44 D10
Marathon *Archaeological site* Greece 79 L9
Marbella Spain 60 J14
Marche-en-Famenne Belgium 65 J17
Mardan Pakistan 116 J2
Mardin Turkey 105 Q9
Margarita Island *Island* Venezuela 44 J4
Margherita Peak *Volcano* Uganda 87
Mariana Trench *Sea feature* Pacific Ocean 8, 128 G6
Marías Is. *Island group* Mexico 38 J10
Ma'rib *Archaeological site* Yemen 109 I15
Maribor Slovenia 74 H2
Marie Byrd Land *Region* Antarctica 50 C10
Marie Galante *Island* Guadeloupe 43 T12
Mariental Namibia 98 I11
Mariestad Sweden 57 K12
Marijampolė Lithuania 80 H10
Marinette Wisconsin, USA 31 L6
Marion Indiana, USA 31 N11
Marion Ohio, USA 31 P11
Marion, L. *Lake* South Carolina, USA 29 P8
Maritsa *River* SE Europe 77 M14
Mariupol' Ukraine 85 L8
Marka Somalia 91 M18
Marmara, Sea of Turkey 104 H5
Marmaris Turkey 104 H10
Marne *River* France 63 M4
Maroua Cameroon 94 H8
Marowijne *River* French Guiana/Surinam 44 O7
Marquesas Is. *Island group* French Polynesia, Pacific Ocean 129 M9
Marquette Michigan, USA 31 L4
Marrakesh Morocco 88 I16
Marsá al Burayqah Libya 89 Q7
Marsa Matrûh Egypt 90 E6
Marsabit *National park* Kenya 97 P3
Marseille France 52 L8, 63 O14
Marsh I. *Island* Louisiana, USA 28 H10
Marshall Islands *Country* Micronesia, Pacific Ocean 128 I7

Marshall Islands 128

ⓐ English, Marshallese · 🕭 Dollar · ♦ 265 · ♥ 65 · ⌂ £1.28 · 🖷 (av.) 7% · 🏚 N/A

Marshfield Wisconsin, USA 30 J7
Martaban, Gulf of *Sea feature* Burma 125 G11
Martha's Vineyard *Island* Massachusetts, USA 27 O11
Martigny Switzerland 68 E12
Martin Slovakia 71 L10
Martinique *Dependent territory* Caribbean Sea 43 T13
Martre, Lac la *Lake* Northwest Territories, Canada 23 K9
Mary (prev. Merv) Turkmenistan 110 J9
Maryland *State* USA 27
Maryville Missouri, USA 33 Q10
Masada Israel 107 L11
Masai Mara *Nature reserve* Kenya 97 N5
Masai Steppe *Physical region* Tanzania 97 O8
Masaka Uganda 97 M5
Masbate Masbate, Philippines 127 M5
Masbate *Island* Philippines 127 M5
Mascarene Is. *Island group* Indian Ocean 101 G11
Mascarene Plateau *Sea feature* Indian Ocean 100 G10
Maseru Lesotho 99 L13
Mashhad Iran 109 Q4

ⓐ Language (official or most commonly spoken) · 🕭 Currency · ♦ Population density per square kilometre · ♥ Average life expectancy · ⌂ Price of 1 dozen hen's eggs · 🖷 Literacy · 🖵 Number of TVs per 1,000 people · ✚ Number of people per doctor · ☠ Death penalty · 🏚 Percentage of urban-based population · ╟ Average number of calories consumed per person

149

Mozyr' *see* Mazyr
Mpika Zambia 97 M12
Mtwara Tanzania 97 Q11
Muang Khammouan (var. Thakhek) Laos 124 M10
Muang Không Laos 125 M12
Muang Lampang Thailand 124 I10
Muang Loei Thailand 124 K10
Muang Nan Thailand 124 J9
Muang Pakxan Laos 124 L10
Muang Phetchabun Thailand 125 J11
Muang Phitsanulok Thailand 125 I11
Muang Xaignabouri Laos 124 K9
Muang Yasothon Thailand 125 L11
Muchinga Mts. *Mountain range* Zambia 97 L13
Muck *Island* Scotland, UK 58 F8
Mufulira Zambia 97 K13
Muğla Turkey 104 H9
Mühlhausen Germany 67 I11
Mulhouse France 63 P6
Mull *Island* Scotland, UK 58 F9
Muller Mts. *Mountain range* Indonesia 126 I11
Multan Pakistan 116 I4
Mun, Mae Nam *River* Thailand 125 K12
Muna *Island* Indonesia 127 M13
München *see* Munich
Muncie Indiana, USA 31 N12
Munich (var. München) Germany 67 J16
Münster Germany 66 E10
Munzur Mts. *Mountain range* Turkey 105 P7
Muonio *River* Sweden 57 N3
Mupa N.P. *National park* Angola 98 H7
Muqdisho *see* Mogadishu
Mur (var. Mura) *River* Austria 69 P8
Mura (var. Mur) *River* Slovenia 74 I1
Murat *River* Turkey 105 Q7
Murchison *River* Western Australia, Australia 132 F10
Murchison Falls *National park* Uganda 97 M3
Murcia Spain 61 M12
Mureş *River* Romania 76 H6
Murfreesboro Tennessee, USA 29 L5
Murgab *River* Turkmenistan 111 K10
Müritz, L. *Lake* Germany 66 L7
Murmansk Russian Federation 52 M7, 82 J5
Murmansk Rise *Sea feature* Barents Sea 54
Muroroa *Island* French Polynesia, Pacific Ocean 129 L10
Murray *River* New South Wales/South Australia, Australia 131, 133 L13
Murray Fracture Zone *Sea feature* Pacific Ocean 129 L5
Murrumbidgee *River* New South Wales, Australia 133 N13
Murzuq Libya 89 O9
Muş Turkey 105 R7
Muscat (var. Masqat) Oman 109 P12
Muscat and Oman *see* Oman
Muskegon Michigan, USA 31 M8
Muskegon *River* Michigan, USA 31 N7
Muskogee Oklahoma, USA 33 Q14
Musoma Tanzania 97 N5
Mussau I. *Island* Papua New Guinea 133 O1
Mutare (prev. Umtali) Zimbabwe 99 N9
Muynak Uzbekistan 110 I3
Mwanza Tanzania 97 M6
Mweru, L. *Lake* Zaire/Zambia 87, 95 O16, 97 K10
Mwene-Ditu Zaire 95 L15
Mweru Wantipa *National park* Zambia 97 K11
Myanmar *see* Burma
Mycenae *Archaeological site* Greece 70 J10
Myingyan Burma 124 F8
Myitkyina Burma 124 H5
Mykolayiv (var. Nikolayev) Ukraine 84 J8
Mykonos *Island* Cyclades, Greece 79 N10
Mymensingh Bangladesh 117 P7
Mysore India 116 J13
Mytilini Lesvos, Greece 79 O7
Mzuzu Malawi 97 N12

N

Naberezhnyye Chelny Russian Federation 83 K11
Nacala Mozambique 99 Q7
Naestved Denmark 56 I16
Nafplio Greece 78 J10
Naga Cebu, Philippines 127 M4
Nagano Japan 123 J10
Nagarjuna Res. *Reservoir* India 117 K11
Nagasaki Japan 123 B14, 128 F6
Nagercoil India 116 J16
Nagorno-Karabakh *Region* Azerbaijan 85 R14
Nagoya Japan 123 I11
Nagpur India 117 K9
Nagqu China 118 I12
Nagykanizsa Hungary 70 J15
Naha Okinawa, Japan 123 A20
Nahuel Huapi, L. *Lake* Argentina 49 H14
Nain Newfoundland, Canada 25 P5
Nairobi Kenya 97 O5
Naissaar *Island* Estonia 80 I11
Najrān Saudi Arabia 108 I14
Nakamura Japan 123 E14
Nakhichevan' *see* Naxçıvan
Nakhodka Russian Federation 112 I7
Nakhon Ratchasima Thailand 125 K12
Nakhon Sawan Thailand 125 I11
Nakhon Si Thammarat Thailand 125 I16
Nakina Ontario, Canada 24 H10
Nakskov Denmark 56 I16
Nakuru Kenya 97 O4
Nal'chik Russian Federation 83 E15
Nam Co *Lake* China 118 I12
Nam Dinh Vietnam 124 N9

Nam Ngum Dam Laos 124 K10
Nam Theun *River* Laos 124 M10
Namangan Uzbekistan 111 O6
Namen *see* Namur
Namib Desert *Desert region* SW Africa 11, 87, 98 H11
Namibe Angola 98 F7
Namibia (prev. South-West Africa) *Country* Southern Africa 98

Namibia 98

🅰 English • 🖭 Rand • ♦ 2 • 💀 58 • ◑ £2.44 • 📖 (m) 74% (f) 71% • 🏠 28%

Nampa Idaho, USA 32 F8
Namp'o North Korea 121 P7
Nampula Mozambique 99 P7
Namur (var. Namen) Belgium 65 H16
Nan Ling *Mountain range* 115
Nan'ao China 128 E6
Nanchang China 121 M12
Nancy France 63 O5
Nanded India 117 K10
Nanjing China 121 N10
Nanning China 121 K14
Nanping China 121 N12
Nansen Basin *Sea feature* Arctic Ocean 54, 103
Nantes France 62 H8
Nantucket I. *Island* Massachusetts, USA 27 P11
Napa Valley *Physical feature* California, USA 37 H14
Napier New Zealand 134 H7
Naples (var. Napoli) Italy 52 L9 73 K13
Naples, Bay of *Sea feature* Italy 73 K13
Napo *River* Ecuador/Peru 44 E9
Napoli *see* Naples
Narach, L. *Lake* Belorussia 81 K10
Narathiwat Thailand 125 J17
Nares Plain *Sea feature* Atlantic Ocean 20
Nares Strait *Channel* Northwest Territories, Canada 23 O1
Narew *River* Poland/Belorussia 71 N4
Narmada *River* India 115, 116 J8
Narsarsuaq Greenland 51 M15
Narva Estonia 81 L2
Narva *River* Estonia/Russian Federation 81 L2
Narvik Norway 57 M3
Naryn Kyrgyzstan 111 R5
Naryn *River* Kyrgyzstan 111 Q5
Nashua New Hampshire, USA 27 N9
Nashville Tennessee, USA 29 L4
Nasik India 116 I9
Nassau Bahamas 43 K2
Nasser, L. *Reservoir* Egypt/Sudan 87, 90 G9
Natal Brazil 46 O9
Natal *Region* South Africa 99 M13
Natal Basin *Sea feature* Indian Ocean 87
Natitingou Benin 93 M11
Natuna *Island* Natuna Is. Indonesia 126 H9
Natuna Is. *Island group* Indonesia 126 G10
Naturaliste, C. *Cape* Western Australia, Australia 132 F13
Naukuuft Park *National park* Namibia 98 I112
Nauru *Country* Micronesia, Pacific Ocean 128 I9

Nauru 128

🅰 Nauruan • 🖭 Dollar • ♦ 422 • 💀 67 • ◑ £1.60 • 📖 (m) 99% (f) 99% • 🏠 100%

Navajo Dam *Dam* New Mexico, USA 35 L7
Navajo Indian Reservation *Reservation* USA 35 K8
Navapolatsk (var. Novopolotsk) Belorussia 81 M8
Navarin, C. *Cape* Russian Federation 113 Q3, 128 J3
Navoi Uzbekistan 111 L7
Nawabshah Pakistan 116 H6
Naxçıvan (var. Nakhichevan') Azerbaijan 85 Q15
Naxos *Island* Cyclades, Greece 79 N12
Nazareth Israel 107 L8
Nazca *Archaeological site* Peru 45 E14
Nazca Plate *Physical feature* 41
Nazilli Turkey 104 H9
N'Dalatando Angola 98 G4
Ndélé Central African Republic 94 K9
N'Djamena (prev. Fort Lamy) Chad 94 H7
Ndola Zambia 97 K13
Neagh, Lough *Lake* Northern Ireland, UK 59 E11
Neapoli Greece 78 J13
Nebitdag Turkmenistan 110 G7
Nebraska *State* USA 33
Nechako *River* Alberta/British Columbia, Canada 22 J13
Neches *River* Texas, USA 35 S11
Neckar *River* Germany 67 G15
Necochea Argentina 49 M12
Negev Desert *Desert region* Israel 107 L12
Negrais, Cape *Cape* Burma 125 E11
Negro *River* Argentina 49 K13
Negro *River* Brazil/Uruguay 48 O9
Negro, Rio *River* S America 41, 46 D7
Negros *Island* Philippines 127 M6
Nei Mongol *see* Inner Mongolia
Neiva Colombia 44 E7
Nejd *Region* Saudi Arabia 108 I9
Nekemte Ethiopia 91 I15
Nellis Air Force Range *Military centre* Nevada, USA 34 G5
Nellore India 117 L12
Nelson New Zealand 134 F9

Nelson *River* Manitoba, Canada 23 O12
Néma Mauritania 92 J7
Neman (var. Nemunas) *River* Belorussia/Lithuania 80 G9
Nemunas *see* Neman
Nemuro Japan 122 O3
Neosho *River* Kansas/Oklahoma, USA 33 P12
Nepal *Country* S Asia 117

Nepal 117

🅰 Nepali • 🖭 Rupee • ♦ 142 • 💀 52 • ◑ £0.38 • 📖 (m) 38% (f) 13% • 🏠 10%

Nepalganj Nepal 117 M5
Neretva *River* Bosnia and Herzegovina 75 K8
Neris *River* Belorussia/Lithuania 80 I9
Nesebŭr Bulgaria 77 O13
Ness, Loch *Lake* Scotland, UK 58 H8
Netherlands *Country* Europe 64-65

Netherlands 64-65

🅰 Dutch • 🖭 Guilder • ♦ 443 • 💀 77 • ◑ £1.08 • 📖 (m) 99% (f) 99% • 🖵 495 • ✚ 414 • ☠ No • 🏠 89% • ʃ| 3151

Netherlands Antilles *Dependent territory* Caribbean Sea 20, 43 O14
Neubrandenburg Germany 66 L7
Neuchâtel Switzerland 68 E10
Neuchâtel, L. of *Lake* Switzerland 68 D10
Neufchâteau Belgium 65 J18
Neumünster Germany 66 H6
Neunkirchen Austria 69 R6
Neuquén Argentina 49 I13
Neuschwanstein *Castle* Germany 67 I16
Neusiedler L. *Lake* Austria/Hungary 69 S5
Nevada *State* USA 34
Nevada, Sierra *Mountain range* Spain 61 K13
Nevada Test Site *Military centre* Nevada, USA 34 G6
Nevel' Russian Federation 82 E9
Nevers France 63 M8
Nevşehir Turkey 105 M8
New Albany Indiana, USA 31 N14
New Amsterdam Guyana 44 N6
New Amsterdam *see* New York City
New Bedford Massachusetts, USA 27 O11
New Britain *Island* Papua New Guinea 131, 133 P2
New Britain Trench *Sea feature* Pacific Ocean 131
New Brunswick New Jersey, USA 27 L12
New Brunswick *Province* Canada 25
New Caledonia *Dependent territory* Melanesia, Pacific Ocean 128 H10
New Caledonia *Island* Melanesia, Pacific Ocean 131
New Caledonia Basin *Sea feature* Pacific Ocean 131
New Castle Pennsylvania, USA 26 G11
New Delhi India 117 K5
New England *Physical region* USA 27 O6
New Guinea *Island* Indonesia/Papua New Guinea 115, 128 I9, 131, 133 M2
New Hampshire *State* USA 27
New Hanover *Island* Papua New Guinea 133 O1
New Haven Connecticut, USA 27 M11
New Hebrides Trench *Sea feature* Pacific Ocean 131
New Ireland *Island* Papua New Guinea 131, 133 P1
New Jersey *State* USA 27
New London Connecticut, USA 27 N11
New Mexico *State* USA 35
New Orleans Louisiana, USA 28 I9, 52 C9
New Plymouth New Zealand 134 G6
New Providence *Island* Bahamas 43 K2
New R. *River* Virginia/West Virginia, USA 29 P3
New Siberian Is. (var. Novosibirskiye Ostrova) *Island group* Russian Federation 51 R7, 103, 113 N4
New South Wales *State* Australia 133
New Ulm Minnesota, USA 30 G7
New York *State* NE USA 27 K9
New York City (prev. New Amsterdam) New York, USA 14, 52 E9, 27 L12
New Zealand *Country* Polynesia, Pacific Ocean 8, 131, 134

New Zealand 134

🅰 English, Maori • 🖭 Dollar • ♦ 13 • 💀 76 • ◑ £0.88 • 📖 (m) 99% (f) 99% • 🖵 442 • ✚ 373 • ☠ No • 🏠 84% • ʃ| 3362

Newark Delaware, USA 27 K14
Newark New Jersey, USA 27 L12
Newark Ohio, USA 31 P12
Newburgh New York, USA 27 L11
Newcastle New South Wales, Australia 133 O12
Newcastle upon Tyne England, UK 59 J11
Newfoundland *Island* Newfoundland, Canada 10, 20, 25 R9, 52 F8
Newfoundland *Province* Canada 25
Newfoundland Basin *Sea feature* Atlantic Ocean 52 G8
Newport Isle of Wight England, UK 59 J17
Newport Oregon, USA 36 G9
Newport Rhode Island, USA 27 N11
Newport Wales, UK 59 H15
Newport News Virginia, USA 29 S5
Newry Northern Ireland, UK 59 E12

Neyshābūr Iran 109 Q4
Ngaoundéré Cameroon 94 G9
Ngauruhoe, Mt. *Volcano* North Island, New Zealand 134 H6
Ngorongoro *Conservation area* Tanzania 97 O6
Ngorongoro Crater *Physical feature* Tanzania 87
Nguigmi Niger 93 R8
Nguru Nigeria 93 P9
Nha Trang Vietnam 125 P14
Niagara Falls New York, USA 26 I18
Niagara Falls Ontario, Canada 25 K14
Niagara Falls *Waterfall* Canada/USA 20
Niagara Peninsula *Physical feature* Canada 25 K15
Niamey Niger 93 M9
Niangay, L. *Lake* Mali 92 L8
Nias *Island* Indonesia 126 C11
Nicaragua *Country* C America 42

Nicaragua 42

🅰 Spanish • 🖭 Cordoba • ♦ 33 • 💀 65 • ◑ £0.64 • 📖 (av.) 66% • 🏠 60%

Nicaragua, L. *Lake* Nicaragua 41, 42 D11
Nice France 63 Q13
Nicobar Is. *Island group* India, Indian Ocean 100 K7, 115
Nicosia (var. Lefkosa; prev. Levkosia) Cyprus 105 L12
Nicoya, Gulf of *Sea feature* Costa Rica 42 D13
Niedere Tauern *Mountain range* Austria 69 P7
Nifa *Archaeological site* Italy 73 I12
Niğde Turkey 105 M9
Niger *Country* W Africa 93

Niger 93

🅰 French • 🖭 Franc • ♦ 6 • 💀 46 • ◑ £1.72 • 📖 (m) 40% (f) 17% • 🏠 20%

Niger (var. Joliba, Kworra) *River* W Africa 53 F11, 87, 93 M9
Niger Delta *Delta* Nigeria 87, 93 O14
Nigeria *Country* W Africa 93

Nigeria 93

🅰 English • 🖭 Naira • ♦ 97 • 💀 52 • ◑ £0.39 • 📖 (m) 62% (f) 40% • 🖵 32 • ✚ 6134 • ☠ Yes • 🏠 35% • ʃ| 2312

Nihon *see* Japan
Niigata Japan 122 J9
Nijmegen Netherlands 65 K11
Nikolayev *see* Mykolayiv
Nikopol' Ukraine 85 K7
Nikšić Montenegro, Yugoslavia 75 L9
Nile *River* Africa 52 N10, 87, 91 G11, 100 C5
Nile *River basin* Africa 11
Nile Delta *Delta* Egypt 87
Niles Michigan, USA 31 M10
Nîmes France 63 N13
Ninety East Ridge *Sea feature* Indian Ocean 100 J10, 115, 130
Nineveh *Archaeological site* Iraq 109 K2
Ningbo China 121 O11, 128 F6
Ningxia Hui Autonomous Region China 120 J8
Ninigo Group *Island group* Papua New Guinea 133 M1
Niobrara *River* Nebraska, USA 33 M9
Nioro Mali 92 I8
Nipigon, L. *Lake* Ontario, Canada 24 H10
Nippon *see* Japan
Niš Serbia, Yugoslavia 75 O8
Nissan I. *Island* Papua New Guinea 133 Q1
Nitra Slovakia 71 K12
Nitra *River* Slovakia 71 K11
Niue *Dependent territory* Polynesia, Pacific Ocean 129 K10
Nivelles Belgium 65 G16
Nizhnevartovsk Russian Federation 112 I9
Nizhniy Novgorod Russian Federation 82 H10
Nizhniy Tagil Russian Federation 112 G8
Nizwā Oman 109 O12
Njombe Tanzania 97 N10
Nkhotakota Malawi 97 N13
Nkongsamba Cameroon 94 E10
Nobeoka Japan 123 D14
Nogales Mexico 38 H3
Nome Alaska, USA 22 J7
Nonacho L. *Lake* Northwest Territories, Canada 23 M10
Nordfjord *Coastal feature* Norway 56 H9
Nordhausen Germany 66 I10
Nordstrand *Island* North Frisian Is. Germany 66 G6
Nordvik *Research centre* Russian Federation 51 I9
Norfolk Nebraska, USA 33 O9
Norfolk Virginia, USA 29 S5
Norfolk I. *Dependent territory* Pacific Ocean 128 I11
Norge *see* Norway
Noril'sk Russian Federation 112 J7
Norman Oklahoma, USA 33 O15
Normandy *Region* France 62 J5
Norman Wells Northwest Territories, Canada 22 J8
Norrköping Sweden 57 L13
Norrtälje Sweden 56 M12
North Albanian Alps *Mountain range* Albania/Yugoslavia 75 M10

🅰 Language (official or most commonly spoken) • 🖭 Currency • ♦ Population density per square kilometre • 💀 Average life expectancy • ◑ Price of 1 dozen hen's eggs • 📖 Literacy • 🖵 Number of TVs per 1,000 people • ✚ Number of people per doctor • ☠ Death penalty • 🏠 Percentage of urban-based population • ʃ| Average number of calories consumed daily per person

151

Panama, Gulf of *Sea feature* Panama 41, 42 G15
Panama, Isthmus of *Physical feature* Panama 41
Panay *Island* Philippines 127 L6
Pančevo Serbia, Yugoslavia 75 N5
Panevėžys Lithuania 80 I8
Pangaea *Ancient Continent* 8
Pangani Tanzania 97 Q8
Pangani *River* Tanzania 97 P7
Pangkalpinang Bangka, Indonesia 126 G12
Pangnirtung Baffin I. Northwest Territories, Canada 23 R6, 51 M13
Panj (var. Pyandzh) *River* Afghanistan/Tajikistan 111 N9
Panjnad Barrage *Dam* Pakistan 116 H4
Pantelleria *Island* Italy 73 H19
Panuco *River* Mexico 39 M10
Panzhihua China 120 I12
Papandayan *Volcano* Java, Indonesia 115
Papeete Tahiti French Polynesia, Pacific Ocean 129 L10
Paphos Cyprus 105 K12
Papua, Gulf of *Sea feature* Papua New Guinea 133 N3
Papua New Guinea *Country* Australasia 133

Papua New Guinea (P.N.G.) 133

ⓐ English • **💷** Kina • **♦** 9 • **♥** 55 • **◔** £2.23 •
💀 (m) 65% (f) 38% • **🏠** 16%

Paraguarí Paraguay 48 N6
Paraguay *Country* S America 48

Paraguay 48

ⓐ Spanish • **💷** Kina • **♦** 11 • **♥** 67 • **◔** £0.37 •
💀 (m) 92% (f) 88% • **🏠** 48%

Paraguay *River* S America 41, 47 G13, 48 N5
Parakou Benin 93 N11
Paramaribo Surinam 44 O6
Paramushir Is. *Island Group* Russian Federation 113 R8
Paraná Argentina 48 L9
Paraná *River* Argentina/Paraguay 41, 47 H14, 48 M10
Paraná *River basin* S America 11
Paranaíba *River* Brazil 46 K10
Pardubice Czech Republic 70 I9
Parecis, Serra dos *Mountain range* Brazil 47 F11
Parepare Celebes, Indonesia 127 L13
Paris (anc. Gallia) France 63 L5
Parker Dam *Dam* Arizona, USA 34 I18
Parkersburg West Virginia, USA 29 P2
Parma Italy 72 F8
Parnaíba Brazil 46 M8
Parnaíba *River* Brazil 41
Pärnu Estonia 80 J3
Pärnu *River* Estonia 80 J3
Paros *Island* Cyclades, Greece 79 M11
Parry Is. *Island group* Northwest Territories, Canada 23 M4
Pas, The Manitoba, Canada 23 N13
Pasadena California, USA 37 L18
Pasadena Texas, USA 35 S13
Pasargadae *Archaeological site* Iran 109 N7
Pasley, C. *Cape* Western Australia, Australia 132 H13
Passau Germany 67 M13
Passo Fundo Brazil 47 I16
Pasto Colombia 44 D8
Patagonia *Physical region* Argentina 41, 49 J16
Paterson New Jersey, USA 27 L12
Pathfinder Res. *Reservoir* Wyoming, USA 32 J9
Patna India 117 N7
Patos Lagoon *Lake* Brazil 47 I16
Patrai Greece 78 H9
Patrai, Gulf of *Sea feature* Greece 78 G9
Pattani Thailand 125 J17
Pattaya Thailand 125 J13
Patuca *River* Honduras 42 E9
Pátzcuaro, L. *Lake* Mexico 39 L12
Pau France 62 J14
Pavlodar Kazakhstan 112 H11
Paysandú Uruguay 48 N9
Pazardzhik Bulgaria 76 J14
Peć Serbia, Yugoslavia 75 M9
Pearl *River* Louisiana/Mississippi, USA 28 J8
Pearl Harbor Oahu Hawaiian Is. Pacific Ocean 129 K6
Peary Land *Physical region* Greenland 51 P12
Pechora *River* Russian Federation 54, 82 L7
Pecos Texas, USA 35 N11
Pecos *River* New Mexico/Texas, USA 35 O12
Pécs Hungary 71 K15
Pedras Salgadas Portugal 60 G6
Pedro Juan Caballero Paraguay 48 N4
Pee Dee *River* North Carolina/South Carolina, USA 29 Q8
Pegasus Bay *Sea feature* New Zealand 134 F11
Pegu Burma 124 G10
Peipus, L. *Lake* Estonia/Russian Federation 81 L3
Peking (var. Beijing) China 15, 121 M7
Pelada, Serra *Mountain range* Brazil 46 J8
Pelagie Is. *Island group* Italy 73 H20
Pelée, Mt. *Volcano* Martinique, Caribbean Sea 9, 41
Peljesac *Peninsula* Croatia 74 J9
Pelly *River* Yukon Territory, Canada 22 I8

Peloponnese *Region* Greece 78 I10
Pelotas Brazil 47 I17
Pematangsiantar Sumatra, Indonesia 126 D10
Pemba Mozambique 99 Q6
Pemba I. *Island* Tanzania 97 Q8
Pendleton Oregon, USA 36 K8
Pennine Alps *Mountain range* Switzerland 68 F12
Pennines *Mountain range* England, UK 54, 59 I12
Pennsylvania *State* USA 26
Penobscot *River* Maine, USA 27 Q5
Penonomé Panama 42 G15
Pensacola Florida, USA 29 K10
Penticton British Columbia, Canada 23 K15
Penza Russian Federation 83 H12
Penzance England, UK 59 E17
Peoria Illinois, USA 31 K11
Pereira Colombia 44 E6
Pergamon (var. Bergama) *Archaeological site* Turkey 104 G7
Perge *Archaeological site* Turkey 104 J10
Périgueux France 63 K11
Perito Moreno Argentina 49 I16
Perm' Russian Federation 83 L11
Pernik Bulgaria 76 I13
Perpignan France 63 M15
Persepolis *Archaeological site* Iran 109 N7
Persia *see* Iran
Persian Gulf (var. The Gulf) *Sea feature* Arabia/Iran 87, 100 F5, 103, 109 M8
Perth Scotland, UK 58 I9
Perth Western Australia, Australia 132 F12
Perth Basin *Sea feature* Indian Ocean 131
Peru *Country* S America 9, 45-46

Peru 45-46

ⓐ Spanish, Quechua • **💷** Sol • **♦** 17 • **♥** 63 •
◔ £0.25 • **💀** (m) 92% (f) 79% • **📺** 97 • **✚** 966 •
❀ No • **🏠** 70% • **🍴** 2186

Peru Basin *Sea feature* Pacific Ocean 129 P10
Peru-Chile Trench *Sea feature* Pacific Ocean 8, 129 Q11
Peru Current *Ocean current* Pacific Ocean 12
Peručić, L. *Lake* Croatia 74 I7
Perugia Italy 72 H10
Pesaro Italy 72 I9
Pescara Italy 73 K11
Peshawar Pakistan 116 I2
Petaluma California, USA 37 G15
Petah Tiqwa Israel 107 L9
Peter the First I. *Dependent territory* Pacific Ocean, Antarctica 50 B9
Peterborough England, UK 59 K14
Peterborough Ontario, Canada 25 K14
Peterhead Scotland, UK 58 J8
Petersburg Alaska, USA 22 I11
Petersburg Virginia, USA 29 R4
Petra Jordan 107 M12
Petropavl *see* Petropavlovsk
Petropavlovsk (var. Petropavl) Kazakhstan 112 G10
Petropavlovsk-Kamchatskiy Russian Federation 113 R7
Petrozavodsk Russian Federation 82 H7
Pevek Russian Federation 51 Q5, 113 P3
Pforzheim Germany 67 F15
Phangan I. (var. Ko Phangan) *Island* Thailand 125 I15
Phet Buri Thailand 125 I13
Philadelphia, Jordan *see* Amman
Philadelphia Pennsylvania, USA 27 K13
Philippeville Belgium 65 H17
Philippine Basin *Sea feature* Pacific Ocean 115, 131
Philippine Plate *Physical feature* 8, 115, 131
Philippine Sea Philippines 127 N4
Philippine Trench *Sea feature* Pacific Ocean 115, 131
Philippines *Country* SE Asia 127

Philippines 127

ⓐ English, Filipino • **💷** Peso • **♦** 210 • **♥** 65 •
◔ £0.79 • **💀** (m) 90% (f) 90% • **📺** 48 • **✚** 6413 •
❀ No • **🏠** 43% • **🍴** 2375

Philippines *Island group* SE Asia 115, 131
Phnom Penh Cambodia 125 M14
Phoenix Arizona, USA 34 I9
Phoenix Is. *Island group* Kiribati, Pacific Ocean 128 J9
Phôngsali Laos 124 K8
Phuket Thailand 125 H16
Phuket I. (var. Ko Phuket) *Island* Thailand 125 H16
Phumĭ Sâmraông Cambodia 125 L12
Piacenza Italy 72 E7
Piatra-Neamţ Romania 77 M4
Piave *River* Italy 72 H6
Pichilemu Chile 49 G11
Picos Brazil 46 M9
Picton New Zealand 134 G9
Piedras Negras Mexico 39 M5
Pielinen, L. *Lake* Finland 57 P8
Pierre South Dakota, USA 33 N7
Pietermaritzburg South Africa 99 M13
Pietersburg South Africa 99 M11
Piła Poland 70 J4
Pilar Paraguay 48 M6
Pilcomayo *River* Bolivia/Paraguay 48 M5
Pilos Greece 78 H12

Pilsen *see* Plzeň
Pinang *see* Georgetown
Pinar del Río Cuba 42 G3
Pinatubo Mt. *Volcano* Philippines 115
Pindus Mountains *Mountain range* Greece 54, 78 H6
Pine Bluff Arkansas, USA 28 I5
Pinega *River* Russian Federation 82 K8
Pineios *River* Greece 78 I5
Pines, I. of *see* Juventud, Isla de la
Ping, Mae Nam *River* Thailand 125 I11
Pingxiang China 120 J14, 121 M12
Pini *Island* Indonesia 126 C11
Pinnacles Desert *Desert region* Australia 131
Pinsk Belorussia 80 J15
Pioner I. *Island* Severnaya Zemlya, Russian Federation 113 K3
Piotrków Trybunalski Poland 71 L7
Piqua Ohio, USA 31 O12
Piraeus Greece 79 K9
Pisa Italy 72 F9
Pisác *Archaeological site* Peru 45 G13
Pistoia Italy 72 G9
Pitcairn Is. *Dependent territory* Polynesia, Pacific Ocean 129 M10
Pite *River* Sweden 57 M5
Piteå Sweden 57 N6
Piteşti Romania 77 K8
Pittsburg Kansas, USA 33 Q13
Pittsburgh Pennsylvania, USA 26 G12
Pittsfield Massachusetts, USA 27 M9
Piura Peru 44 B10
Placentia Bay *Sea feature* Newfoundland, Canada 25 T10
Plainview Texas, USA 35 O9
Plate *River* Argentina/Uruguay 41, 48 N10
Platte *River* Nebraska, USA 20, 33 N10
Platte, South *River* Nebraska, USA 33 L10
Plattsburgh New York, USA 27 M6
Plauen Germany 67 K12
Plenty, Bay of *Sea feature* New Zealand 134 I5
Pleven Bulgaria 77 K11
Ploča, C. *Cape* Croatia 74 H8
Plock Poland 71 L5
Ploieşti Romania 77 L8
Płońsk Poland 71 M5
Plovdiv Bulgaria 77 K14
Plungė Lithuania 80 G7
Plymouth England, UK 59 G17
Plymouth Montserrat 43 S11
Plzeň (var. Pilsen) Czech Republic 70 G9
Po *River* Italy 54, 72 G7
Po Delta *Delta* Italy 54
Pobeda Peak (var. Pik Pobedy) *Peak* China/Kyrgyzstan 103
Pobedy, Pik *see* Pobeda Peak
Pocatello Idaho, USA 32 H8
Podgorica (prev. Titograd) Montenegro, Yugoslavia 75 L10
Podlasie *Region* Poland 71 O5
Poinsett, C. *Cape* Wilkes Land, Antarctica 50 G10
Pointe-à-Pitre Guadeloupe 43 T11
Pointe-Noire Congo 95 F14
Poitiers France 62 J9
Pol-e Khomrī Afghanistan 111 N10
Poland *Country* C Europe 70-71

Poland 70-71

ⓐ Polish • **💷** Zloty • **♦** 126 • **♥** 71 • **◔** £0.42 •
💀 (m) 99% • **📺** 293 • **✚** 479 • **❀** Yes • **🏠** 62% •
🍴 3505

Polatsk (var. Polotsk) Belorussia 81 M8
Polis Cyprus 105 K12
Polotsk *see* Polatsk
Poltava Ukraine 85 K5
Polygyros Greece 79 K4
Polynesia *Region* Pacific Ocean 129 K10
Pomerania *Region* Germany/Poland 70 I3
Pomeranian Bay *Sea feature* Germany/Poland 70 H2
Pompeii *Archaeological site* Italy 73 K13
Ponca City Oklahoma, USA 33 P13
Ponce Puerto Rico 43 Q9
Pontchartrain, L. *Lake* Louisiana, USA 28 I9
Pontevedra Spain 60 F4
Pontiac Michigan, USA 31 O9
Pontianak Borneo, Indonesia 126 H11
Pontic Mountains *Mountain range* Turkey 105 N5
Pontine Is. *Island group* Italy 73 I13
Poona *see* Pune
Poopó, L. *Lake* Bolivia 41, 45 H15
Popayán Colombia 44 D7
Poplar Bluff Missouri, USA 33 S13
Popocatépetl *Volcano* Mexico 20, 39 N12
Popondetta Papua New Guinea 133 O3
Poprad Slovakia 71 M10
Porbandar India 116 H8
Porcupine *River* Canada/Alaska, USA 22 H6
Pori Finland 57 N10
Poronaysk Russian Federation 113 Q10
Porpoise Bay *Sea feature* Wilkes Land, Antarctica 50 G11
Porsangen *Coastal feature* Norway 57 O1
Porsgrunn Norway 56 I12
Port Alice Vancouver I. British Columbia, Canada 22 I14
Port Antonio Jamaica 43 K8
Port Arthur Texas, USA 35 S13
Port Augusta South Australia, Australia 133 L12
Port-au-Prince Haiti 43 M8
Port-de-Paix Haiti 43 M7
Port Dickson Malaysia 125 J19

Port Elizabeth South Africa 99 K16
Port-Gentil Gabon 95 E13
Port Harcourt Nigeria 93 O13
Port Hedland Western Australia, Australia 132 F8
Port Hope Simpson Newfoundland, Canada 25 R7
Port Huron Michigan, USA 31 P8
Port Lincoln South Australia, Australia 133 K13
Port Louis Mauritius 101 G11
Port Moresby Papua New Guinea 133 N4
Port Nolloth South Africa 53 M14
Port of Spain Trinidad & Tobago 43 S16
Port Said (var. Būr Sa'īd) Egypt 52 N9, 90 G6, 100 D4
Port Sudan Sudan 91 I11
Portalegre Portugal 60 G10
Portales New Mexico, USA 35 N9
Portimão Portugal 60 F13
Portland Maine, USA 27 O8, 52 E8
Portland Oregon, USA 36 H8
Porto (var. Oporto) Portugal 52 J9, 60 F6
Pôrto Alegre Brazil 47 I16
Porto-Novo Benin 93 M12
Pôrto Velho Brazil 46 D9
Portoviejo Ecuador 44 B9
Portsmouth England, UK 59 J17
Portsmouth New Hampshire, USA 27 O8
Portsmouth Ohio, USA 31 P13
Portugal *Country* SW Europe 60

Portugal 60

ⓐ Portuguese • **💷** Escudo • **♦** 113 • **♥** 75 • **◔** £0.95 •
💀 (m) 89% (f) 82% • **📺** 177 • **✚** 381 • **❀** No •
🏠 34% • **🍴** 3495

Portuguese Guinea *see* Guinea-Bissau
Porvenir Chile 49 J19
Posadas Argentina 48 N7
Posonium *see* Bratislava
Potash Italy 73 K18
Potenza Italy 73 M13
Potenza *River* Italy 72 J10
P'ot'i Georgia 85 O12
Potosí Bolivia 45 H15
Potsdam Germany 66 L9
Poughkeepsie New York, USA 27 L11
Poŭthĭsăt Cambodia 125 L13
Powder *River* Montana/Wyoming, USA 33 K6
Powell, L. *Lake* Utah, USA 34 I5
Poyang Hu *Lake* China 115, 121 M11
Poza Rica Mexico 39 O11
Požarevac Serbia, Yugoslavia 75 O6
Poznań Poland 70 J5
Pozo Colorado Paraguay 48 M5
Prachin Buri *Archaeological site* Thailand 125 J12
Prachin Buri Thailand 125 J12
Prachuap Khiri Khan Thailand 125 I14
Prague (var. Praha) Czech Republic 70 H9
Praha *see* Prague
Praia Cape Verde, Atlantic Ocean 52 I10
Prato Italy 72 G9
Pratt Kansas, USA 33 O13
Pravats (var. Pravets) Bulgaria 76 J13
Pravets *see* Pravats
Prešov Slovakia 71 N11
Prescott Arizona, USA 34 I8
Prespa, L. *Lake* SE Europe 75 N13, 78 G2
Presque Isle Maine, USA 27 Q2
Preston England, UK 59 I13
Pretoria South Africa 99 L12
Preveza Greece 78 G7
Priene *Archaeological site* Turkey 104 G9
Prijedor Bosnia and Herzegovina 75 I5
Prilep Macedonia 75 O12
Prince Albert Saskatchewan, Canada 23 M13
Prince Charles I. *Island* Northwest Territories, Canada 23 Q6
Prince Edward Island *Province* Canada 25
Prince Edward Is. *Island group* South Africa, Indian Ocean 101 E14
Prince George British Columbia, Canada 22 J13
Prince of Wales I. *Island* Northwest Territories, Canada 23 N5
Prince of Wales I. *Island* Queensland, Australia 133 M4
Prince Patrick I. *Island* Canada 51 N8
Prince Rupert British Columbia, Canada 22 I12, 129 M3
Princess Charlotte Bay *Sea feature* Queensland, Australia 133 N5
Princeton New Jersey, USA 27 L13
Príncipe *Island* Sao Tome & Principe 87, 95 D12
Pripet *River* E Europe 81 L15
Priština Serbia, Yugoslavia 75 N9
Prizren Serbia, Yugoslavia 75 N10
Progreso Mexico 39 S11
Prome Burma 124 F9
Prosna *River* Poland 71 K6
Provence *Region* France 63 P13
Providence Rhode Island, USA 27 O10
Provideniya Air Base *Military centre* Russian Federation 113 Q2
Provo Utah, USA 34 J3
Prudhoe Bay Alaska, USA 51 O6
Prudhoe Bay *Sea feature* Alaska, USA 22 I16
Prut *River* E Europe 77 O5
Pruzhany Belorussia 80 I14
Prydz Bay *Sea feature* Indian Ocean Coast, Antarctica 50 F4
Przheval'sk Kyrgyzstan 111 S4
Pskov Russian Federation 82 E8
Psich *River* Belorussia 81 M13
Ptuj Slovenia 74 I2

ⓐ Language (official or most commonly spoken) • **💷** Currency • **♦** Population density per square kilometre • **♥** Average life expectancy • **◔** Price of 1 dozen hen's eggs • **💀** Literacy • **📺** Number of TVs per 1,000 people • **✚** Number of people per doctor • **❀** Death penalty • **🏠** Percentage of urban-based population • **🍴** Average number of calories consumed daily per person

153

St Laurent-du-Maroni French Guiana 44 O6
St Lawrence *River* Canada 10, 20, 25 O11, 52 E8
St. Lawrence, Gulf of *Sea feature* Canada 20, 25 Q10
St Lawrence I. *Island* Alaska, USA 22 E5
St. Lawrence Seaway *Waterway* Ontario, Canada 25 L13
St. Lô France 62 I4
St. Louis Missouri, USA 33 S11
St-Louis Senegal 92 F7
St Lucia *Country* Caribbean Sea 43 T13

St. Lucia 43

a English • 🕭 Dollar • ♦ 249 • ♥ 72 • ◎ £1.47 •
🐛 (m) 81% (f) 82% • ⌂ 46%

St. Malo France 62 H5
Ste Marie, Cap *see* Vohimena, C.
St Martin Guadeloupe 43 S10
St Matthew I. *Island* Alaska, USA 22 D5
St. Moritz Switzerland 68 I11
St. Nazaire France 62 H8
St Paul Minnesota, USA 30 H6
St Paul I. *Island* Indian Ocean 101 I13
St. Peter Port Guernsey, UK 59 H18
St Petersburg Florida, USA 29 N13
St. Petersburg (prev. Leningrad) Russian Federation 82 F7
St Pierre St Pierre & Miquelon 25 S10
St Pierre & Miquelon *Dependent territory* SE Canada 25 S10
St. Quentin France 63 M3
St Vincent *Island* St Vincent & The Grenadines 43 S14
St Vincent and the Grenadines *Country* Caribbean Sea 43 T14

St Vincent and the Grenadines 43

a English • 🕭 Dollar • ♦ 318 • ♥ 71 • ◎ £1.47 •
🐛 (m) 96% (f) 96% • ⌂ 27%

St. Vincent, Cape *Coastal feature* Portugal 54, 60 E13
St Vith Belgium 65 L17
Saintes France 62 I10
Sajama *Mountain* Bolivia 41
Sakākah Saudi Arabia 108 I6
Sakakawea, L. *Lake* North Dakota, USA 33 M4
Sakarya *River* Turkey 104 J6
Sakhalin *Island* Russian Federation 113 Q9, 28 H4
Sala y Gomez Ridge *Sea feature* Pacific Ocean 41
Salado *River* Argentina 41, 48 K8
Şalālah Oman 100 F6, 109 M15
Salamanca Spain 60 I7
Salamat *River* Chad/Sudan 94 J8
Salamis *Archaeological site* Cyprus 105 L12
Saldanha South Africa 98 I15
Saldus Latvia 80 H6
Sale Victoria, Australia 133 N14
Salekhard Russian Federation 112 H7
Salem India 117 K14
Salem Oregon, USA 36
Salerno Italy 73 L13
Salerno, Gulf of *Sea feature* Italy 73 K14
Salihorsk (var. Soligorsk) Belorussia 81 L13
Salima Malawi 97 N13
Salina Kansas, USA 33 O12
Salina Utah, USA 34 J4
Salina *Island* Lipari Is. Italy 73 L16
Salinas California, USA 37 H16
Salinas Mexico 39 P12
Salinas Grandes Salt Marsh *Physical feature* Argentina 41
Salisbury England, UK 59 I16
Salisbury *see* Harare
Salisbury I. *Island* Northwest Territories, Canada 25 K1
Salmon *River* Idaho, Washington, USA 32 F6
Salo Finland 57 O11
Salonika *see* Thessaloniki
Salso *River* Italy 73 K18
Salt *River* Arizona, USA 34 J9
Salt Lake City Utah, USA 34 J3
Salta Argentina 48 I6
Saltillo Mexico 39 M7
Salto Uruguay 48 N9
Salto del Guairá Paraguay 48 O5
Salton Sea *Lake* California, USA 20, 37 N19
Salvador Brazil 47 N11, 53 H12
Salween (var. Nu Jiang) *River* China 119 K12, 120 H13, 124 H9
Salzburg Austria 69 N6
Salzgitter Germany 66 I9
Samā'il Oman 109 P12
Samaná Dominican Republic 43 O8
Samar *Island* Philippines 127 N5
Samara Russian Federation 83 J12
Samarinda Borneo, Indonesia 127 K11
Samarkand (var. Samarqand) Uzbekistan 111 M7
Samarqand *see* Samarkand
Sāmarrā' Iraq 109 K4
Sambre *River* Belgium/France 65 G16
Samobor Croatia 74 H3
Samos Samos, Greece 79 P10
Samos *Island* Greece 79 P10
Samothraki *Island* Greece 79 N3
Samsun Turkey 105 N5
Samui I. (var. Ko Samui) *Island* Thailand 125 I15

San Ambrosio, Isla *Island* Chile 129 Q11
San Andreas Fault *Physical feature* USA 8
San Andres Mts. *Mountain range* New Mexico, USA 35 L10
San Angelo Texas, USA 35 P11
San Antonio Chile 48 G10
San Antonio Texas, USA 35 Q13
San Antonio *River* Texas, USA 35 Q13
San Antonio Oeste Argentina 49 K13
San Benedetto del Tronto Italy 72 J10
San Bernardino Tunnel *Tunnel* Switzerland 68 H11
San Bernardino California, USA 37 L18
San Bernardo Chile 48 H10
San Carlos Nicaragua 42 E12
San Carlos Venezuela 44 H5
San Carlos de Bariloche Argentina 49 H14
San Clemente California, USA 37 L19
San Cristóbal Venezuela 44 F5
San Diego California, USA 37 L19, 129 N5
San Felipe Chile 48 G10
San Felipe Venezuela 44 H4
San Félix, Isla *Island* Chile 129 Q11
San Fernando Chile 49 H11
San Fernando Luzon, Philippines 127 L3
San Fernando Spain 60 H14
San Fernando Trinidad & Tobago 43 S16
San Fernando de Apure Venezuela 44 I5
San Francisco California, USA 9, 37 H15, 129 N5
San Francisco de Macorís Dominican Republic 43 O8
San Gorgonia Pass *Mountain pass* California, USA 37 L18
San Ignacio Belize 42 C6
San Joaquin *River* California, USA 37 I16
San Jorge, Gulf of *Sea feature* Argentina 49 K16
San Jose California, USA 37 H15
San José Costa Rica 42 E13
San José del Guaviare Colombia 44 F7
San José I. *Island* Mexico 38 H7
San José I. *Island* Panama 42 G15
San Juan Argentina 48 H9
San Juan Peru 45 E14
San Juan Puerto Rico 43 Q9
San Juan *River* Nicaragua 42 E12
San Juan *River* New Mexico/Utah, USA 35 K6
San Juan Bautista Paraguay 48 N9
San Juan de los Morros Venezuela 44 I5
San Juan Is. *Island group* Washington, USA 36 H5
San Juan Mts. *Mountain range* Colorado, USA 35 M6
San Lorenzo Honduras 42 C9
San Luis Argentina 48 J10
San Luis Obispo California, USA 37 I17
San Luis Potosí Mexico 39 M10
San Marino San Marino 72 I9
San Marino *Country* S Europe 72 I9

San Marino 72

a Italian • 🕭 Lira • ♦ 328 • ♥ 76 • ◎ £1.02 •
🐛 (m) 98% (f) 98% • ⌂ 90%

San Matías, Gulf of *Sea feature* Argentina 49 K14
San Miguel El Salvador 42 C9
San Miguel *River* Bolivia 45 K14
San Miguel de Tucumán Argentina 48 I7
San Nicolás de los Arroyos Argentina 48 L10
San Pedro Paraguay 48 N5
San Pedro Sula Honduras 42 C8
San Pietro *Island* Italy 73 C15
San Rafael Argentina 48 I11
San Remo Italy 72 C9
San *River* Cambodia/Vietnam 125 N12
San *River* Poland/Ukraine 71 O8
San Salvador El Salvador 42 B9
San Salvador *Island* Bahamas 43 M3
San Salvador de Jujuy Argentina 48 I6
San Sebastián (var. Donostia) Spain 61 M3
San'ā Yemen 108 I15
Sanaga *River* Cameroon 94 F10
Sanandaj Iran 109 L4
Sandakan Borneo, Malaysia 127 K8
Sandanski Bulgaria 76 I15
Sandnes Norway 56 H12
Sandoway Burma 124 E9
Sandviken Sweden 57 L11
Sanford Maine, USA 27 O8
Sângeorz-Băi *Spa* Romania 77 K3
Sangha *River* Congo 95 I12
Sangir *Island* Indonesia 127 N9
Sangir Is. *Island group* Indonesia 127 N10
Sangre de Cristo Mts. *Mountain range* Colorado/New Mexico, USA 35 M6
Sangro *River* Italy 73 K12
Sankt Gallen Switzerland 68 H8
Sankt Pölten Austria 69 R5
Sankt Veit Austria 69 P9
Şanlıurfa Turkey 105 P9
Sant' Antioco Sardinia 73 C16
Santa Ana California, USA 37 L19
Santa Ana El Salvador 42 B9
Santa Barbara California, USA 37 J18
Santa Catalina I. *Island* Mexico 38 H7
Santa Clara Cuba 42 I4
Santa Clara Valley *Physical feature* California, USA 37 H15
Santa Cruz Bolivia 44 J15
Santa Cruz California, USA 37 H16
Santa Cruz *River* Arizona, USA 34 I11
Santa Elena Venezuela 44 L7

Santa Fe Argentina 48 L9
Santa Fe New Mexico, USA 35 M8
Santa Fe *see* Bogotá
Santa Maria Brazil 47 H16
Santa Maria California, USA 37 I17
Santa Maria *Volcano* Guatemala 41
Santa Marta Colombia 44 F4
Santa Rosa Argentina 49 K11
Santa Rosa California, USA 37 H14
Santa Rosa Honduras 42 C8
Santa Rosalia Mexico 38 G5
Santander Spain 61 K3
Santarém Brazil 46 H8
Santarém Portugal 60 F10
Santee *River* South Carolina, USA 29 P8
Santiago Chile 48 H10
Santiago Dominican Republic 43 N8
Santiago Panama 42 F15
Santiago de Compostela Spain 60 F4
Santiago de Cuba Cuba 43 K6
Santiago del Estero Argentina 48 J7
Sant Jordi, Golf de *Sea feature* Spain 61 O7
Santo Domingo Dominican Republic 43 O9
Santo Domingo de los Colorados Ecuador 44 C8
Santorini *Volcano* Greece 54
Santos Brazil 47 K14
Santos Plateau *Sea feature* Atlantic Ocean 41
Sanya China 121 K16
São Francisco *River* Brazil 41, 47 L11
São José dos Campos Brazil 47 K14
São Luís Brazil 46 L8
São Paulo Brazil 14, 47 K14
São Roque, Cabo de *Cape* Brazil 46 P8
São Tomé São Tome & Principe 95 D12
Sao Tome and Principe *Country* C Africa 52 L12, 95

Sao Tome and Principe 95

a Portuguese • 🕭 Dobra • ♦ 124 • ♥ 67 • ◎ £0.63 •
🐛 (m) 73% (f) 42% • ⌂ 33%

São Tomé, Cabo de *Cape* Brazil 47 M14
São Tomé I. *Island* 87
Saône *River* France 63 O7
Sapporo Japan 122 K4
Sapri Italy 73 M14
Sara Buri Thailand 125 J12
Saqqara *Archaeological site* Egypt 90 F7
Sarajevo Bosnia and Herzegovina 75 K7
Saransk Russian Federation 83 H11
Saratoga Springs New York, USA 27 M9
Saratov Russian Federation 83 H12
Saravan Laos 125 N11
Sarawak *Region* Borneo, Malaysia 126 I10
Sardinia *Island* Italy 54, 73
Sargasso Sea Atlantic Ocean 52 G10
Sargodha Pakistan 116 I3
Sarh Chad 94 J9
Sārī Iran 109 O4
Sarikei Borneo, Malaysia 126 I10
Sariyer Turkey 104 I5
Sarnen Switzerland 68 G10
Sarnia Ontario, Canada 24 J14
Sarroch Sardinia 72 D16
Sartang *River* Russian Federation 113 N7
Sárvíz *River* Hungary 71 K14
Sarykamysh, L. *Lake* Turkmenistan/Uzbekistan 110 I1f
Saskatchewan *Province* Canada 23
Saskatchewan *River* Canada 23 N13
Saskatoon Saskatchewan, Canada 23 M14
Satu Mare Romania 76 I2
Saudi Arabia *Country* SW Asia 108-109

Saudi Arabia 108-109

a Arabic • 🕭 Riyal • ♦ 7 • ♥ 65 • ◎ £0.62 •
🐛 (m) 73% (f) 48% • 📺 283 • ✚ 633 • ☠ Yes •
⌂ 77% • 🍴 2874

Sault Sainte Marie Ontario, Canada 24 I12
Sault Ste. Marie Michigan, USA 31 N4
Saurimo Angola 98 I4
Sava *River* SE Europe 74 J4
Savanna-la-Mar Jamaica 42 J7
Savannah Georgia, USA 29 O9
Savannah *River* Georgia, USA 29 O8
Savannakhét Laos 125 M11
Save *River* Mozambique/Zimbabwe 99 N10
Savona Italy 72 D8
Savonlinna Finland 57 Q9
Saxony *Region* Germany 66 H8
Saynshand Mongolia 119 N6
Scandinavia *Region* N Europe 54, 56-57
Scarborough Trinidad & Tobago 43 T16
Schaffhausen Switzerland 68 G8
Schärding Austria 69 P5
Schefferville Quebec, Canada 25 O6
Scheldt *River* W Europe 65 F14
Schenectady New York, USA 27 L9
Schiermonnikoog *Island* West Frisian Is. Netherlands 64 J5
Schleswig Germany 66 H6
Schouten Is. *Island group* Papua New Guinea 133 N1
Schwaner Mts. *Mountain range* Indonesia 126 I12
Schwarzwald *see* Black Forest
Schweinfurt Germany 67 H13
Schwerin Germany 66 J7
Schwerin, L. *Lake* Germany 66 J7
Schwyz Switzerland 68 G10

Scilly, Isles of *Island group* England, UK 59 D17
Scioto *River* Ohio, USA 31 O11
Scoresbysund Greenland 51 O15
Scotia Plate *Physical feature* 89, 41
Scotia Sea Atlantic Ocean 50 C6, 53 G16
Scotland *Country* UK 58
Scott Base *Research centre* Antarctica 50 E11
Scottsbluff Nebraska, USA 33 L9
Scottsdale Arizona, USA 34 I9
Scranton Pennsylvania, USA 27 K11
Scupi *see* Skopje
Scutari, L. *Lake* Albania/Yugoslavia 75 L10
Sea of Galilee *see* L. Tiberias
Seaford Delaware, USA 27 K16
Seal *River* Manitoba, Canada 23 O11
Seattle Washington, USA 36 H6, 129 N4
Segovia Spain 61 K7
Segozero, L. *Lake* Russian Federation 82 H7
Segura *River* Spain 61 L11
Segura, Sierra de *Mountain range* Spain 61 L12
Seikan Tunnel *Tunnel* Japan 122 K6
Seinäjoki Finland 57 N9
Seine *River* France 54, 63 M5
Sekondi-Takoradi Ghana 93 L13
Selayar *Island* Indonesia 127 L14
Selebi-Phikwe Botswana 99 L10
Selkirk Manitoba, Canada 23 O14
Selma Alabama, USA 29 L8
Selous *Game reserve* Tanzania 97 P10
Selvas *Physical region* Brazil 41
Semarang Java, Indonesia 126 H15
Semey *see* Semipalatinsk
Semipalatinsk (var. Semey) Kazakhstan 112 H12
Semnān Iran 109 O4
Sên *River* Cambodia 125 M12
Sendai Japan 122 L8, 128 G5
Senegal *Country* W Africa 92

Senegal 92

a French • 🕭 Franc • ♦ 40 • ♥ 48 • ◎ £2.00 •
🐛 (m) 52% (f) 25% • ⌂ 38%

Senegal *River* W Africa 87, 92 G7
Senja *Island* Norway 57 M2
Sennar Dam *Dam* Sudan 91 H13
Senta Serbia, Yugoslavia 75 M3
Seoul South Korea 15, 121 P7
Sept-Îles Quebec, Canada 25 O9
Seraing Belgium 65 I16
Seram *Island* Indonesia 127 O12, 131
Seram Sea Indonesia 127 O12
Serbia *Republic* Yugoslavia 75 N6
Seremban Malaysia 125 J19
Serengeti *National park* Tanzania 97 N6
Serengeti Plain *Physical region* Tanzania 87
Sérifos *Island* Cyclades, Greece 79 L11
Serov Russian Federation 112 G8
Serowe Botswana 99 L10
Serres Greece 79 K2
Sétif Algeria 89 L4
Setubal Portugal 60 F11
Seul, L. *Lake* Ontario, Canada 24 G9
Sevan, L. (var. Ozero Sevan) *Lake* Armenia 85 Q14
Sevan-Hrazdan *HEP scheme* Armenia 85 Q13
Sevastopol' Ukraine 84 J13
Severn *River* England, UK 59 I15
Severn *River* Ontario, Canada 24 H7
Severnaya Zemlya (var. North Land) *Island group* Russian Federation 51 S10, 103, 113 K4
Sevier L. *Lake* Utah, USA 34 I4
Sevilla (var. Seville) Spain 60 I13
Seville *see* Sevilla
Seward Alaska, USA 22 G8
Seychelles *Country* Indian Ocean 100 F9

Seychelles 100

a Seselwa • 🕭 Rupee • ♦ 256 • ♥ 71 • ◎ £1.91 •
🐛 (m) 55% (f) 60% • ⌂ 52%

Seyhan *River* Turkey 105 M9
Sfântu Gheorghe Romania 77 L6
Sfax Tunisia 52 L9, 89 N5
Shache (var. Yarkand) China 118 E8
Shackleton Ice Shelf *Coastal feature* Indian Ocean Coast, Antarctica 50 H10
Shadehill Res. *Reservoir* South Dakota, USA 33 M6
Shahjahanpur India 117 L5
Shahr-e-Kord Iran 109 N6
Shāmīyah Desert *Desert region* Syria 107 P6
Shandong Pen. *Physical feature* China 121 O8
Shanghai China 15, 121 O10, 128 F6
Shannon Ireland 59 B13
Shannon *River* Ireland 59 C13
Shantou China 121 N14
Shaoguan China 121 M13
Shaoxing China 121 O11
Shaoyang China 121 L12
Sharjah United Arab Emirates 109 O10
Shark Bay *Sea feature* Western Australia, Australia 132 E10
Shashe *River* Botswana/Zimbabwe 99 L10
Shasta L. *Lake* California, USA 37 H12
Shebeli *River* Ethiopia/Somalia 87, 91 M16
Sheboygan Wisconsin, USA 31 L8
Sheffield England, UK 59 J13
Shelby Montana, USA 32 H4
Shelikof Strait *Channel* Alaska, USA 22 F8
Shenandoah *River* Maryland/Virginia, USA 29 Q3

---

a Language (official or most commonly spoken) • 🕭 Currency • ♦ Population density per square kilometre • ♥ Average life expectancy • ◎ Price of 1 dozen hen's eggs • 🐛 Literacy • 📺 Number of TVs per 1,000 people • ✚ Number of people per doctor • ☠ Death penalty • ⌂ Percentage of urban-based population • 🍴 Average number of calories consumed daily per person

155

ⓐ Language (official or most commonly spoken) • ⓔ Currency • ✦ Population density per square kilometre • ⬤ Average life expectancy • ◔ Price of 1 dozen hen's eggs • ✇ Literacy • ⌧ Number of TVs per 1,000 people • ✚ Number of people per doctor • ❂ Death penalty • ⌂ Percentage of urban-based population • ⇃ Average number of calories consumed daily per person

157

a Language (official or most commonly spoken) • 🏛 Currency • ♦ Population density per square kilometre • ♥ Average life expectancy • ⬦ Price of 1 dozen hen's eggs • ♥ Literacy • 🖵 Number of TVs per 1,000 people •
♣ Number of people per doctor • ❁ Death penalty • 🏠 Percentage of urban-based population • ⑪ Average number of calories consumed daily per person

159

NORTH AMERICA

CANADA
PAGES 22-25

UNITED STATES OF AMERICA
PAGES 26-37

MEXICO
PAGES 38-39

CENTRAL AND SOUTH AMERICA

ANTIGUA & BARBUDA
PAGES 42-43

BAHAMAS
PAGES 42-43

BARBADOS
PAGES 42-43

BELIZE
PAGES 42-43

COSTA RICA
PAGES 42-43

JAMAICA
PAGES 42-43

NICARAGUA
PAGES 42-43

PANAMA
PAGES 42-43

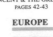
ST. CHRISTOPHER & NEVIS
PAGES 42-43

ST. LUCIA
PAGES 42-43

ST. VINCENT & THE GRENADINES
PAGES 42-43

TRINIDAD & TOBAGO
PAGES 42-43

BOLIVIA
PAGES 44-45

CHILE
PAGES 48-49

PARAGUAY
PAGES 48-49

URUGUAY
PAGES 48-49

THE ATLANTIC OCEAN

CAPE VERDE
PAGES 52-53

ICELAND
PAGES 52-53

EUROPE

DENMARK
PAGES 56-57

FINLAND
PAGES 56-57

NORWAY
PAGES 56-57

BELGIUM
PAGES 64-65

LUXEMBOURG
PAGES 64-65

THE NETHERLANDS
PAGES 64-65

GERMANY
PAGES 66-67

AUSTRIA
PAGES 68-69

LIECHTENSTEIN
PAGES 68-69

SWITZERLAND
PAGES 68-69

CZECH REPUBLIC
PAGES 70-71

BOSNIA & HERZEGOVINA
PAGES 74-75

CROATIA
PAGES 74-75

MACEDONIA
PAGES 74-75

SLOVENIA
PAGES 74-75

YUGOSLAVIA
PAGES 74-75

BULGARIA
PAGES 76-77

ROMANIA
PAGES 76-77

GREECE
PAGES 78-79

AFRICA

MOLDAVIA
PAGES 84-85

UKRAINE
PAGES 84-85

ALGERIA
PAGES 88-89

LIBYA
PAGES 88-89

MOROCCO
PAGES 88-89

TUNISIA
PAGES 88-89

WESTERN SAHARA
PAGES 88-89

DJIBOUTI
PAGES 90-91

GHANA
PAGES 92-93

GUINEA
PAGES 92-93

GUINEA-BISSAU
PAGES 92-93

IVORY COAST
PAGES 92-93

LIBERIA
PAGES 92-93

MALI
PAGES 92-93

MAURITANIA
PAGES 92-93

NIGER
PAGES 92-93

EQUATORIAL GUINEA
PAGES 94-95

GABON
PAGES 94-95

SAO TOME & PRINCIPE
PAGES 94-95

ZAIRE
PAGES 94-95

BURUNDI
PAGES 96-97

KENYA
PAGES 96-97

MALAWI
PAGES 96-97

RWANDA
PAGES 96-97

SOUTH AFRICA
PAGES 98-99

SWAZILAND
PAGES 98-99

ZIMBABWE
PAGES 98-99

THE INDIAN OCEAN

COMOROS
PAGES 100-101

MADAGASCAR
PAGES 100-101

MALDIVES
PAGES 100-101

MAURITIUS
PAGES 100-101

SEYCHELLES
PAGES 100-101

IRAN
PAGES 108-109

KUWAIT
PAGES 108-109

OMAN
PAGES 108-109

QATAR
PAGES 108-109

SAUDI ARABIA
PAGES 108-109

UNITED ARAB EMIRATES
PAGES 108-109

YEMEN
PAGES 108-109

AFGHANISTAN
PAGES 110-111

PAKISTAN
PAGES 116-117

NEPAL
PAGES 116-117

SRI LANKA
PAGES 116-117

CHINA
PAGES 118-121

MONGOLIA
PAGES 118-119

NORTH KOREA
PAGES 120-121

SOUTH KOREA
PAGES 120-121

TAIWAN
PAGES 120-121

THE PACIFIC OCEAN

BRUNEI
PAGES 126-127

INDONESIA
PAGES 126-127

PHILIPPINES
PAGES 126-127

FIJI
PAGES 128-129

KIRIBATI
PAGES 128-129

MARSHALL ISLANDS
PAGES 128-129

MICRONESIA
PAGES 128-129

NAURU
PAGES 128-129